THE ROAD TO EGDON HEATH

The Aesthetics of the Great in Nature

Frozen wastelands and scorched deserts, once considered cursed and avoided at all cost, are now sought out or seen as the epitome of a highly spiritual kind of beauty. In *The Road to Egdon Heath*, the first of a two-part study, Richard Bevis shows that this modern sensibility has its roots in late Renaissance science and natural philosophy. Concentrating on the eighteenth and nineteenth centuries, he traces its development up to 1878 and one of its earliest conscious articulations, Thomas Hardy's description of Egdon Heath in *The Return of the Native*.

Bevis examines a wide range of English, European, and North American texts, literary works as well as religious, scientific, and travel writing. He surveys the literature on mountain climbing, sea voyages, desert travel, and polar exploration, and its metaphorical uses in poetry and fiction. Relying on Addison's term "the Great" rather than "the sublime," he shows how works such as Darwin's journals, Lyell's studies in geology, and de Saussure's books on the Alps helped form an outlook on nature that also found frequent literary expression.

A wide-ranging, interdisciplinary work in the history of ideas, *The Road to Egdon Heath* traces the growth of an aesthetic sensibility that is now widespread but that was only embryonic in the Renaissance. This sensibility underlies not only much of modern literature but also our modern ideas about conservation, ecology, and environmentalism.

RICHARD BEVIS is professor emeritus of English, University of British Columbia.

McGill-Queen's Studies in the History of Ideas

THE ROAD TO EGDON HEATH
The Aesthetics of the Great in Nature

Richard Bevis

McGill-Queen's University Press

Montreal & Kingston · London · Ithaca

© McGill-Queen's University Press 1999
ISBN 0-7735-1800-2
Legal deposit second quarter 1999
Bibliothèque nationale du Québec

Printed in the United States of America on acid-free paper

This book has been published with the help of a grant from the Humanities
and Social Sciences Federation of Canada, using funds provided
by the Social Sciences and Humanities Research Council of Canada.

McGill-Queen's University Press acknowledges the financial support of the Government
of Canada through the Book Publishing Industry Development Program for its activities.
We also acknowledge the support of the Canada Council for the Arts
for our publishing program.

Permission to publish the quotations from Basho (pages 22–3) has been granted
by Professor Makota Ueda, author of *Matsuo Basho*, and by Penguin UK,
publisher of *Basho. The Narrow Road to the Deep North and Other Travel Sketches*.
The lines from "Northwest Passage" by Stan Rogers (page 254) are used
by permission of Fogarty's Cove and Cole Harbour Music Ltd.

Canadian Cataloguing in Publication Data
Bevis, Richard W.
The road to Egdon Heath: the aesthetics of the great in nature
(McGill-Queen's studies in the history of ideas; 25)
Includes bibliographical references and index.
ISBN 0-7735-1800-2
1. Nature (Aesthetics) 2. Nature in literature.
3. Landscape in literature. 4. Landscape. I. Title. II. Series.
PN48.B49 1999   809'.9332   C99-900097-7

This book was typeset by Typo Litho Composition Inc.
in 10/12 Baskerville.

Contents

To Vivian, Linda, Bill, Lu,
and
all the other companions
of my occasional forays
into the Great.

Preface

Despite its title, this book is not about Thomas Hardy, but about a broad, diffuse phenomenon in (mainly western) aesthetics that Hardy tried to describe at roughly the midpoint between its discernible origins and ourselves. In the years 1876–78, when Hardy was considering the meaning of great barrens like Egdon Heath in *The Return of the Native,* Charles Doughty was wandering through Arabia Deserta with the Bedouin, Herman Melville meditated on desertic landscapes in *Clarel,* John Wesley Powell produced his report on the arid lands of the western United States, and two expeditions probed the Arctic. All of these contributed to the movement (if that is not too formal a term) discussed here. Had I based my title on another writer and started with Longinus or Thomas Burnet or Marjorie Hope Nicolson, the argument would have been, finally, much the same.

Hardy's discussion of Egdon Heath is, however, a highly conscious synthesis of evolving western attitudes towards the most daunting aspects of nature, and one that was seminal for me. In 1964 I saw a paperback edition of the Garnett abridgment of Doughty's *Travels in Arabia Deserta* in a Berkeley bookstore. I did not yet know that wonderful book, but was much taken with its cover: Edward Gorey's rendering of the jagged desert mountains of Arabia, which seemed oddly familiar. In a moment I recognized the emotion they aroused as akin to what I had felt on midwinter pilgrimages across the Sierra Nevada mountains to Death Valley, and during a summer in Yellowstone, between the Absarokas and the Tetons. Still, the moment might have passed without further connections had it not been for Hardy. As it happened, I had read *The Return of the Native* for the first time that year, and recalled his remarks about the peculiar power of gaunt wastes such as Egdon Heath over

modern minds. Those few moments by a bookstore window set me wondering about the taste for vast, bare natural phenomena – where it originated, how widely it was distributed, and so on – and that wonder has
not gone away. Using Hardy in the way I have is an act of piety as well as
a recognition of his insight and importance.

I did not really pursue these questions; they seemed to pursue me.
That same year I came across Marjorie Nicolson's *Mountain Gloom and
Mountain Glory*, an account of how the eighteenth-century English
learned to revere mountains, had my first, humbling encounter with a
big one, Mount Shasta, and read John Muir. Over the next few years I
saw something of the Middle Eastern deserts that had moved Doughty,
climbed Mount Kilimanjaro, read Gertrude Bell and T.E. Lawrence.
Now and then, modern culture handed me something unexpected.
During the first moon walk, Neil Armstrong noted, "It has a stark beauty
all its own. It's like much of the high desert of the United States." Subsequent reading, and travels to the Sahara, Alaska and the Andes, kept
bringing me back to the first chapter of *The Return of the Native*.

Briefly, Hardy describes Egdon Heath, a "vast tract of unenclosed
wild," as "grand," observing that its quality of "chastened sublimity" –
found also on moors, seas, mountains, and Arctic wastes (coded as
"Thule") – is more in tune with thoughtful modern minds than are ancient Greek ideals of natural beauty ("Tempe"). He predicts that eventually the "commonest tourist" will prefer Iceland, the Alps, and desolate
beaches to verdant spas. From the first I was inclined to take this hypothesis seriously, advanced as it was by one of the parents of literary modernism, and to examine other data on the subject. Hardy's statement is
not limited to Victorian England, or to literature, but presumes to
include other times, places, cultures, and languages. I found the "under-
pinnings" of his ideas in Greek philosophy and aesthetics, in Renaissance cosmology, science, art and theology, and in travel literature; *belles-
lettres* were a late contributor. After 1712, when Addison tentatively formulated a new aesthetic category above beauty, English and Continental
(later American) literature played a larger role, but scientists, philosophers, theologians, and travellers remained crucial to the shift in attitudes.

Many recent writers and naturalists have reacted to barren landscape
in ways that seem to bear out Addison and Hardy. A piece on the
Arabian desert in *Harper's* describes the Empty Quarter as having the
"primal allure of emptiness ... that elsewhere might only be experienced on open seas, high mountains, or polar ice" (Iseman 1978, 46).

Armstrong's phrase "stark beauty" is applied by George Schaller to Tibet's Chang Tang desert in an article in *National Geographic* (Schaller 1993, 76). One of the most prolific and influential purveyors of responses to wild nature, the *National Geographic* frequently asserts the holiness of such places: the Chang Tang is a "High and Sacred Realm," the Nahanni River in northwest Canada an "aisle inside the earth's own temple" (Schaller 1993, 62; Chadwick 1981, 416).

Often the language of those who report on the great empty spaces is aesthetic and spiritual. "Freed from constraints of time and place" in the Alaska wilderness, Douglas Chadwick discovered that the "real treasure" of travel there is "the awareness of how intensely alive your mind, your body, and the world around you can be" (1979, 746, 761). In trying to describe his reactions to the Sahara, Alain Woodrow (1979) quotes Charles de Foucault, a religious hermit, on the spirituality of the desert and Albert Camus on its "useless and irreplaceable beauty." Peter Iseman found sunrise in Arabia's Hejaz Mountains a "strange, impressive scene [that] lets the mind soar, out of time, in an ecstasy of desolation" (1978, 46). Ecstasy, I hardly need to say, is not the only possible reaction to desolation.

With language and perceptions like these virtually all around us now, we may take for granted Hardy's assertion that we have abandoned the Greeks' Tempe for a new aesthetics of Thule, but this would be a mistake. The road to Egdon Heath was long and difficult to build; much had to happen to make possible such attitudes as Armstrong's, Iseman's, and Schaller's. In 1979 a chartered jet full of tourists crashed in Antarctica, killing all on board. Apart from questions about the weather and human error, we ought to ask why three hundred people were willing to pay a considerable sum to be flown over that cold, empty continent for an hour. For that matter, why do so many people now take arduous trips to great barrens throughout the world with the trekking companies that have sprung up since the 1970s? Why would anyone seek an "Experience de Solitude au Sahara" and find a deep spiritual appeal in that "lunar landscape" (Woodrow 1979), or perceive the harsh Chang Tang desert as "sublime," "beautiful," or "sacred"? It was such questions, as well as Hardy's ruminations, that fuelled my research.

Some features of this book require a word of explanation. It undertakes to survey a sprawling mass of material – hundreds of disparate sources from several countries, languages and centuries – and how to present my findings has long been a major concern. I wanted to write a history of ideas book, like A.O. Lovejoy's *The Great Chain of Being*,

Samuel Monk's *The Sublime,* Nicolson's *Mountain Gloom and Mountain Glory* (a work I have sought to extend in scope and in time), or Christopher Thacker's *The Wildness Pleases.* But could any mind hope to absorb the whole corpus of (even western) literature on mountain climbing, sea voyages, desert travel, and polar exploration, along with its metaphorical uses in poetry and fiction, and the large body of theory and commentary on it? Could any reader be expected to sit through a presentation of the whole subject?

Fortunately I came across useful models. Clarence Glacken's *Traces on the Rhodian Shore* imposes order on a subject as large as mine ("Nature and Culture in Western Thought" to 1900) by finding logical subdivisions of the topic. My colleague Eva-Marie Kröller's approach to some related problems (*Canadian Travellers in Europe*) showed me how material could generate form. In my case that has meant a circular structure (using Hardy as both alpha and omega), an introduction that outlines the whole argument, basically chronological organization with the anatomization of ideas and spaces in each period, the special studies in authors and groups. Although my "Road to" title may suggest parallels with J.L. Lowes's *The Road to Xanadu* or Paul Carter's *The Road to Botany Bay,* I am not studying the influences on an author or how a culture names places, but tracing the growth of a certain kind of aesthetic sensibility.

Given the nature of Hardy's assertion, it was not easy to limit my scope; any and all reaction to the Great had at least to be considered. My commentary is based on well over four hundred sources (a source being anything from a line of Blake to four volumes of French prose) containing thousands of recognizable aesthetic responses. Eventually it became necessary to divide the topic, which I did by avoiding Hardy's prediction and confining myself to his historical statement. Thus I deal with the background of "Egdon Heath" in this volume, leaving the fate of his predictions and all post-1878 material for a sequel. Together the volumes will show that the development Hardy alerted us to underlies a great deal of modern thought about nature that is usually classified as conservation, ecology, or environmentalism.

No one needs to tell me that I could have carried the material I have gathered farther or treated it differently. Most of my readers have pointed me to further reading, not all of which I could include here. Ideological critics may wish I had pursued the political implications of the subject, comparatists may find the book Anglocentric, and so on. To all such I can only say that the subject is vast, that I have merely surveyed it, and that the work I have left untouched may still be done.

Any book this long in the works acquires more debts than it can discharge. Besides the many authors who provided raw material and suggested ways of understanding it, various friends, colleagues, and relatives lent their attention and experience to assist me. The line stretches from my research assistants at the American University of Beirut in the 1960s to readers and editors at university presses, among whom I must mention Aurèle Parisien and Joan McGilvray at McGill-Queen's for their support and guidance. My colleagues John Wilson Foster and Christine Parkin, Robert Weyeneth of the University of South Carolina, my brother Bill of the University of Montana, and my daughter Linda gave several chapters the kind of careful, challenging critiques that are invaluable to every writer. My errors are my own; my achievements are partly theirs.

A NOTE ON STYLE

The numbers in parenthetical references signify pages unless otherwise indicated. The dates in parenthetical references are those of the edition used. The date of original publication is given in Works Cited.

Single quotation marks (' ') indicate my own translations from other languages. Otherwise, translators are noted in the Works Cited.

Joos de Momper (the Younger), *Large Mountainous Landscape* (early seventeenth century), shows an interest in the pictorial and emotive appeal of mountain masses, vaguely treated. See p. 36. (From Walter S. Gibson, *Mirror of the Earth* [Princeton: Princeton University Press, 1989], 6:1. Published by permission of Princeton University Press)

Frederick W. Beechey, *HMS Hecla and Griper in Winter Harbour* on Parry's first voyage (1821). Note that the cooks are being watched by a wolf or fox, symbolizing the dangers of the ships' isolation. See p. 155. (Parry, *Journal*, 122)

David Roberts, *Jericho* (ca. 1840). The melancholy atmosphere surrounding the ruins in the desert is similar to that of Shelley's *Ozymandias* and Edwin James's account of the American West. See p. 132. (David Roberts, *The Holy Land* [London: Cassell, Petter, Galpin, n.d.], facing 46)

Elisha Kent Kane, *Ice Bergs Near Kosoak* (1856). A moment of peaceful sailing among awesome perils near Lifeboat Cove. See p. 260. (Kane, *Arctic Explorations*, 2:56)

E. K. Kane, *Parting Hawsers Off Godsend Ledge* (1856). A (melo)dramatic representation of the dangers of Arctic sailing. See p. 260. (Kane, *Arctic Explorations*, 1:71)

Auguste Bisson, *Glacier des Boissons* (1861). An early photograph of an Alpine glacier shows its vast scale, dwarfing the humans. See pp. 251–2. (Alpine Club Library, London, repr. Whyte Museum of the Canadian Rockies)

Edward Whymper, *Matterhorn from ... Theodule Pass* (1871). The illustration (by a member of the first party to ascend the Matterhorn) emphasizes the insignificance of climbers in the Alpine vastness. See p. 309. (Whymper, *Scrambles amongst the Alps*, facing 36)

John Wesley Powell, *The Heart of Marble Canyon.* An illustration of the magic and the majestic scale of the canyon. The gloom and glory motif is suggestive of Ruskin. See p. 305. (J. Powell, *Canyons of the Colorado* [1895; repr. NY: Argosy-Antiquarian, 1964], 210)

THE ROAD TO EGDON HEATH

Introduction:
Tempe and Thule

Certain passages in the major authors of most literatures possess a tonal resonance that preserves an important aspect of their age. The disillusioned laugh of Chaucer's Troilus, the poignant questions of Ronsard, the ravings of Lear, the musings of Faust, Pope on the human condition, Wordsworth on the French Revolution, Jane Austen's "truth universally acknowledged" and Virginia Woolf's "room of one's own" have implications that reach far beyond the works in which they appear. It is significant that many such passages from the nineteenth century onwards – Arnold's darkling plain, Eliot's wasteland, Frost's desert places – use vistas of natural voids to make their point. One purpose of this book is to investigate why some kinds of physical space have come to possess a peculiar attraction for modern writers.

Thomas Hardy's description of Egdon Heath in the first chapter of *The Return of the Native* (1878) has this quality of a "meta-statement" about nature. Besides being an introduction to the most powerful force in the novel, it is also one of the first great dark passages in modern literature, gravely announcing a major shift in western aesthetics. Hardy begins by describing the twilit heath as a "Titanic form" that is "majestic without severity, impressive without showiness, emphatic in its admonitions, grand in its simplicity. The qualifications which frequently invest the facade of a prison with far more dignity than is found in the facade of a palace double its size lent to this heath a sublimity in which spots renowned for beauty of the accepted kind are utterly wanting" (Hardy 1980, 2). This much is fairly orthodox, and may be understood as continuing an historical tradition. Hardy is drawing on the well-established aesthetics of the sublime, conventionally distinguished from the beautiful. Any number of eighteenth- or nineteenth-century authors known to

Hardy, from Burke (or even Addison) to Ruskin, might have formed the conception, if not written the passage, up to this point.

What follows, however, is a development in a different, more dissonant key: "Fair prospects wed happily with fair times; but alas, if times be not fair! Men have oftener suffered from the mockery of a place too smiling for their reason than from the oppression of surroundings oversadly tinged. Haggard Egdon appealed to a subtler and scarcer instinct, to a more recently learnt emotion, than that which responds to the sort of beauty called charming and fair" (Hardy 1980, 2). Here the perception has acquired a late-Victorian colour: the sadness of sublimity seems appropriate, while beauty becomes a shallow prettiness that mocks "reason" and reality. In *Tess of the D'Urbervilles* (1891), Hardy would elaborate on the "more recently learnt emotion," calling it "the ache of modernism."

Hardy now stops to consider the possible appearance of a new aesthetics of barrenness:

Indeed, it is a question if the exclusive reign of this orthodox beauty is not approaching its last quarter. The new Vale of Tempe may be a gaunt waste in Thule; human souls may find themselves in closer and closer harmony with external things wearing a sombreness distasteful to our race when it was young. The time seems near, if it has not actually arrived, when the chastened sublimity of a moor, a sea, or a mountain will be all of nature that is absolutely in keeping with the moods of the more thinking among mankind. And ultimately, to the commonest tourist, spots like Iceland may become what the vineyards and myrtle-gardens of South Europe are to him now; and Heidelberg and Baden be passed unheeded as he hastens from the Alps to the sand-dunes of Scheveningen. (Hardy 1980, 2)

Even with its subjunctives and conditionals this is a striking pronouncement for 1878, rich with unexplored ramifications. The notion of an aesthetic shift from Tempe to Thule is both vague and piquing: what exactly did that mean to Hardy, and to others, if others were involved? What could cause such a change? Why would an author or a culture turn from a classical Greek vale (Tempe) to the Arctic icefields (Thule) for their images, standards, and settings? How does aesthetics, the science of the beautiful, operate after "orthodox beauty" has ceased to reign? And do these remarks have any relevance outside Europe?

Such questions, raised by one of the foremost pioneers of modernism in both poetry and prose but certainly not limited to him or to literature in their implications, deserve to be taken seriously and are long overdue for examination. This book is an attempt to address these issues, to ascertain how western culture reached the point where Egdon Heath was both a logical outcome and a cultural barometer.

Though Hardy's mood in *The Return of the Native* had proximate causes in his own life, his reflections on Egdon Heath also form part of the Victorian reaction to seventeenth- and eighteenth-century treatments of "the sublime" as a quality of art and nature capable of evoking a level of response superior to that elicited by "the beautiful." The "simplicity" and "dignity" of Egdon, the fact that it seems "majestic" and "grand," would establish that lineage even if the word "sublimity" were not used twice in the passage. We know that Hardy had studied Edmund Burke's *Philosophical Enquiry into the ... Sublime and Beautiful* (1757), and he appears to have used it both for themes and style (S.F. Johnson 1958). Burke's thesis is that sublimity arouses deeper and larger emotions, including fear, than does beauty, which gives relatively shallow feelings of joy and pleasure.

According to Marjorie Hope Nicolson, Hardy may also have read Joseph Addison's essays on "the pleasures of the imagination" in *The Spectator* (1712; cited in S.F. Johnson, 61n.12). Addison, a major source for Burke's essay, was the prime delineator of the category of landscape that Burke and Hardy call "sublime," that is, capable of evoking the sublime emotions (awe, astonishment, fear, wonder). Addison himself termed this category "the Great" (still a synonym for sublimity in Burke), listing as examples plains, deserts, mountains, and oceans. Hardy generalizes from the mood of Egdon Heath to that of "a moor, a sea, or a mountain," one of the clearest indications that he is thinking in these inherited categories. The landscapes he specifies are the Alps, "the sand-dunes of Scheveningen" on the shore of the North Sea (both recognizable instances of "the Great"), Iceland, and "Thule," i.e., the Arctic. The North was a later addition to Addison's "Great," although the voyages on which its inclusion was based had already been undertaken and reported in 1712.

Hardy modifies the early form of the Great in other ways. Egdon's sublimity is permeated with sadness and "sombreness"; it is "chastened." Interesting choice of word: in 1878 "chastened" still meant "rendered chaste or pure" as well as "chastised." This process of chastening sublimity had begun with Byron and Percy Shelley, one of Hardy's favourite poets, who almost always associated sublimity with suffering (Prometheus) or some dark perspective on the human condition (Alastor, Ozymandias). This darkened sublime, however, was by no means universal among writers; Hardy *chose* to follow Shelley in this matter, rather than, say, Coleridge, in whom sublimity is typically associated with fearful exaltation and exultation (see "Vale of Chamouni," for example). Hardy wants to modernize sublimity as a category of experience by purging it of some of the buoyancy and faith of its eighteenth-century youth.

Hardy also claims that the kind of landscape represented by the heath is especially suited to his time; "Haggard Egdon appealed to ... a more recently learnt emotion." The idea of a culture *evolving* from ideals of beauty towards "chastened sublimity" (as opposed to their being coexistent categories) may have originated with Hardy as part of his personal response to the Victorian ethos, especially the conflict between science and religion, as well as to private griefs such as Horace Moule's suicide and his own loss of faith. The period of Hardy's maturity coincided with "the first stage of flux resulting from the overthrow by science of standards accepted for many generations"; he was caught up in the sceptical and iconoclastic mood of "the more thinking among mankind" (Rutland [1938] 1962, 45). His readings in evolutionary science, astronomy, and the "higher criticism" of the Bible underlie the conviction that times are not fair. "Fair prospects" would only mock what reason has now discovered, so "harmony with external things" requires Thulean landscapes. Something of the grandeur and resonance of Shelley's vision in *Prometheus Unbound* is lost, or at least darkened, in Hardy's vision, for humanity has outgrown not only the classical Vale of Tempe, but classical heroism, and joy, as well.

"Egdon Heath," then, was a relic not only of the Domesday Book's "Bruaria," as Hardy says, but of earlier authors; its mindscape preserves traces of Addison, Burke, Shelley, and other aestheticians, poets, novelists, theologians and philosophers. And the historical resonance of Hardy's heath grows when we turn from the passage's details to its large assumptions, several of which could be called "geological," in the literal sense of *geo-logos*: the story or organizing conception of the earth ("In the beginning was the Logos"). The "face on which Time makes but little impression" is a heath. Western literature had not always deemed what the Oxford dictionary calls a "bare flat waste tract of land" a fit subject for serious meditation at the opening of a major work, but the growth of "land-consciousness" in the nineteenth century provided essential materials for the road to Egdon Heath. This uninhabited tract is given qualities that, while gloomy enough to suggest "the facade of a prison," are pronounced well suited to the modern temper. Hardy's desire for harmony between humanity and nature, while in one sense a rediscovery of the Greek ideal of the integrated community (the *polis*), is also a product of the rise of geology and heightened awareness of land in eighteenth- and nineteenth-century Europe and North America.

This sensitivity to correspondences of mind with nature takes its most "modern" form when Hardy suggests that Egdon Heath seen during a stormy winter night "was found to be the hitherto unrecognized original of those wild regions of obscurity which are vaguely felt to be compassing us about in midnight dreams of flight and disaster, and are never thought of after the dream till revived by scenes like this." That is, the heath, as the natural embodiment of a primal fear, is a near relation not only of night but (in twentieth-century terms) of Carl Jung's archetypes and T.S. Eliot's "objective correlatives." Such metaphorical uses of landscape to express mood had gained currency during the eighteenth and nineteenth centuries among a broad spectrum of western writers.

Hardy is not talking to or about poets and philosophers exclusively, however, but about thoughtful travellers and ("ultimately") "the commonest tourist." Travellers were vital to the development of "land-consciousness"; they could test in the field the theories of aesthetic philosophers about how we respond (or "should" respond) to the great natural phenomena. Hardy knew that Addison, Shelley, Ruskin, Arnold, and others had been moved to write some of their most influential and valued work by their encounters with the Alps, and less literary travellers also played a role in the shift of attitudes towards nature that Hardy posits.

We have done what we can on the heath: it is time to explore the road thither. Once the Great has been defined as an aesthetic category, we will be able to recognize its origins in some early discussions of and notable encounters with its various components (Part One). Addison's and other early theories of the Great or sublime are analyzed in Part Two, along with some influential expressions of the idea in eighteenth-century English literature, and the contributions of European scientists and writers, and English travellers and explorers, in the same period. Around the turn of the nineteenth century, as the original concept becomes more subjective in philosophy, it is darkened by poets and travel writers to something Hardy would begin to recognize (Part Three). The further development of this "chastened" Great and the emergence of a heightened "land-consciousness" in nineteenth-century science, nature philosophy, literature, and travel are the themes of Part Four. When we eventually return to Egdon, we will find it richer, and discover additional significance in details that we now take for granted.

PART I

Underpinnings

Addison's essay on "the Great" as a pleasure of the imagination did not spring *ex nihilo* in 1712. Earlier poets, scientists, philosophers, theologians, and travellers also discussed kinds of landscape for which "beautiful" was not *le mot juste,* mentioning some of the same emotions that Addison, Burke, and even Hardy do. Part One considers what evidence we have that these scattered mentions began or became a coherent aesthetic entity, "the Great," and examines some of the data that shaped this entity before Addison gave it a local habitation and a name.

The Great as Aesthetic Category

In order to evaluate Hardy's proposition, we need to ascertain the class of things to which Egdon Heath properly belongs, that is, the group of phenomena (places, thoughts, feelings, writings) with which his fictional landscape and its emotional attributes are affiliated. Like eighteenth- and nineteenth-century scientists such as Linnaeus, Cuvier, Lyell, and Darwin, who had to classify their data before they could ascertain its meaning, we need a taxonomy. Hardy ascribes a timely kind of value – (chastened) sublimity, dignity, and grandeur – to a vast, empty, lonely, gloomy landscape, a heath; later he generalizes from Egdon to moors, seas, and mountains as natural stimuli of similar aesthetic experiences. The prime question is whether others grouped these landscapes, and how they felt about them. The estimable pages of the *British Journal of Aesthetics* and the *Journal of Aesthetics and Art Criticism* do not help us much here; we can answer only by examining a broad selection of expository and imaginative literature dealing with heaths/moors/deserts, seas, and mountains. This alone will tell whether the aspects of nature Hardy lists had coherence and meaning for others.

I have already suggested that Egdon Heath is linked to Burke's "Sublime," which descended from what Addison called "the Great." The latter is more useful, being the bedrock term, less tainted by confusingly disjunctive applications to natural stimulus and personal response, and less impeded by the semantic baggage that has piled up around the sublime. For sublimity has become a modern academic hobby horse whose meaning varies with the rider: we have the Marxist and other political sublimes, the mathematical, the negative, and other Kantian sublimes, even the androgynous sublime. All of these have only a tangential (and complicating) relation to the "chastening" of natural sublimity at issue here. Our first question, then, is whether the Great as defined by Addison remained or became a viable category.

The answer seems to be that the original elements of the category were *gradually* perceived as comparable in effect, and received additions. Of the natural scenes specified by Addison, mountains and seascapes had awed many observers well before his time. In the West, at least, deserts took longer, partly because few Europeans had contact with them until the nineteenth century; when enough of them did, the response was as Addison had predicted. His essay in number 412 of the *Spectator* mentions the heavens in connection with "Beauty or Uncommonness," not the Great. Yet the night sky was widely revered before Addison wrote, and his famous poem "The spacious firmament on high" is a clear example of spiritual response to the astronomical Great, so we have preliminary grounds for including it, a choice amply confirmed by many observers. More understandably, he omitted the polar wastes, little known in the early eighteenth century. Like the desert, they were a nineteenth-century passion, and were then quickly perceived as sublime. By Hardy's day, these five kinds of material nature – mountains, seas, deserts, the heavens, the poles – had cohered as an expanded Great, capable of eliciting from many travellers, readers, and theorists some of the emotions he and Addison mention.

Of these five, mountains have inspired the most voluminous library. The scientific, the religious, the adventurous, and the ambitious had all been drawn to the Alps, mainly, by the end of the eighteenth century. Writers have been allowed to define "mountain" for themselves; some of the seventeenth- and eighteenth-century British examples may seem to us to be "hills," but the distinction is not, as it turns out, important at the level of aesthetic response.

By now, texts about deserts of one kind or another (moors and heaths in England) run mountain books a close second, but were less prominent before Hardy; the great surge in desert writing did not begin until after the mid-nineteenth century. Here definition is more of a problem: early uses of "desert" are apt to stay close to the original meaning of "a deserted place," rather than anything remotely Saharan. Robinson Crusoe's verdant island was a "desert" in the eighteenth century; Addison himself refers to some "solitary rocks and mountains" near Genoa as "Deserts." So would a given traveller's response to a certain desert be relevant to Addison's Great, or comparable to Hardy's reaction to a heath? One must take each case individually and try to ascertain whether a particular usage makes modern or ancient sense. However, readers can judge for themselves from the quotations.

The heavens were well established as a source of Great or sublime emotions before Addison, and it is a tenable proposition that the night sky, which was venerated in ancient religion and whose contemplation required no travelling, was the earliest source of Great aesthetics. Many passages in the Renaissance philosophers dwell on their awe of the nocturnal firmament. References to oceans are almost as numerous as those to the sky. Europe had several major seafaring nations by the end of the sixteenth century, and volumes about voyages found many readers. Discussions of Arctic and Antarctic regions, however, were relatively few before 1878; the great age of polar travel came a generation later with Nansen, Amundsen, Scott, and Shackleton.

The coherence of the five areas of the Great is established by writers linking two or more of them as phenomena producing similar emotions. Mountains are associated with sea and sky, for example, as early as Longinus, who said, probably in the third century AD, that oceans, stars, and volcanoes are the sights we most admire. Matthew Arnold's Victorian Empedocles, yearning to unite himself with mountains, sea, and stars, finally leaps into Mt Etna's crater. That these are simple physical conjunctions – one usually sees the sky, and sometimes desert or ocean, from a mountaintop – does not make them worse data on the Great. Many climbers have remarked on the integrity of such a vista.

Deserts are usually linked with mountains – a fairly common landscape pairing outside Europe, and in the eighteenth century mountains could still be "Desarts" – or paralleled with the ocean. The latter occurs as early as Thomas Shaw (1738), who notes that the mirages of Arabia appear as large sheets of water, and that magnification is common to both kinds of topography. In the nineteenth century this became a standard comparison with travellers to the Mideast (Flaubert, Kinglake, Melville) and to America's Great Plains, where Captain Lewis noted the prairie's oceanic appearance, and "prairie schooners" crossed a "sea of grass" until someone shouted "Camp ahoy!" Prairies are not technically deserts, but their vast extent of open space, "unbounded views," and lack of population provided the requisite conditions for the effects Addison describes.

The heavens, and the feelings they give, have long been compared to deserts. Jonathan Richardson, a writer on painting, refers to the "Vast Desert of the Sky" in 1725. Nineteenth-century poets might perceive the sky as "deserted" by God (James Thomson, "City of Dreadful Night"

[1874]), or parallel it with the "desert" of their own griefs (Stephane Mallarmé, "L'Azur" [ca. 1863]). And to early explorers the Arctic often seemed a "snowy desert." E.K. Kane observed that the return of animal life after the polar winter was like finding an oasis, and Isaac Hayes called the area "a vast frozen sahara." Jules Verne brought this image into fiction (*The Desert of Ice*, 1864), and later it became standard among writers on Antarctica.

Oceans were frequently linked to mountains, not only along precipitous coasts but far inland. Early visitors to the Alps compared the peaks themselves or their glaciers to a stormy sea suddenly petrified or frozen. Wordsworth's careful phrase for one Alpine view, "a sea-like reach of prospect," was more commonly generalized to "an ocean of mountains" (Whymper 1871). Shelley's letter to T.L. Peacock about Vesuvius (22 December 1818) likens the appearance of cold lava to that of the sea.

All five areas that I include in the Great were also linked with each other in larger groupings between Addison and Hardy. The trio of mountain, sea, and sky has been mentioned; that of desert, mountain, and sea was established in Addison's *Spectator* essay of 1712, and in Edward Young's *Night Thoughts* (1742). Romantic poets – Scott in "Lord of the Isles," Shelley in "Mont Blanc" – hailed mountain, sea, and desert as emblems of free, wild nature, and Richard Burton called them "scenes ... which endure as long as Memory lasts" (1855). The Reverend A.P. Stanley described the desolate volcanic steppe of northern Arabia as both the "Alps unclothed" and "an ocean of lava" (1856).

Even larger clusters of Great areas occur in the poets and philosophers. Shelley's Alastor shows a strong affinity for mountain, desert, sea, and sky, which Tennyson lists as sources of sublimity ("On Sublimity," 1827) and J.S. Mill as natural phenomena productive of "awe" ("Nature" 1851–58). The award for virtuosity, however, goes to James Thomson; his "City of Dreadful Night" gives its "enormous mountains," "bleak uplands," "desert ocean," and empty sky the polar touch of "endless nights."

What the "Egdon Heath" passage joins together in the way of landscapes, then – a desert heath, whose effect is compared to that of seas, mountains, and a "gaunt waste in Thule," and a floor whose roof is the sky – had been united before. Hardy was adept at aesthetic synthesis, but his achievements in that sphere were not unprecedented; an enlarged version of Addison's Great existed for him to use. What makes *The Return of the Native* original is Hardy's ability to step aside from his concatenation of landscapes and give an historical perspective on what they mean.

Knowing the Planet:
Early Travel and Exploration

Addison defined "the Great" (or sublime) for the eighteenth century and described our astonishment in its presence; Hardy found a "chastened" version of this idea apt for his time. But for as far back as history and legend record, we have wondered at the stars, crossed deserts, oceans, or mountains when the need arose: where do we first find traces of the interests and attitudes described by Addison, and why did they develop? We need to know something of the palaeo-history of the Great in order to understand the movement that it became. This knowledge can be gleaned from records of early travel to vast barren places, and from embryonic European aesthetic systems seeking the meaning of nature.

SEA VOYAGES AND THE NORTH

About 330 BC the Massalian Greek geographer and astronomer Pytheas sailed north from Gibraltar, perhaps to Norway or the Arctic Ocean, or just to the northern British Isles (like most early travel literature, his text does not always distinguish between hearing of places and actually seeing them). He described a land of cold, snow, and ice called "Thule" (Hardy's "gaunt waste"), which remained mythic for centuries, though it was identified with Norway and then Iceland as exploration moved west. The Irish monks and Scandinavian explorers who opened Iceland and Greenland to colonists between the eighth and twelfth centuries brought at least the margins of the boreal regions into the orbit of history and geography, but generated chronicles and legends rather than a literature of study or appreciation. The voyages of Ottar and Wulfstan, Leif Ericsson's probe towards the New World, and its continuation by John Cabot likewise bring us no closer to the concept or affect of the Great.

Renaissance Europe began to gather the data from which Addison would work. Elizabethan England took an entrepreneurial and imaginative interest in northern seas, sponsoring the voyages of navigators, chiefly Martin Frobisher (1575–78) and John Davis (1585–87), in search of a Northwest Passage to the Orient, and devouring collections of travel literature such as Richard Hakluyt's *Principal Navigations* (1589–1600). Davis described his first landfall on Greenland as a place "vast and void," where the noise of grinding ice floes "bred strange conceites [imaginings] among us"; he named it "Desolation" (Lopez 1986, 327). Some such description lies behind a famous speech in Shakespeare's *Measure for Measure* (act 3, sc. 1, lines 122–3), where Claudio imagines that to die might be "to reside / In thrilling region of thick-ribbed ice."

The Dutch mariner Gerrit de Veer's "True and Perfect Description" of William Barents's three voyages towards the Arctic (1594–96) is one of our earliest accounts of how Thule treated ill-prepared explorers. This plain, unadorned seaman's log records weather, courses, soundings, and the wonders – goldstone and rock crystal, seahorses and parhelia – that became the staples of Arctic narratives. De Veer's story of the enforced winter on the island of Novaya Zemlya north of Russia, during which Barents died, is little but storms and suffering, marauding bears and foxes. In June, hoping to escape from this "wild, desart, irkesome, fearfull, and cold country" (de Veer 1876, 185), the survivors embarked in small boats and limped back to Amsterdam. The polar regions have tended to inflict on their challengers a level and a duration of suffering rarely matched elsewhere in the Great; at this early stage the survival imperative ruled out any aesthetic response, which usually requires a degree of detachment, or at least safety.

Stuart England continued the Elizabethan passion for maritime exploration. Samuel Purchas made a career out of publishing multi-volume editions of *Hakluytus Posthumus or Purchas His Pilgrimes*, whose pages would stir Coleridge. The voyages and sufferings of Henry Hudson (1607–10), William Baffin, and Robert Bylot (1615–16) in search of the Northwest Passage advanced geographical knowledge and piqued imaginations with their descriptions. One of Hudson's men, John Playse, was deeply impressed by the west coast of Spitsbergen. Its "crests of everlasting snow" seemed "magic," and the whole coast had "a kind of majesty" (quoted in Markham 1921, 121). Similarly, Davis had written that the Arctic was "the place of greatest dignitie" on earth (Lopez 1986, 333). "Dignity" and "majesty" would in the nineteenth century be subsumed under "grandeur" in the lexicon of responses to the Arctic.

The best late-seventeenth-century accounts of the nordic-maritime variety of the Great also proved influential. Frederick Marten of Hamburg's striking description of Spitsbergen in 1671 contains several details that adumbrate later accounts of polar regions. Spitsbergen appeared forbiddingly uninhabitable but provided effects both rich and strange. At first sight, its mountains' feet seemed fiery, while their tops were in fog; yet the marbled snow "gave as bright and glorious a shining or gloss to the Air or Skies, as if the Sun had shin'd" (in *Account* 1711, 18). There were "great Ice-hills" as high as mountains, with "great Ice fields" lower down (41). Glaciers, with their "glorious blew colour," were wondrous novelties, part of a chiaroscuro effect: dark snow with blue cracks below, "foggy clouds" hovering in the middle, "very bright" snow and fiery rocks above reflecting the pale sun (20). Extraordinary, too, were the stones that "glister[ed] like Silveroar" on the beach (21), the sapphire and emerald hues of the sea, and the blue of the ice underwater, "the deeper ... the purer" (41). Everywhere Marten was deceived by the vast distances and altitudes, as if Spitsbergen were another order of reality, distinct from the world he knew.

Capt. John Wood left a briefer account of Novaya Zemlya, where he was stranded for 10 days in 1676. His verdict on the island was, like de Veer's, understandably negative: "the most miserable Country that lyeth on the Foundation of the Earth" (in *Account* 1711, 193). Yet Wood was clearly impressed by the almost preternatural quality of the experience, especially the "strange shapes" of the icebergs (162). Most of the island was "perpetually" snowcovered, and two feet down they found earth that never thawed, permafrost, "which ... was never heard of before" (193). Inland they could see mountains "covered with Snow, which ... hath lain there ever since the Creation" (194). Wood was almost obsessed by the ageless hegemony of the snow, but he too found richness in the "very good Black Marble, with White Veins" of the beaches, and purity in sea water so clear that he could see shells on the bottom 80 fathoms down (195).

Marten's and Wood's accounts have more than intrinsic interest. Published by the Royal Society in 1694, they were reissued in 1711 and used by Alexander Pope to ornament a famous passage in "The Temple of Fame," written a year before Addison published his *Spectator* essay on the aesthetics of the Great. European mariners were thus early contributors of primary material relevant to that field, although Addison seems to have missed them.

MOUNTAIN TRAVEL

Humans venerated mountains long before anyone thought of climbing them; they were, after all, sacred places, linking earth to heaven (Eliade 1959, 37). In fact the veneration (part reverence, part fear) demonstrably delayed mountaineering. For all their literary and mythological use of mountains, almost no Greeks or Romans other than Lucretius, Hadrian, and Philip of Macedon are known to have climbed one (Hyde 1915; Bishop 1963, 103). Most large peaks – Mont Blanc, Everest/ Jomolungma, Chimborazo, Olympus, Mount Shasta, and so on – have generated legends of a domain of gods or spirits at the top that long discouraged ascents, at least with local cooperation. The crosses placed on many Alpine (and other) heights are telling. In the seventeenth century the glaciers of Chamonix were still exorcised, and tales of demons and dragons persisted thereabouts until the eighteenth, colouring narratives of early climbs (Engel 1971, 15–16, 22). Presumably the mountains needed consecration against the awful, mysterious powers that might reside there. Below the flames of Dante's *Inferno* (which reflects mediaeval Catholic belief), Satan lies frozen into eternal ice, like a body in a glacier.

The "awe-fullness" of mountains was fearful, but its other face was that of reverence and majesty, as seen in the legend of King Menelik I of Abyssinia, reputed progeny of Solomon and the Queen of Sheba. Returning with his army from conquering much of East Africa, he encamped on a barren volcanic plateau some fourteen thousand feet up on Mount Kilimanjaro ("the shining mountain"). This seems odd, as Kilimanjaro stands alone on a wide plain, and an army need not climb it at all, but the legend concerns what suits a king, not practicalities. Menelik, old and tired, felt close to death: "King I am and as a king I wish to die," he told his followers. He bid his army farewell and ascended the peak, accompanied by warlords, and slaves carrying treasure. His soldiers watched from below as the royal party ascended the snowfields and disappeared into the clouds. In the evening the warlords returned, saying that the king had entered the crater with his slaves and treasure. The legend concludes that an offspring of Menelik will someday climb Kilimanjaro, reclaim the jewels, and restore the glory of Abyssinia (Reusch 1965; 1954, 25, 51).

Italian poets were Europe's earliest known climbers. Dante seems to have gone up Mount Bismantova (Dante 1954, *Purgatory* canto 4, line 26), and in 1336 Petrarch made a much-debated ascent of Mont Ventoux in the Alpes de Provence. Which is more important: his choice to climb and his initial enjoyment of the view (Bergin 1970, 47), or the moment when, on the summit, he pulls out his copy of Augustine's *Confessions* (ca. 397-98 AD), reads that "men admire high mountains and great seas and rivers and the movements of the stars, but neglect themselves," feels abashed, and rejects the pleasure of the climb as irrelevant to the great question of salvation (Nash 1967, 19–20)? Or was this rather a "densely allegorical" report (Schama 1995, 419) of an "imaginary ascent" (Frasso 1974, 17)? Petrarch compares the climb to a spiritual ascent on the way up, and is "stunned" both by the vista from the peak and by the passage from Augustine (Bishop 1963, 108, 109, 111), who evidently recognized the affective power of nature. Augustine's point is not salvation but the marvel of the human faculties of memory and visualization. The fascination of the episode is the way it juxtaposes mediaeval and Renaissance attitudes towards nature: rejection, attraction.

A generation after Petrarch, Fazio degli Uberti described some mountain views and what sounds like altitude sickness. In the fifteenth century Aeneas Sylvius Piccolomini – Pope Pius II – included in his *Memoirs* (n.d.) a long appreciation of his summer quarters on Monte Amiata, a verdant refuge from Siena's heat, but records no reaction to his repeated crossings of the Alps on diplomatic missions. Leonardo da Vinci, a mind for all seasons, climbed "Mon Boso" near Monte Rosa around 1500 and speculated on its geology, recognizing marine fossils for what they were (Freshfield 1920, 6–8; Read 1963, 3–5). The *scientific* study of mountains dates from Leonardo, who did drawings of the Alps and used jagged mountains as backgrounds in religious paintings.

Not until the sixteenth century did interest in mountains begin to quicken. Aegidius Tschudi (1528) and Johann Stumpf (1544) may have been the first Alpine tourists; each later wrote of his travels, and Stumpf mapped the Alps (De Beer 1930, 25–6; Schama 1995, 429). But Europe's mountain *literature* dates from 1543, when Conrad Gesner published *De Montium Admiratione* (*On the Admiration of Mountains*), in which he vows to climb at least one a year for exercise and spiritual delight. Mountains lift the spirit to God, and have so many delights and marvels, such as perpetual snows, that they seem to belong to another world. "The consciousness is in some vague way impressed by the stupendous heights," he says, "and is drawn to the contemplation of the Great Architect" of "the Theatre of the World" (quoted in Freshfield 1920, 9). Thus the veneration of mountains as signposts to God, common among later climbers, is at least four centuries old, but Gesner's idea of "natural science" is mostly speculation (mountains sweat like bodies) and classical references, and he conveys no concrete sense here of being on any specific mountain.

That lack is remedied in his *Descriptio Montis Fracti* (*Description of the Riven Mountain*), published in 1555. The mountain is Pilatus, near Lucerne, which he climbed on 20 August 1550. Again he has general praise for mountains, which gratify all the senses by compressing great variety of terrain and weather into a small compass, and for climbing: in the silence of the high solitudes you can hear the music of the spheres, and it is "pleasant thereafter" to tell your friends about it (Gesner 1937, 27, 30; Freshfield 1920, 10). Gesner then narrates how his party passed the highest huts carrying their alpenstocks, climbed above all paths, and finally reached the top, where grass still grew and people had scratched their names on the rocks (Gesner 1937, 33). Any weekend climber will recognize this as recounting the ascent of a low but real peak. While the historian of ideas may prefer the more reflective *Admiration of Mountains*, both works introduce themes – delight, spirituality, transcendence of ordinary experience – that figure prominently in later writing about the Great.

Evidently others were climbing by then. Benoit Marti, revising Gesner's image significantly, praised the Alps as "the Theatre of the Lord" and said he had made some ascents (1557); Josias Simler of Zurich described early mountaineering and its equipment in 1574, quoting Gesner (Freshfield 1920, 11–13). During the turbulence of the Reformation, which inhibited European travel, some Englishmen crossed the Alps, and one of them, John Evelyn, left interesting comments in his *Diary*. In Etruria, his party ascended through thick cloud and emerged "into a most serene heaven, as if we had been above all human conversation"; the world of peaks above the clouds was "one of the most pleasant, new, and altogether surprising objects that I had ever beheld" (Evelyn 1889, 1:103). Yet the nearest of these peaks was a "horrid rock," and the appearance of the Alps was "as if Nature had swept up the rubbish of the earth" to clear the Italian plains (104, 239). In 1646 he rode by "strange, horrid, and fearful crags and tracts," making a "dangerous" and "terrible" passage of the "vast," cold, barren mountains and everlasting "ocean of snow" (239–40, 242). On the whole, the Alps were "melancholy and troublesome" (243).

In the Alps, as in northern waters, the real beginning for the English was the Restoration period: once their civil broils ended, they could direct their energies outward. Of the four Englishmen who recorded their impressions of the Alps between 1670 and 1690, the most influential was Thomas Burnet. His *Telluris Theoria Sacra* (1680–81; translated as *The Sacred Theory of the Earth*, 1684–89) describes travels through the Alps and Apennines, where "those wild, vast and indigested heaps of Stones and Earth, did so deeply strike my fancy" (imagination) as to demand further study, for they seemed not "the same Earth" he had known (T. Burnet 1965, 110–11). For Gilbert (later Bishop) Burnet, "the very sight" of the Italian Alps was "enough to fill a man with horror" (1687, 98) – a good example of the strong but mainly negative reactions of many early English visitors. Otherwise he had little to say about the Alps, though he did later approach a smoking Mount Vesuvius and stood "amazed" at the sheer vastness of the phenomenon (214). The third earl of Shaftesbury's impressions of his Alpine crossing took the form not of travel narrative but of a philosophical rhapsody to Nature, including mountains, in *The Moralists* (1709), a very influential text. I shall return to Thomas Burnet and to Shaftesbury later.

John Dennis set down specific reactions to the Savoyard Alps in a letter of 25 October 1688, while his walk on the 21st through a "dreadful" (fearful) canyon with "amazing" views was still fresh in his mind. On a dangerously narrow path, he felt a "delightful Horrour, a terrible Joy," was both "infinitely pleased," and "trembled"; the high summits "seem'd at once to forbid and invite" (Dennis 1943, 2: 380). This kind of oxymoron remained a frequent response to the Alps in the eighteenth and nineteenth centuries. Making the renowned passage of Mont Cenis, Dennis was impressed beyond words: if nature really created these mountains thus in the beginning, he says, then "her careless, irregular and boldest Strokes are most admirable," and "she moves us less, when she studies to please us more." Meads and streams may delight our reason, but the Alps transport as they horrify, joining "Harmony" with "Horrour." Or, if these mountains are actually the ruins of the "old World" (Thomas Burnet's theory), they are also "the greatest wonders of the New" (381). Dennis is important as one of the earliest travellers to articulate the simultaneous sensations of what Ruskin would later call "mountain gloom and mountain glory."

This book affords few glimpses of the role of the Great in non-western cultures. An exception must be made, however, for Matsuo Bashō (1644–94), a Japanese poet who described his arduous journeys and climbs in prose narratives interspersed with haiku. As a poetic recounter of hard travels, Bashō was well ahead of anyone in western Europe; as an existential and literary minimalist, he has no western counterpart until the twentieth century (Ezra Pound was one of the first western writers to appreciate him). Bashō's importance to us lies in his pioneering role as a travel writer drawn to the primitive and austere in nature, one for whom the road, both a metaphor of spiritual questing in life and a structural principle, may possibly afford a "vision of eternity" (Yuasa 1966, 37).

The titles of Bashō's travel books are indicative of his style and philosophy. In *Records of a Weather-Exposed Skeleton* he tries to renew himself by following the example of a mediaeval priest who walked great distances and attained ecstasy under the "pure beams" of the moon (Bashō 1966, 51). The landscape and the journey towards purity are both allegorical and physical, there and in *Records of a Travel-Worn Satchel*, whose poems yearn for union with the snow's whiteness.

> Deep as the snow is,
> Let me go as far as I can
> Till I stumble and fall,
> Viewing the white landscape.   (76)

As it is for Poe and Melville, white is the ultimate mystery. In *The Narrow Road to the Deep North*, Bashō feels the "purifying power" of a temple near the summit of a mountain "covered with age-old pines and oaks" (122). The theme of the book is a "quest for the ultimate beauty of nature and of man," a beauty "rarely found outside of rugged, primitive nature" (Ueda 1970, 137). Bashō's haiku are bare and lonely; stripped of any humanity other than the perceiver's – Bashō said he was weary of society – they focus on stark, austere landscapes.

Many of Bashō's haiku are set on storm-beaten mountains:

> Blowing the gravel
> Off the rocks of Mount Asama
> An autumn gale.

Or

> Against the wintry gust
> How sharp are the rocks
> Amid the cedars!

But he treats other bare landscapes with the same seriousness:

> On a journey, ailing –
> My dreams roam about
> Over a withered moor.   (Quoted in Ueda 1970, 54, 35)

All Bashō wants in such locations is to endure, to enter into the spirit of the place and to learn something about it and about himself. The kinds of questions his western contemporaries asked about mountains – why they were created, what use they were, how our feelings about them could be explained – were needless for him. What is remarkable in Bashō is just this humble acceptance of the most barren formations in nature as having equal rights to the planet with himself, and very likely a good deal to teach him if he is worthy and listens intently.

DESERTS

The desert's spiritual overtones in Judaeo-Christian scripture did not soon attract travellers there, though some early Christian hermits such as St Anthony did seek refuge and a meditative regime in the austerity of the wilderness. After the establishment of Islam, a few Crusaders and pilgrims saw Middle Eastern deserts, but the Ottoman conquest discouraged western access for centuries. While we hear of the occasional adventurer – Ludovico de Varthema travelled in the Arabian Peninsula in 1503 and wrote a long-lived and accurate, if scanty, account – David Hogarth dates European exploration of Arabia only from the Danish expedition in the 1760s. The cultural and natural barriers that rendered deserts remote (and visitors scarce) caused them to enter the west's nature aesthetic more slowly than did mountains, seas, or the heavens.

When Europeans did visit desert landscapes (mainly the Middle East and North Africa until the nineteenth century), they rarely thought them worth comment. Bertrandon de la Brocquière rode from Gaza into the Sinai with French and Arab companions in 1432 but said only, "We thus travelled two days in the desert, absolutely without seeing any thing deserving to be related" (1848, 289). Joseph Pitts, a captured English sailor, was taken to Mecca as a slave in the 1680s, but likewise says nothing of the desert in his *Account of the Religion and Manners of the Mahometans* (1704). A reader who picks up almost any nineteenth-century narrative of travel in the same locales will notice how much more interested the later travellers are in geology and in landforms.

If an Englishman noticed the desert in this period, it was usually through a mist of cultural preconceptions. In his dedication to *A Relation of a Journey Begun Anno Dom. 1610*, the most popular English travel book on the Mideast in the seventeenth century, George Sandys wrote that the region has, "through vice and ingratitude," declined from its biblical splendour to a despotic wasteland of deserts and sinkholes. Such "great and deserved" calamities should serve as "threatening instructions" for Europe (Sandys 1621, n.p.). In his (and others') "sacred geography," the climatic, topographical, and botanical realities of the Mideast become manifestations of God's displeasure and an argument for a new crusade.

Most English travellers carried a comparable weight of religious baggage. Henry Maundrell, chaplain to an English trading company in Aleppo, rode to Jerusalem in 1697 and published an account of his journey that was read for half a century. Maundrell too laments the departed glory of the land and blames its present waste on the infidels. He reacts strongly against the "mountainous desart" east of Jerusalem (associated with Christ's Temptation) as a "most miserable dry barren place," though he is responding chiefly to the "great convulsion" of the *mountains* there (Maundrell 1963, 106–7). Maundrell saw less of the desert than did Sandys, who journeyed in Egypt; like most pilgrims, he went, Bible in hand, to see the holy places. An appended journal of his travels east of Aleppo says nothing of the desert through which he must have passed for days: it was not part of the Holy Land and did not interest him.

Deserts, then, found no western apostles to witness to their power during the Renaissance, certainly no counterpart of Conrad Gesner or John Dennis in the Alps. Most travellers before the mid-eighteenth century viewed the desert with a shudder of disgust; none found it admirable or sublime. But the formation of an aesthetic of nature involves more than travellers' reports, and so we now turn to theories, asking what early writings about the components of the Great would have led readers to want or expect.

3

Coming to Terms:
Philosophy, Religion, and Science

It must always have been a circle. While the adventurous travelled and reported their reactions, a broad spectrum of intellectuals (some of them also travellers) were reflecting on the meanings of the natural phenomena that eventually coalesced as "the Great." Their speculations shaped the parameters of response to the various facets of the physical world, making it more likely that one of their readers would feel a given emotion at a given place and time, or even go here rather than there. Later travellers then ratified, amended, or voted down the theories as seemed best, influencing future discourse.

For a later, more compartmentalized age it would be possible and desirable to separate the philosophical, theological, aesthetic, and scientific components of western attitudes towards nature, but before 1700 those disciplines had not separated. Donne's "new philosophy" that "calls all in doubt" was science. "Religious philosophy" would describe many of the writings discussed here, but often, as in the Bible, they have aesthetic and quasi-scientific dimensions as well. How could we limit such compendious writers as Lucretius, Dante, Milton, or Burnet to one compartment? What we mean by a "Renaissance mind" is one that oversteps conventional boundaries, and that is what most of these early philosophers of nature did, before, during and after the Renaissance.

THE BIBLICAL AND CLASSICAL HERITAGE

Most of the writers discussed in this book were steeped in the Bible, which treats landscape, sea, and sky in all their manifestations, but particularly the desert, as expressions of a transcendental deity. "The cultural influence of the desert on the Bible cannot be overestimated"

(Mackenzie 1965, 195) because of the Hebrews' encounters with Yahweh there. Ancient Israel conducted a kind of moral trade with the wilderness, exporting "scapegoats" laden with the community's sins, importing prophets of great purity and ethical rigour. Besides its associations with hardship and demons, the desert in both testaments is "the place where man meets God" and "a type of the Christian experience" (196); it figures largely in the prophets' imagery (see, for example, Isa. 35) and was where John and Jesus began their missions. Paul may have withdrawn to the Arabian desert after his conversion (Gal. 1:17). It is a place of purification, refuge, and testing; the test may be failed, but the rewards could be immense, for God is like a well in "a dry and thirsty land," as David sang in the wilderness of Judah (Ps. 63). Of all the landscapes of biblical literature, the desert is the one most often mentioned in a spiritual context.

Of mountains we hear less, although Mount Sinai is where Moses met Yahweh, received the commandments, and had a vision of heaven (Exod. 24:10). Nicolson gives a good summary of biblical references (1963, 42–5), and indeed is indispensable on the history of western attitudes to mountains. High places in general were sacred, used for worship – "I will lift up mine eyes unto the hills, from whence cometh my help" (Ps. 121) – or defence. The rest of the Great figures less prominently. The heavens were where God dwelt and the good might go, while the sea was feared as a monster redolent of chaos, restrained only by God. Of course these images affected writers variously, but most European travellers were at least familiar with them and thus predisposed to look through landscape to its metaphysical meaning.

The philosophical tradition is more diverse. In the *Phaedo* (388–68 BC) Plato seems no admirer of physical nature: the earth is "spoiled and eaten away" like undersea rocks, and as the submarine world is "not comparable in any way with the beauties of our region," so ours cannot be compared with the perfect realm on high (Plato *Phaedo*, 110). But the details of his discussion allow another reading. We normally live "in the hollows" of the earth, breathing bad air and drinking bad water, the "sediment of the ether" above (109C); in fact, "we live ... like ants or frogs around a swamp," and "because of our weakness and slowness we are not able to make our way to the upper limit of the air" (109B, D). Then Plato raises an interesting possibility: "If anyone got to this upper limit," and "if his nature could endure to contemplate" what he saw, "he would know that there is the true heaven, the true light and the true earth," which are "far superior to the things we know" (109E–110).

Of course Plato was advocating an ascent to the sunny realm of Ideas, not a climb of Parnassus or Olympus. But the thrust of the image is upward to a summit, and when Alpine climbing became popular, mountaineers testified to such a realm as Plato described, purer and truer than our world, but not one for the feeble and sluggish: only for those able to make the effort and bear the sight. If this is not influence – and many of the climbers had been educated at universities where Plato was taught – it is certainly a remarkable concurrence. The idea of a sacred ascent "transcending the profane world" has long been widely distributed in the world's cultures and religions (Eliade 1959, 41).

In the Hellenistic period, two philosophers contributed ideas that eventually formed part of Great aesthetics. Lucretius' *De rerum natura* (ca. 55 BC) is an elegant Latin poem depicting a universe of infinite vacancy where the gods live aloofly, untroubled by earthly affairs. Lucretius recommended the study of natural science as an antidote to superstition, and speculated on the mechanism of earthquakes and volcanoes. Recovered in 1417, *De rerum natura*, with its rationalism, vast scale, and secular vision, encouraged the awakening interest in natural science (especially astronomy) and proved compatible with the new expanded model of the universe and with deism.

The impact of the treatise *On Sublimity* by the mysterious Longinus (third century AD?) was demonstrably greater. Translated into French by the respected critic Nicolas Boileau in 1674, it was thence "Englished" in 1712, the year of Addison's essay in number 412 of the *Spectator*, by his friend Leonard Welsted, a desert traveller, who tried to illustrate Longinus's points (Russell in Longinus 1965, xv). *On Sublimity* deals mostly with sublime effects in literature, although the analysis could be applied to natural objects with little change. The one section that discusses landscape says that the natural phenomena we most admire are oceans, stars, and volcanoes (Longinus 1965, 42, sec. 35.4): that is, the Great. The short, undeveloped passage possibly inspired and certainly corroborated the aesthetics of Thomas Burnet, Dennis, Addison, and Burke. Longinus, who may have been from the oasis of Palmyra in the Syrian desert, became almost a cult figure and "the sublime" virtually synonymous with tremendous scenes and experiences. Sublimity was the response most often associated with the Great up to Hardy's time.

In discussing Petrarch, I noted a remarkable passage in the *Confessions* of St Augustine, heir to both the biblical and classical traditions, that implies the concept of Great landscape. Variously translated and inter-

preted, it can be rendered, "Men go out and gaze in astonishment at
high mountains, the huge waves of the sea, the broad reaches of rivers,
the ocean that encircles the world, or the stars in their courses. But they
pay no attention to themselves" (Augustine 1964, 216, bk.10, sec. 8).
While Petrarch, reading this passage on Mont Ventoux in 1335, felt that
it rebuked his admiration of the vista and turned to his soul, the context
shows that Augustine is celebrating the marvel of human response to
and visual recall of great natural phenomena, rather than the phenomena themselves. He does not condemn the study of nature, but asks us
to recognize what we contribute to it, a point developed by Kant. Thus
we know that the psychological and emotional bases on which Great aesthetics would be built existed for the ancient Mediterranean peoples.

EUROPEAN IMAGININGS AND DISCOVERIES

Around 1314, Dante, drawing on Catholic theology and tradition, provided an allegorical interpretation of mountaineering by imaging Purgatory as a "mountain which cures / by being climbed" (1954, *Purgatory*,
canto 13, lines 2–3), each ledge being an antidote to one of the Seven
Deadly Sins. The purifying and curative effects of mountaineering would
become a basic tenet of climbers in the nineteenth century. Even some of
the disciplines employed on Mt Purgatory – loading heavy weights on the
proud, making the slothful develop habits of speed and the gluttonous
practice restraint – have turned out to be useful on real climbs.

Other areas of the Great also became literary metaphors in the early
Renaissance. In Eustache Deschamps's "Lay du desert d'Amours," written
in the fourteenth or fifteenth century, his love has the beauty of the stars,
but he has lived to an age (he is thirty) when love has become a desert.
'Come not into this desert,' he warns; nothing grows or lives in its dessication (Deschamps 1880, lines 236–48). Yet there is also something about
this place that 'closely accords with his soul' ("qui fort m'agrée"), an idea
that later poets such as Leconte de Lisle and Théophile Gautier would
develop into a love/hate relationship with barren landscapes. At the beginning of the seventeenth century, Shakespeare sent King Lear onto an
English heath at the nadir of his fortunes to learn something about the
"poor, bare, forked animal" in that empty space he had not learned elsewhere. "Is man no more than this?" asks Lear of the ragged, raving Edgar.
"Thou art the thing itself" (act 3, sc. 4). Shakespeare too intuits a connection between the heath and the human condition.

But it was above all Renaissance science that created the enlarged conceptual field in which the "aesthetics of the infinite" (Nicolson 1959) grew and the attitudinal climate that allowed it to flourish. In 1571 Peter Severinus, a Danish physician, argued the importance of travel and the empirical method for anyone who wanted to understand the world. Sell your possessions and burn your books, he urged his readers, "buy yourselves stout shoes, get away to the mountains, search the valleys, the deserts, the shores of the sea ... watch and experiment without wearying. In this way, and no other, will you arrive at a knowledge of things and of their properties" (quoted in Geikie 1897, 6). Before Bacon or Descartes, centuries before "Go and see" became the watchword of the geologists, Severinus espoused a scientific approach to nature and experience.

The late sixteenth and early seventeenth centuries gave European cosmology a thorough shaking up that required radical readjustments in many areas. The Copernican revolution, which un-centred the earth, is the prime example of such re-visions, although Copernicus himself was relatively conservative in describing the universe as *immensum*, 'immeasureable' (Koyré 1994, 32). A less well known but more revolutionary thinker, Cardinal Nicholas of Cusa (whom Giordano Bruno, Kepler, and Descartes considered the first to deny the mediaeval conception of a limited universe), called it *interminatum* ('interminate' or 'boundless'; pp. 6, 8). He reserved infinity for God, but calling the universe 'boundless' is already bolder than simply saying we cannot measure it. Then Bruno made the dangerous leap to asserting that space is an infinite void, thus transferring to the physical universe what had previously been an attribute of God (Lovejoy 1936, 116; Koyré 1994, 35–40). This inclusion of hitherto divine qualities within an enlarged concept of nature was a fundamental precondition for the evolution of the Great from the older ideal of beauty.

In the same period, technological advances, especially in optics, were contributing to the intellectual upheaval. The discoveries of "new" stars by Tycho Brahe (1572), Kepler (1604), and others helped to undermine the concept of an immutable cosmos and encouraged evolutionary thought. Yet most scientists were cautious, not iconoclastic. Kepler gave both scientific and metaphysical reasons for denying that space might be infinite and confessed his horror of the idea (Koyré 1994, 58, 61). Galileo's *Sidereus nuncius* (*The Message of the Stars*, 1610), with its accounts of recently discovered stars and planets, and mountains on the moon, had considerable impact across Europe, but, though his data suggest a universe of great size, Galileo settled for Nicholas's word: 'boundless.' Of course the book had to be passed by Church censors for publication. Descartes, who also had to placate theologians, called God 'infinite' and the universe 'indefinite' in extent (101–9).

By the mid-seventeenth century, science and religious philosophy were deeply engaged in debating the new cosmology, and aesthetic consequences could begin to be seen. Blaise Pascal, himself a formidable scientist, reacted strongly against the enlarged universe. In his *Pensées* 91 (1657–60) he says, "Le silence éternel de ces espaces infinis m'effraye" – 'The eternal silence of these infinite spaces terrifies me' (Pascal 1976). This is in the "Man without God" section, and some scholars have argued that this is the *libertin* (freethinker) speaking, not Pascal. In that case, Pascal is imagining how the idea of an infinite cosmos strikes terror into the godless soul, and grasping his own faith more firmly. The notion of being surrounded by a blank void – the Great as existential terror – still haunted some nineteenth-century poets and novelists.

Others were less *effrayé*, though equally impressed. Bernard le Bovier de Fontenelle's *Entretiens sur la pluralité des mondes* ('Conversations on the Multitude of Worlds,' 1686), a popular defence of Copernicus and Descartes published soon after Halley's comet stirred additional interest in astronomy, takes the form of six conversations between a scientist and a lady. The first gives a powerful sense of space as it shows that the earth rotates and revolves around the sun; the second and third, drawing on Galileo, give details of the lunar world and speculate on the possibility that the moon and other planets are populated. The lady's imagination, already overwhelmed ("accablée") by these ideas (Fontenelle 1955, 107), is further stunned by more information about the other planets in the fourth conversation, and by the theory that the stars are the suns of other worlds in the fifth. The vast empty reaches ("grand espace vide") between systems are presented as both terrifying and exciting (130). On the last evening the "philosopher" shows the significance of marine fossils found on mountains now far inland. Fontenelle's impressive synthesis of current developments in science forced his readers to enlarge their previous concepts of cosmic time and distance enormously.

Boileau's decision to translate Longinus in 1674, then, was part of a widespread interest in natural grandeur.

ENGLISH COSMOLOGY

England contributed substantially to Renaissance speculation about the nature and extent of creation that underlies the idea of the Great, and felt the associated intellectual upheaval. "In these last hundred years," wrote John Dryden late in the seventeenth century, "almost a new Nature has been revealed to us." Thomas Digges, who extended Copernicus's ideas, published a *Perfit Description of the Celestial Orbes* (1577), which managed to assert the infinity of the universe while remaining sufficiently pious to avoid trouble with the Church. William Gilbert's influential work on magnetism, *De magnete* (1600), also upheld the idea of infinite space, to Kepler's dismay.

An even more important figure was the Cambridge Platonist Henry More, credited by Nicolson with inventing the "aesthetics of the infinite." His *Democritus Platonissans* (1646) went far towards building a theology of infinity into the findings of the new astronomy. The world and time, he said, are infinite; God virtually *is* space, and all of His power is in every atom of matter, which is eternal. In More, space is hallowed as the abode and representation of Deity, something that gives a shadowy notion of God. The microcosm of this idea was the "illusion of infinity" given by vast landscapes, which might seem mere wastes to man but were still expressions of God's art (Tuveson 1951, 23–5, 33; Nicolson 1959, 122, 136–8). The book led to an interesting correspondence in 1648–49 with Descartes, who argued against More's infinite void space.

More's later writings identify space "with the divine extension itself" (Koyré 1994, 135). His *Enchiridium metaphysicum* (1671) boldly "asserts the real existence of infinite void space" and makes it eternal, though it backs away from his earlier statement that the *world* is infinite (137, 153). As in the case of Bruno, the attribution of qualities previously held to be divine prerogatives (eternity, infinity) to the physical universe was seminal for the concept of the Great, and helps to explain the awe it evoked. The influence of More's ideas on aesthetics is beyond doubt: he and his fellow Platonist Ralph Cudworth both taught Thomas Burnet at Cambridge, and later Burnet taught Addison. Cudworth's views on nature also influenced Shaftesbury (C. Moore 1953, 68–71).

While the Platonists were discussing cosmology at Cambridge, the "compleat scientist" Robert Hooke was teaching earth history, physics, navigation, and astronomy in London. His course of lectures to the Royal Society in 1667–68 introduced his audiences to evolutionary ideas in several fields. Analyzing the available data on mountains (especially volcanoes), fossils, and earthquakes, he concluded that "a great part of the Surface of the Earth hath been since the Creation transformed and made of another Nature ... Parts which have been Sea are now Land" (Hooke 1705, 290), as Leonardo da Vinci and Fontenelle had noted. Since both species and landforms have come and gone in historical time, the earth must be very ancient: mountains are the "warts" of its old age, fossils the "most lasting [ancient] Monuments of Antiquity," far older than the pyramids (348, 335). Hooke urged scientists to seek "proximate [natural] Causes," rather than invoke miracles to explain gaps in knowledge, but he avoided any assertion that might contradict the Bible (423–4; Albritton 1986, 52).

Not all cosmologists were philosophers or scientists; John Milton cast a long shadow in aesthetics, as in literature. One of the first poets to convey the affective content of the new astronomy's "infinite sublime" (Nicolson 1959, 273), he remained a potent influence on sensitive readers for centuries. *Paradise Lost* (ten books, 1667; twelve books, 1674) draws on Lucretius and Dante but also dramatizes the enlarged sense of space and time associated with Giordano Bruno and Henry More. In Book Two, for example, Satan travels from Hell into the "wild Abyss" of Chaos, a "vast vacuity" that is "neither sea,/ Nor good dry land," through which he must stride/swim/fly like the archetype of all explorers (Milton 1953, bk. 2, lines 910, 932, 939–40). Across this "darksome desert" he blazes the trail that would later become "a broad and beaten way" (lines 973, 1,026). Milton imparts a feeling of spaciousness to earth, too. Readers can share Satan's wonder at the vista where "Eden stretched her line / From Auran eastward to the royal towers / Of great Seleucia, built by Grecian kings" (bk. 4, lines 205, 210–12): a secular view of space and time whose sacred counterpart is the vast historical panorama that Michael shows Adam from a hilltop in Books Eleven and Twelve.

That scene foreshadows Satan's temptation of Christ atop a mountain in the Judaean wilderness, narrated in *Paradise Regained* (1671). There again the emphasis is on earth's scale – "so large/ The prospect was, that here and there was room / For barren desert, fountainless and dry" (1953, bk. 3, lines 262–4) – as Satan points out Assyria, Persia, Arabia, and the rest. Travel to the actual Mideast was still difficult in the 1670s, but the resonant allusions and evocative imagery of Milton's verse provided an imaginative surrogate: a notable exception to Francis Palgrave's generalization that from 1660 to 1730 English verse rarely, and then narrowly, depicted landscape (1897, 166–7).

The impact of the new science and philosophy is felt in other seventeenth-century English religious writers as well. Henry Vaughan's "The World" (1650), for example, is a mystic's dream vision in which "Eternity" appears as "a great Ring of pure and endless light," below which Time moves "Like a vast shadow," bearing the misery and pettiness of earth (Vaughan 1963, line 2). But pious men could view the same data differently. Thomas Traherne, like Henry More, assumes the infinity of space in *Centuries of Meditations*, yet finds only joy in contemplating the beauties of creation, "a glorious mirror" and a foretaste of heaven (1908, pt. 2, meditation 17). Nature may be fallen, only "the remainders of Paradise" (2.17), yet "this visible World is the body of God" (2.21). The future of the aesthetic movement being traced here lay with such deism, not with Vaughan's *contemptus mundi*, which Traherne condemned as an "abominable corruption" (1.31).

The condition of the earth, and the reasons for it, worried several poets. John Donne's "An Anatomy of the World" (1611) depicts a planet disjointed by the Fall and revealed by science as "spent" and "rotten," with "all coherence gone"; mountains and ocean trenches disfigure it like "warts, and pock-holes" (1978, lines 205, 209, 242, 213, 300). In *Poly-Olbion* (1622), Michael Drayton admits that mountains help defend a country against invaders, but finds them "presumptuous," "monstrous," and "grim" (1889, 1:65, 229; 2:164). Andrew Marvell believed that the earth was smooth before the Fall, and that the present "rude heap" of "Gulfes, Deserts, Precipices" was a product of original sin ("Upon Appleton House"). Gardens and parks, echoes of Eden, delight us; a mountain is an "excrescence" whose deformed, "hook-shoulder'd height" is frightening ("Upon the Hill and Grove at Bill-borow"). John Dryden agreed: "High objects may attract the sight; but it looks up with pain on Craggy Rocks and Barren Mountains" (1966, dedication to *The Indian Emperor*, 1667). This gloomy English view of mountains, however, was about to change.

THOMAS BURNET AND THEORIES OF THE EARTH

Out of Thomas Burnet's clerical piety and his European travels of 1671–74 came a remarkable book. *Telluris theoria sacra* (1680–81), which, at the request of Charles II, Burnet translated as *The Sacred Theory of the Earth* (1684–89), made the meaning of high mountains (and of Great landscape in general) a subject of discussion throughout Europe. Some of the encomia and attacks on the book were so extravagant, and

some modern summaries of Burnet's position are so oversimplified, that
it is important to review what he actually said, which is remarkable partly
for its ambivalence.

From the standpoint of Great aesthetics, the chapter "Concerning the
Mountains of the Earth" is seminal. "The greatest objects of Nature,"
Burnet writes, "are the most pleasing to behold"; next to the heavens,
nothing gives him "more pleasure than the wide Sea and the Mountains
of the Earth," there being "something august and stately" in them "that
inspires the mind with great thoughts and passions" (1965, bk. 1, 109).
Why? Burnet's view is that anything possessing "the shadow and appearance of INFINITE," that is, any phenomenon "too big for our comprehension," fills the mind to overflowing with "stupor and admiration"
and makes us "think of God and his greatness" (109–10). This goes well
beyond Longinus and Augustine, if not Gesner, and was certainly the
fullest aesthetic analysis undertaken to that time in England. For Joseph
Addison, growing up in the shadow of Burnet and his work, it must have
seemed only natural to call his highest category of aesthetic experience
"the Great."

But Burnet reveals radically mixed feelings about mountains, which
he believed were "the taller parts" of the "great ruines" of the earth's
youth before the Fall (110, 112). (Plato's discussion of the upper and
lower worlds in the *Phaedo* may be in the background here.) To counter
any illusions that the earth's surface is smooth and regular, Burnet provides sketches of terrestrial hemispheres, "such bare draughts as shew us
Nature undrest" (110). Ranges such as the Alps are, he says, "a multitude of vast bodies thrown together in confusion" (111); geology had
not yet made sense of such landscapes. Beauty should not be expected.
Having seen at close range "how barren, how desolate, how naked" the
Alps are, possessing "neither form nor beauty, nor shape, nor order"
(112), Burnet calls for topographical maps and relief globes of these
"ill-figured" mountains and other irregularities (seas and "vast desarts of
Sand") to show "what a rude Lump our World is" (118).

But why dwell on the rudeness of the earth? In Book Two Burnet suggests that the prelapsarian earth had no seas or mountains, but was a
smooth, fertile, forested plain, watered by rivers fed by condensation: a
belief shared by Marvell and others in the period. Rugged mountains
are thus a reminder of the Fall, a standing reproach. Though the universe was made not for man but for some larger Divine purpose (bk. 2,
xi), the inorganic creation merits study and contemplation, for "*The
Course of Nature is truly the Will of God*" (221; Burnet's emphasis). Thus

Burnet's "physico-theology," like his aesthetics, is bipolar. Fallen Nature ought to, and in some cases does, horrify us, yet it is edifying, and the heavens manifest Divine power and purpose.

Burnet's ambivalence reflected a debate over the meaning of nature that was as old as Scripture, and his version of earth history did not go uncontested. Erasmus Warren's *Geologia* (1690) envisions a kinder God than Burnet's, one who would not fling natural ugliness in our faces for an old affront; modern nature, though changed, is no less beautiful for its irregularities (Ogden 1947, 142–5; Nicolson 1963, 263–8). Warren confines himself to the English countryside, ignoring the Great, but John Ray, whose *Wisdom of God Manifested in the Works of Creation* (1691) argued that mountains are both useful and ornamental, says that he travelled through Alpine snow for four days one March and observed butterflies on the summits (Ray 1735, 215–20). Ray's thesis, developed in a series of "discourses," was that if we "converse with Nature as well as Books," we can infer a deity who is benevolent and wise as well as powerful (quoted in Willey 1962, 41).

"Mountain gloom" was less widespread than one might assume from the scattered evidence of seventeenth-century travellers; Burnet's sacred theory did not represent the full spectrum of opinion about mountains, which had many defenders. John Beaumont's *Considerations on ... The Theory of the Earth* (1693) held that mountains have their uses and their beauties (Collier 1968, 85, 91; Ogden 1947, 147–8). John Woodward's *Essay towards a Natural History of the Earth* (1695) differs with Burnet on the alleged ugliness of mountains, while agreeing that nature bears the impress of man's fall (Glacken 1967, 409–11; Collier 1968, chapter 13). William Whiston, a student of Isaac Newton, argued that the present earth is quite good enough for such a creature as man in his *New Theory of the Earth* (1696), a popular emendation of Burnet (Glacken 1967, 411–12).

These commentators generated a controversy that set the European intellectual community to debating the earth's changes and their meaning. In replying to his critics, Burnet relied more on nature than on Scripture, which ruined his ecclesiastical career but did him no harm with scientists (for awhile) or poets. Robert Hooke took a critical interest in the book, and Newton wrote Burnet a generally favourable letter (Albritton 1986, 58; Nicolson 1959, 235n.24). Richard Steele and Joseph Warton classed Burnet with Plato, Cicero, and Milton; Addison wrote a Latin ode in his honour and adapted Burnet's remarks on aesthetics to his own purposes in *Spectator* number 412. Poets such as James

Thomson, Wordsworth, and Coleridge (who considered turning the *Theoria* into blank verse) were moved by Burnet's descriptions of earth's ancient convulsions.

By the nineteenth century the scientific reception had cooled – Charles Lyell described the *Sacred Theory* as "a fine historical romance" – but an imaginative writer such as Jules Verne could still use it to decorate science fiction. Leslie Stephen treated Burnet as an important early teacher whom we have outgrown (1894, 24–9). Katherine Collier's *Cosmogonies of Our Fathers* (1934) was the beginning of scholarly recognition; in the 1950s Ernest Tuveson and Marjorie Nicolson established Burnet's importance for eighteenth-century aesthetics. Both Paul Shepard's *Man in the Landscape* (1967), which shows how Burnet linked astronomy to aesthetics, and Claude Albritton's *The Abyss of Time* (1986) place Burnet in a scientific context and grant his historical importance.

LANDSCAPE PAINTING

Some art historians have shown that the sensibilities of Gesner, Burnet, and other early Alpine travellers had analogues in landscape painting as well as in science and religious philosophy (Schama 1995, chapter 7). Pieter Breughel the Elder (late sixteenth century) was "one of the first to depict mountain scenery by itself," and by the early seventeenth century mountains were "probably the most conspicuous feature of [European] landscapes," except in Holland (Ogden and Ogden 1955, 44–5). Several of Joos de Momper's mountainous landscapes, for example, give a strikingly emotive view of hills and peaks. Such landscapes were well known and well liked in England; the influence of Nicholas Poussin, Claude Lorrain, and especially Salvator Rosa not only on painting but on taste in general, on ways of seeing and writing, was so great that they have been credited with effectively founding the "picturesque" and "sublime" schools of English nature writing after Milton (Manwaring 1925, 3–4). John Dennis, argued Manwaring, though spiritually ready for Alpine sublimity, lacked the vocabulary to articulate it until Salvator helped him to see, and Addison's *Spectator* number 412 is as redolent of Claude Lorrain's images as of Burnet's language (5–6, 124).

That there is a similarity of tone and emotion between visual representations and written impressions of mountains late in the seventeenth century is fairly clear. An aura of spirituality, even of religious ecstasy in the wilder locales, is common to both, for instance. The terms critics use to describe shifts in taste among some English writers around 1700 – sublime, wild, primitive – are also applied to innovations in European land-scape painting of the previous generation, and the fondness of some writers for emotional oxymoron ("terrible beauties") is foreshadowed by Salvator Rosa's response of *orrida bellaza* ('horrid' or 'wild beauty') at the Terni waterfall (Manwaring 1925, 169; Schama 1995, 456).

But exactly what weight should we give these parallels? It is not always clear whether the issue is influence or "the spirit of the age," and, if the former, who influenced whom. Adrian van Diest, whose "Mountain Landscape" has the kind of scenery that moved Burnet and Dennis, may have read Dennis's description of his Alpine travels and so have been following, not leading (Ogden and Ogden 1955, 140, 146). Yet a painter who reads a book, or an author who sees a painting, does not *have* to imitate it. When the choice of subject matter, the point of view, and the response sought from the audience appear remarkably similar in the writer and the painter, this may be due to one having seen or read the other, or to the proclivities of the period. Whether the writers discussed in this study were feeling a particular or a general influence, however, matters less than the phenomenon of their enthusiasm for the developing "aesthetics of the infinite," that is, for what was about to be identified as "the Great." Travellers and artists were being drawn to certain types of wild landscape well before Addison drafted his manifesto rationalizing this attraction.

PART II

Recognizing Greatness: The Eighteenth Century

Using as materials the seventeenth-century developments in science, religion, philosophy, and travel discussed in Part One, eighteenth-century Europe began to construct a road that would eventually reach Egdon Heath. The poems, letters, essays, and expeditions of that period testify to a growing interest in the largest natural phenomena and their possible meanings for humanity. Marjorie Nicolson documented the shift in British attitudes towards mountains over the century (1959), but the factors that underlay that change operated in other countries and for some other geographical features as well.

4

The Great and the Sublime:
British Aesthetics

Generally speaking, three important developments in eighteenth-century British intellectual life furthered the shift in attitudes towards nature that underlay the phenomenon Hardy described: the appearance of aesthetics as an independent branch of philosophy; an increased tendency to reverence nature as a deity; and an emerging consensus that certain kinds of topography could produce religious or quasi-religious emotions. Each of the authors treated in this chapter exhibits, in varying degrees, all three tendencies.

SHAFTESBURY AND NATURE

After a long period of neglect, the writings of Anthony Ashley Cooper, third earl of Shaftesbury, are again being treated with respect, as they were in his own time. Ernst Cassirer hailed him as "the first great aesthetician" in England (Grean 1964, xxxv); his substantial influence on important theorists (Addison, Burke, Diderot, Lessing, Kant) and poets (Goethe, Wordsworth) is now widely recognized (Thacker 1983, 37–9, 77, 229; Grean 1964, xiii–xiv). Shaftesbury's unabashed, ecstatic deism encouraged "natural" as opposed to Bible-centred religion, steering piety towards nature. He has been credited with fathering the essential Romantic attitudes to nature, including the cults of sublimity, wildness, and inspiration, which superseded the symmetries of neoclassical aesthetics (Thacker 1983, 12–18).

Wealthy and wise but not healthy, Shaftesbury led an uneasy if privileged life. He studied classics with his private tutor, John Locke. After attending Winchester for three years, he travelled in Europe (including the Alps), followed by five years of private philosophical study during

which he began to write on ethics. He served six years in Parliament, but
the worsening of his asthma drove him into early, though productive, retirement. Shaftesbury's major writings were published or revised from
1705 to 1711, when he collected them as *Characteristicks of Men, Manners, Opinions, Times.* Then he went to Italy for his health (and further
revisions), dying there at age forty-two.

Shaftesbury's social and ethical writings are confined to the perspective of an aristocratic horizon and marred by a blurring of the distinction between what is and what ought to be. His treatment of nature in
The Moralists (1709) would be open to a similar objection if Theocles'
paean to "glorious Nature" (Shaftesbury 1964, vol. 2, pt. 3, sec. 1)
were not so patently an attitude, a personal impression of the natural
world; the question of its validity as a description of "objective nature"
hardly arises. The heart of Shaftesbury's message is his divinization of
nature, which seemed to him "all-divine," a viceroy or "wise substitute
of Providence": "impowered creatress!" he enthuses, "Or thou impow-
ering Deity, supreme creator!" (2:98). That God rules nature is clear,
and orthodox, but whereas either member of this Holy Duality may
equally well be invoked, nature is easier to image and perhaps provides
images of God, as a "boundless ... ocean," or "an infinity" of stars (98,
112–13).

Developing the important idea – derived from Nicholas of Cusa
through the Cambridge Platonists (Tuveson 1960, 60) – that nature is
to be regarded as a sign of God's power and goodness, not of His curse,
Shaftesbury argued that the study of nature was "the *only* means [my
emphasis] which cou'd establish the *sound Belief* of a Deity" (quoted in
Willey 1962, 68–9). Several far-reaching corollaries follow from the central premise: church and scripture are relegated to the margins of belief; feelings of exaltation are less likely to arise from reading than from
encountering nature, which is far above art; and a wilderness, or wildness of any kind, is preferable to the artifice of a garden (Shepard 1967,
83, 164).

Along with his general reflections on nature, Shaftesbury offered specific commentary on three areas of the Great. Astronomy is highly valued because the heavens' immensity and infinitude of bodies teach us
about the nature of the Creator: "How glorious it is to contemplate him
in this noblest of his works apparent to us, the system of the bigger
world!" (Shaftesbury 1964, 2:112). The sun is hailed as "Mighty being!
brightest image and representative of the Almighty," an image well
rooted in Plato and ancient religion, but the new astronomy has taught

Shaftesbury that "even the smallest spark [star] of this bright galaxy may vie with this our sun": a perception that must enlarge our wonder and adoration. God is apostrophized as "the author and modifier," the "sovereign and sole mover" of "these stupendous bodies" (113).

Of course, there was nothing unusual in reading the heavens as a *codex dei* (book of God) by 1709; Shaftesbury's originality appears when he turns to the "vast deserts" of the Mideast (which he had not seen). At a time when deserts, if discussed at all, were viewed by Europeans as waste and ugly places, symbols of sin, Shaftesbury pursued his argument to its logical conclusion. If nature is "all-lovely," it follows that "all ghastly and hideous as [deserts] appear, they want not their peculiar [i.e., have their own] beauties. The wildness pleases" (122). This short sentence has the sound of tumblers falling. In deserts, "we seem to live alone with Nature"; we "contemplate her with more delight in these original wilds than in the artificial labyrinths and feigned wildernesses of the palace." The divinely ordained landscape, whatever its form, is superior to human imitations (artificial grottoes, formal gardens), and thus "fit to raise our thoughts in admiration of that divine wisdom" underlying its creation. If we do not understand the "uses" of deserts or appreciate their "peculiar beauties," "we are yet assured of the perfection of all" (122). No doubt this is easier to say away from the Sahara, and travellers were slow to endorse this point, but a *theory* of appreciation henceforth existed.

It was a foregone conclusion which side of "the mountain question" Shaftesbury would take, but his line of defence is interesting. After evoking the "trembling steps" and "giddy horror" with which we tread the brink of Alpine precipices (which he *had* seen), he argues that mountains teach us mutability: "Here thoughtless men, seized with the newness of such objects, become thoughtful, and willingly contemplate the incessant changes of this earth's surface" (2:123). The "use" of those heaped boulders, torn-up trees, and subterranean torrents is to demonstrate "the fleeting forms of things, and the decay of this our globe," reminding us of the End of all. Ingeniously, Shaftesbury both accepts Burnet's imagery and turns it to show God "educing good from ill": "the apparent spoil and irreparable breaches of the wasted mountain show [us] the world itself only as a noble ruin, and make [us] think of its approaching period [end]." A great mountain functions as a huge *memento mori*, directing our thoughts forward, not (as in Burnet) back.

Shaftesbury's defence of the place of mountains in God's plan may seem tepid to us, but overall his "mystique of nature" as "a means of grace" (Tuveson 1960, 55) sensitized his readers to the holiness of even the great "waste" places of the natural world. For a sickly earl who did his travelling in his teens, and whose short life was largely occupied by politics or ethical philosophy, this was an impressive personal accomplishment, one that contributed to a cultural movement.

JOSEPH ADDISON AND THE GREAT

At one time it was fashionable to condescend to Addison's mind and career; in some circles it still is, despite the appreciation of Virginia Woolf ("alert to his fingertips") and C.S. Lewis. He was portrayed to generations of students as a middlebrow popularizer of others' ideas, a teatable philosopher. That estimate, however, is untenable in the present context. While we know that Addison did not *originate* the idea of the natural Great, but inherited relevant material from diverse thinkers, he reworked what he received in ways that are undeniably fresh and original. Addison was the first English writer to treat aesthetics as an autonomous subject and shadowed forth the modern fascination with the vast or Great in nature (Tuveson 1960, 92; 1951, 20). A list of those demonstrably indebted to his writings reads like a *Who's Who* of eighteenth-century aesthetics: Mark Akenside, John Baillie, Edmund Burke, Lord Kames, Immanuel Kant. That Addison accomplished what he did in the context of some of England's first periodical journalism does not taint his achievement, but makes it more remarkable.

Read in chronological order, Addison's writings on the Great reveal a gap between early experience and later theory. His reports on his travels in Switzerland and Italy (1699–1703) do little to prepare us for his essay in number 412 of the *Spectator*. In a letter to Wortley Montagu from Geneva in December 1701, he calls his crossing of the Alps "very troublesome"; still "giddy with mountains and precipices" after days of "shivering among the *eternal snows*," he is "pleased with the sight of a plain" (Addison 1893, 5:336–7). In *Remarks on Several Parts of Italy, Etc.* (1705), Addison says he enjoyed his first passage of the Apennines but found his second "tedious" (1:414–15, 502). Crossing the Alps in December, he pronounced them "vast heaps ... thrown together with ... much irregularity and confusion" (agreeing with his former teacher Thomas Burnet), though the lakes delighted him (507). From Lake Geneva, a view of the "irregular" and "misshapen" Alps gave him "an agreeable kind of horror" (510–11). His language is close to that of John Dennis, whose letter describing his crossing had been published in 1693. Dennis and

Addison were among the first to apply this kind of emotional oxymoron to the Alps; it soon became a standard epithet.

When, years later, Addison began to write reflectively of his Alpine experiences, his tone was very different. In *The Tatler* no. 161 (April 1710), a dreamer finds himself in the high Alps, where he discovers the home of the goddess of Liberty, her eyes darting a "shining and glorious" light. But the essays on "the pleasures of the imagination" in *The Spectator* (nos. 411–21, June-July 1712) are the heart of Addison's aesthetics. Number 411, a general introduction to the relevant physiology and psychology, follows John Locke in arguing for the primacy of sight among the senses; "a more delicate and diffusive kind of Touch," it fills the mind with images and ideas, which provide imaginative pleasures (Addison 1965, 3:536). These may arise either from scenes before us (primary) or, as Augustine marvelled, from recollected images (secondary). If the pleasures of the imagination are grosser than those of the understanding (i.e., conceptual thought), they are equally strong, and more refined than the pleasures of sense. They give a man "a kind of Property in every thing he sees" (538).

In number 412 Addison founds his aesthetics on this base by dividing pleasurable sights into the Great, the Uncommon, and the Beautiful. He does not rank them, but discusses Greatness first, and in subsequent essays develops its connection with the Deity. The fundamental requirement for this category is "the Largeness of a whole View," such as the vistas afforded by "open Champian [champaign, i.e., extensive plain] Country, a vast uncultivated Desart, ... huge Heaps of Mountains, high Rocks and Precipices, or a wide Expanse of Waters" (540). These share a "rude kind of Magnificence" that produces "a pleasing Astonishment" in the beholder; we "feel a delightful Stillness and Amazement in the Soul at the Apprehension of them," for the human mind "naturally hates" everything that suggests restraint, including a narrow view, whereas "a spacious Horison is an Image of Liberty" (541). Liberty – the subject of a famous speech by the hero of Addison's tragedy *Cato* (1712), applauded by both Whigs and Tories – rules the psychology of the Great from her Alpine palace. Broad vistas, Addison believes, "are as pleasing to the Fancy [imagination], as the Speculations of Eternity or Infinitude are to the Understanding," constituting a secular or natural counterpart of the highest meditations we can attain.

Things that are "*new* or *uncommon*" (e.g., spring buds, water in motion) refresh us with "agreeable Surprise" or "Variety," he explains, while "beautiful" objects strike "more directly to the Soul," giving us "secret Satisfaction and Complacency," "Chearfulness and Delight" (542). Beauty is a matter of taste, but one kind arises from symmetrical proportions. (This praise of beauty seems bland, but Addison's contemporaries valued cheerfulness and symmetry more highly than we do.) Significantly, symmetry is made an attribute of the neoclassical concept of beauty, *not* of Addison's original contribution, the Great, which is "rude" and "uncultivated," yet finally superior (540). He acknowledges that the imagination is no purist about these categories; what pleases it most is two or three qualities combined in one object: "a troubled Ocean, a Heaven adorned with Stars and Meteors" (541). Yet while the uncommon may "improve" or the beautiful "finish" the other qualities, the Great will not *subserve* in this manner.[1]

Number 413 confirms the primacy of Great nature, which prompts the mind to contemplate the Creator: this is precisely the non-biblical, non-rational proof of God sought by deism (Tuveson 1960, 101; Nicolson 1963, 315). Later papers elaborate on both the natural stimulus and the human response. Addison's famous ode in *Spectator* number 465 (magnificently set by Haydn) uses the skies as an example of the process:

> The Spacious Firmament on high,
> With all the blue Etherial Sky,
> And spangled Heav'ns, a Shining Frame,
> Their great Original proclaim.   (Addison 1965, 4:144)

Number 489 adds that the ocean gives an "agreeable Horrour" – the same mixed emotion that Addison felt in the Alps – which "prompts the Understanding" to thoughts of God (233–4).

In number 414 Addison agrees with Shaftesbury that nature is superior to art: vaster, bolder, and more various. But since art pleases us most when it most closely resembles nature, he discusses the pleasures that the imagination derives from great, uncommon, or beautiful buildings,

---

1. In *The Beautiful, Novel, and Strange* (1996), Ronald Paulson argues that, of Addison's three categories, the Uncommon or Novel "interested him most," as the most literary category (pp. 49, 53), which may well be true. To believe that the Novel somehow "resolves the unresolvable experience of the Great," and that "the awe of greatness is essentially the curiosity of the Novel *un*satisfied" (49–50), however, I would need more evidence than he provides. The idea that the Great is "only an expansive version of the Novel," and that its epistemology "clearly subordinates it to the Novel" (49–50), puzzles me, but to fix and agree on this hierarchy seems finally unnecessary, either to his argument or to mine.

statues, pictures, words, and music (nos. 415–16). "Great literature" is treated in number 417, where Homer and Milton are cited as poets who "enlarge [the] Imagination" (3:564). Homer in particular "strikes the Imagination wonderfully with what is Great" and "fills his Readers with Sublime *Ideas*" (564–5). (Addison's friend Leonard Welsted translated Boileau's rendering of "Longinus on the Sublime" in 1712.) One of Addison's similes connects Homer closely to the natural Great: "Reading the *Iliad* is like travelling through a Country uninhabited, where the Fancy is entertained with a thousand Savage Prospects of vast Desarts" (564–5).

The remaining essays in the group also treat the (secondary) artistic imagination, without forgetting that its basis is nature. In number 418, however, Addison adopts Sidney's position that the poetic imagination, because it requires "something more perfect in Matter, than what it finds there," *idealizes* Nature, "mending and perfecting" her (569). This is not an amendment to the process described in number 412, where the natural Great provided a stimulus strong enough to stun the soul, but an admission that the secondary imagination, recollecting in tranquillity, must leap in to compensate for the absence of the natural stimulus. And in number 419, the practitioner of "*the Fairie* [supernatural] *way of Writing*" creates "new Worlds" out of his own imagination (570, 573). Akenside, Kant, and the Romantics would develop these ideas and further the debate over the relative contributions of nature and the imagination to Great aesthetics.

Number 420 asserts that nonfiction – history, philosophy, travel reports, scientific writing – can also "gratifie and enlarge the Imagination" by illuminating the Creation (574). It is above all "the Authors of the new Philosophy" with their telescopes who engage both our reasoning and speculative faculties as we try to follow them "almost to an infinitude" (575). (Addison refers to "Infinite Space." This idea, which had been perilous for Bruno and controversial for Henry More, seems to have created no stir at all by 1712.) The statement that "we are filled with a pleasing Astonishment, to see so many Worlds hanging one above another, and sliding round their Axles in such an amazing Pomp and Solemnity" removes any doubts that the heavens should be considered part of the Great, "pleasing Astonishment" being precisely the phrase used in number 412 to introduce the idea. Our imaginations reach their limits here; "we are lost" and "confounded" by space, though Addison insists that the Understanding (reason) can take over when Fancy "finds her self swallowed up in the Immensity of the Void" (576). How this will work, why it must be so, we are not told, but he was probably thinking of Newton's laws.

Addison closed the series with the observation (no. 421) that metaphors of nature please both reason and imagination if they are accurate and sufficiently general, a belief that encouraged literature with a strong natural basis. After discussing Great nature as an incentive to religion in numbers 465 and 489 (see above), Addison moved on to other endeavours, but "the Great" was fairly launched, and his aesthetic manifesto continued to influence fellow enquirers, including Burke and Kant, throughout the century (Elioseff 1963, 114–19; Nicolson 1963, 313).

BURKE AND THE SUBLIME

Edmund Burke, one of the most remarkable men of the eighteenth century, published *A Philosophical Enquiry into the Origin of Our Ideas of the Sublime and the Beautiful* (1757) when he was twenty-eight but may have started work on it when he was eighteen, so it is not surprising that his influential treatise was highly derivative, rather than daringly original (Boulton 1987, viii, xviii; Sigworth 1971, 312; Monk 1960, 235). It drew on the psychology of sensations sketched in Locke's *Essay on Human Understanding*, as developed in aesthetics by Shaftesbury, Addison, and others (Nicolson 1963, 313), and perhaps on John Baillie's *Essay on the Sublime* (Boulton 1987, xvii; Monk 1960, 73–4). Baillie treated the literary sublime as the imaginative equivalent of the natural sublime, wherein "vast extended Views, *Mountains*, the *Heavens*, and an immense *Ocean*" (Addison's Great) elevate the soul and make the mind conscious of its own vastness (Baillie 1953, 4–6). We may wonder how sublimity can do this and still be "a solemn *Sedateness*" that "*composes*" the mind (11, 7), but Baillie's central thesis, that "Vast Objects occasion vast Sensations" (7), had been gaining adherents in England since the late seventeenth century.

In addition, Burke drew on travel writers, including Shaftesbury, Addison, Burnet, and Dennis (Tuveson 1960, 171). The perceptions and moods that had become staples of English poetry since the 1720s, especially in the works of James Thomson, Edward Young, Mark Akenside, and Thomas Gray, also pervade the *Enquiry* (Monk 1960, 88–90; Nicolson 1963, 313, 358). John Dennis's *Grounds of Criticism in Poetry* (1702), David Hume's *Treatise of Human Nature* (1739–40), and William Smith's 1739 commentary on Longinus have been identified as other influences

(Boulton 1987, xvi–xvii). The end result at times seems a pioneering effort in aesthetics, at others just a synthesis of existing attitudes.

Burke's introduction "On Taste" (added to the second edition, 1759) seeks the operative principles of the imagination, though ultimately (1987, pt. 4, sec. 1) he settles for the "efficient causes" of certain effects, final causes being beyond human knowledge. For Burke, the most powerful passions are those involving "*pain* and *danger*" to the individual (1.6; 1987, 38). This belief generates his principal thesis: *whatever is terrible*, exciting ideas of alarm and suffering, *is sublime*, and will produce stronger emotions than any other stimulus, including pleasure (1.7, 2.2 and 4.5). Burke argues, though, that pain and danger, which at close range are terrible, can, at a certain distance and with some "modifications" (40; see also pt. 4, sec. 6), be a source of delight: an argument sometimes used to explain the appeal of tragedy. Applied to Alpine travellers such as Burnet, Dennis, and Addison, this idea provides a framework for understanding both the stronger, darker emotions they felt in the mountains, and their subsequent reflections on the experience; it also bears on what Hardy says about the appeal of Egdon Heath.

Part Two of the *Enquiry* explores the psychological and aesthetic dimensions of sublimity. Burke, who uses "Great" and "sublime" as synonyms (3.27), agrees with Addison that "the great and sublime in *nature*" produce an "astonishment" wherein the mind is "entirely filled with its object" (2.1, 57). Burke attempts to isolate the qualities or kinds of things that terrify us sublimely. Above all, he says, we find obscurity more moving than clarity: "A clear idea is ... a little idea" (63). Thus infinity and eternity, or any approach to them, move us precisely because we cannot comprehend them. Power is always sublime, and most of all Divine power, because it is absolute (2.5). Large-scale deprivations such as emptiness, darkness, solitude, and silence are sublimely terrible, and "Greatness of dimension is a powerful cause of the sublime" (72). Vertical extension (height or depth) seems more sublime than horizontal extension, though why this should be so he cannot determine.

Most of the later sections draw inferences from these fundamentals. Extremes of light or darkness and rapid transitions between light and dark (lightning) transcend our sensory capacities and produce sublime obscurity; gloomy and cloudy scenes are more sublime than their opposites because more obscure. Infinity combines obscurity and vastness. Smooth, polished surfaces are not sublime but beautiful, a weaker quality because it is founded on pleasure, not pain (3.27; Thacker 1983, 78–9). Reiterating the important role of (distanced) terror in producing sublimity, Burke suggests that vast objects are sublime because the eye is almost pained in viewing them. His aesthetics seems particularly physiological, his sublime something we feel physically (Monk 1960, 97–8; Tuveson 1960, 168).

Burke's essay had a significant impact on European aesthetics (Lokke 1982), helping to define the more affective sense of the natural sublime that was emerging from the mainly rhetorical conception found in Longinus; its terms and distinctions appear in writers as diverse as Johnson, Ann Radcliffe, Wordsworth, Diderot, Lessing, and Kant (Boulton 1987, xxiii–xlviii; Monk 1960, 84–7, 94). Several of the qualities that Burke found productive of sublimity – chiefly power and vastness – have been widely endorsed by posterity, both in the study and in the field. The *Enquiry* gave "sublime" its associations with wildness, divinity, and terrible greatness (Thacker 1983, 77). Burke's impact lingered even after his analysis had been superseded: in the 1820s Tennyson supplied his poem "On Sublimity" with an epigraph from the *Enquiry*. In retrospect, Burke's emphasis on the fearful, his analysis of how scenes and objects really affect us, and his distinctions between the sublime (or Great) and the beautiful seem his most significant contributions to the tradition that Addison defined and the Romantics "chastened" (Monk 1960, 92–3; S.F. Johnson 1959).

The conservative political views of Burke's later career have been read back into the *Enquiry* by ideological critics from Mary Wollstonecraft (see chapter 10), who considered sublimity masculine (de Bruyn 1996, 206–7), to Terry Eagleton (1990, 52–60). While these polemical readings lie off the road to Egdon Heath, it is true that the Great was – like so much else – mainly a male concern in its first century. That began to change in the 1790s with Ann Radcliffe – and Mary Wollstonecraft.

NORTHERN VIEWS:
GERARD, KAMES, BLAIR, PRIESTLEY

Most later eighteenth-century British aestheticians acknowledged the importance of Shaftesbury, Addison, or Burke and continued their interest in the Great, but broke little new ground. All were northerners; perhaps the austere topography of north Britain acted on them as Alpine passes had on their predecessors.

Alexander Gerard, a Scottish preacher and professor, treated the "Taste of Grandeur and Sublimity" in his *Essay on Taste* (1759) as a sense "higher and nobler" than others, valuing objects that "possess *quantity*, or amplitude, and *simplicity*, in conjunction": ocean, sky, the Alps, "or the immensity of space uniformly extended without limit" (1764, 11). Acknowledging the influence of Baillie, Gerard uses the association of ideas to explain our responses to such scenes (Boulton 1987, xxix). Natural grandeur, by suggesting divine omnipotence, gains the "power to exalt the disposition of the observer"; "the mind expands itself to the extent of that [vast] object, and is filled with one grand sensation" (Gerard 1764, 14, 12): as clear a description as had been provided of how the Great might work for the theist. Gerard held that whatever excites emotions similar to those aroused by vast natural phenomena – thinking of eternity, reading great literature, seeing a great army – can be sublime. There is less terror and pain than in Burke, more joy, nobility, and pride in the capacity to respond to the divine symbol (Monk 1960, 110).

Another influential Scot, Henry Home, Lord Kames, drew on Addison, Baillie, and Gerard for his treatment of beauty and sublimity in *Elements of Criticism*. Sublimity is more "serious" and "vivid" than beauty in that our "capacious and aspiring" minds are drawn to "great and elevated" things, which create an emotional counterpart in us (Kames 1824, 101–3). Extensive vistas of ocean, sky, or high mountains can "raise the strongest emotion of grandeur." Of Burke's stress on fear there is no trace.

Hugh Blair's "Lectures on Rhetoric and Belles Lettres" at Edinburgh, delivered from 1762 onwards and published in 1783, had a long life in reprints and provide a valuable summary of contemporary opinion on the sublime. "Sublimity in Objects" takes the deist line that God gave us a taste for natural grandeur in order to promote worship of Himself. Acknowledging Addison and the poet Mark Akenside as important predecessors, Blair agrees that sublime nature (wide plains, high mountains, sky, ocean, and "All vastness") produces an "internal elevation and expansion," filling the beholder with astonishment and awe quite unlike the emotions aroused by beauty (Blair 1824, 35). Several of Burke's "sublime qualities" are endorsed – infinity, eternity, power, deprivation, obscurity, and vastness – but terror is once more marginalized; the core of Blair's sublime is power. Lecture Four treats literature that describes objects or emotions "of a sublime nature" (42–3). To the usual examples – Homer, the Bible, Milton – Blair adds James Macpherson's *Ossian* (see chapter 5), whose publication he had encouraged and hailed.

No one would call Blair an innovator; he exhibits the academic and religious establishment incorporating sublime aesthetics within a traditional framework: the study of rhetoric. In the Nonconforming

Yorkshire Socinian Joseph Priestley, on the other hand, we have a figure outside the system. Priestley devoted one of his "Lectures on Oratory and Criticism" (1777) to the sublime, and the treatment is in part familiar. Again we hear of minds enlarged by mountains, broad plains, ocean, sky, and space, giving us a pleased consciousness of our own mental powers. Again the Bible, Milton, and *Ossian* exemplify the literary sublime. But Priestley's mind was more original and multifaceted than Blair's; we feel the energy that drove him to write histories of both Christianity and electricity in the notion that "Great objects please us ... by the exercise they give to our faculties" (quoted in Sigworth 1971, 431). He thinks of the attributes of Great nature – chiefly height and vastness – as archetypes from which we draw metaphors for human achievement: "a great man," for example, or "a lofty spirit" (435–6). Association of ideas links natural size and power to their human counterparts.

In the course of the eighteenth century, then, British aestheticians defined and analyzed an important new category of experience: the spiritual encounter with grand natural phenomena (the Great or sublime), generating profound, quasi-religious emotions. There was broad agreement as to where these experiences occurred and why God allowed us to have them, but division over their intellectual and emotional content, the analyses ranging from pride and religious ecstasy through liberty to sublimated terror. The common underlying assumption was that Great nature was an integral part of an innocent and exalted process, a Godly instrument whereby transcendental insights could be obtained. Georgian accounts of such revelations generally conform to the responses that Rudolf Otto, in *Das Heilige* (1917), found to be characteristic of sacred experience: awe and religious fear before the *mysterium tremendum* and *mysterium fascinans* (Eliade 1959, 9). That some eighteenth-century Europeans felt these emotions not in church but in the vastness of nature foreshadowed the nineteenth century's fascination with geology.

5

Wild Writing:
The Great in Georgian Literature

The development of a cultural sensibility that responded reverently to the Great was not left to writers on aesthetic philosophy; poets contributed a great deal to the spread of new ideas about nature. In eighteenth-century England, the two groups fed each other: mid-century poets such as Thomson and Akenside freely used Shaftesbury and Addison, while later aestheticians (Blair, Priestley) drew inspiration from these same poets, as well as from earlier essayists. Given the sales figures and allusions that we have, it is likely that more of the reading public became familiar with natural sublimity, and was moved by it, through verse than through prose.

POPE'S ETERNAL SNOWS

The odds were against Alexander Pope figuring in this story: he was too sickly to travel, and he was a Catholic Tory when most enthusiasts for the Great were Anglican Whigs. But Pope was part of Addison's Whig circle until about 1712, read widely in science and travel as well as in *belles lettres*, and exhibited some deist tendencies despite his upbringing (see "The Universal Prayer," ca. 1715). His formidable imagination could grasp and vivify any concept that might give pleasure or instruction, including the power of the Alps and the Arctic to provide supra-human analogues for human experience.

In *An Essay on Criticism* (1711), for example, Pope compares a long course of study to an Alpine climb:

> In *fearless Youth* we tempt the Heights of Arts,
> While from the bounded *Level* of our Mind,

> *Short Views* we take, nor see the *Lengths behind,*
> But *more advanc'd*, behold with strange Surprize
> New, distant scenes of *endless* Science rise!
> So pleas'd at first, the towring *Alps* we try,
> Mount o'er the Vales, and seem to tread the Sky;
> The Eternal Snows appear already past,
> And the first *Clouds* and *Mountains* seem the last:
> But *those attain'd*, we tremble to survey
> The growing Labours of the lengthen'd Way,
> Th'*increasing* Prospect *tires* our wandring Eyes,
> Hills peep o'er Hills, and *Alps* on *Alps* arise!
>
> (1968, lines 220–32)

This passage (modelled on one in Lucretius) continues the allegorical tradition stemming from another Catholic poet, Dante, of treating mountain climbing as symbolic of the struggle to rise above mundane levels, and suggests that Pope was familiar with accounts of Alpine travels.

The Temple of Fame (1715) began as an imitation of Chaucer's *Hous of Fame* but then took its own direction. One of the most striking differences between the two poems is Pope's use of travel literature to give topographic specificity to the setting of Fame's temple. Instead of Chaucer's unlocalized "roche of yse," Pope asks that we imagine such a scene as mariners had reported in the Barents Sea:

> So *Zembla's* Rocks (the beauteous Work of Frost)
> Rise white in Air, and glitter o'er the Coast;
> Pale Suns, unfelt, at distance roll away,
> And on th'impassive Ice the Lightnings play:
> Eternal Snows the growing Mass supply,
> Till the bright Mountains prop th'incumbent Sky:
> As *Atlas* fix'd, each hoary Pile appears,
> The gather'd Winter of a thousand Years.   (1968, lines 53–60)

Pope's note here argues that, although "strict Verisimilitude" is not required in such cases, his simile "renders it not wholly unlikely that a *Rock* of *Ice* should remain for ever, by mentioning something like it in the Northern Regions, agreeing with the Accounts of our modern Travellers." He is alluding to the narratives of Captains Wood and Marten, published by the Royal Society in 1694 and reissued in 1711 (Tillotson 1954, 2:384; see chapter 2). Pope's letter of 21 December 1712 probably refers to these: "The severity of the cold has turned my studies to those books, which treat of the descriptions of the Arctic regions, Lapland, Nova Zembla and Spitsberg; deserts of snow, seas of ice and frozen skies" (quoted in Sherburn 1956, 1:166). Pope's "Zembla" conflates scenic details from Wood's account of Novaya Zemlya and Marten's description of Spitsbergen: "Pale Suns" that do not warm, "Eternal Snows" (also a stock phrase of Alpine travellers), and a chiaroscuro landscape that glitters brightly despite "incumbent" clouds. Other details from their narratives, such as the preservative qualities of permafrost, the appearance of precious minerals, the atmosphere that deceives about size and distance, and the purity of the environment, turn up elsewhere in the poem.

The broad relationship between the original poem and Pope's "imitation" is instructive. Chaucer's geography is vague (a desert in Book One, a high rock of ice near a street in Book Three); Pope tries to create a realistic environment for Fame's temple. Where Chaucer's eagle-borne "Geffrey" looked down on a generic landscape of fields, plains, hills, and mountains, Pope's vision comprises "naked Rocks, and empty Wastes" (1968, line 15). Chaucer's rock of ice now has "ambient Clouds" around a "tow'ring Summit," much like Marten's description of Spitsbergen. Though the passage on Zembla is cast as a simile, the next line, "On this Foundation *Fame*'s high Temple stands" (61), drops the notion of similitude and places the visionary temple on the actual Novaya Zemlya, at the edge of the known world. Pope's Arctic, then, owes more to the action of recent travel literature on his imagination than to the few sketchy hints in Chaucer's poem. This kind of influence was not new: instances of travellers supplying English poets with material go back at least to Shakespeare.

During the period when he was composing these works, Pope kept in touch with Addison's circle; he sent Richard Steele a draft of *The Temple of Fame* in 1712, the year of the "Pleasures of the Imagination" series (Tillotson 1954, 2:236). Apart from some curiosity about the new astronomy in 1714, however, there is little evidence that Pope maintained his interest in the Great, the "Nature" of *An Essay on Man* being too abstract to fit within the subject as defined. The political events of 1714 confirmed his Tory sympathies and isolated him from Whigs. And among the baggage that Pope seems to have jettisoned when he joined the Tory opposition was the Whiggish affinity for the Great.

JAMES THOMSON AND DEIST VERSE

Deists held that we can deduce "th'Eternal from his works," as Sir Richard Blackmore put it in *The Creation*, a "physico-theological" poem (1713, bk. 1, line 12). Admiring the heavens' "wide realms of vast immensity," Blackmore asks, "Can this be done without a guide divine?" (lines 21, 211) Among the earthly marvels to be venerated are "th'uplifted mountains" (line 424). Blackmore's "defence" of mountains is conventionally utilitarian (they provide water), but his admiration of sky and mountains as "sublime" aligned him with Addison and other versifiers of deist beliefs.

James Thomson's *The Seasons*, the century's best-known deist poem, is a bibliographer's nightmare. "Winter" (1726) ran through five editions before the first collected *Seasons* appeared in 1730. Thomson revised that in 1744, 1745, and 1746 (the prime text), and oversaw two editions of his *Works*. Changes to the poem are substantial over those two decades as Thomson incorporated his broadening experience (he first visited the Continent in 1730) and readings in philosophy, science, and travel literature. Many of the writers already discussed – Lucretius, Burnet, Milton, Shaftesbury, Addison – were used; Dennis was an admired friend (Sambrook 1981, xvii–xxv; Nicolson 1963, 309). In turn, many of the English authors discussed below would be touched by *The Seasons*.

Various scholars from McKillop (1942) on have studied the changes that Thomson made. Marjorie Nicolson observed that in successive editions, vistas grow "more spacious" and mountains "more majestic" as the poem lengthens; nature itself becomes "more sublime" (1963, 335). Sambrook's finding that secondary causes gradually become more important than the First Cause, and that post-1730 revisions have more Newtonian science and less religion (1981, xx, xxiii), needs to be read with the understanding that neither Newton nor his followers saw a necessary conflict between religious piety and science. The latter simply noted the ways in which the natural world expressed the Creator, whom it was the business of theology to study. Thus *The Seasons* could receive twenty years of "secular accretions" and yet remain "a religious didactic poem" in intent (xviii).

Thomson began publication of *The Seasons* with "Winter." Although wintry touches were sometimes used for decorative effect in early eighteenth-century verse (e.g., Pope's *Temple of Fame*), and winter had a niche in the pastoral tradition, evocations of actual winters were virtually unknown, and certainly an odd way for a poor Scots divinity student to try to enter London's "wintry World of Letters" (Thomson 1981, 304). The Shaftesburian declaration of the preface that the most elevated, philosophical, and poetic subject is "the *Works of Nature*" provides the key. For Thomson, nature is magnificent, inspiring, "In every Dress ... greatly charming!" (305). This is why "the best" poets have always delighted in "Retirement, and Solitude" in "unfrequented Fields, far from the little, busy, World." This patent distortion of the careers of Chaucer, Shakespeare, Dryden, Pope, and others serves to reveal Thomson's attitudes and values. His "nature," religion, and program are Shaftesbury's (Thacker 1983, 37–8). *The Seasons* would celebrate the holy handmaid nature "In every Dress" at *some* point; that Thomson chose to undertake the toughest assignment first was perhaps a matter of character.

Thomson's winter is geographical as well as seasonal: the poem ranges widely, not only over the "loose disjointed Cliffs, / And fractur'd Mountains wild" of Britain, which he knew firsthand, but "o'er the spacious Regions of the North" (1981, line 834) of Europe, where he depended on his reading. The section on the "*Frigid Zone*," lines 794–987, draws on Peter the Great's account of his "arctic excursion" (Sambrook 1981, xxvii). In fact, "Winter" is a general tour of the Great at its most severe and demanding. Besides mountains, Thomson glances at "the howling Waste / Of mighty Waters" (1981, lines 165–6), the "wild dazzling Waste" of snowcovered plains (line 239), the night sky disclosing "Infinite Worlds" (line 739), and the frozen Arctic Ocean, "a bleak Expanse, / Shagg'd o'er with wavy Rocks" (lines 917–18).

Thomson was both philosophically and pictorially driven to embrace winter. He hails the *whole* of nature as a "great Parent," "mighty" and "majestic," who fills the "astonish'd" soul with "pleasing Dread" (lines 106–10), but since he wants to recommend spiritual rigour, winter is a particularly good time. Frosty winter days, clear after a storm, are "joyous," strengthening our bodies, animating our blood, refining our spirits and quickening our brains (lines 692–701); at night the whole cosmic panoply "Shines out intensely keen" (line 740). Thomson's Arctic, with its "vivid Moons, and Stars that keener play" on the "radiant Waste" of snow, has an elemental sharpness (lines 861–2). In the "wild stupendous Scene" of the polar regions – Iceland's volcano "*Hecla* flaming thro' a Waste of Snow," Tartary's primordial snows and icy mountains – where Winter holds "unrejoicing court," images make the philosophical point (lines 887–911).

At times, Thomson's winter may seem to symbolize the human condition, but it is a casual, wavering symbol. Hunters and their dogs, crueller than nature, actually "desolate the Fields" more than winter does (line 791). The inhabitants of the Far North include both the melancholy "*Russian* exile" (line 801) and the idealized, well-adjusted Lapps; asking only what "simple Nature gives, / They love their Mountains and enjoy their Storms" (lines 845–6). In the elaborate metaphor that closed the poem from 1726 to 1746, winter becomes one of the seasons of man: old age, before the "unbounded Spring" of eternal salvation (lines 1,032, 1,069). Later editions blur the image, though; winter is *all* of time. Thomson described winter very well, but could not quite decide what it represented.

If "Summer" (1727), in many ways of course the tonal opposite, offers less of the sublime, it has a wild side. Verdure clothes the earth and the livin' seems easy on a warm day in the fields; lulled by pastoral glades, we are surprised to find ourselves at the top of a waterfall on a "Mount," where the "azure Sheet" slides over the edge and "thundering shoots" in an "impetuous Torrent, down the Steep" (Thomson 1981, lines 592–5), breaking the placid surface of the poem. There is a "prospect" over "Plains immense," "interminable Meads, / And vast Savannahs" that seem "a verdant Ocean" (lines 690–3). In such places, says Thomson, "great *Nature* dwells / In awful Solitude" (lines 702–3). From this Miltonic vista he leaps to the tropics, throne of summer, evoking "the joyless Desert" (line 819), along with hurricanes, mighty rivers, volcanic eruptions, and earthquakes. Then the poem comes home to more manifestations of natural power: thunderstorms and avalanches shake Wales, "and *Thule* bellows through her utmost Isles" (line 1,168) as summer storms hit the Hebrides.

Among the ways in which Thomson's verse differed from the ruling Augustan mode was its preference for solitude over society, a taste that developed alongside the interest in Great landscapes. A love of being alone, implicit in the nature worship and occasional misanthropy of *The Seasons*, is acknowledged in the original "Winter," where the Miltonic speaker pleads, "solitary, and in pensive Guise, / Oft, let me wander o'er the russet Mead" (1981, lines 40–1). The narrator in "Summer" also "lonely loves / To seek the distant Hills" at sunset "and there converse / With Nature" (lines 1,380–2). In "Spring" (1728), Thomson's persona turns with a shudder from the unhealthy town to the verdant countryside, declaring that civilization has deteriorated since the Golden Age. The speaker in "Autumn" (1730) inherits the lines from "Winter" quoted above and presents fall as a good time to retire to lonely natural retreats where "Voices more than human" can be heard (line 1,035).

And the "Hymn" on the seasons (1730) reminds us that "GOD is ever present, ever felt, / In the void Waste as in the City full" (lines 105–6).

Admittedly, not all of this desire for solitude is a yearning after Great landscapes; "Spring" and "Summer" especially, and naturally, emphasize bucolic verdure. Lyttelton's Hagley park is a "*British Tempe*" ("Spring"), the antipole to the Hebrides' Thulean storms. Yet even in "Spring" there are moments when a different aesthetic operates. The "grand" rainbow (line 204), the mention of "awful NEWTON" (line 208), and the "amazing" cliffs of the Hebrides (line 756) move the poem from pastoral beauty towards the sublime, albeit briefly.

"Autumn," the last written of the four, embraces the wild and barren as fully as does "Winter"; the speaker rejoices in the "naked" woods and fields, announcing, "The desolated Prospect thrills the Soul" (line 1,003). The excited phrasing is a residue of the excursion into the Great that precedes it, in which the world's major mountain ranges are evoked, their "horrid, vast, sublime" forms (line 711) half hidden by primordial fogs as they recycle the world's water from "eternal Snows" to ocean. Thomson calls the roll of the most renowned massifs, from the Alps to the Andes and Mountains of the Moon: "Amazing Scene!" he exclaims (line 807). When the mists clear, he gives a "romantic View" of Scotland's mountains (line 880).

Thomson, "the finest English mountain poet before Wordsworth" (Nicolson 1963, 352), also took an aesthetic interest in other areas of the Great. In "Autumn," his imagination is caught both by the "Infinite Wings" of the massive bird migrations to the North Atlantic islands, "the naked melancholy Isles / Of farthest *Thule*" (a phrase that Charlotte Brontë remembered), and by the "rolling Wonders" of the heavens: "World beyond World, in infinite Extent" (Thomson 1981, lines 869, 863–4, 1,354–5). "Autumn," which begins quietly with the sickle and sheaf on the yellow plain, ends with an apostrophe to *cosmic* "NATURE! all-sufficient! over all!" (line 1,352).

That Thomson revered the whole cycle of Creation is clearest in the "Hymn" that he appended to *The Seasons* in 1730. The seasonal succession is "the *varied* GOD"; to welcome spring and shun winter would be to treat divine worship as a smorgasbord. Since "The rolling Year / Is full of Thee" (lines 2–3), no part may be rejected. Thomson recapitulates the characteristics of each season: spring's beauty, summer's glory, autumn's bounty. Awe and majesty belong to winter storms, when, "Riding sublime, THOU bidst the World adore" (19), but the season of great privations will give way to the season of gentle beauty, by the grace of God. Forgetting this, one could, like Hardy, become obsessed with sereness and winter.

"Liberty" (1735–36) envisages her as a goddess with a penchant for mountainous countries, as Addison did. The "shaggy mountains charm" Thomson's persona more than do the plains (1908, pt. 4, lines 344–5), which had certainly not been the usual reaction half a century earlier. But *The Seasons* stands as Thomson's final (as well as first) and finest tribute to the role of wild nature in showing God to us.

Lesser poets also wrote imaginary voyages (partly based on real travels) through the sublimities of nature, a type that began for most Georgians with Shaftesbury's *The Moralists*. David Mallet's *The Excursion* was written at the behest of Thomson, who urged his friend to found his poem on sublimity, use material from Thomas Burnet, and "leave no great scene unvisited" (Nicolson 1963, 333, 231). Mallet, who was well travelled and well read in science, complied. *The Excursion* emphasizes the deist leap from natural phenomena such as tempests and earthquakes "to nature's God" (Mallet 1759, 72). The first canto sets one scene by a ruin on a heath at midnight, describes winter's Arctic home, complete with "Zembla's cliffs," and surveys Desolation's court in the deserts of Tartary. A volcanic eruption, taken as a symbol of nature's destructive powers, is evoked with an intensity that echoes Milton's depiction of chaos in *Paradise Lost*, but with enough detail to suggest personal observation, perhaps of Vesuvius (90–2).

Mallet tries to imagine all in nature that is "beauteous, great, or new" (93), an echo of Addison's *Spectator* no. 412. In Canto Two he traverses the heavens, nature's chief wonder, "Seen with transcendent ravishment sublime." Thoroughly excited now, he can only exclaim over divine qualities – "Thou art infinite!" "Simplicity divine!" – and pay homage to Newton. The spectacle of a dying sun reminds him of the universal conflagration to come at the end of time, when the comet's (seemingly) "infinite excursion" must cease, and there remains only the eternal God who "fills th'immensity of space" (100, 100–1, 106, 110). For a short time Mallet looked like "the master of the new combination of science and sublimity" (Nicolson 1963, 340).

The five cantos of Richard Savage's *The Wanderer. A Vision* (1729) are a bumpy ride on the poet's "wild Fancy" over a "strange, visionary Land" (1962, Canto 4, lines 1–2). He whisks us to "wintry Wilds," describes Frost's throne "on an Alp of Ice" amid "cheerless Scenes by Desolation own'd," and climbs a mountain, among whose cliffs and cataracts "Horror o'er the firmest Brain prevails!" (canto 1, lines 27–8,

47–8, 120). Then it's off to the ocean and up to the stars, where "HALLEY's Soul" strays among new suns, like his comet, and "Sees God in *All!*" (lines 149–52) Savage had a vivid imagination with a low flashpoint; the poem is riddled with exclamation marks. After perusing Mallet's and Thomson's works, the speaker makes a night journey beneath wondrous heavens and evokes an arctic springtime, stressing the scenic appeal of icebergs. Judging from the Turneresque descriptions (see, for example, canto 5, lines 227–36), Savage possessed an artist's eye; perhaps in landscape painting his imagination would have found its true *métier.* But his deist determination to "see God in all" is clear.

EDWARD YOUNG AND THE CHRISTIAN GREAT

Edward Young's *Night Thoughts on Life, Death, and Immortality* was a phenomenally popular poem in its day, with dozens of printings; its admirers included Pope, John Wesley, Fanny Burney, Dr Johnson, Wordsworth, Coleridge, and Blake, who illustrated it. This popularity waned as devotional literature lost its appeal, but *Night Thoughts* remains a valuable record of how a Great theme (the heavens) could move an eighteenth-century Anglican to religious ecstasy. Young combined Biblical and secular influences: Locke, Burnet, Cambridge Platonists, religious poetry (Cornford 1989, 3; Nicolson 1963, 364), even some of the deism that he officially opposed. He has been described as both "par excellence the poet of the Sublime," and the "poet of the Christian sensibility par excellence" (Nicolson 1963, 362; Cornford 1989, 13). In him those categories are not mutually exclusive.

The nine sections of *Night Thoughts* were published serially in 1742–46 and collected in 1750. *Night Thoughts* was originally the subtitle; in most early editions the running title was *The Complaint.* Young's "complaint" is that of the sentient sufferer – Pascal's "Man without God" or Eliot's wastelander – against the miseries of unredeemed existence (only in Night IX is the "Consolation" of Christianity fully extended). Parts of Night I (1742) have a modern ring; Young, like St Exupéry, is struck by how little of the earth humans have civilized: "the rest a *Waste,* / Rocks, Deserts, frozen Seas, and burning Sands" (Young 1989, sec. 1, lines 285–6). Moreover, this "melancholy" globe seems to the speaker "a true Map of man" (line 289) in its proportion of delight to woe. Many later travellers and writers would agree that there was a correspondence of some kind between the planet and humanity.

Though Young's Christianity was conventional, in Night the Fourth (1743) he tells his student Lorenzo, "I send thee not to Volumes for thy Cure; / Read Nature" (sec. 4, lines 702–3). The idea of a "book of nature" was at least as old as St Bernard, but in deism it acquired a centrality and weight not granted by traditional scripture-based religion. If "Nature is Christian" (line 704), Shaftesbury and other deists were right. At times the rather deistic Lorenzo seems not wholly "other," but an aspect of Young's own personality (Cornford 1989, 7), though elsewhere Young preaches the full Christian doctrine, from sin to salvation.

Whereas other "Nights" run to about 400 to 1,400 lines, the ninth ("The Consolation," 1746), which provides most of the Great material in the poem, has over 2,400. Apart from some Burnetian evocations of the ancient globe and the Day of Judgment, with God seen in volcanic eruptions, Young concentrates on the "gloomy Grandeurs" of the night sky (1989, line 561). The nocturnal heavens can serve us as "The *Temple*, and *the Preacher!*" (line 770), a source of awe and a preparation for heaven. They are also "The Garden of the DEITY" (line 1,042) and "an Ocean wide / Of deep Astonishment!" (lines 1,233–4), though generally Young disparages the *earthly* Great.

In fact, Young cannot quite decide whether "Creation" is a worthy theme (lines 565–7) or a mere "Nothing" (line 1,590). The problem is both the relation of two different scales, and the inherent ambiguity of the word "creation." "God created the heavens and the earth," and Young does not always specify which creation he means, though he values them quite differently. When he says, "All Things speak a GOD," but in lesser ones we "trace out *Him*," whereas "in Great, *He* seizes Man," we have to deduce from context that the Great means the firmament (lines 774–5). "The Grand of Nature," which serves as "th'Almighty's Oath, / ... to silence *Unbelief*" (lines 845–6), is usually the heavens. Yet the ancients are said to have taught wisely that nature mirrors God as the sea does the sun, and "The *Course* of *Nature* is the *Art* of GOD" (line 1,269). Young believes that "*Nature* herself does Half the Work of *Man*" by manifesting the creator, though the "Seas, Rivers, Mountains, Forests, Desarts, Rocks" are but motes on a universal scale (lines 907–17). Moved by vastness, Young was obsessed by infinity.

"*Great* Objects make / *Great* Minds," Young wrote optimistically (lines 1,064–5). Nineteenth-century writers a good deal less certain of this effect still tended to concur with him on the essential spirituality of Great nature and the value of solitary exposure to it. Young is one of the most intensely and conventionally religious of the authors found on the road

from Burnet to Hardy, and one of the most insistent on the philosophical superiority of "The spacious firmament on high" to any phenomenon of sublunary nature.

Of those who versified the ideas of Shaftesbury and Addison, Mark
Akenside was considered by his contemporaries to be as interesting as
Thomson or Young (whom he admired), though quite distinct from
them. If Thomson was a naturalist and Young a preacher, Akenside was a
Neoplatonist, tracing the earthly incarnations of divine forms. Though
he borrowed the title of his major poem from Addison, Akenside had
his own agenda in aesthetics and psychology. His originality lay in his
ability to affirm the importance of the natural sublime, while holding
aloof from both physical landscape and Christianity. Akenside's poetry
was well known to Burke and later aestheticians.

The Pleasures of Imagination (1744) occupied Akenside for much of his
life. He may have begun it at seventeen, published it at twenty-three
(Gilfillan 1857, vi–x), and kept going back to it. In the expanded posthumous edition of 1772, Book One is dated 1757, Book Two 1765,
Book Three and 130 lines of a new Book Four, 1770. One change was to
drop "the wonderful" (Addison's "uncommon") from the roster of pleasures, leaving only the sublime and the beautiful. Akenside's readers
from the eighteenth century to the twentieth, however, have preferred
the original three-book version of 1744, which I follow.

In Book One, Akenside divides the pleasures that nature and art can
give into "the Sublime, / The Wonderful, the Fair" (1857, lines 145–6).
What is important for our purposes is the primacy Akenside gives the
first category. "Wherefore darts the mind, / With such resistless ardour
to embrace / Majestic forms," he asks rhetorically ("majesty" was a standard attribute of the Great). "Who that, from Alpine heights" can survey
"mountains, plains" and "continents of sand, will turn his gaze / To
mark the windings of a scanty rill / That murmurs at his feet?" (lines
169–71, 177–83) And why are we fascinated by vastness in general, such
as those heavenly "fields of radiance" whose light has been travelling for
six thousand years? Because, says Akenside, it is the soul's divinely in-
stilled wish that "every bound at length should disappear" (lines 204–5,
220): an elaboration of Addison's idea that the mind naturally seeks liberty. Majesty and vastness are sparks that jump from God's mind to ours.
Akenside glosses sublimity as "vast, majestic pomp," while beauty is "The

least and lowliest" of nature's charms, unrelated to the soul's high aspirations (lines 440, 446–7).

Akenside differs from most other eighteenth-century theorists before
Kant – though he is close to Addison's "secondary imagination" (*Spectator* no. 418) – in the degree of his emphasis on the *mind's* role in the
power of the Great. In Akenside, *we move ourselves* when prompted by
Great scenes. "Mind, mind alone," he insists, "The living fountains in
itself contains / Of beauteous and sublime" (1857, bk. 1, lines 481–3).
It follows for him that we can be more deeply stirred by stories of human
virtue and passion than by anything in nature. Almost every writer we
encounter in this study assumes some degree of interaction among natural forms, a higher principle, and the human perceiver; Akenside
ranks the second and third above the first.

Book Three tries to clarify the role that nature does play in our lives.
Owing to a "secret harmony" between the spiritual and material worlds,
such that we "behold, in lifeless things," a "semblance" of ourselves, nature has a "grateful charm" for human senses (lines 280–5). Akenside
values nature, then, as a mirror of humanity. Why does the play of sun
and shadow on a broad plain impart a "sense of winning mirth"? And
"Whence is this effect, / This kindred power of such discordant things"
as nature and ourselves? (lines 302, 306–7). Such effects, such harmonies, force us to ask the largest questions, and those, he believes, lead us
to God: "Whence but from Thee, / O source divine of ever-flowing
love!" (lines 487–8).

Nature is a means to an end, teaching diverse lessons. From her gen-
tler beauties the mind imbibes harmony; from "ampler prospects,"
where sublime nature puts on "Eternal Majesty," we take something
"mightier far / ... and nobler" (lines 609–15). As nature is subordinate
to God, pastoral prettiness is inferior to the Great. Here Akenside is in
step with the aesthetics of Shaftesbury, Addison, and Thomson, though
on other topics he marches to a different drummer.

ACADEMIC POETS AND THE GREAT

During the mid-eighteenth century, several scholar-poets at the English
universities developed their own versions of Addison's aesthetics of nature. The best known of these, Thomas Gray, published little in his lifetime that has relevance here, though some of his later odes and
imitations have Great settings. "The Bard" (1757), in particular, may
have influenced Macpherson and Scott, and its dramatic mountain

scene was painted "sublimely" (Thacker 1983, 83; Schama 1995, 469–71). But Gray's letters and journals recounting his excursions into Great landscape, published posthumously, reveal a sensibility *prepared* to be thrilled by mountain wildness in a way that Burnet and Dennis, or anyone who had not read Shaftesbury, Addison, and Thomson, could hardly have been (Nicolson 1963, 354–5; Thacker 1983, 138–41; Schama 1995, 449–50).

Gray's Grand Tour (1739–41) took him into the Alps several times, and his letters of October-November 1739 mark a distinct development in susceptibility to Great landscape among Englishmen. Though Gray was generally timid, he and Horace Walpole "took the longest road" through the Savoyard Alps to Geneva "on purpose to see a famous monastery": the beginning of the English fascination with the Grande Chartreuse (Gray 1935, 1:122). This meant six miles on horseback up a track less than six feet wide, with a steep cliff on one side and a "monstrous precipice" above a torrent on the other: "one of the most solemn, the most romantic, and the most astonishing scenes I ever beheld," full of "strange views" of crags and cataracts, Gray reported. At the monastery, the visitors found all "orderly and simple" around the silent monks, then descended through "clouds that were then forming" (1:122). Several features of this narrative – the reiterated strangeness of the environment, the implied danger, the beholder's astonishment, the silence and simplicity – dovetail with other descriptions of the Great by explorers (Wood and Marten) and poets (Thomson).

Gray's letter of 16 November contains another account of the same excursion, which he likens to a "journey through Greenland." Although he has not yet encountered the great Italian "works of Art," Gray admits, "those of Nature have astonished me beyond expression" (128). On the climb to the monastery, "I do not remember to have gone ten paces without an exclamation ...: Not a precipice, not a torrent, not a cliff, but is pregnant with religion and poetry." Religion? "There are certain scenes that would awe an atheist into belief." This letter also mentions fear, the distanced fear of Burke's *Enquiry*: "You have Death perpetually before your eyes, only so far removed, as to compose the mind without frighting it." Aestheticians might reject Burke's *fearful* sublime from their quiet studies; Gray would not. He was in the Alps again in early November, and though the whole foggy week was not worth the single day at the Grande Chartreuse, yet "there was still somewhat fine remaining amidst the savageness and horror" of the Arc valley (7 November).

When Gray returned to the Grande Chartreuse in 1741 he left an Alcaic ode in Latin in the visitors' book, whether prepared or *extempore* we do not know. Most of it is an apostrophe to the "*severi relligio loci*" ("Holy Spirit of this stern place" in Starr and Hendrickson's translation). Whether the speaker is drawn to the place despite or because of its rigour is not clear, but he is sure that it must be "no insignificant divinity that holds sway over untamed streams and ancient forests," and that "we behold God nearer to us, a living presence, amid pathless steeps, wild mountain ridges and precipitous cliffs" than in the most magnificent temple (Gray 1966, 151–2). The ode's striking spirituality belongs more to the tradition of holy mountains than to Christianity.

Age did not wither Gray's ability to respond to grand natural phenomena. His tour of the Scottish Highlands in 1765 took him up the Tay valley between chains of mountains and produced "one of the most pleasing days I have pass'd these many years," he noted (Gray 1935, 2:892). "In short since I saw the Alps I have seen nothing sublime till now" (894): Burke and others had established *the* word for such experiences since his first trip. Back in London, though, Gray wrote of the Highlands in even stronger terms, this time using religious and paradoxical rather than fashionable language: "The Mountains are extatic, & ought to be visited in pilgrimage once a year. none [*sic*] but those monstrous creatures of God know how to join so much beauty with so much horror" (899). The Greek root of "ecstatic" (here loosely applied to the *mountains*) means standing outside of one's self.

In October 1769, two years before his death, Gray visited the English Lake District, carrying his "Claude-glass": a tinted mirror that softened and composed the observed land into a sepia-toned landscape (Manwaring 1925, 182; Thacker 1983, 142; Schama 1995, 11–12), rendering life as art. He panted up Dunmallert, overlooking a lake "majestic in its calmness," among mountains "rude & aweful" (Gray 1935, 3:1,077). Later he walked to Borrowdale, awed by the "turbulent Chaos of mountain behind mountain roll'd in confusion," pleased by the "shining purity" of the lake, and reminded of the Alps (1,079–80). The Ambleside road showed him "the mountains all in their glory!" (1,097). He was particularly moved by Helm Crag's "strange broken outline," "like some gigantic building demolished," its stones "flung cross each other in wild confusion" (1,098).

Gray's "Journal to the Lakes," published in 1775, helped establish them as the Mecca of English sublime scenery; that is, it affected the way the lakes were perceived. As the Great began to enter general culture, it provided every literate traveller with a new aesthetic vocabulary, a glossary of suggested responses. The concept of the Great is a subset of a powerful archetype – our relation with the supra-human – but no archetype is too powerful to be debased by trivialization and clichés. Words like "sublime" might now be parroted by some eighteenth-century counterpart of the posturing George Pontifex in Samuel Butler's *The Way of All Flesh*. When the protagonist of Eliza Haywood's *Life's Progress Through the Passions* (1748) crosses into Italy, "The stupendous mountains of the Alps" give him "perhaps a no less grateful sensation" than the plains of France, and "he did not fail to make reflections suitable to the different occasions" (1974, 102). Is this sensibility, parody, or tourism? Elizabeth Montagu found the "terrible sublime" in Germany and Scotland in the 1760s: can we treat her as an independent witness, or was she just looking through lenses provided by Burke and Claude (Ross 1965; Tuveson 1960, 159)? There is no easy prophylaxis against mechanical reflexes; each case poses its own challenge.

The influential primitivism of the Warton brothers at Oxford offered further emotional guidance for encounters with wildness. Joseph Warton's *The Enthusiast; or, The Lover of Nature* (1744) venerates pure unspoiled places (an "enthusiast" being a religious zealot). As in Locke, and John Winstanley's "The Happy Savage" (1732), the "state of nature" was benign, though irrevocably departed; Warton idealizes non-urban, prelapsarian life. Anything natural trumps everything artificial or civilized: even a "Pine-topt Precipice" or "bleak Heath" surpasses Versailles (J. Warton 1973, lines 26–31). Some modern readers find the speaker ironically distanced, but the poem's rhetoric is all on his side, and *The Enthusiast* was read as another endorsement of the superior merits of wild nature to civilization's proudest accomplishments. Warton's *Essay on the Genius and Writings of Pope* (1757, 1782), which ranked him below poets of nature such as Shakespeare, also suggests that he identified closely with his "enthusiast."

Thomas Warton, Jr, shared the darker shadings of his brother's tastes. The speaker in *The Pleasures of Melancholy* (1747) is drawn to the "solemn glooms" of ruined abbeys, "twilight cells and bow'rs" (T. Warton 1973, lines 17–19), where nature has returned to claim its due. A pensive soul who wants appropriate surroundings to heighten his sensibilities – a note heard increasingly often from this time – he finds a bare and chastened nature attractive. Egdon Heath at dusk would, in fact, suit him well. "Tempe … Adieu," he declares, "no more I court thy balmy breeze" (lines 26–7). Night is more congenial than day, December than spring; Pope pleases him less than Spenser, who sent Una wandering "Thro' wasteful solitudes, and lurid heaths" (line 159). The Siberian exile is probably "far happier" than the "potent satrap" ruling Moscow, and the hermit overlooking Persepolis' ruins than the shepherd near Athens (lines 228, 241).

If the Wartons sometimes strike naive or extreme poses, they indicate the direction that English and French (later German) literary culture was taking and would take in the nineteenth century. Their celebration of solitude amid wild nature developed Shaftesbury's central theme, and was in turn endorsed by a growing stream of critics and artists tributary to the Romantic movement. Hence they, and Gray, often appear in anthologies as "pre-Romantics."

C.S. Lewis once remarked on the success of a now-obscure mediaeval allegory: "When the demand is very strong a poor thing in the way of supply will be greedily embraced. Thus the intense desire of the eighteenth century for literature of a certain kind led them to accept MacPherson's *Ossian*" (1958, 66). The whole truth is more complex, but Lewis had a point. James Macpherson published *Fragments of Ancient Poetry, Collected in the Highlands of Scotland* (1760) with the backing of Edinburgh's intellectual élite, including Hugh Blair the rhetorician and David Hume, whose letter (citing Adam Smith) persuaded Thomas Gray that the poems were authentic, that is, translations of ancient originals. Macpherson went on to publish the "Gaelic epics" *Fingal* (1761) and *Temora* (1763), and a collected edition, *The Works of Ossian* (1765). On the Continent, "Ossian" was preferred reading for Goethe's young Werther, and for Napoleon. Many British readers were also impressed, although Dr Johnson never believed that Macpherson's "fragments" were "ancient" folk poems. Thacker, who gives "Ossian" a full chapter, states that the poems "were largely [Macpherson's] own invention" (1983, 103).

Macpherson's candour aside, what qualities of the poems explain their reception? A mastery of sublimity and pathos rivalling Homer's, Blair maintained. A "rude yet noble and impressive magnificence" in descriptions of landscape (Palgrave 1897, 175), which drew upon and further popularized the paintings of Salvator Rosa (Manwaring 1925, 176). Primitivism, novelty, spontaneity, and emotionalism, says Thacker (1983, 104–7). Depictions of wild nature are central to the effect. Open the Ossianic volumes almost anywhere and you find yourself among heaths, mountains, cliffs and sea, moon and winds: "The whirlwind is heard on the heath. Dark rolls the river thro' the narrow plain. A tree stands alone on the hill" (Macpherson 1760, 23). Blair, an enthusiastic classifier, lists twenty-two recurrent elemental images.

It is difficult to fathom the charm that Gray found in Macpherson's prose. The narrative and speeches use Great and barren landscapes as backdrops, but it is all much of a piece, and a little goes far. To me it reads like a bad translation or imitation of Homer, with less plot and more decoration. Macpherson's "epic" is a combination of scenic effects and, at times, something close to rant. His commitment to simplicity of statement (for example, in the Songs of Selma) is laudable and occasionally effective, but instead of sublimity there is an intense longing for sublimity. Macpherson's compound of Shaftesbury, Burke, and Celtic legend represents a passionate wish for a venerable Scottish example of primary epic. He was buried in Westminster Abbey, and despite various attacks on the antiquity of the poems, new editions of "The Works of Ossian" as "translated" by Macpherson kept appearing.

THE NOVEL AND MR AMORY

Until the 1790s the English novel was generally interested in society, not Great nature. Thomas Amory's *The Life and Opinions of John Buncle* (1755), however, is an exception to every rule. Buncle spends a hundred pages walking through fanciful mountain country "wilder than ... the Alps," ostensibly in Westmoreland and Yorkshire (Amory 1904, 45). He may not see humans or houses all day and feels altitude-sick at the passes, but he finds the landscape "grand, wonderful, and fine" (75). Buncle climbs the highest mountain in the land, which rises a mile and a half from its base (the highest peak in Britain is Ben Nevis, ca. 4,400 feet). Amory's message is that the world is full of natural wonders – cloud-piercing peaks, deep lochs, springs gushing from subterranean passages, earthquakes – and that all such phenomena evince "the immediate operation of the Deity" (79). Amory sends Buncle on and on through a depopulated, "amazing" landscape of gorges, falls, and caves to witness God's work.

DR JOHNSON IN SCOTLAND

Samuel Johnson's strong temperamental attachments to traditional Christianity, neoclassical aesthetics, and the pleasures of urban life make him an unlikely participant in the story of western culture's gradual approach to Great landscapes, and his contributions to the discussion of wild nature did not break new ground. But Johnson thought and spoke with such massive, articulate, informed independence that his views on any question carry weight.

In 1773 Johnson toured the Scottish Highlands and Hebrides with James Boswell, his disciple, biographer-to-be, and gadfly. Johnson reported his reactions in letters and in *A Journey to the Western Islands of Scotland* (1775); Boswell waited until after Johnson's death to publish his *Journal of a Tour to the Hebrides* (1785). Part of the interest of the expedition is this double vision, the dialogue and debate between the aging Tory and the young proto-romantic who had sought out Rousseau and wanted to believe in Macpherson. Ask them, for example, why they travelled. "We saw in every place, what we chiefly desired to know," says Johnson, "the manners of the people" (1970, 48). Boswell remembered it somewhat differently: "[Johnson] always said, that he was not come to Scotland to see fine places [e.g., parks, palaces]; but wild objects, – mountains, – waterfalls, – peculiar manners." He adds, "I have a notion that he at no time has had much taste for rural beauties. I have myself very little" (Boswell 1970, 230). Here "rural beauties" means small, artificial prettinesses, as distinguished from "wild objects."

Another kind of dynamic exists *within* Johnson's writings. While never enamoured of Scotland's barren grandeur *per se*, Johnson moved from initial repulsion to a degree of acceptance during his journey, or between the tour and the writing. The flexibility for which he has been praised (Thacker 1983, 177–8), however, is a phenomenon of the *Journey* not evident in the letters, where he concedes "a kind of dreadful magnificence" to Loch Ness's tributary early in the journey, but is unmoved by the "savage solitude" of mountains and heaths, and becomes displeased with the "gloomy barrenness" and loneliness of the Hebrides (Littlejohn 1965, 102, 104, 109, 111). Boswell depicts Johnson as depressed during the windstorms on Col ("This is a waste of life": 1970, 358). Johnson, a man of strong emotions, may have felt an existential discomfort with this "islanded" situation; years earlier he had written, "I have ever since [the death of my wife] seemed to myself broken off from mankind a kind of solitary wanderer in the wild of life" (Littlejohn 1965, 26).

The same trip unfolds rather differently in Johnson's *Journey*. At first he seems horrified by the denudation of Scotland: "The whole country is extended in uniform nakedness" (1970, 9). And he never entirely overcomes this disgust; on Mull, towards the end, his reaction to a "bleak and barren" heath is to speculate whether it could be planted "to give nature a more cheerful face" (126). Anything approaching desert seems to have threatened him personally; "the dreariness of solitude" (30) is more than mere description of the Highlands. But he is capable of stepping back and seeing how his own background has conditioned him. Thus, "an eye accustomed to flowery pastures and waving harvests is astonished and repelled by this wide extent of hopeless sterility" concedes that an eye otherwise accustomed might react differently (34). To other kinds of Great phenomena Johnson responds more complexly. At Slanes Castle on the coast, he envisions how "the eye" would "enjoy all the terrifick grandeur of the tempestuous ocean"; in the Hebrides, he imagines "enjoying" the "magnificence" of a sea-tempest (16, 62).

It is mountainous country, though, that he comes nearest to appreciating. Initially, the cliffs by Loch Ness tower "in horrid nakedness" amid "general barrenness," but at the Fall of Fiers the rugged country "strikes the imagination with all the gloom and grandeur of Siberian solitude" (26, 29), a response consonant with Great aesthetics. Johnson describes the general appearance of mountainous regions as "that of matter, incapable of form or usefulness, dismissed by Nature from her care, disinherited of her favours, left in its original elemental state, or quickened only with one sullen power of useless vegetation." Yet until we know the "realities" of mountains, he says, we cannot tell if our ideas of them are "just." Moreover, "regions mountainous and wild, thinly inhabited, and little cultivated, make a great part of the earth, and he that has never seen them, must live unacquainted with much of the face of nature, and with one of the great scenes of human existence" (35).

Johnson's own situation now reappears, tonally altered. Amid the "rudeness, silence, and solitude" of a Highland glen, a scene such as "a writer of Romance might have delighted to feign," he first thinks of writing an account of his expedition (at a time when his creative output had slowed to pamphleteering and desultory work on *Lives of the English Poets*), for "the imaginations excited by the view of an unknown and untravelled wilderness are not such as arise in the artificial solitude of parks and gardens" (36). What even this small wilderness shows us, he decides, is our own weakness, and "what are these hillocks to the ridges of Taurus, or these spots of wildness to the desarts of America?" Johnson also notes that mountain dwellers tend to remain free, and, like the mountains themselves, possess the interest of the "original elemental state" (38–41).

In the Hebrides Johnson's reactions were mixed. The journey had the interest of time travel to a "feudal" age, yet only a "mere lover of naked nature" would find the Islands alluring (69, 142). Back on the mainland, he seemed to regain strength. The noise of rain, wind, and torrents during a night ride "made a nobler chorus of the rough musick of nature" than he had ever heard (144): a reaction one would sooner expect from John Muir. And what impressed Johnson at Hawkstone Park in 1774 was its "terrific grandeur," "awfulness," and horrors, which gave him "a kind of turbulent pleasure between fright and admiration" (Thacker 1983, 144–5). We may wonder if he would have been capable of this reaction before his ride through the Highlands.

Johnson's final account is not easy to settle; it is certainly not all "dyspeptic complaints" and a "torrent of irascibility" (Schama 1995, 471). Thomas Curley concludes that he "could respond to sublime scenery as strongly as any nature enthusiast," yet "was not a sentimentalist" about it (1976, 213–14). Boswell quotes him as asking rhetorically, "Who *can* like the Highlands?" (1970, 416), but Johnson describes more wild nature at Loch Ness and Fiers than does Boswell. There is some evidence that, in time or in retrospect, Johnson learned to appreciate wild nature. Beyond question, the Great could engender strong feelings in him, feelings that (as we would expect from all we know of his life) were precariously balanced between "gloom and grandeur."

COWPER, CRABBE, AND THE NATURE OF NATURE

Towards the end of the eighteenth century, it becomes possible to glimpse the shape of some nineteenth-century attitudes towards nature. The poems of William Cowper and George Crabbe constitute a dialogue on the question of what nature essentially is and how we are related to it, a dialogue held while the Georgian style was being invaded by Romantic impulses.

Cowper's *The Task* (1785) is still affiliated with earlier modes of thought and feeling. He stresses some of the same points as Thomson – that we can derive pleasure from observing ordinary nature, that urban vice threatens rural virtue, and so on – believing that these had become mere clichés or literary artifices that needed revivifying. Since "God made the country, and man made the town," "health and virtue" are essentially bucolic, although "The town has ting'd the country" now with its corrupt manners (Cowper 1934, bk. 1, line 749, bk. 4, line 553). Thus far Cowper is content to restate Georgian platitudes, to continue a tradition.

But Cowper felt that his contemporaries neglected the God behind (and in) nature: "Man views it, and admires; but rests content / With what he views. The landscape has his praise, / But not its author" (5:791–3). The contention of deists like Shaftesbury and Thomson that to love nature *was* to love God is rejected; Books 5 and 6 admonish, "Acquaint thyself with God, if thou would'st taste / His works" (bk. 5, lines 779–80). Without scripture, the book of nature only misleads us, Cowper believed. He and the deists agreed that "The beauties of the wilderness are his" (bk. 6, line 186), but Cowper required the naturalist-poet to give explicit and reiterated recognition to the Author. "Nature is but a name for an effect, / Whose cause is God," and "Familiar with th'effect we slight the cause" (lines 223–4, 121). He did not acknowledge that either "book" or path would suffice.

In another respect, however, Cowper seems allied with Thomson; three of *The Task*'s six books describe various times and moods of winter. "Oh winter," he exclaims, "I love thee"! (bk. 4, lines 120, 128). Cowper is narrower than Thomson, though; snow falls beneficently, insulating the earth and his cottage, within which he tends a fire and watches dusk deepen through frosty windows. On winter mornings he sallies out to admire icicles and the ice-forms along streams, wherein nature outdoes the ice palace that the Russians built on the Neva in 1740: a rare allusion to something outside his neighbourhood (bk. 5, line 130). This rather tame nature Cowper found good and Christian. But in 1799, drawing on a newspaper article and perhaps Erasmus Darwin's *The Botanic Garden* (Cowper 1995, 3:356), he composed a remarkable poem, "On the Ice-Islands Seen Floating in the Germanic Ocean." The staid, reclusive Cowper's imagination was so stirred by these second-hand accounts of the Great that he wrote both Latin and English versions. He has many questions – "What portents, from what distant region, ride / Unseen, till now, in ours, th'astonish'd tide?" (212, lines 1–2) – and references to Proteus, Apollo, and Winter in connection with these "horrid wand'rers of the Deep" (line 57), while the God of the Bible is conspicuous by His absence.

Realism about nature – in the sense of a determination to make empirically truthful observations of physical nature – was crucial both to the development of the earth sciences and to the aesthetic shift that Hardy describes. Crabbe's *The Village* (1783) wants to set "truth and nature" against the ancient myths of the pastoral and paint "the real picture of the poor" (1988, bk. 1, lines 5, 19). He depicts a "niggard" nature along the "frowning coast" of East Anglia where poor farmers try to wrest a living from "the sterile soil" (lines 131, 49, 72). "Rank weeds" and thistles overrun "blighted rye," and a "thin harvest" is won from "burning sand" (lines 65–9). Crabbe avoids sublimity, which would have given his grim poem an unwanted note of uplift, but *The Village* is nevertheless a distant ancestor of Egdon Heath. Crabbe darkens, "chastens," the Shaftesburian worship of "NATURE" in a way that anticipates Hardy and the nineteenth century.

In *The Borough* (1810), which again explores the country near Aldeburgh, there is some Burkean material (and language) when the speaker turns to look at the sea. The flowing tide "fills the Channel vast and wide," and the sea is "vast, sublime in all its forms [moods]" (1988, bk. 1, lines 38, 165). Some inflation is evident; "the Channel" is a river mouth, "the sea" is the English Channel, and the Dedication says that you can see "works of grandeur and sublimity" from near Belvoir Castle. Alpinists, astronomers, and blue-water mariners may smile, feeling that Crabbe has learned a language that he is overeager to apply. But when he exclaims, "Terrific splendour! gloom in glory drest!" over the spectacle of a shaft of moonlight falling on "wild Waves" in winter (lines 261–4), Crabbe is in the mainstream of poetic responses to the natural sublime from Thomson onwards, and close to the vision of Turner and Ruskin. Crabbe is reported to have been among Hardy's early reading (Rutland 1962, chapter 1).

Cowper and Crabbe show that the aesthetic movement we have traced from Burnet and Shaftesbury was continuing, but that it was now being revised and not just maintained. By the time *The Borough* was published, in fact, a new, "Romantic" generation of poets had appeared with much to say about the Great that both used and modified the tradition they had inherited.

6

Breaking Loose:
European Developments to Goethe

The eighteenth-century Continental portion of the road to Egdon Heath was built chiefly by scientific travellers and climbers who published narratives or interpretations of their experiences. Philosophy and aesthetics played a lesser role than in England, French theorists being slower to adopt new ideas about old subjects. Jean-Pierre de Crousaz's *Traité du Beau* (1715) defines beauty in conventional neoclassical terms: unity, regularity, proportion; mountains are described only as *lacking* these qualities (1715, 29–33, 82). Though de Crousaz mentions *The Spectator* politely, he takes no cognizance of Addison's "Pleasures of the Imagination," creates no category above or beyond beauty. In the Leibniz-Clarke correspondence (published 1715–17), the Englishman Samuel Clarke upholds Newton's notion of infinite space as an attribute of God, while Leibniz maintains the traditional denial of absolute space (Koyré 1957, 243–8). Nor does the Abbé Pluché's eight-volume *Spectacle de la Nature* (1732–33) take any aesthetic interest in great landforms. The seas are described and the heavens piously admired, but mountains, glaciers, and deserts are not deemed worthy of discussion.

DE MAILLET AND BUFFON

The new ground was broken by peripatetic natural scientists. Benoît de Maillet was French consul in Egypt from 1692 to 1708, later inspector of French establishments in the Near East and North Africa (1715–20). During this time he worked out a theory of earth history based on his own observations and enquiries (Albritton 1986, 68). After retiring in 1720, de Maillet allowed manuscripts to circulate that apparently influenced Buffon (Carozzi 1968, 4). Yet *Telliamed; or Conversations Between an*

Indian Philosopher and a French Missionary on the Diminution of the Sea was not published until 1748, after Buffon's *Théorie de la terre*, and then in a version toned down by an ecclesiastical editor (Albritton 1986, 72–3). Fortunately, modern students can work with A.V. Carozzi's "reconstitution" of the "original text" from later manuscripts (1968, 10, 31).

The three "conversations" – really monologues by the Indian – chiefly discuss geology, biology, and astronomy. Though much of de Maillet's "science" looks fanciful today, he clearly tries to reason from his evidence and tiptoe around Genesis. The section on "The Great Mountains" concludes that they were formed under water, or by subsequent erosion, and that these processes are continuing (de Maillet 1968, 83–8). The second conversation suggests that the inside of the earth may reproduce the features and organisms of the outside, then refutes this "inner earth" theory in an apparent attempt to disarm criticism. The final section ranges from speculations about space and time to the emergence of terrestrial life from the sea. *Telliamed* was controversial for its higher estimate of the earth's age than the Bible seemed to authorize, its un-biblical hypothesis that human beings were probably descended from marine forms, and the generally secular, empirical cast of the discussion.

De Maillet (despite the play on his name) attempts to distance *Telliamed*'s heresies from himself and to anticipate objections. The speaker, who has now gone home to India, insists that his reasonings do not contradict Genesis; the "six days" of Creation must be understood metaphorically. An afterword by the "French missionary" challenges Telliamed's "pleasant dreams," and a final comment by the manuscript's addressee notes Telliamed's closeness to some of Spinoza's ideas: the symbol of dangerous free-thinking. Even with these hedges, and his editor's cutting of de Maillet's millions and billions of years to thousands and millions – or vague euphemisms – *Telliamed* provoked a violent reaction, foreshadowing the nineteenth-century confrontations between science and religion (Carozzi 1968, 30, 3). But its role in treating astronomy and the earth sciences independently of Genesis was important; an empirical and experiential approach to nature is part of the aesthetic movement under discussion here. De Maillet was an advocate of "Go and see," a doctrine that eventually led to new ways of seeing and new modes of feeling about nature.

Georges-Louis Leclerc, Comte de Buffon, travelled in the Alps in the early 1730s and probably knew de Maillet's work when he wrote *Théorie de la terre* (1744, included in his *Histoire naturelle*, 1749), which argues that only vast periods of time can explain earth's changes. His published estimate was 75,000 years, but manuscripts say up to three million (Al-britton 1986, 85). Buffon agreed with de Maillet that our continents were once under the seas, which formed them. Perhaps more important in the long run, though, was Buffon's belief that "il faut le prendre tel qu'il est," and "conclure du présent au passé" ('we must take things as they are, and infer the past from the present'; Buffon 1744, 1:43). This is in embryo the doctrine of "the adequacy of present causes," which held that we need not suppose supernatural events in the past to explain the present earth. Though he was moved by Burnet's *Sacred Theory*, Buffon had more in common with the deists than with the "fallen earth" school; he called nature "*le trône extérieur de la magnificence Divine*" ('God's visible throne'; Glacken 1967, xiv).

In "Des Époques de la nature," published 30 years later, Buffon shows how to reconcile science and scripture. After delineating six long stages in earth history and wondering whether this "haute ancienneté" ('great age') clashes with sacred traditions (Buffon 1778, 3:492), he proclaims his piety and, developing de Maillet's point, analyzes Genesis to show that its six "days" could well be his six periods. Buffon's influence was profound, in France and elsewhere. In 1816 Shelley, confronting Alpine glaciers for the first time, recalled Buffon's evocation of the world ending in ice (P.B. Shelley 1964, 1:499). Both Buffon and de Maillet were part of the gradual marshalling of evidence about the earth's antiquity – a development that helped shape Hardy's veneration of Egdon Heath as a vestige of "prehistoric" time.

STUDYING THE EARTH

The science of geology, which would radically reshape nineteenth-century reactions to nature, was founded or at least anticipated by eighteenth-century Europeans. Jean-Étienne Guettard (1715–86) virtually invented palaeontology (fossil geology), made the first geological survey and map of France (1751), and ascertained the volcanic nature of the Auvergne region. The doctrine of geological succession (the logical sequence of rock strata) can be traced to a 1756 treatise by Johann Lehmann. Nicholas Desmarest (1725–1815) continued Guettard's research on erosion and vulcanism in the Auvergne, compared it to Irish formations, and enunciated the principles on which modern geology was founded: "the adequacy of present causes," and "Go and see." Pierre Pallas noted the geological sequence of mountain ranges during his survey of Russia (1768–74), while G.C. Fuchsel demonstrated the sequence of strata in Germany and anticipated Lyell's uniformitarianism (Geikie 1897, 12–39, 56–78, 80–99). J.F.W. Charpentier produced the world's first coloured geological map in 1778.

Abraham G. Werner (1749–1817), the most influential of them all, was a charismatic teacher of mineralogy at Freiberg from 1775, drawing pupils from as far away as Britain, and a classifier of Linnaean proportions, but he was also a mischievous theorist from insufficient data (Bailey 1962, 21–2). His supposedly theory-free approach, "geognosy," contained unexamined assumptions – for example, that all rocks were deposited by a "universal ocean" – that ignored Guettard's and Desmarest's work in the Auvergne, set back the principle of geological succession, and forced the next two generations of geologists to fight useless battles over "Neptunism" and "Vulcanism." Though Werner's work has its modern defenders (Greene 1982, 26–30), he shows how dangerous a popular teacher who follows an inner light can be. Werner generalized broadly but travelled little, and rarely submitted his views to the scrutiny of his peers. One of his pupils, Robert Jameson, taught Werner's Neptunism at Edinburgh well into the nineteenth century, but his best students eventually undermined his views by modifying their own after broader study and travel (Geikie 1897, 137): Jean François D'Aubuisson, Leopold von Buch, and Alexander von Humboldt abandoned "Wernerism" and helped found modern empirical geology.

That science was more important than philosophy in establishing Great aesthetics in Europe is clear whenever we pick up a philosopher. Baron d'Holbach's *Système de la Nature* (1770), notorious for its materialism, impressed Shelley, but the nature that D'Holbach reveres is the abstraction of philosophical systems; it does not include physical nature. Jacques H.B. Saint-Pierre was a deist who studied nature's beautiful and 'divine work' as proof of a beneficent Providence, yet his *Études de la Nature* (1789) is full of geographical errors and mistaken assumptions about the earth. Not until the end of the century do we find general philosophy that bears on the line of development from Burnet to Hardy.

THE LURE OF THE ALPS

In the first half of the eighteenth century the trickle of Alpine writings began to swell. Johann J. Scheuchzer, a Zurich scholar, published accounts of his *Journeys in the Swiss Alps* (1702–11) and a *Natural History of Switzerland* (1706–08). Scheuchzer enthused over the Alps, classified their dragons (cat-faced, malodorous, etc.), and admired the sublimity of volcanoes (Engel 1971, 22; Thacker 1983, 19–20, 146; Schama 1995, 412). Further descriptions of the Alps were given by J.H. Hottinger (1706), Abraham Stanyan (1714), and J.G. Altmann (1730, 1751), the last two contributing to the *État et les délices de la Suisse* series. An anonymous "Voyage dans les montagnes occidentales du Paris de Vaud" (1737) speaks of their "*horribles beautés*" (Mornet 1907, 52), an oxymoron used by Burnet and Dennis and often repeated independently. In 1754, Élie Bertrand gave both medical and aesthetic reasons for visiting mountains, which he called the bones of the macrocosm (Engel 1930, 18–19).

An English party that visited Chamonix in 1741 is often credited with popularizing the region. The leader, William Windham, published a report in the *Journal helvétique* in 1743, and a pamphlet, *An Account of the Glacières or Ice Alps in Savoy*, in 1744. Windham tells how they climbed for four and a half hours to gain a "full view" of the glaciers, which were unlike anything he had ever seen; even travellers' descriptions of Greenland's seas, or analogies with, for example, a stormy lake "frozen all at once," fell short of the reality (Windham 1744, 107). He then proceeds to describe the scene quite circumstantially (some of the details being incorporated by James Thomson into later editions of "Winter"). The party, which included the flamboyant eastern traveller Richard Pococke, descended onto glacial ice, saw crevasses, and heard rumblings before returning to Chamonix via another summit. Windham's account was translated, cited before the Société royal in 1750, and mentioned by the Duc de la Rochefoucauld when he visited Chamonix in 1762 (Mornet 1907, 274).

The most influential European writer on the Alps in this period was the Swiss poet and naturalist Albrecht von Haller, who had visited England and read Shaftesbury and Pope by the time he began to write (Siegrist 1967, 7–8). *Die Alpen* (1729) drew more visitors to the Alps than any previous work and popularized ideas about the innocence of primitive life there that Jean-Jacques Rousseau later broadened. *Die Alpen* is a sort of high-altitude pastoral idyll, a paean to life and nature in the upper Swiss villages, which are portrayed as superior to their counterparts below. It is not a celebration of peak-climbing: "alps" (*Alpen* or *Gebürg*) were mountain meadows where flocks could pasture, as in "Ein fruchtbares Gebürg," 'a fruitful high pasture' (von Haller 1965, line 346).

Yet some aspects of von Haller's rhetoric became the staples of later mountaineering books: the metaphorical sense of an 'elevated world' ("der erhabnern Welt," line 312), for example, and the idea that the rigorous climate somehow creates happiness and purity. Fate has given you "kein [no] Tempe" (line 35), von Haller tells the villagers, yet long winters and perpetual ice have improved your morals (lines 36–40). Thule is, at least, character-building. And high peaks, 'covered to the sky with eternal ice' (line 342), are close at hand to be enjoyed. From a mountain summit at dawn, says von Haller, one sees, "Mit immer neuer Lust," 'with pleasure ever new,' Nature's magnificent formations ("was die Natur am prächtigsten gebildet": lines 321–4). There a 'gentle giddiness' ("sanfter Schwindel") troubles our weak eyes, unaccustomed to the glare of a broad horizon (lines 329–30). Implicitly, von Haller corrects Addison: the *imagination* may yearn for this "Image of Liberty," but the flesh is weak.

One example of von Haller's extensive influence will have to stand for many. It is said to have been *Die Alpen* that drew Archdeacon William Coxe to the region (Freshfield 1920, 26). Coxe's *Sketches of the Natural, Civil and Political State of Switzerland* (1779) was translated with an extensive commentary by L. Ramond de Carbonnières (who wrote several vivid books about his own climbs) as *Lettres sur l'État politique, civil et naturel de la Suisse* (1781–82). This was the guidebook that Wordsworth used in the Alps and to which he pays tribute in "Descriptive Sketches" (1793).

In 1761 Jean-Jacques Rousseau brought out his novel *Julie, ou la nouvelle Héloïse. Lettres de deux amants habitants d'une petite ville aux pieds des Alpes* (*Letters of Two Lovers, Inhabitants of a Small Town at the Foot of the Alps*). Rousseau, a Genevese, was not a mountaineer, and his book is denigrated as Alpine description by climbers, but he helped give the Alps a literary currency alongside the scientific and climbing interests fostered by von Haller and, later, H.B. de Saussure. For Rousseau's St Preux, it is "les lieux sauvages qui forment à mes yeux les charmes" ('the wild places that for me make the charm') of the Vaux country (Rousseau 1960, 43: pt. 1, letter no. 18). As Shaftesbury had said, "the wildness pleases." Rousseau invited the public to explore the Valais, an "unknown" district that "deserves notice" (letter no. 21), and they soon complied.

The twenty-third letter describes St Preux's climb along rough paths through canyons and past waterfalls, where all seasons and climates can occur at once, and optical illusions abound. He ascends through cloud to summits where he can look down on tempests forming. Mountain air makes the spirit more serene, St Preux observes; the surrounding objects encourage thought that is "grand et sublime" and purify the soul. This important note, audible as early as Gesner (1543), had not been expressed so fully or influentially before (von Haller finds purity in residents, not in visitors). The dark side of the experience is the bond St Preux feels with bleak crags and early winters as he faces the hopelessness of his passion. (For Hardy, it is we moderns who feel this.) At times Rousseau uses landscape metaphorically; Parisian society is "ce vaste désert" ('this great desert': pt. 2, letter no. 14). And his general proposition that nature is most charming in unfrequented places such as mountain summits and desert islands, not in parks and gardens, became a romantic assumption, the opposite of the neoclassic position; it fed into the kind of free-floating nineteenth-century misanthropy that encouraged flight from a corrupt civilization.

DE SAUSSURE AND MONT BLANC

Albrecht von Haller had, besides his literary impact, a direct influence on the patriarch of Alpine climbing and the study of mountains. In 1758 he met Horace Bénédict de Saussure; they became friends on the basis of a mutual love of the natural sciences and of the Alps. De Saussure had grown up outside Geneva, enjoying long rambles and views of Mont Blanc from his family's summer home. In 1760, aged twenty, he visited Chamonix and "les montagnes maudits" (as the Mont Blanc range was then known) for the first time, to collect specimens for von Haller. Stunned by the spectacular peaks and glaciers, he did some climbing and announced a prize for the first ascent of Mont Blanc: the formative event of his life and of the next three decades of Alpine mountaineering. De Saussure then returned to Geneva (becoming professor of Philosophy and Natural Science at the Academy), revisiting Chamonix whenever he could. He concentrated more and more on geology, and nourished his passion for Mont Blanc, "a sort of illness" (Freshfield 1920, 83).

Climbing in the 'cursed mountains' proceeded slowly; few were prepared to brave the venerable superstitions. Among the first aspirants were the Deluc brothers, amateur scientists from Geneva who may have supplied Rousseau with details of the Valais in 1754 (Engel 1971, 29, 38). The Delucs viewed Mont Blanc "with admiration as well as horror" from a nearby ridge in 1765 (Freshfield 1920, 178) and ascended Le Buet in 1770. Jean-André Deluc published his first report on their high-altitude research in 1772. Several books on Alpine glaciers publicized the region further in the 1770s, and A.C. Bordier's *Voyage pittoresque aux Glacières de Savoie* (1773) anticipated the fluid theory of glacial flow (Freshfield, 194). Serious attempts on Mont Blanc itself commenced in 1775. One of the leading figures was Marc-Théodore Bourrit: guide, author, artist, and braggart. His *Description des aspects du Mont Blanc* (1776) and illustrations for de Saussure's volumes helped popularize the Alps and mountaineering, despite his self-serving inaccuracies.

Meanwhile de Saussure, who had rarely missed a climbing season, brought out the first of his *Voyages dans les Alpes*, detailing his explorations, in 1779. (Those not wishing to tackle the four volumes in French can follow his progress in Douglas Freshfield's biography, a project suggested to him by John Ruskin, for whom the *Voyages* were an Alpine Bible.) A "Preliminary Discourse" sets out de Saussure's motives. Geologists know that our globe has undergone great revolutions during its long life, he notes, bowing to Buffon; mountains are especially interesting in this regard, if seen "dans leur ensemble" ('as a whole'). This requires tiring, dangerous climbs, yet the soul is nourished by "ces grands spectacles": an erupting volcano dwarfs human activity, a glacier is like a sea suddenly frozen, and the Alps reveal the skeleton of the globe. Mountains of primitive granite are the most interesting, since they are nearest the origin of things. A prescient remark: as primitivism grew more popular, so would Great landscapes. De Saussure also mentions a 'theory of the earth' he was developing (1779, v–xix), but never finished.

Volume one includes an "Essay on the Natural History of the Environs of Geneva" and a "Tour around Mont Blanc." The former, mostly scientific, sometimes stops to admire the scenery and practically call for tourists. Once, describing La Dole's "magnifique spectacle," de Saussure remembers a time when only the summits projected above the cloud-filled valleys, and he felt strangely fearful, like a castaway on a rock in a stormy ocean seeing the coast of a distant continent; then the clouds lifted, revealing a pastoral valley. There is no transcendental meditation; all this is ascribed to 'chance' (242–3). In the "Tour," he expresses the hope that better knowledge of Mont Blanc will assist his theory of the earth and unlock the secrets of the formation and structure of the whole chain. He then narrates the last of his three circumambulations (undertaken in 1778), with companions who possessed "sensibilité pour les grands beautés de la Nature" ('feeling for the great beauties of nature': 300). De Saussure hails the pure air and scenic grandeur of Chamonix – 'a new world,' 'an earthly Paradise' (359) – and observes that

gigantic scale deceives ("trompe") one's judgment of distances: a phenomenon often noted by mountaineers and polar explorers.

During the 1780s the pace of Alpine activity quickened. In 1781
Bourrit published his *Description des Alpes pennines*, H. Renfner translated
J.G. Sulzer's Alpine travels, and Ramond de Carbonnières, the "first
poet of mountaineering" (Engel 1971, 39), brought out his version of
Coxe's *Switzerland.* In the second volume of his *Voyages* (1786), de Saussure chronicles attempts to climb Mont Blanc, which became more serious from 1783. His own 1785 climb bogged down in heavy snow, but he
recalled the magnificent view from his cabin at the Aiguille du Goûter:
in the evening, he beheld the "cadavre" of the universe at his feet, and
felt 'a kind of terror' of the 'vast space' (de Saussure 1786, 475–8;
Freshfield 1920, 202). This volume is notably more emotional and self-
aware than the first; he would like to describe his excursions onto two
glaciers, but they had so little in common with ordinary experience,
were such an unusual mixture of 'admiration and terror' inspired by immensity, that he cannot. Yet his sense that the pure air, majestic silence,
and "la nudité même de ces rochers élevés" ('the very bareness of these
uplifted rocks') – constitute "un autre monde oublié par la Nature"
('another world, forgotten by nature': de Saussure 1786, 25–6) – has
many parallels among later mountain writers.

The first ascent of Mont Blanc was finally achieved by François Pac-
card and Jacques Balmat in the summer of 1786; de Saussure himself
reached the top in 1787 and quickly wrote a *Relation Abrégée* of the experience, reprinted in volume four of the *Voyages* (1796). He was struck
chiefly by the ocean of pure white snow, the cold silence of the high
camp, and, on top, the "grand spectacle," including the relationship between the high peaks that he had been yearning to see for a decade. He
could hardly believe he was not dreaming; one glance showed the structure of the range and erased more doubts than years of work could have
done (1796, 4:145–7). Von Haller had written that the sage could not
look anywhere in the Alps without finding a marvel. De Saussure marvelled, but he also found the answers to many scientific questions.

The ascent of Mont Blanc did not end his work. Perhaps his "most
daring adventure" was spending two and a half weeks in a hut at the Col
du Géant, at an altitude of eleven thousand feet, to make observations
(Freshfield 1920, 250). The last night was 'ravishingly beautiful'; a full
moon brought out colours that repaid all his pains. "Quel moment pour
la méditation!" he exclaims. "L'âme s'élève, les vues de l'esprit semblent
s'agrandir, et au milieu de ce majesteux silence, on croît entendre la

voix de la Nature et devenir le confident de ses opérations les plus se-
crètes" ('What a moment for meditation! The soul ascends, thought
seems to expand, and amidst this majestic silence, we come to hear the
voice of nature and become privy to her most secret operations': de Saussure 1796, 4:224–5). It is a remarkable outburst after many pages of
strictly scientific writing, one that seems to confirm from the field what
were after all mostly the *predictions* of Addison and Shaftesbury about
how the soul would respond to a close encounter with the Great. We can
date the inception of the modern tradition of mountain-climbing narratives from the *Voyages*: de Saussure's emotions, if not his motives, would
be ratified many times over by his successors.

By the end of the eighteenth century, it is no longer feasible to survey
all Alpine literature, let alone all mountain writing. Clair-Éliane Engel's
bibliography of French and English "litterature alpestre" (1930) lists
only 20 accounts of (actual) mountain travel between 1700 and 1770,
then 17 more in the next decade, and 64 between 1780 and 1800, with
11 titles in 1787 alone. While Bourrit, J.-A. Deluc, Ch.-J. Mayer, and
many others wrote more books about the Swiss Alps, Ramond treated
the Pyrenees, de Saussure the Italian mountains, and Goethe the Harz
range (see below). The geographical and generic "database" was broadening rapidly; more people were climbing, travelling, and writing, for
more reasons, in more places, than ever before.

FARTHER AFIELD

The well-publicized drama of Mont Blanc, like a hero in folklore, tends
to usurp our attention; Europe and the world had a good deal more of
the Great to offer. Italy's active volcanoes, Etna and Vesuvius, interested
both professional scientists, such as de Saussure, and *virtuosi*, or amateurs. In 1717 George Berkeley wrote an account of his visits that same
year to Vesuvius during an eruptive period, and Sir William Hamilton,
the British envoy at Naples, sketched Vesuvius at intervals from 1767 to
1791 (Smith 1960, 9). Whereas seventeenth-century observers had typically been horrified by volcanoes, Hamilton pronounced Vesuvius' eruption "glorious, and sublime" (Thacker 1983, 146–9). Late eighteenth-
century travellers had been primed for such responses by Burnet, Shaftesbury, Addison, and Burke.

Among eighteenth-century European intellectuals who described
wild nature, none was more influential than Johann Wolfgang von
Goethe. During a solitary excursion to the Harz Mountains in Decem-

ber 1777, young Goethe climbed their highest elevation, the Brocken. He produced a drawing of the mountain, and a poem, "Harzreise im Winter" (1777), that impressed Brahms and Rilke (Zeydel in Goethe 1957, 4–5). In its final section the speaker ascends, apostrophizes a summit, and worships a distant, mysterious deity. He beseeches this 'Father of Love' to open the eyes of the thirsty man in the desert to its thousand springs; to light the lonely man "Über die grundlose Wege / Auf öden Gefilden" ("Over bottomless spaces / On plains of the desert," translates Zeydel, but "grundlose Wege" is 'groundless' or 'baseless' paths or ways); and to bear him aloft with the storm. On the mountain's snowy peak, he finds an altar, and the god "Mysteriously revealed / Over the wondering world" (Goethe 1957, 37). The idea of a vague, intense spirituality attaching to mountains was already becoming established in European literature. Goethe later used the Brocken as a setting for *Walpurgisnacht* in Part One of *Faust* (1797).

Goethe also used his *Harzreise* in the undated "Essay on Granite," a type of rock that he says we respect for its mysterious origins and its presence at the top and bottom of mountains. The poet announces his turn from the study of the changeable human heart to that of nature's "oldest, firmest" child. He travels to "a high bare peak" amid granite mountains, the "most ancient, most dignified monuments of time," standing in solitude like men who want to open their souls to only the deepest truth (Goethe 1958, 590–1). On this "eternal altar, built directly on the foundations of the world" yet close to the sky, he feels "attuned to higher meditations on nature," reveres the "being of all beings," and envisions the geological changes of "past centuries": the upthrust, cleavage, and erosion of mountains, the retreat of "ancient waters," the raging of volcanoes (591–2). Truly "nothing is in its ancient state." Nineteenth-century evolutionary geology would agree.

The impulse that took Goethe to the Harz and other natural sites in Switzerland and Italy was both scientific and philosophical. Nearing middle age, he became more interested in Buffon's work, botany, and mineralogy or geology, but his study of nature was also a worship of it. Fascinated by Giordano Bruno, Goethe developed a "poetical Pantheism" in which "the whole universe was conceived as divine" (Lewes 1965, 525). About 1780 he produced a paean to "Natur" as a quasi-divine principle, mighty and various. Her "constant life" is "eternally changing," yet she "remains where she was," "her laws immutable" (Goethe 1897, 6,454). "She is all things" and all times; "In her everything is always present." This nature, whose laws give form to art and the mind, is very nearly the all-mothering spirit of Pope and other deists in the early part of the century, yet it retained its appeal for the Victorians. Goethe's vision of nature as the body whose soul is God was a powerful influence on Thomas Carlyle, and the evolutionist T.H. Huxley quoted "Natur" in the first number of *Nature, A Weekly Illustrated Journal of Science* (1869).

The conjunction of mountain and desert imagery in "Harzreise im Winter" is surprising because so little was being published in Europe about deserts (Goethe's inspiration was biblical). It is as if that gene had not yet developed. The de la Verendrye family walked over hundreds of miles of America's Great Plains to within sight of the Rocky Mountains between 1738 and 1743, but the closest their reports come to aesthetic appreciation is to call the prairie "magnifique" (Verendrye 1925, 32, 55). The Danish expedition to Arabia (1761–67), for all its achievements, has almost nothing to say about the peninsula's deserts (Hansen 1964). The foundations of the nineteenth century's orientalism were being laid in Antoine Galland's translation of *Les Mille et une nuits* (1704), Pétis de la Croix's *Contes turcs* (1707), and especially his *Contes persans* (1710–12), which accustomed readers to landscapes (typically paradisal gardens or "dangerous" deserts) that symbolized character and situation (Maynard 1979, 93–103), yet they did not encourage the apprehension of desertic themes or landscapes as other than hostile, nor give any specific information about them.

Though deserts remained unappreciated, explorers were pushing into new areas of the Great, a precondition for the kind of aesthetic appreciation that Europeans were developing for mountains. There was notable progress into the subpolar seas and lands that would capture the public imagination in the nineteenth century and cause Hardy to use "Thule" as shorthand for moors, seas, and mountains. Danish colonists began to settle Greenland in 1721; these settlements facilitated arctic voyages and, eventually, Nansen's crossing. Vitus Bering sailed through his strait to reach 67° north latitude in 1728. In 1734 the English Admiralty offered a prize for the discovery of the Northwest Passage, stimulating travel (as de Saussure would on Mont Blanc), and sent Cook into the Antarctic Ocean in the 1760s (see chapter 7). Lyakhov, a Russian, discovered the New Siberian Islands in 1770. Two years later Solander and Joseph Banks, both associates of Cook, led a voyage to Iceland that included Uno von Troil, chaplain to the King of Sweden and a student of natural science. His *Letters on Iceland*, translated from the German in 1780, is an interesting record not only of that expedition, but of a late-eighteenth-century European intellectual's knowledge of earth science and feelings about Great nature.

At first sight, the coast of Iceland was "not pleasing," but "uncommon and surprising," with signs of vulcanism and "high rocky mountains covered with eternal snow" stretching to the horizon (von Troil 1780, 3). Addison could have written what follows: "Beauty is pleasing both to our eyes and our thoughts; but gigantic nature often makes the most lasting impression" (4). Feeling "as it were, in a new world," he made the first ascent of the five-thousand-foot Mount Hecla, then quite active (5). Pursuing the theme of earth's fire, von Troil discusses geysers (which the natives considered entrances to Hell, but which he, paying "chearful homage" to nature's "Creator," found "beautiful"), and the pillars at Staffa (Scotland) and the Giant's Causeway (Ireland), which he identifies as volcanic basalt (10–16). Von Troil says that his party was the first to visit Staffa, and subjoins Banks's account of Fingal's Cave. He notes that the Hebrides' "wild romantic and enchanting scenes of nature" produced Fingal and Ossian (21); the scholarly cleric could cite Macpherson and Thomson as well as Buffon. The verdict on Iceland's "barren mountains" and "dreary rocks" is "horrid" (24–5), yet they were full of scientific interest for von Troil, who speculated about the connection between volcanoes, earthquakes, and geysers.

Astronomy, like most other physical sciences, made progress in eighteenth-century Europe, but there seems to have been less intellectual excitement over its findings than in the seventeenth century, when the great breakthroughs in optics were new. In Voltaire's *Micromegas* (1752), for example, where one might anticipate an aesthetic response to cosmic space from one of the century's liveliest minds, imaginative evocation of the universe is minimal. The voyage of Micromegas from Sirius here occasions a jibe at William Derham, the English astro-theologist, and a parody of Fontenelle, no more. Voltaire's interest is clearly the moral, not the physical, universe.

As for the ocean, some mid-century observers enthused over views of stormy seas from the coast of Europe; one M. Guibert sounds like Addison as he describes such a scene filling his thought and pushing it "into infinity," "like the sight of the heavens and the thought of eternity." Painters were then beginning to give the "violent beauties" of ocean tempests the kind of sublime treatment accorded mountains (Mornet 1907, 287–90). But such emotional effects required a certain distance. One of the few writers to analyze the experience of travelling by sea was Bernardin de St Pierre. His *Voyage à l'Île de France* (1773) exudes the kind of gloom that turns up in many early accounts of ocean and desert travel: "Il n'y a guère du vue plus triste que celle de la pleine mer. On s'impatiente bientôt d'être toujours au centre d'un cercle dont on n'atteint jamais la circonférence" ('Hardly any sight is sadder than that of the open sea. It is boring to be always at the centre of a circle whose circumference is never reached': Bernardin 1773, 45). He acknowledges the magnificent beauty of the sky, especially at sunset, night, and dawn, but his response lacks any spiritual dimension. For the most part the sea, like the desert, was still awaiting its epoch.

7

Enlarged Views:
English Travel and Exploration

We have already seen some eighteenth-century Englishmen responding to mountainous landscapes: Addison, Gray, and Windham to the Alps, Johnson and Boswell to Scotland, Berkeley and Hamilton to Vesuvius. Berkeley advised Alexander Pope in 1714 that it might be "worth a poet's while to travel, in order to store his mind with strong images of nature," for "to describe rocks and precipices, it is absolutely necessary that he pass the Alps" (1848, 1:20). A few (including Gray) visited the Lake District, with mixed results. Heading west from York in 1773, William Hutchinson initially found the "prospect" of hills and heath "dreary," all "barrenness and deformity," "wilderness and horrid waste" (1774, 10–11). But after miles of "melancholy," Starbury Crag seemed "nobly awful," and when sunset reddened the mountains, Hutchinson's thoughts rose to the "mighty author" of all (72, 79). Like Burnet, he saw cliffs as "the pillars of the antediluvian world" (135). His party climbed "Awful Skiddaw," admiring its "majesty," and "rejoice[d]" in the "grand spectacle" of other "stupendous" mountains (143, 159). It remained a gloomy region, but Hutchinson felt the glory, too.

If eighteenth-century British travellers played a lesser role than the Swiss in exploring and responding to mountains, they were important in other spheres. Britons began to pay more attention to the desert than had been the norm, though still little enough, and through Captain Cook's voyages they extended not only geographical knowledge but imaginative life into Antarctic waters for the first time.

OBSERVING THE DESERT: SHAW AND PLAISTED

In some ways, true desert proved the most resistant area of the Great. Early travellers there were not immediately awed into reverence, as

mariners were by icebergs, or torn by strong mixed emotions, like walk-
ers in the Alps; there were questions of perception, as well as difficulties
of access. As mentioned in chapter 2, Renaissance visitors either did not
think the desert worth commenting on, or, around the "Holy Land,"
tended to see a biblical curse rather than a landscape. The level of re-
porting was no higher in the early eighteenth century. Aaron Hill's *Full
and Just Account of the Present State of the Ottoman Empire* (1709), supposedly based on his own travels, says nothing about Ethiopian landscapes
and offers no personal reaction to the sight of the Pyramids. He affirms
the barrenness of "Goshen [Egypt] and Libya" without providing details, saying simply that he went overland from Egypt to Palestine
through "*desart Sands* and *miserable Countries*" (Hill 1709, 274). Hill informs us that "Arabia the Stony" is "*desolate, and barren,*" with waves of
sand rolling up and down it, while "Arabia the Desart" is a plantless
waste where corpses blow around in the wind and hobgoblins prowl
(303, 307–9). He had visited neither place.

   Thomas Shaw's *Travels, or Observations Relating to Several Parts of Barbary
and the Levant* (1738) represents a considerable advance on such perfor-
mances: he traversed more real desert than did his predecessors, and was
more broadminded and perceptive about it. A Fellow of Queen's College, Oxford, who could enrich his text with oriental and classical scholarship as well as scriptural citation, Shaw felt the kind of ambivalent
responses to deserts that Burnet had to the Alps. He found the way from
Cairo to Mount Sinai "long and dreery," the "desolate mountains,"
"naked Rocks and Precipices" east of Jerusalem "frightful," and Arabia
Petraea south of Damascus "a lonesome, desolate wilderness" (1738, iv,
334, 377). Yet the Sinai desert is pronounced "a beautiful Plain," and between Cairo and Suez can be seen "Beautiful Pebbles ... superiour to the
Florentine Marble" (350, 383). Of course beauty is not the Great, but the
difference between these adjectives and those employed by earlier travellers, or by Shaw himself when speaking generally, is striking; his openness
or neutrality of vision and his eye for detail are rare in this period.

   For example, while many travellers compare the desert to the sea,
Shaw works out the analogy with unusual thoroughness: "Where any
Part of these Deserts is sandy and level, the *Horizon* is as fit for astronomical Observations as the Sea, and appears, at a small Distance, to be no
less a Collection of Water. It is likewise equally surprizing, to observe, in
what an extraordinary Manner every Object appeared to be magnified
within it. ... This seeming Collection of Water, always advances, about a
Quarter of a Mile before us, whilst the intermediate Space appears to be

in one continued Glow" (378–9). While Shaw remains the detached, scholarly observer, the intellectual and visual interest he finds in the desert presages its appeal to those later travellers who noticed that their powers of perception were *heightened* by the sparseness of the landscape.

One quality that he noted figures more often in polar than in desert exploration: atmospheric purity, inducing a kind of immutability. The dry heat, he found, inhibited disease bacteria, so that "few Persons are seized with any Illness, during their travels through these lonesome, sultry Deserts," and for the same reason carcasses exist in an almost mummylike "State of Preservation" (379). To the extent that even a partial defeat of time and decay images eternity, this is a movement towards the aesthetics of the Great, wherein the imagination seizes upon natural metaphors of the infinite and eternal. Shaw, then, supplies desert literature with several new features that would later be common: beauty of detail, interesting effects of perception, and a preserving purity.

That Shaw's work did not signal a *general* advance in British responses to deserts is clear from Richard Pococke's massive *Description of the East* (1743), which imparts reams of historical and anthropological information, but has almost nothing to say about the desert, or his response to it. A much humbler tome, Bartholomew Plaisted's short "Narrative of a Journey from Basra to Aleppo in 1750" (1757) is more rewarding. A surveyor and sea captain returning from India to England, he belonged to the largest European group to use "the Great Desert Caravan Route" in that period: British East India Company officials and other servants of the Empire. They started making the arduous overland journey as an alternative to the sea route in the late sixteenth century, but political unrest made it unpopular until the mid-eighteenth century (Carruthers 1929).

Plaisted, who spent 25 days with a large caravan crossing seven hundred miles of desert in what are now Iraq and Syria, is in many ways an excellent source: blunt and businesslike, without religious preconceptions; almost devoid of emotion except for occasional fury at thieving Arabs and irritation with the inaccuracies of the French traveller Tavernier; concerned chiefly with setting down the details of the route for the benefit of posterity. After his homely preface we do not expect, nor do we receive, an aesthetic treatise. The nearest approach is one remark about the desert air being "always pure and serene," so that stars do not twinkle and rust does not form: the theme of preservation again (Plaisted 1929, 92).

What Plaisted provides is abundant, intensive observation. He describes, ploddingly enough, the natural features of each day's march:

gravel and sand, then "loose sand with shrubs," then sand dunes, some heath, a marshy spot, five trees, some chalk-white hills, a stony plain (69). By the third week he notes "a champion country" with shrubs and firm soil. Plaisted's empirical observations debunk common myths about the desert. It is not sandy but stony ("the greatest part is a hard sandy gravel like some of our heaths in England"), not featureless but varying, with "a change of the soil every hour," and not without water (90, 73). He paid constant attention to the land, noting fluctuations in soil and topography more carefully than had any of his predecessors. Plaisted shows no tendency to dismiss the desert as a monotonous, cursed, or uniformly hostile waste and thus takes a first step towards the kind of geologic awareness that the later desert mystics, the Doughtys and Lawrences, display. Adapting Ruskin and Nicolson, we can see the beginning of a movement away from "desert gloom" towards something more positive.

Yet other British travellers of the period contribute little to this meagre yield. Robert Wood, an illustrator, skirted the western edge of the Syrian desert at mid-century, but his only sense of the sublime came from the skies, a region seldom mentioned by eighteenth-century observers in terms suggestive of the Great. Wood liked to sleep on roofs, because in the "desarts of Arabia" the heavens have more beauties and the earth fewer than elsewhere (1757, 15). On the Canadian tundra, Samuel Hearne reached the Arctic Ocean via the Coppermine River in 1771 and Alexander Mackenzie via the Mackenzie in 1789, both impressive achievements, but their journals contain little aesthetic material. Hearne (who quotes Young's *Night Thoughts*) has nothing to say about the Barrens and finds the Arctic coast "dreary"; the only view he seems to have liked was an "extensive prospect" over lake and forest, "beautifully contrasted" with snowy hills (1958, 14). Mackenzie occasionally describes nature, seemingly without appreciation, but mostly narrates facts. At century's end, desert, prairie, and tundra had not found their lovers.

OPENING THE ANTARCTIC: COOK'S SECOND VOYAGE

Voyages and voyage literature, like mountain books, burgeoned during the eighteenth century to the point where one cannot hope to read and describe them all; the tradition founded in Hakluyt was thriving. (In the introduction to his *Voyage towards the South Pole* [1777], Capt. James Cook devotes the first twenty-odd pages to a survey of his predecessors in the search for a southern continent.) English navigators benefited greatly from government support, delivered by the Admiralty and the Royal Navy. Admiral Anson's voyage around the world (1740–44), the showpiece of the first half of the century, was upstaged by the three expeditions of Captain Cook (1768–79), which attained the epic status and broad following of the quest for Mont Blanc. His second voyage (1772–75) included the first venture into the Antarctic Ocean, and on his third voyage he sailed through Bering's Strait and reached the Arctic Ocean's ice pack, both venues of the Thulean Great.

Of the copious materials produced by and about the expeditions, the writings of Captain Cook are among the least interesting. Like most master mariners, he was, as he says, "a plain man" (Cook 1777, 1:xxxvi), not given to introspection, effusions, or dramatic accounts of dangerous moments that might appeal to the public but raise questions at the Admiralty about his stability. Most travel writers either flesh out a diary into a fuller book or suppress their private thoughts, but there is little difference between Cook's journals and the published *Voyage*: both are reticent. Cook rarely expressed emotional or aesthetic reactions to the ocean or to the weather; his first sight of an Antarctic iceberg was recorded without remark. In the book he adds that watching the sea break against icebergs pleases the eye, yet fills the mind with horror (23). He makes several such distinctions: ice-covered rigging is "agreeable" to the eye, for example, but chills the mind (36).

In January 1773 Cook and the *Resolution* achieved the first crossing of the Antarctic Circle, turning back in heavy ice only 75 miles from Antarctica. Cook wondered at the vast extent of the icefield, but it was the officer of the watch who called the Southern Lights "beautiful"; to Cook, they "curiously illuminated" the sky (1777, 53, 64). Cook's greatest self-indulgence in his journal was to admit that icebergs afford "romantick Views" that require a painter, and that their dangerous beauty evokes "admiration and horror" (1961, 1:98–9): a pairing reminiscent of Alpine narratives. The waterspouts of New Zealand, though, one of which just missed the ship's stern, produced nothing but objective description in both journal and book. The following December Cook was again within the Antarctic Circle and among icebergs three hundred feet high, which he found "astonishing" (1777, 1:256). In January 1774 the *Resolution* reached 71°10′ South latitude before being turned back by "prodigious ice mountains" (1777, 1:267). Convinced that any southern continent must be distant and hopelessly icy, Cook wrote that he was "not sorry" to be stopped so decisively (1961, 321–2; 1777, 1:269–70).

Cook's strongest reactions to any aspect of nature occurred around Tierra del Fuego (Cape Horn) and the adjacent islands. Coasting the fjords of southern Chile, Cook gave the name Cape Desolation to a headland of "the most desolate and barren country I ever saw ... entirely composed of rocky mountains without ... vegetation, ... horrible precipices, whose craggy summits spire up to a vast height ... hardly any thing in Nature can appear with a more barren and savage aspect" (1777, 2:173–4). A few days later he pronounced "the whole country ... a barren rock, doomed by Nature to everlasting sterility" (179; the journal passages are virtually identical in this section). South Georgia and "Southern Thule" islands evoked similar responses: "savage and horrible," "wild rocks," "everlasting snow" (213), "the most horrible Coast in the World" (1961, 632). It is not a question, then, of Cook "liking" barren landscape, any more than Burnet "liked" the Alps, or Addison, infinity, or Hardy, Egdon Heath: the word suggests something amiable. They were, rather, struck, staggered by bouncing off a formidable entity, strangely moved. The difference is that Cook sees no divinity, nothing positive, in the scene; it is not epiphanic for him.

Through the words or pictures of almost anyone else on the voyage, we see the expedition in higher colours. Lieutenants Clerke and Pickersgill regularly portray icebergs, storms, waterspouts, and near-mishaps more excitedly than does their leader, conveying a wide-eyed sense of the voyage's perils and novelties. Without Cook's self-control and supreme responsibility, they are more vulnerable and exclamatory. One of the scientists on board, the Swede Anders Sparrman, described how the setting sun "transformed [an iceberg] into the loveliest scene imaginable," a composite of crystal, gold, yellow, and "rich purple" (quoted in Smith 1960, 44). This is something Cook never did.

A Voyage Round the World (1777) by the naturalist George Forster has been called "the most readable of all accounts of Cook's voyages" (Smith 1960, 39). Forster too is more dramatic than his captain, with a penchant for scenic detail. Where Cook "saw an Island of Ice to the Westward" (1961, 1:57), Forster saw "prodigious pieces of ice," which showed a "beautiful sapphirine or ... berylline blue" in the sunshine, but in the fog made a "dismal scene" (1777, 1:94, 101, 97). The "gloomy," "desolate" world of fog and beautiful, terrible bergs sharpened Forster's sense of human frailty; when two men in a rowboat were temporarily lost among icebergs in fog he was deeply stirred, and while the expedition's two ships were separated, each was described as being "alone on this vast and unexplored expanse" (104–5, 117, 99, 115).

The sea full of icebergs looked to Forster as the Alps had to Thomas Burnet: "like the wrecks of a shattered world" (538). Coleridge, who once considered turning Burnet's *Theoria* into blank verse, used Forster's book as a source of scenic detail for "The Rime of the Ancient Mariner."

In his response to Cape Horn, Forster was closer to Cook. The "black" and "barren" islands of Tierra del Fuego had a "very unfavourable aspect," and the "Coast of Desolation," with its high snow-covered mountains and dark rocks, deserved the name Cook gave it, though Cook's whimsical "York Minster" becomes a "dreary chaotic rock": i.e., redolent of Chaos (Forster 1777, 2:484, 486). It was officially summer, but Forster found that the country "looked wild and horrid in its wintry dress," reminding him of the Alps (490; there are many such instances of Europeans comparing polar or subpolar regions to their mountains). The affective content of these passages is strong, and may appear disproportionate – to someone who has not coasted Tierra del Fuego in a sailing vessel. Vast scale and some of the darker emotions (fear, gloom), then, characterize Forster's recollections of the high southern latitudes.

It fell to the expedition's painters to provide images of what Cook declined to evoke and other writers only suggested. William Hodges tried to break free of his classical training in the southern seas, applying established formulae (such as Salvator Rosa's "sublime" effects) to new subjects, or transcending the formulae (Smith 1960, 41–51). Even when engraved, his paintings of icebergs retain the emotional expressiveness that Cook lacks. In some of Hodges's early canvases, striving men or the ship *Resolution* loom large in the foreground, but in later ones they are dwarfed by natural forms (cf. plates 30, 32, and 34). If the treatment of light, sky, and sea anticipates Turner (see Hodges's "Cape of Good Hope," for example), the minimizing of the human impact is reminiscent of Breughel's "Fall of Icarus." This effect is particularly evident in Hodges's and Joseph Gilbert's views of Tierra del Fuego, South Georgia, the Sandwich Islands, and waterspouts. In their "Christmas Sound" paintings, the *Resolution*, dwarfed by mountains and sea, is little more than a speck. One might write a long volume on natural philosophy and the relation of man to nature without expressing more than these few washes and canvases do; certainly they are worth thousands of Cook's words in conveying emotion and attitude.

The fascination of the material from Cook's voyages is seeing observers of various temperaments respond to the same natural phenomenon. We can use these diverse reports on shared encounters with the Great as a navigator does triangulation: to learn something by viewing an object from different angles. They show us that (as Kant would soon argue) the experience we call "sublimity" is highly subjective; ultimately we are talking not about nature itself, but about the human mind and nervous system. And the very material that is on one level a record of completed reactions is, on another, a commencement: the stimulus for a whole new set of responses. For Cook's voyages were famous even before they were completed; the books describing his expedition immediately influenced a wide audience that included the next generation of artists and travellers. Cook's achievements and death drew tributes from poets, painters (such as Johann Zoffany), and dramatists. John O'Keefe's pantomime *Omai; or a Trip Round the World* (1785) included scenes of the "snowy rock of Kamchatka and a 'dreary ice island'" (Smith 1960, 81).

One text that responded to Cook's voyages, Anna Seward's "Elegy on Captain Cook" (1780), has an interest beyond its modest poetic merits: her taste in sublime scenery. "The Goddess of the new Columbus" bestrides the "rude summit" of an "icy rock" along a "frozen shore," darting "radiant glances" over the "hoar waste" in order to point the *Resolution* to a "mazy path" through "The floating fragments of the frozen bed." Cook himself, standing "Firm on the deck" despite all dangers, "Round glitt'ring mountains hears the billows rave, / And the vast ruin thunder on the wave" (quoted in Smith 1960, 85). If "vast ruin" and "floating fragments" mean icebergs, they echo Forster's phrase "wrecks of a shattered world," with *its* echo of Burnet. This and other images make it probable that Anna Seward had read Forster and Cook, and had therefore seen the engravings from Hodges and Gilbert. There were rumours after her death that her Litchfield neighbour, Erasmus Darwin, the poetic scientist whose work got Cowper interested in icebergs, had collaborated on the poem (Ashmun 1931, 74–6), which would be an interesting nexus between natural science, travel, and Great aesthetics. Dr Johnson (also from Litchfield) praised the passage on the polar seas in his post-Hebridean mood.

When we look at eighteenth-century English travellers in the light of Addison's *Spectator* essay number 412, then, we see a mixed picture. A few visitors to the mountains felt their power, but were less bold and articulate than their Continental counterparts, and the connection between the desert and the Great remained tenuous. The literature of the polar seas, however, gives clear if scattered evidence that some explorers did feel the emotions that Addison and Burke said Great landscape should evoke. So if, on some fronts, Georgian travellers confirmed Addison, in other ways they revised him. Deserts and oceans, which he had included in his new category, rarely moved travellers as did the polar regions, which he had omitted. Only with regard to high mountains did he anticipate the tastes of his century. The next, however, would bear him out more generally.

PART III

From Sublimity to Barrenness: The Romantic Period

Among its plethora of meanings, "Romantic" connotes a turning from the claims of society towards the needs, talents, and imagination of individuals, from an objective to a subjective emphasis. In the late eighteenth and early nineteenth centuries, many Europeans realized that human perception makes a large contribution to some phenomena that had been ascribed to nature. As William Blake put it, "Where man is not, nature is barren," "barren" being understood as "devoid of meaning." Ecology objects that Blake's clauses should be reversed: "Where nature is barren, man is not." That could have been the motto of those nineteenth-century travellers for whom barren nature had a fascination based partly on its inability to support human habitation: either they could thus see certain truths more clearly, or they were fleeing humanity. In Blake's formulation, we bring meaning to nature, but some of the English Romantic poets lost confidence that *Homo sapiens* could convey a meaning worthy of nature. Whatever the train of causation, in this period the eighteenth century's quasi-religious veneration of sublimity crests, is chastened, and begins to yield to intimations of barrenness within and without.

8

Mind and Earth:
Philosophy and Science

The philosophical ideas that connect Burke to Romantic literature came mostly from Scotland, whose contributions to aesthetics in the late eighteenth century were considerable, and from Germany, whose thought had wide influence in nineteenth-century England. Although Goethe remained a prestigious figure, his view of nature as a kind of spiritual mother, connecting us with God and giving laws to art and the mind, was of little interest to the new generation of formal inquirers into the aesthetics of nature. What unites these philosophers – besides their grounding in eighteenth-century British aesthetics – is the belief that the sensibility of the observer, not any outside object or process, is the crucial determinant of aesthetic phenomena. This subjectivism helped to shape the generations of writers called "Romantic," who also made the quality of individuals' feelings and perceptions the measure of many, if not of all, things.

THE GREATNESS IN US: ALISON AND KANT

From the standpoint of aesthetics, the new era of subjectivism began in 1790, when Archibald Alison published his *Essays on the Nature and Principles of Taste* and Immanuel Kant his *Critique of Judgement.* The complex thought of Alison, a Glaswegian who became a minister, has a number of aspects and affiliations. Clearly he was aware of the entire spectrum of eighteenth-century psychology from Locke to Priestley, though historians differ on how much he derives or departs from his sources. Usually treated as an associationist (Hipple 1957; Hussey 1927), Alison has also been called an idealist (Monk 1935). What matters here, however, is not his relation to his sources but the content of his synthesis. His formulation, whatever its origins, was influential: Wordsworth and Coleridge knew his work, which was still prominent in Ruskin's time.

Alison defines taste as an emotion, within which exists "the emotion of sublimity" (1971, 475). Such emotions (which "serve to exalt the human mind from corporeal to intellectual pursuits") are produced by "qualities" in "objects," yet are often "dependent upon the state of our own minds" (475–6). Alison discusses both the qualities that stimulate these emotions and the "faculty" that receives them, insisting that earlier accounts of this process have oversimplified it (476–9). He argues that, although association *begins* with a simple emotion, this excites the imagination, and the interaction of the two produces a complex emotion. For him, "the qualities of matter are not beautiful or sublime in themselves, but as they are ... the signs or expressions of qualities capable of producing emotion" (480). Alison fuses categories that are usually distinguished (beauty and sublimity are "Ideas of Emotion"), but apart from this difficulty, and the apparent circularity of his formulation ("qualities" are "signs" of "qualities"), we understand that he wishes to assign primacy to the perceiver, not to the world.

If matter and mind are related through association, it must be understood that this relation is complicated and highly subjective, not automatic or universal. Alison insists that "the diversity of effects that one object may have upon many people proves that the object itself is really indifferent; one idea has never been permanently or constantly beautiful or sublime" (Kallich 1948, 317). "Indifferent" may be too strong; later Alison explains how we come to associate certain "Ideas of Emotion" with certain objects: "the constant connection we discover between the [material] sign and the thing signified" (the quality that produces emotion) eventually makes the first "expressive to us" of the second, encouraging us to read back the signified emotion into the sign (316). This would be clearer if Alison had not used the word "quality" for two entities he was at pains to distinguish, but perhaps he took this way to express our connection with the world. He does give helpful examples of "qualities" generally found sublime, many of which occur in field descriptions of the Great: danger, power, solemnity, desolation, magnitude, majesty, melancholy. Alison agrees with Addison that the ocean is a "sign" of infinity.

In some ways, then, Alison's work confirms earlier treatments of our relation to the natural sublime – familiar emotions and stimuli reappear, and the mechanism is implicitly deist (Hipple 1957, 180) – but his *Essays* have original dimensions that some call "romantic" (Kallich 1948, 138). The emphasis on the sublime's subjectivity, though not unprecedented, is stronger than before, and the "taste" for it, treated more subtly than in most previous writers, depends on the imagination, not on judgement. The long description of the "romantic ecstasy" generated by intense aesthetic experience anticipates the early Wordsworth (317–18). And in his view that only the mature, well-educated, large-minded individual could fully comprehend the sublime, Alison had virtually no predecessors.

That same year, Immanuel Kant devoted nearly a hundred pages of his *Critique of Judgement* to an "Analytic of the Sublime," making sublimity part of a large, prestigious philosophical system for the first time. Read in the context of eighteenth-century British aesthetics, however, Kant's treatment often sounds familiar. He basically accepts Addison's psychology of aesthetic experience and his distinction between beauty and Greatness (Hipple 1957, 84; Nicolson 1963, 313; Gracyk 1986). To Kant, "sublime" means "absolutely ['beyond all comparison'] great"; *natural* sublimity conveys the idea of infinity to the imagination (1952, 94, 103). He maintained that the physical universe was of infinite extent, and his limitless sublime is an emotional analogue of this universe. But "rude nature" is also sublime when its "irregular disorder and desolation" demonstrate "magnitude and power," as in great storms, volcanoes, troubled oceans, overhanging rocks, and high waterfalls (92, 100, 110). Though it is not the same as Addison's list, there is considerable overlap. Thus it is incorrect to say that the Analytic "introduces an aesthetic without nature" (Lyotard 1994, 54).

Kant's British roots go deep. The idea that sublimity sets the mind vibrating between attraction and repulsion echoes what Burnet, Dennis, and others felt in the Alps. Kant argues that we are not afraid of the sublime (as Burke claimed), yet concedes that we experience an *imaginative version* of fear (1952, 110, 120–1), and though he wants to distinguish his transcendental aesthetics from Burke's physiological/psychological approach (130–1), is himself often psychological. Many of the emotions (admiration, awe, solitude) and natural qualities (desolation, magnitude, simplicity) that Kant associates with the Great had been mentioned by British aestheticians and travellers. (Kant adds that sublime 'solitude' should not be confused with 'misanthropy' [129], an increasingly crucial distinction in the nineteenth century.) Finally, like Alison, Kant emphasizes that sublimity resides in the mind, especially in the imaginative faculty, not in nature, and that the sublime calls for higher mental culture in the observer than does beauty.

Kant's work has undergone close critical scrutiny in this century. E.F. Carritt contended that once Kant's debts to Addison, Kames, and Blair are subtracted, he offers "few original ideas" about beauty and sublimity (1925, 323). He noted that the sedentary philosopher had seen little wild landscape, and argued that Kant made his topographic lists from British aestheticians, de Saussure's *Voyages* and Savary's *Lettres sur L'Égypte* (325). The one type of Great that Kant could see without travelling was the night sky, and he "felt for the starry heavens an awe and reverence only comparable with that which he felt for the moral law" (319). Of course the sky seems to have represented the infinite and eternal everywhere in primitive religion (Eliade 1959, 118).

If Kant's treatment of sublimity is largely a synthesis of others' views, his expression sometimes has an individual ring, as when he describes the sublime experience as a "momentary check to the vital forces" followed by their strong return, a kind of "negative pleasure" (1952, 91). The same passage connects the sublime with "reason," yet in the First Analytic he derives Beauty from understanding and imagination (Miall 1980, 139). The concept of a "rational sublime" is problematical, since most aestheticians had made sublimity a non-rational or supra-rational phenomenon. Kant held that the sublime involves an ascendancy of reason over sense and sensibility. Whatever Kant meant by "reason" here (apparently "the mind" or "ideas"), its ascendancy is only theoretical and temporary, for it is precisely when reason is unable to estimate magnitude and the imagination has to take over that the observer is led *ad infinitum*, into sublimity. Moreover, aesthetic judgment is called intuitive, not mathematical; the aesthetic must be distinguished from the logical, and insensitivity to sublimity suggests lack of feeling (Kant 1952, 116). These latter statements accord with the main tradition, before and after Kant.

One of Kant's assertions has provoked a strong rebuttal from a modern writer on the history of natural aesthetics. As part of his argument for human dignity and importance in relation to nature (which he felt were threatened by Burke's emphasis on fear), Kant insisted that the sublime of God and religion does not call for self-abasement, but for self-respect; the sublime is a consciousness of our superiority over nature (113–14). Few if any theorists or travellers have endorsed the final clause. Paul Shepard attacked Kant for setting man above nature; Kant and his followers, Shepard claimed, denied that nature was a source of knowledge for man (1967, 157, 229). To this it may be answered, first, that Judaism and Christianity set man over nature long before Kant (though some theologians deny this now); second, that he is not responsible for what his "followers" maintained; and finally that he does not *everywhere* deny that we can learn from nature. Although Kant's sublime is ultimately mental, "rude nature" excites sublime ideas, provides the best examples of sublimity, and conveys the idea of infinity to the aesthetic imagination.

Kant's treatment of sublimity (along with much else in his Analytics) was taken up by Hegel, Goethe, and Schiller – from whom it spread into nineteenth-century aesthetics, touching Carlyle and Emerson – and by some English poets. As a young man Coleridge read Kant and told Wordsworth about him. Ironically, they could have found many of the ideas in then-unfashionable writers such as Addison and Kames (Carritt 1925, 323–6), but a contemporary German was more exciting.

Dugald Stewart's discussion of the sublime in his *Philosophical Essays* (1810) – the climax, perhaps, of the Addisonian tradition (Tuveson 1960, 180) – makes "Generalizations of Sublimity, in consequence of associations resulting from the phenomena of gravitation"; Stewart believed that "great Altitude" is the etymological, physical, and theological root of the sublime, which elevates the mind (1818, 409, 378). Sublimity is thus part of the religious instinct, which looks upwards for the deity; mountains, ocean, and sky are sublime because they force the idea of the Creative Power upon us. Stewart thought that the idea of sublimity is then applied to eternity and other divine attributes. Among his admirers in the next generation was its leading geologist, Charles Lyell.

During the period when Goethe flourished and the English Romantics were young, then, aesthetic philosophy continued to discuss the sublime and to identify the Great as the prime stimulus of the experience, much as Addison had done. Sublimity was now assumed, usually without demonstration, to be the acme of human response to nature; it arose from the depths of (and revealed something about) the soul. Although each philosopher's list of evocative and responsive qualities was somewhat different, nature's vastness and power were typically associated with awe, ecstasy, and admiration. The principal development at this time was increased emphasis on the subjectivity of the phenomenon; it was not a universal gift, not simply the by-product of, say, visiting the Alps. Maturity and education might be required. Sublime scenes were clearly important, and ought to be confronted by anyone wishing to know all of life and human capacity, but nothing was guaranteed. Perhaps one might take away from the Great only what one brought to it.

A NEW THEORY OF THE EARTH:
HUTTON AND PLAYFAIR

Around the beginning of the nineteenth century, the "fathers of modern geology" (as they are sometimes called) attempted to separate that field from "physico-theology" and make it one of the empirical sciences. Their efforts were opposed by those who feared that scripture and morality would thus be undermined, and the resultant controversies continued with little respite from the end of the eighteenth century to Darwin and Hardy, by which time the storm included biology and astronomy. The interests of these men differed sharply from those of Kant and Alison, yet, working in another branch of "philosophy," they too influenced travellers' tastes in landscape.

The man usually credited with creating modern geology is James Hutton, another talented Scot. Trained in chemistry, law, and medicine, he took an MD but never practised. A profitable venture in manufacturing and the inheritance of a farm allowed him to please himself, so he became a farmer. To Hutton this meant touring Britain and the Low Countries, investigating agricultural practices and geological formations; he was, he admitted, "very fond of studying the surface of the earth" (Albritton 1986, 91). In 1768 he left his farm for Edinburgh, where he spent his time talking with Adam Smith, James Watt, Robert Adam, and, most important for Hutton's development, James Hall and John Playfair, whose interests included geology. With them he debated the ideas he had been developing. In 1788, at the age of sixty-two, Hutton published his "Theory of the Earth" in essay form. Not a *sacred* theory, and not even very theoretical; Hutton reasons but from what he knows, which is that the earth is a beautiful machine within the natural system. The machine is eroded by water but rebuilt by its central heat, of which volcanoes are the safety valves. Its age must be great, and there is no sign of its end.

Hutton's theory is essentially an engineer's description of the terrestrial mechanism. No dogma, no speculation, no miracles or catastrophes in the legendary past: just observation, physical laws, and natural change. What can be seen now enlightens us about the past, as Buffon had said. In 1794 James Kirwan, also of Edinburgh, launched a counterattack, arguing that the earth lacks sufficient heat to run Hutton's machine, nor does either Genesis or reason authorize the vast periods of time envisaged by Hutton (97). Hutton defended himself by developing his ideas in a book-length *Theory of the Earth* (1795). Behind this individual clash lay a broader debate between "Neptunist" and "Plutonist" camps. Neptunists tried to explain all geological formations in terms of water action; Plutonists or "vulcanists" brought in heat, such as volcanic action. In Hutton's theory, water eroded the land and built sedimentary layers on the sea bottom, but the Neptunists' or diluvialists' water of choice was Noah's Flood. Their commitment to the Bible contrasted sharply with Hutton's desire for an empirical synthesis of all existing geological data (Gillispie 1959, 41; Dean 1981, 112).

Elements of the geological past and future coexist in Hutton. His assumptions are basically those of an optimist and deist – God in His goodness made nature benign; earth's "purpose" is to sustain our lives – yet his effect was revolutionary. He quickly became the leading vulcanist (or vulcanists became Huttonians), espousing a longer time-scale and everything else the theo-geologists feared. His argument that "every thing is in a state of change" struck his contemporaries and the next several generations forcibly (Albritton 1986, 99). Hutton's theory that the powers that had shaped the earth could still be seen ("the adequacy of present causes") inspired more travel, and led to the "uniformitarianism" of Charles Lyell (Shepard 1967, 133; Read 1963, 17; Gillispie 1959, 126).

The best friend Hutton's reputation ever had was John Playfair, whose *Illustrations of the Huttonian Theory of the Earth* (1802) did for him what T.H. Huxley did for Darwin. Playfair, an Edinburgh minister who believed that science and religion should be kept separate, was the ideal popularizer: an associate who understood the scientist's work, resented the attacks on him, and could explain his ideas to a general audience more lucidly and eloquently than could the master himself. Together they found the famous "unconformity" (disjoined strata) at Siccar Point, for example, but while Hutton's account is technical and flat, Playfair makes us feel "the immeasurable force which has burst asunder the solid pavement of the globe," and the depths of "the abyss of time" that make the mind "giddy" (quoted in Albritton 1986, 103). Hutton is the pioneer thinker leading the way (his friend compares him to Newton), but Playfair, who provided the first clear exposition of the significance of Hutton's work and most of the biographical material we have, understood the "pleasures of the imagination." After Hutton's death in 1797, Playfair vigorously resisted the assaults of Neptunists (including the Alpinist J.-A. Deluc, see chapter 6), and fortified the vulcanist position.

Hutton and Playfair acquired allies on the Continent in the first years of the nineteenth century. Jean François D'Aubuisson de Voisins (1769–1819) and Leopold von Buch (1774–1853) both studied under

Abraham Werner at Freiberg (see chapter 6) and so began as Neptunists, but both concluded after visiting the Auvergne that basalt was volcanic (not aqueous, as Werner maintained): the beginning of their
apostasy. Von Buch's gradual conversion to Hutton's views was particularly important; he became Germany's leading geologist and was a
friend of the enormously influential Alexander von Humboldt, another
of Werner's former students.

EXAMINING THE EARTH: WILLIAM SMITH

Another progenitor of scientific geology, William Smith, a self-educated
Oxfordshire engineer and surveyor, begot stratigraphy, historical geology, and palaeontological method (Albritton 1986, 112–13; Gillispie
1959, 83). Smith's work, appearing a generation after Hutton's, was
founded on equally close inspection of the land, but their spheres of interest were different. If Hutton was more empirical than the physico-
theologians, Smith was even more so, with still less theory. His work
grew out of a childhood hobby (collecting fossils) and his later employ-
ment, surveying mines and constructing canals, all of which brought
him into repeated contact with various strata. This proved an educa-
tional combination. In the early 1790s, "he discovered that each formation contained distinctive species" of fossils by which it could be
identified: in modern terms, the "principle of faunal sequence" (Albritton 1986, 106; Drachman 1930, 40).

Using this powerful tool, Smith drew a geological map of the Bath region about 1799, but a great deal happened in geology before he published his most important findings. The Geological Society of London
(which did much to further Hutton's ideas) was founded in 1807; its
Transactions began to appear in 1811. Georges Cuvier and Alexandre
Brogniart published an essay on the geology of the Paris region (1808)
that essentially demonstrated faunal sequence (Albritton 1986, 105).
In 1809 William McClure produced the first geological maps of the
eastern United States. The Neptunist-Plutonist wars continued, J.-A. Deluc attacking Hutton in his *Treatise on Geology* (1809), Robert Bakewell,
a surveyor, arguing the vulcanist position in his *Introduction to Geology*
(1813), and so on. The Reverend Joseph Townsend (Smith's Playfair)
even presented his friend's ideas to the public (1813) before Smith finally issued his *Delineation of the Strata of England and Wales* (1815), "the
first [map] to represent on a large scale the geological relations of so
extensive an area" (110), and a "memoir" explaining the map.

Smith later published two books on stratified fossils, and *Deductions from Established Facts in Geology* (1835), his only speculative work. Smith's ideas are a curious *mélange*, typical of the transitional geology of the day. On the one hand he, along with Lamarck and Cuvier, helped to found palaeontology and provide geology with its descriptive method; on the other he remained a creationist, believing in a series of supernatural historical catastrophes, including the Flood, though it was "no more than an episode ... in a long chain of such events" (114–15). He would not estimate the earth's age, but placed "the creation" *late* in his chronicle of geologic history. Rev. Mr Townsend called his two volumes, which first publicized Smith's work, *The Character of Moses Established for Veracity as an Historian* (1813, 1815); they treated earth history before and after the Deluge.

Smith, then, was not a revolutionary: like Hutton, he proclaimed his orthodoxy, and looked orthodox to a friendly minister willing to grant science a separate sphere from scripture. But just that separation was emerging as a crucial issue, and would remain so for much of the century. Could geology and biology operate independently of Genesis? Were scientists responsible for the religious implications of their data? The relations between theology and geology at that time seem curious now – if we forget that deism viewed nature as a revelation of its Creator. William Paley's *Natural Theology* (1802), a book that reached orthodox Anglican conclusions by reason alone, was admired by Darwin; T.H. Huxley said that it admitted evolution "proleptically" (Drachman 1930, 36). Professor William Buckland of Oxford, who wrote *Vindiciae Geologicae* (1820) to explain "the Connexion of Geology with Religion" and *Reliquiae Diluvianae* (1823) to present geological evidence of the Flood, was the teacher, then colleague, of Charles Lyell, whose *Principles of Geology* (1830 ff.), dedicated to Buckland, actually undercut his principles in favour of Hutton's.

In the early nineteenth century, philosophy began to split into the humane and empirical branches that now constitute the arts and sciences. While Alison and Kant looked inward, emphasizing the operations of the psyche as the key to understanding how nature impinges on us, Hutton and Smith advocated travel, fieldwork, close scrutiny of external nature. Of course geologists' minds had to compare and deduce, but the ideal was to minimize human interference (especially from scripture) in what should be an essentially *objective* procedure. The educated traveller would henceforth try to combine close inspection of natural phenomena with introspection, outward with inward attention.

The philosophers and geologists are actually closer to Egdon Heath than they may seem. Aesthetics and science filtered down to poets and general readers in countless ways. Through the media of Coleridge and Carlyle, for example, Kant's ideas, incorporating those of Addison, Kames, and others, reached most English-language readers of the nineteenth century; Hutton's theory passed from Lyell to Tennyson, and thence to many others in England, Europe, and America. Geology had a double impact on the next generations. It urged them to "go and see" the land – especially where it was bare and contorted, hence readable – and, with its theological disputes, surrounded such visitations with an air of vague but unmistakably urgent spirituality. Thus the ghost of deism slipped quietly into science.

9

Poetic Feet:
England's Peripatetic Bards

By the time England's Romantic poets began to write, the evolution of the attitudes we have traced from the seventeenth century was well underway. Even William Blake, a Londoner, believed that "Great things are done when men and mountains meet; / This is not done by jostling in the Street." Some variety of wild nature had pleased numerous writers and travellers, as Shaftesbury foretold; Addison's Great was firmly established in aesthetics as the sublime; and landscapes were being examined more carefully than ever before. This movement bore literary fruit in the Romantics, but some of their works also sound the sterner tones that Hardy heard as a "chastened sublimity."

"HOLY GROUND": WILLIAM WORDSWORTH

From almost any perspective on English poetry and culture around 1800, William Wordsworth is a pivotal figure. For Basil Willey (1940), the eighteenth-century divinization of nature culminated in him; for Marjorie Nicolson he sums up "mountain glory" and the "aesthetics of the infinite" (1959); for Christopher Thacker, *The Prelude* completes "a century's study of nature" founded in Shaftesbury's thought (1983, 229). As for influence, he was both a prime source of "the concept of nature in nineteenth-century English poetry" (Beach 1936) and the patron saint of the taste for landscape and travel in America (Shepard 1967, 91). While much of Wordsworth's bequest to western civilization's aesthetics of nature confirmed earlier trends noted here, some parts of it opened new prospects.

Treating Wordsworth in a chronological or developmental way is difficult because of his tendency to revise the texts of May in December:

both "Descriptive Sketches" and *The Prelude* exist in early and late forms. It is clear, however, that "the essential Wordsworth," the poet whose imagination leaps up to behold wild nature, begins with his Alpine journey in 1790, when the twenty-year-old student sent his sister Dorothy an account of crossing the Simplon Pass: "Among the more awful [i.e., awe-full, or awing] scenes of the Alps, I had not a thought of man, or a single created being," he wrote; "my whole soul was turned to him who produced the terrible majesty before us" (quoted in Nicolson 1963, 382). Wordsworth begins, then, as a deist, whom nature leads to God. Mark Rutherford observed that Wordsworth's "real God" was not the Church's, but "the God of the hills" (quoted in Willey 1962, 258, 275).

Over the next two years, Wordsworth composed "Descriptive Sketches. Taken During a Pedestrian Tour Among the Alps" (1793), which he revised much later (1849–50). Though both concentrate on describing the Alps and their mystique, the early and late texts differ significantly. For example, the 1849–50 version begins by asserting that if there is "holy ground" on earth, where "solitude" prepares the soul for heaven (perhaps an echo of Marvell's "The Garden"), "nature's God" has given it to us on the "mountain-side"; but it omits the ocean sunsets and "moonlight Upland" of 1793 (which does not mention solitude). The revision generally gives more lines to the traveller, fewer to natural description. Both versions hail "the Alps, ascending white in air," and depict the Grande Chartreuse and "Uri's Lake," a "savage scene" where "The rocks rise naked as a wall" (1849–50, line 230) and "creation seems to end." Burnet's horror of chaotic crags is not so much rejected or outgrown as assimilated.

Like earlier writers, Wordsworth enthrones Freedom in the Alps; liberty is the theme of the poem's human aspect. The Alpine peasant, "slave of none," bears "traces of primeval Man" in his "simple dignity" and "eye sublime" (1849–50, lines 441–5). The qualities of the natives, then, accord with those of the mountains. Both versions present the mountain dweller as a noble savage and credit the exalting influence of the Alps: "For images of other worlds are there; / Awful the light, and holy is the air" (1849–50, lines 455–6; 1793, lines 544–5). They make their inhabitant a kind of spiritual hero who "holds with God himself communion high" in "The sky-roofed temple of the eternal hills," with its "sea-like reach of prospect": a trio of Great landscapes. Addison had noted that "a spacious horizon is an image of liberty"; Wordsworth ends both versions with a paean to Freedom and the free.

As in the letter to Dorothy, however, the human is dwarfed here. After hailing Alpine freedom, Wordsworth returns to inorganic nature, and a note to line 347 (1793) warns that the "sublime" Alps are "insulted" by the faddish term "picturesque" (popularized by William Gilpin), which suggests that painterly technique can capture them. Alone atop a "naked cone" (1849–50, line 304), the speaker watches a chamois-hunter and versifies Ramond's vision, in his reworking of Coxe's *Switzerland*, of silent, "vacant worlds," and heavenly bodies appearing at dusk over a wide expanse of "icy summits" (1793, lines 373–84). There is even a touch of misanthropy in his evocation of Underwalden Canton: "sure there is a secret Power that reigns / Here, where no trace of man the spot profanes" (lines 424–5). In the stillness of a mountain evening, with the soul rapt in "severe delight," "Deep ... calls to Deep across the hills" (lines 431, 433), evoking the cosmic Deep of Genesis.

Similarly, the tribute to the noble Alpine peasant is followed by more Great scenery: Chamonix's "Five ice-streams" are "A scene more fair than what the Grecian feigns / Of purple lights and ever vernal plains" (1793, lines 684–5; 1849–50, lines 573–4). If this refers to Tempe, then Wordsworth anticipated Hardy's discovery that "Thule" could have aesthetic qualities superior to the classical standard of natural beauty (though Hardy would have avoided the word "fair"). The passage on Mont Blanc is shortened in the 1849–50 text, but in both versions the mountain is perceived as combining "havoc" with "serenity": the kind of ambivalence that produced John Dennis's complex response and Wordsworth's "severe delight." With its sometimes clumsy neo-Augustan diction, "Descriptive Sketches" is not one of Wordsworth's best poems, but the aesthetic ideas and emotions are already close to those of Books Six and Fourteen of *The Prelude*.

The long poem that Wordsworth composed between 1798 and 1805, published with revisions after his death as *The Prelude; or, Growth of a Poet's Mind* (1850), develops these early reactions to the Alps and takes a broader approach to Great phenomena. In Book Six, "Cambridge and the Alps," he returns to the setting of "Descriptive Sketches." The 1805 version acknowledges the "awful solitude" of the Grande Chartreuse (Wordsworth 1971, line 419); the 1850 version adds lines explaining why this is such a "soul-affecting *solitude*" (line 421): when French revolutionaries wanted to close the monastery, Nature's voice "from her Alpine throne" cried, "stay your sacrilegious hands!" (lines 425–31). Nature's reason is Wordsworth's theme in Book Six, and whenever he discusses mountains: "be this one spot / Of earth devoted to eternity!"

(lines 434–5); the Alps are "types and symbols of Eternity" (line 639). He also celebrates the "imaginative impulse" emanating from the "majestic" glaciers and "shining cliffs, / The untransmuted shapes of many worlds" (lines 462–4); imagination is as central as eternity in both versions. Wordsworth "grieved" to see the mere "soulless image" of Mont Blanc, a sense impression usurping the Idea (imbibed from Ramond), "grieved" that his party had crossed the mighty Alps without even knowing it (1850, lines 525–6, 586–91; these passages differ little from the 1805 version).

A passage in Book Seven suggests that Wordsworth perceived mountains as belonging to a larger aesthetic category. His praise of the "deep solemnity" of London's nights, with "sounds / Unfrequent as in deserts" (1850, lines 655, 661–2), leads to a consideration of how we develop the personal resources to cope with urban life. The answer is "From early converse with the works of God," particularly those exhibiting "simplicity and power" (1805, lines 718–20). The example used in the 1805 version is the "pure grandeur" and "majesty" of mountains and "ancient hills" (lines 722–6); the 1850 version, picking up the parallel of nocturnal London with the desert, and the dream-vision in Book Five of the Arab on "a boundless plain / Of sandy wilderness, all black and void" (lines 71–2), adds, "On his desert sands / What grandeur not unfelt, what pregnant show / Of beauty, meets the sun-burnt Arab's eye" (lines 745–9). Between 1805 and 1850, a good deal more writing on the desert had appeared (see chapter 14). Book Seven (1850) completes its list of God's majestic works with the sea, so Wordsworth's catalogue is Addison's Great and Hardy's Thule.

Book Eight ("Love of Nature Leading to Love of Mankind") explains the importance of spacious horizons for humanity. Seen upon "the Plain / Endless," or in any "vast space," man can appear "A solitary object and sublime," like the cliff-top cross near the Grande Chartreuse (1850, lines 192–3, 202, 272–5; the wording is the same in 1805). Humans were "Ennobled outwardly" to the young poet by being seen as "purified" and "Removed," and "through objects that were great or fair": that is, sublime or beautiful (lines 276, 304–5, 316; same wording in 1805). Here Wordsworth provides a way of understanding a preference for underpopulated barrens as something other than mere misanthropy.

The closing books of *The Prelude* testify in both versions to the power of mountains over Wordsworth's imagination. In Book Thirteen he remembers how, as a child, he took the "disappearing line" of a public road "that crossed / The naked summit of a far-off hill" as "an invitation into space / Boundless, or guide into eternity" (lines 146–51). Here the bareness and openness of the vista create just the effect Addison had described, which Wordsworth had also felt in the Alps. Book Fourteen opens by narrating a nocturnal climb of Mount Snowden, at first in a thick fog, with the climbers trudging a bit apart. Wordsworth was in front, when "at my feet the ground appeared to brighten," and they broke through the fog:

> For instantly a light upon the turf
> Fell like a flash, and lo! as I looked up,
> The Moon hung naked in a firmament
> Of azure without cloud, and at my feet
> Rested a silent sea of hoary mist.   (lines 38–42)

Hills and headlands, their backs visible above the "solid vapours," range westward to the Atlantic; the moon dims the stars in a clear sky; and the noise of torrents and ocean surf roaring at the heavens through a rift in the clouds unites all.

This epiphanic scene, with what follows, is a *locus classicus* of the Great deeply felt, of natural religion, and of the spontaneous overflow of powerful feelings recollected in tranquillity. For when the "vision" had "partially dissolved" and was "in calm thought / Reflected, it appeared to me the type / Of a majestic intellect" (or "the emblem of a mind / That feeds upon infinity"): "a mind sustained / By recognitions of transcendent power, / In sense conducting to ideal form" (1850, lines 63–7, 70–1, 74–6). And what is this mind? In 1805, it is God (line 72), but in 1850 it is "Nature ... putting forth, / 'Mid circumstances awful and sublime," "One function ... of such a mind" (lines 79–80, 78). That function is to show us that the "power" that nature has over our senses is "the express / Resemblance [1805: "a genuine counterpart / And brother"] of that glorious faculty / That higher minds bear with them as their own" (1850, lines 88–90; 1805, lines 88–9): imagination. And what Wordsworth *saw*, "higher minds" can *project*: "They from their native selves can send abroad / Kindred mutations" (1850, lines 93–4).

In *The Prelude*, then, Wordsworth confirms through his own experience much of the aesthetics and psychology of responses to nature that had developed from Addison to Kant. He is conscious of the sublime as a kind of landscape-induced exaltation that can connect him – briefly but recurrently – with transcendental knowledge of eternity and infinity. His most striking addition to earlier field descriptions of natural sublimity is his insistence that an encounter with the Great is an analogue of the powers of the imagination, although he holds short of Idealism. For Wordsworth, there is definitely something out there that stimulates us, but we are usually "creator and receiver both" of nature (1850, bk. 2, line 258).

The Excursion (1814) also contains a great deal about the value of mountains. Infinity, awe, and spiritual power are themes of the portrait of the "Herdsman on the lonely mountain-tops" in Book One. There "did he *feel* his faith," where biblical wonders were made manifest. "There littleness was not; the least of things / Seemed infinite." Rather than having to believe, "he *saw*." No wonder, then, that his soul became "sublime and comprehensive" (Wordsworth 1936, bk. 1, lines 219–34). Beach says that Wordsworth (unlike Hardy) emphasizes nature's benevolent design, adducing a passage in Book Four that begins, "These craggy regions, these chaotic wilds, / Does that benignity pervade, that warms / The Mole" (Beach 1956, 166–7, 185). While generally true, this is oversimplified. Before the Wanderer finds his mountain valley, he is "Dispirited" by the "savage region," a "tumultuous waste of huge hill tops"; only after he sees the "sweet Recess" with its cabin does he pronounce the scene innocent, "an image of the pristine earth, / The planet in its nakedness" (Wordsworth 1936, bk. 2, lines 323–61). And the epiphanic vision ("Glory beyond all glory ever seen") of "Clouds, mists, streams, watery rocks and emerald turf," things "Such as by Hebrew prophets were beheld," comes only after a storm that almost kills an old man (lines 830–77).

Some of Wordsworth's short poems are relevant here. After touring the Highlands with his sister and Coleridge in 1803 and visiting Ossian's supposed burial site, William composed a tribute, "Glen-Almain" (1807). Initially, the speaker is surprised by the bard's place of interment: he who sang of war should have rested "Where rocks were rudely heaped" and "sight were rough," not in this "calm, Narrow Glen." Yet its deep silence is "austere," so in that respect it *is* an appropriate site. Both the problem and the resolution of "Glen-Almain" are rather contrived, but it testifies to the influence of Macpherson at the time, and the qualities associated with Ossian – roughness, silence, austerity – are all attributes of Great aesthetics. Minor lyrics such as "View from the Top of Black Comb" (written 1813; published 1815), "To –, on Her First Ascent to the Summit of Helvellyn" (1816; 1820), and several in *Memorials of a Tour on the Continent, 1820* show that mountains remained compelling for him.

Wordsworth spoke out on the effects of tourists and other issues affecting his home and heartland in *A Guide through the District of the Lakes in the North of England* (1810). The fifth edition of the *Guide* (1835) is quite ambivalent about visitors, giving "Directions and Information for the Tourist," yet discussing "The Country disfigured," "Causes of false Taste" and problems of development. In "Miscellaneous Observations," he compares Lake District and Alpine scenery. The beauty of English mountains is "more interesting" and well suited to painting, Wordsworth says, with a "tranquil sublimity" based on form and due relation, whereas the sublimity of the desolate Alps comes from bulk (1974, 231–6). In retrospect, the fearfulness of the Alps loomed larger than their inspiration, and his remark that a depressing barrenness may exclude the sublime (359) suggests that there were aspects of the Great that he could no longer accept. The young Wordsworth had found the Alps' "naked rocks" not depressing but "fair" and "holy."

The appendix on sublimity and beauty would be a major document if it were not a fragment. Generally, Wordsworth takes the subjectivist line: aesthetic feelings arise from the mind's laws, not from objects. A scene may be both sublime and beautiful, in which case the sublimity will strike us first, the beauty later (357, 349, 360). A mountain that is merely "grand" at a distance becomes sublime when we get close enough to perceive its great duration and power, which will produce either exaltation, or dread and awe (351). The effect of power comes from a sense of "intense unity" and leads to "repose"; *pace* Burke, pain and fear are not paths to the sublime (354). This analysis is full of problems. The "grand" that Wordsworth separates from the sublime was traditionally a defining quality of sublimity. He fails to distinguish between his "dread" and Burke's "fear," or to recognize the role of fear in his boyhood response to a towering mountain while rowing on a lake, described in *The Prelude*, Book Two. And though it is "of infinite importance to the noblest feelings of the Mind ... that the forms of Nature should be accurately contemplated" (350), the contemplation of nature is admittedly a question of varying tastes.

In his last decade, Wordsworth tried to defend the Lakes against a further influx of tourists, writing two letters to the *Morning Post* in 1844 opposing the extension of the railway to Windermere. Gone is even the qualified welcome of the *Guide*: he has seen the threat, and irony, of "tourism." The first letter notes that the district has no mines or industry; its "staple" is "beauty." But the taste for sublime scenery is culturally acquired, not innate; except for one passage in Burnet, he says, it hardly predates Thomas Gray, and no good will come of suddenly letting large numbers of persons without it into the region. Besides, the "intrusion" of a railroad will "sacrifice" much of the region's "quiet and beauty," destroying the very object of their quest (Wordsworth 1896, 386–91). The second letter repeats the point that aesthetic culture cannot be rushed or packaged. The kind of utilitarianism represented by the railway proposal is the enemy of all higher thought and feeling; the Lakes are "temples of Nature" that should be held sacred, not defaced as Alpine passes have been. Already "we have too much hurrying about in these islands" (395–404). The world is too much with us.

Besides opposing the desecration of wild country, Wordsworth was also revising "Descriptive Sketches" and *The Prelude* in the 1840s, in some cases expanding on his early tributes to the joys of contact with Great natural forms. Those works are thus the omega as well as the alpha of his own aesthetics, and show that Wordsworth remained to the last a transcendentalist for whom wild nature was a quasi-religion and poetry a mode of worship. Traveller, aesthetician, and poet, he saw in the Great what Addison had seen in 1712: that it lifts one above mere beauty, and everything human, to a realm of spiritual knowledge that stretches mind and soul to their limits.

"GIFTED KEN": SAMUEL TAYLOR COLERIDGE

While Wordsworth improved the Great's best-known trail, through the mountains, his friend and collaborator S.T. Coleridge reached back and outward to less-fashionable areas: seas, deserts, and the subterranean world. For Coleridge, though, it was not necessary to experience Great nature physically; the Idea was, in fact, better, and that might arise from reading. This belief, once ascribed to his interest in Kant and German philosophy, can be traced to his early studies in Henry More and the Cambridge Platonists (Abrams 1958, 59, 346n.57; Nicolson 1963, 114–15). As Coleridge wrote in "Apologia pro vita sua" (1800), the poet "emancipates his eyes"

> From the black shapeless accidents of size –
> In unctuous cones of kindling coal,
> Or smoke upwreathing from the pipe's trim bole,
> His gifted ken can see
> Phantoms of sublimity.   (1912, lines 3–8)

A man who can see the sublime in a wreath of pipesmoke has no call to go scrambling up mountains. Judging by his letters, Coleridge's chief impressions, after a few climbs in Wales in 1794, were of fatigue and thirst.

Coleridge seems always to have been drawn to Addison's Great. His "mind had been habituated *to the Vast*," he said, from childhood, when his father told him tales of the night sky (Coleridge 1895, 1:16). Some of his first poems were a sonnet "To the Autumnal Moon" and an "Imitation of *Ossian*"; he planned (but did not complete) a set of hymns to the elements. He wrote that his mind "ached to behold and know something *great*, something *one* and *indivisible*" (quoted in Willey 1964, 12). If the last phrase suits the ocean, sky, and desert better than it does mountains, it describes the concepts of infinity and eternity that Burnet and Addison considered analogous to Great nature.

A classic of early psychological criticism, John Livingston Lowes's *The Road to Xanadu* (1927), did most of the work necessary to connect Coleridge with the aesthetics of the infinite. Lowes used the poet's notebook to trace many of his images to their sources, demonstrating that Coleridge was deeply influenced by Thomas Burnet, read widely in history, science, and travel, and passed details from these books through his poetic imagination. Lowes's index lists almost three dozen navigators and collections of voyages whence Coleridge drew material and includes some familiar names: Hakluyt, Purchas, William Barents, Gerrit de Veer, Captains Marten, Wood, and Cook, George Forster, Samuel Hearne. An undated epigram bracketed his own vocation with that of a recent Arctic explorer: "Parry seeks the polar ridge, / Rhymes seeks S.T. Coleridge" (quoted in Lowes 1959, 536n.35). Coleridge "travelled" to the north with Maupertius, David Crantz, and Mary Wollstonecraft, to Hindustan with Thomas Maurice, to the heavens with William Herschel and Erasmus Darwin. He borrowed descriptions of the *sounds* of icebergs and earthquakes from at least ten explorers.

The earliest poem that combines Coleridge's feelings for the elements with his reading is the "Ode to the Departing Year" (1796), a curse on England for having joined in the attack on France. Coleridge imagines how the dragon Destruction, while waiting for England's time to come,

> with many a dream
> Of central fires through nether seas up-thundering
> Soothes her fierce solitude ... as she lies
> By livid fount, or red volcanic stream,

changed from a "fire-flashing fount / In the black Chamber of a sul-
phur'd Mount" (1912, lines 141–4). The Lowes traced this imagery to the
section "Concerning the Conflagration" in Burnet's *Sacred Theory of the
Earth* and an account of a new volcanic island in the *Philosophical Transactions of the Royal Society*: the mythical and scientific approaches to earth
history (Lowes 1959, 458n.28). Coleridge's phrase "shattered fragments
of memory" (which suggested to Lowes his psychological approach) may
echo Burnet's description of our fallen world, or Forster's of icebergs.

Coleridge was fascinated by the theories about the inside of the earth
found in Burnet, Erasmus Darwin, and Athanasius Kircher's *Mundus
Subterraneus* (1665). The lines in "Kubla Khan" describing how a "deep
romantic chasm" emitted the sacred river Alph in spasmodic bursts, for
example, may be based on Kircher's text and plates (Nicolson 1963,
171). The texture of the allusion is dense, however: the same lines reminded E.H. Coleridge of a scene in William Bartram's *Travels through
North and South Carolina* (1791), a work that Lowes thought suggested
Kubla Khan's pleasure garden, which S.T. Coleridge's preface says
came from a passage in *Purchas his Pilgrimage* (Coleridge 1912, 297n.4;
Lowes 1959, 332–4). The "caves of ice" may derive from Maurice's *History of Hindustan* (1795), the Abyssinian maid and Mount Abora from
Milton combined with James Bruce's *Travels to Discover the Source of the
Nile* (1790), while his underground river rose in Burnet, Bruce,
Kircher's *Oedipus Aegypticus*, Pliny, and Strabo (Lowes 1959, 346–62).
Coleridge spread his net widely in the recondite literature of travel and
scientific romance, giving glimpses of a wondrous world beyond the
senses.

Sources aside, the poem systematically intermingles human artifacts
(Kubla Khan's "stately pleasure-dome" and garden, the Abyssinian dam-
sel's song, the poet's mimesis) with the vast works of nature for which Coleridge had said his mind ached: the "mighty fountain" pulsing from the
chasm, carrying "Huge fragments" of rock like pieces of hail, plunging
"Through caverns measureless to man / Down to a sunless sea." Though
nature excites the poet to exclamation ("But oh! that deep romantic
chasm ...! / A savage place!"), he keeps reverting to juxtapositions of art
and nature: "The shadow of the dome of pleasure / Floated midway on
the waves"; "A sunny pleasure-dome with caves of ice!"; and "I would
build that dome in air, / That sunny dome! those caves of ice!" (Coleridge 1912). The poem in a sense realizes the wish in pronouncing it.

Coleridge also wrote "The Rime of the Ancient Mariner" in 1797–98.
He had no more been to sea than to Xanadu; again he borrowed

images, facts, even language from travel books. This time his chief inspiration was the voyages of the navigators; many details about the appearance, noises, and fogs of polar icefields originated in the pages of de Veer, Marten, Wood, Cook, Forster, and others (Lowes 1959, 128–37, 286, 297–303). Once more, though, the interconnections are complex; the idea of *preserving* the dead ("Nor rot nor reek did they") is more likely to have come from a desert traveller such as Josephus Acosta (267) or Thomas Shaw (chap. 7) than from a mariner, who would have buried them at sea. And Thomas Burnet was a spiritual father of this poem, too: the epigraph from his *Archeologiae Philosophicae*, or 'Ancient Teaching on the Origin of Things' (1692), notes how pleasant it is to imagine 'a greater and a better world, so that the mind, too habituated to the minutiae of daily life, will not contract to little thoughts.'

The "Ancient Mariner" renders aspects of the Great that had until then received little or no literary treatment so that we can grasp them. Coleridge used an antique form, the ballad, to give the sense of Cook's pioneering ventures into southern seas, and imagined how it might have felt to *be* there:

> And now there came both mist and snow,
> And it grew wondrous cold:
> And ice, mast-high, came floating by,
> As green as emerald.
>
> And through the drifts the snowy clifts
> Did send a dismal sheen:
> Nor shapes of men nor beasts we ken –
> The ice was all between.
> ...
> It cracked and growled, and roared and howled,
> Like noises in a swound!   (Coleridge 1912, lines 51–8, 61–2)

For that matter, "We were the first that ever burst / Into that silent sea" (lines 105–6) brings the daring of the enterprise home to the pulse more directly than any voyage narrative had been able to do.

In 1801 Coleridge went to the ocean at Scarborough. "On Revisiting the Seashore" reports that "Thoughts sublime" came to him on the "echoing strand" there (1912, lines 15–16). Years later, in *Biographia Literaria* (1817), he defined "sublime" as "boundless or endless allness" (1907, 2:309). The awkward phrase conveys the familiar idea that sub-

limity involves feelings of the infinite and eternal, which Addison had
said the ocean inspires.

"Hymn before Sunrise, in the Vale of Chamouni" (1802), Coleridge's
principal mountain poem, is another synthesis of his readings. He had
not visited the Alps; his hymn is an expanded translation of a German
poem, Friederika Brun's "Ode to Chamouny," but from this and other
works he knew what the sight of Mont Blanc *should* evoke. Its summit
and shape are pronounced "awful," still in the old sense of "awe-
inspiring." The qualities associated with the peak are the staples of
eighteenth-century mountain writing: it rises "silently," remains "calm,"
dates from "eternity," lives in an atmosphere of "pure serene," and has a
natural holiness that excites "adoration" (the answer to a series of "Who
made thee?" questions is "God").

Coleridge's deism is complexly metaphysical, however: while "still
present to the bodily sense," Mont Blanc itself "vanish[ed] from [his]
thought"; he "worshipped the Invisible alone" (1912, lines 14–16). Yet
all this time it was "blending with [his] Thought," so that his "dilating
Soul" passed into "the mighty vision" and "swelled vast to Heaven!"
(lines 19–23). Mont Blanc is imaged as a king (God's earthly vicar), as a
"cloud of incense," as an "ambassador from Earth to Heaven," and as
one of the "thousand voices" with which earth praises God (lines 80, 82,
85). The vividness of the hymn's rendering of the actual place was vali-
dated by John Tyndall (see chapter 15), a dedicated Victorian climber
and scientist who laid over for a day at Chamonix in order to view the
sunrise as described in the poem.

Coleridge wrote less about travel, physical nature, and Great aesthetics than did Wordsworth, but what he did produce went a long way, owing to his extensive influence on important Victorian intellectuals as
diverse as J.S. Mill, Thomas Arnold, Newman, and Carlyle.

"ROOTED IN BARRENNESS": LORD BYRON

In his first successful poem, *English Bards and Scotch Reviewers* (1809),
George Gordon, Lord Byron, attacked Sir Walter Scott's *The Lay of the
Last Minstrel* and *Marmion* (1808), though *Marmion*'s image of time passing as "we glide down to the sea / Of fathomless eternity" (Scott 1904,
canto iv), and its depiction of a winter storm in which a shepherd per-
ishes, are in Byron's mature vein. Scott's most Byronic poem came later,
in the year the two became friends: *Lord of the Isles* (1815) evokes the
wild Scottish coast and islands in ways redolent of Ossian and Burke. Af-

ter Bruce pronounces the beach on Skye "sublime in barrenness" (pt. 3, line 13), the narrator describes "stern" ravines and "naked" precipices. Later the "Queen of Wilderness" is enthroned among Caledonian lakes, cataracts, mountains and "deserts" where "Sublime but sad delight," loneliness and fear oppress you, and "savage grandeur wakes / An awful thrill" (pt. 4.1). Here the sublime is "chastened" by association with threats of danger, and some of its power comes from its darkness.

Byron himself plays a major role in Marjorie Nicolson's *Mountain Gloom and Mountain Glory,* which begins by quoting Childe Harold: "To me, high mountains are a feeling." Nicolson's Byron, the poet passionate for wilderness, developed alongside and to some extent out of the scandalous, tortured Byron of Mario Praz's *The Romantic Agony* (1933). The first two cantos of *Childe Harold's Pilgrimage* (1812), published before Byron's marital troubles began, show some interest in Great scenes. "Oh, there is sweetness in the mountain air, / And life, that bloated Ease can never hope to share" (Byron 1980, canto 1, lines 349–50) is no more than any weekend walker in the uplands might say, yet even here "stern Albania's hills" (second canto) are darkly sublime, their "gathering storms," wolves, eagles, and even "wilder men" evoking admiration and dread (2.370–85). And from the "dark barriers of that rugged clime" to Illyria, Harold "passed o'er many a mount sublime," including "bleak Pindus" (2.406–15).

Several sections foreshadow the later, antisocial Byron. Solitary rambles "Where things that own not man's dominion dwell" (e.g., a "trackless mountain") are actually "not solitude," since we "Converse with Nature's charms" there. It is living unattached "midst the crowd" that isolates us: "This is to be alone; this, this is solitude!" (2.219–34). The hermit on Mount Athos is "More blest" than such wretches (2.235). In "Chimera's alps" ("Nature's volcanic amphitheatre"), by a dark river at the supposed site of the mythical Hades, Byron/Harold feels at home: "Pluto! if this be hell I look upon, / Close sham'd Elysium's gates, my shade shall seek for none" (2.452–9). It is not these associations that make the place attractive, however; the appeal is underpopulation. There are no cities, and "here men are few" (2.462). Posing or not, Byron is moving towards the misanthropy found in his later work and increasingly in the Victorians.

Several aspects of the Great are treated in Byron's verse romances of the next few years. "The Corsair" (1814) opens with the protagonist's paean to the "dark blue sea," with which he identifies – "Our thoughts as boundless, and our souls as free" (Byron 1981, lines 1–2) – but then turns to tales of piratical life. "The Siege of Corinth" (1816) offers a more varied scenic palette: cold moonlight illuminates the mountain behind Corinth, where "Blue roll the waters, blue the sky," spangled with "spiritually bright" stars. Who ever saw them, the narrator asks, without wishing to "mix with their eternal ray?" (lines 199, 202, 206). This yearning for eternity is thematic. The night before the great battle, the protagonist ("Alp") keeps vigil under "the silent sky," looks over the Gulf of Lepanto to the "High and eternal" snows of Parnassos (lines 320–1) and contrasts them with human transience. Later the narrator describes how the sea "changeless rolls eternally" under the moon (lines 381–5). The assault of Alp's forces the next day is compared to an Alpine avalanche, though, for by this time Byron was under the spell of the Alps.

Byron's separation from Lady Byron and ostracism from London society in 1816 finally induced the expatriation that he had meditated since at least 1814, when he wrote to a friend, "Why should I remain or care? ... My life here is frittered away ... I am sadly sick of my present sluggishness, and I hate civilization" (quoted in Rutherford 1961, 38). After publishing "Corinth," he left England for good and went to Geneva. His letters, journals, and poems show that the effect of the Alps, the Shelleys (with whom he spent much of the summer), and reading Wordsworth was to make him more responsive to nature. Mont Blanc he at once pronounced "superior" to anything he had seen before (Byron 1976, 5:78). In June he and Shelley toured Lake Leman by boat, a copy of Rousseau's *Nouvelle Héloïse* in hand. Byron admired the "accuracy of his descriptions" and the beauty of this "Paradise of Wilderness" (82, 94).

In September Byron rode horseback through the Bernese Alps with Hobhouse and "repeopled [his] mind with Nature" (98–9). The Jungfrau's glaciers, seen through a storm, were "all in perfection"; the time when the Alps imaged Chaos had passed. He climbed a seven-thousand-foot peak that was "shining like truth," and a nearby glacier seemed "like a *frozen hurricane*" (100–2). Images of heaven, hell and paradise permeate his letters. Yet when he finally returned to "insipid civilization," he admitted that he had been unable to forget his "own wretched identity in the majesty and the power and the Glory" (103, 105).

Both self-absorption and the Alps are prominent in canto three of *Childe Harold* (1816). Harold is now less a character, more a persona; his preference for lonely wastes over the "agony and strife" of "the peopled desert" is recognizable as Byron's (1980, lines 690–1). As in the letters,

Lake Leman has "too much of man" (line 648) for comfort. Byron claims that this is not misanthropy – "To fly from, need not be to hate, mankind" – yet he "hate[d] civilization," feeling that it is "better ... to be alone, / And love Earth" (lines 653, 671–2). Byron/Harold identifies with wild nature in general ("Are not the mountains, waves, and skies, a part / Of me and of my soul, as I of them?"), but sees the "loftiest peaks," isolated, storm-smitten, far above man, as his personal metaphor (line 397). He pays magnificent tribute to the Alps, which have "throned Eternity in icy halls / Of cold sublimity" (stanza 62). "All which expands the spirit, yet appals, / Gather around these summits" (lines 596–7), as did tortured souls like Harold, Manfred, and Frankenstein.

Byron's combination of personal travelogue and metaphorical mountains is unique. The noblest of humanity are imaged as "the mountain-majesty of worth," and the speaker hopes that their names and deeds will endure "In the sun's face, like yonder Alpine snow, / Imperishably pure beyond all things below" (lines 642–3). To distinguish his lines from the old cliché "eternal snows," Byron added a footnote: "This is written in the eye of Mont Blanc (June 3d, 1816) which even at this distance dazzles mine. (July 20.) – I this day observed for some time the distinct reflection of Mont Blanc and Mont Argentière in the calm of the lake, which I was crossing in my boat." The traveller-poet, having been there, knows whereof he speaks; his poem, like the lake, reflects the reality of the Alps.

Except for a brief homage to the beauty of the stars as inspiring reverence (stanza 88), canto three is devoted to mountain worship. The Persians were right to make mountains their altars, "there to seek / The Spirit," for human temples are weak and foolish by comparison (lines 854–5). Byron describes a nocturnal storm in the Alps with a glee not matched until Tyndall: "Far along, / From peak to peak, the rattling crags among, / Leaps the live thunder!" (lines 863–5). The deistic "let me quit man's works, again to read / His Maker's spread around me" (stanza 109) uses mountains to symbolize the spirit's goal: "The clouds above me to the white Alps tend, / And I must pierce them, and survey whate'er / May be permitted, as my steps I bend / To their most great and growing region" (lines 1,017–20).

The appeal of Great phenomena for Byron was never *limited* to mountains, however. "Darkness" (1816) envisions the world's end after the sun cools, an event then being predicted by some astronomers. Both the temporal and spatial scales are sublimely vast, but it is a very grim sublime. Against a backdrop of stars that "wander darkling in the eternal space," the "icy earth" hurtles through darkness (Byron 1986, lines 2–4). In fear of "their desolation," humans go mad, burning forests and towns, killing and eating each other, but dying of famine. Finally "The world was void," a mere "chaos of hard clay" (lines 69, 72): Darkness rules. It is Pope's vision of *moral* Night at the end of *The Dunciad* translated into a physical apocalypse, and, in its science-based grimness, a preview of the mood of Hardy's generation. Byron seems almost pleased to contemplate the end of humanity, and is certainly excited by the scale of the catastrophe.

The dramatic poem *Manfred* (1817), though written in the Alps and the most thoroughly Alpine of all Byron's poems, employs other great desolations – deserts, oceans, the human spirit – as well; it is one of the first western literary works to make a thematic and pictorial icon of barrenness. Readers saw Manfred as Faustian, but Byron wrote to Murray (7 June 1820) that "it was the *Staubach* and the *Jungfrau*, and something else [presumably guilt over his affair with his half-sister Augusta], much more than *Faustus*, that made me write *Manfred*" (in Noyes 1956, 831). In act one, scene two, Manfred is alone on the cliffs of the Jungfrau, surrounded by mists and glaciers. A passing chamois-hunter prevents his attempted suicide with the admonition, "Stain not our pure vales with thy guilty blood" (in Noyes 1956, line 111). Identifying with Great landscapes but not with this von Haller-Rousseau-Wordsworth tradition of Alpine purity, Manfred says that his own "actions" have "made" his life "one desart, / Barren and cold, on which the wild waves break" (act 2, sc. 1, lines 55–6). Did he *make* this coastal desert, though, or was he born to it? Later he says that even in youth his "joy was in the Wilderness" (2.2.62), not in man.

Act two, scene three, set on the summit of the Jungfrau, also gathers sublime components: the "First Destiny" describes the effect of moonlight on "The glassy ocean of the mountain ice" where no mortal has trod, and on the "steep fantastic pinnacle, / The fretwork of some earthquake" (2.3.1–10). Byron once described poetry as "the lava of the imagination whose eruption prevents an earthquake." Back in Manfred's castle, his attraction to such landscapes becomes clearer as he declares his own barren affinities: "my nature was averse from life; / And yet not cruel; for I would not make, / But find a desolation" (3.1.125–7; cf. 2.1.55–6). His life has been like a fiery desert wind, sweeping over the "wild and arid waves" of "barren sands" (3.1.127–34), and in this persuasion he dies. The juxtapositions of ocean, desert, heavens, and mountains in *Manfred* demonstrate that the Great was a coherent aesthetic category for Byron; in retrospect, we can see its assimilation to, and by, his inner "desert places" as beginning the modern usage of the vast and barren by poets such as Eliot and Frost.

The fourth and final canto of *Childe Harold's Pilgrimage* (1818) reinforces several of these points. Byron notes that the Alpine fir grows on high, exposed ledges, seemingly "Rooted in barrenness," and insists "the mind may grow the same" (1980, lines 174, 180). He remains fascinated by mountains – ranking various ranges in terms of sublimity – but yearns for deserts and oceans, too. "Oh! that the Desert were my dwelling-place," exclaims Byron (forgetting Harold), that I could live with the elements and "one fair Spirit," but otherwise "forget the human race" (lines 1,585–6). Though he still claims that he "love[s] not Man the less, but Nature more" (line 1,598), the feeling for humanity seems academic compared to the emotional investment in the wilds. "There is a pleasure in the pathless woods, / There is a rapture on the lonely shore" (lines 1,594–5) leads into a hymn to the everlasting ocean (stanza 182) as a "sublime" mirror of God and "The image of Eternity" (lines 1,643–4).

The verse drama "Cain" (1821), a comparatively narrow but intense experience of the Great, exhibits an almost seventeenth-century feeling for the cosmic void. In act two, Lucifer flies Cain through the universe; earth becomes a "small blue circle" that dwindles to a point (Byron 1968, 2.1.29). Struck with the beauty of the "blue wilderness" and "intoxicated with eternity," Cain "aches to think" of space (2.1.102, 108–9). Lucifer tells him that earth is the "wreck" of earlier creations (2.1.153): Byron's preface says that he "partly adopted" Cuvier's thesis of the world having been destroyed several times before Adam and refers to evidence from strata and fossils. In 2.2 they reach Hades, whose "dim worlds" Cain pronounces silent, vast, and "full of twilight" (2.2.1, 12). In 1858, when John Tyndall was crossing the Strahleck glacier in fog, he suddenly realized why the scene seemed familiar. It was Byron's Hades, "interminable gloomy realms / Of swimming shadows and enormous shapes" (2.2.30–1): a valid transference, since Byron was projecting his own Alpine experiences onto space. The void also seems to Cain "the phantasm of an ocean" (2.2.186).

"Cain" does not end with a sense of interstellar space, however; the protagonist returns to earth and his old dilemmas as unhappy as ever, but now equipped with dark allusions to infinity and eternity. After murdering Abel and being branded, he gathers his family and heads

"Eastward from Eden," because " 'Tis the most desolate and suits my steps" (3.1.552–3). Again a correspondence between an inner and an outer barrenness is dramatized, and the suggestion that barren (will) seek barren had a powerful effect on the poet's admirers. There was much of Byron in his Cain: exiled, guilty, mated with his sister, uprooted in barrenness and seeking desolation.

THE HARMONIOUS WILDERNESS: PERCY BYSSHE SHELLEY

Byron's companion-in-exile and kindred spirit, Percy Shelley, was a devotee of mountains and of Great nature generally. He came to this devotion both through science (chemistry was his particular passion) and through his Neoplatonic interests; Shelley's nature-worship comprised ideology as well as physical adventure. Both astronomy and spiritual quest inform *Queen Mab* (1813), a dream-vision in which (eight years before "Cain") the poet sees the Fairy Queen fly "through the midst of an immense concave" wherein the earth is a speck among "Innumerable systems" and "countless spheres." He tells the "Spirit of Nature," "In this interminable wilderness / Of worlds, at whose immensity / Even soaring fancy staggers, / Here is thy fitting temple" (P.B. Shelley 1989, sec. 1, lines 265–8). This keen sense of a dwarfing void comes closer to the mood of Fontenelle's *Entretiens* than to comparable but solidly theistic passages in Pascal, Milton, and Addison.

In the second section, the poet tries to imagine infinity: "Countless and unending orbs / In mazy motion intermingled." Great space does not terrify him as it did Pascal's "Man without God"; Shelley embraces the void: "Above, below, around, / The circling systems formed / A wilderness of harmony" (2.77–9). From this distance, the ruined cities of the deserts are perceived as monuments to vanity (foreshadowing "Ozymandias"). Vastness is here neither a mere stage effect nor an indulgence of the imagination, but a way to achieve perspective by lifting the "soul above this sphere of earthliness" (4.17). The hopeful vision of the future is couched in the language of the Old Testament prophets: deserts shall bloom, polar wastes thaw, fertile isles arise from the sea. But the present "a pathless wilderness remains / Yet unsubdued by man's reclaiming hand" (9.144–5), an image that contrasts with the harmonious wilderness of space and the view of human history in earlier sections. As in *Prometheus Unbound*, "Thule" is now, "Tempe" only something to be invoked. Byron's "Cain" and Hardy's "In Vision I Roamed" are spiritual heirs of *Queen Mab*.

The theme of *The Assassins* (1814), a fragmentary prose romance, is the spirituality of solitudes. The Assassins (a sect of early Christians) flee from the Roman army to the mountains of Lebanon, "the solemnity and grandeur" of whose "desolate recesses possessed peculiar attractions" (P.B. Shelley 1965, 6:156). Yet the "happy valley" they settle in seems anything but "desolate"; despite ruins and wild beasts, it is lush and well watered. All around, "icy summits darted their white pinnacles into the clear blue sky," but the "chaotic [natural] confusion and harrowing sublimity" of these transported Alps just increase "the delights of [the valley's] secure and voluptuous tranquillity" (6:158–9). These "wild and beautiful solitudes," "hallowed ... to a deep and solemn mystery," are well suited to the "searching spirits" of the refugees, who learn to "identify" their god with "the delight that is bred among the solitary rocks" (6:160, 162). Shelley could have taken the description of Mount Lebanon from travel books or from Beckford's *Vathek* (see chapter 10), and, like Coleridge, may have conflated African with Asian material.

Although their morality is exalted and their conduct gentle, Assassins will not "temporise with vice," so those who do venture out into "the wilderness of civilised society" murder the vicious, earning the group its unsavoury reputation (6:164). Shelley breaks off soon thereafter, leaving major questions unanswered. If the "hallowed" qualities that attracted the Assassins belonged to the "desolate recesses" of the mountains, was settling in the verdant valley a moral error responsible for their decline? And if they were happy in their valley, why did they go out into society and commit murder? In any case, Shelley seems to have been seeking sublimity; given his early fondness for Gothic fiction, perhaps he hoped to create another *Vathek*.

Alastor; or, the Spirit of Solitude (1816) has value as an autobiographical metaphor, and as an interpretation of nature and time. Mary Shelley thought the poem's solemnity, "worship of the majesty of nature," and solitary broodings "more characteristic" of Percy than anything else he wrote (P.B. Shelley 1921, 31). His own preface calls it an allegory of youthful purity "led forth" by a strong, well-educated imagination "to the contemplation of the universe" (1989, 1:462). After confessing his own love of nature, the speaker tells the story of Alastor, who leaves home to wander alone, showing a penchant for volcanoes, snowfields, "bare pointed islets" in bitumen lakes, Mideastern wastes, "desert hills" in Africa, and icy pinnacles in Asia (lines 85–6, 115).

Alastor's erotic dream produces a keen sense of loss, imaged as void space: in the "cold white light of morning," he "Gaze[s] on the empty

scene as vacantly / As ocean's moon looks on the moon in heaven"
(lines 201–2), as earthly reflection does on higher reality. This is the English beginning, perhaps, of the phenomenon traced by Robert Adams
in *Nil: Episodes in the Literary Conquest of Void* (1966). Alastor pursues his
vision through more desolate landscapes until he finds an inland sea
and a small boat. Thinking to "meet lone Death on the drear ocean's
waste," he sails through sun and storm towards the "etherial cliffs" and
"icy summits" of the Caucasus, where Prometheus would be unbound
(lines 305, 352–3). Wind and currents take Alastor down a canyon to an
Edenic glade, where he abandons his boat and follows a brook, despite a
gradual change in his surroundings that resembles ageing: a section
that adumbrates twentieth-century canyon treks. When Alastor reaches
"black and barren pinnacles," the gorge opens to vistas of night sky over
"Islanded seas, blue mountains, mighty streams, / Dim tracts and vast,"
beyond the "naked and severe simplicity" of the foreground (lines 545,
554–60). Here he finds a peaceful death.

Shelley's vision includes a fascination with the kind of natural phenomena that eighteenth-century aestheticians had called the Great or
sublime, but with a twist. His emotional valences are rarely those of the
pioneer theorists, though there is some overlap with early field descriptions. References to infinity and eternity and the rest of the deist panoply are absent, as is the beauty/horror oxymoron that flourished from
Burnet to Byron. What Shelley gives us instead is the darker emotional
palette that appealed to Hardy: solitude amid empty, barren wastes, intimations of gloom and fear such as tinted the first European accounts of
the Arctic, the Alps, and the desert, even age and death. These themes
are not less compelling for being unpleasant, and they were, literally,
"attractive" to a significant number of major nineteenth-century writers.
Why they became so is a question that can be illuminated better by examining individual lives and works than by essaying general answers.

1816 – the year of the Swiss summer with Mary and Byron, but also of
suicides and other family troubles – was above all the year of the Alps for
Shelley. In mid-May, he described for T.L. Peacock the "white wilderness" of the Jura ridge, which they crossed en route to Geneva; it was
"awfully desolate" in the "wonderful su[blimity]" and "natural silence of
that uninhabited desert" (Shelley 1964, 1:475–6). During an excursion
with Byron to Chillon, Shelley was moved both by the "wilder magnificence" of the Savoy Alps and by Rousseau's *Nouvelle Héloïse* (481). His
excitement increased when he went to Chamonix, from which he wrote
to Byron, extolling the splendour of the valley of the Arve and the

"grandeur in the very shapes" of the "immense" mountains, especially Mont Blanc (494–5).

He wrote Peacock that the "vast ravine" of the "terrible Arve," the "deserts of snow" near Mont Blanc, and an avalanche gave him "a sentiment of extatic wonder, not unallied to madness": "I never knew I never imagined what mountains were before," he stammered. "Nature was the poet" (496–7). It was not a question of "mere magnitude," but of "majesty" and "awful grace" added to the mountains' "unutterable greatness" (497–8). Unable to close, he resumed the letter two days later in order to recount a visit to two glaciers whose great size and destructive power had provided a "vivid image of desolation," though he would "not pursue Buffon's sublime but gloomy theory" that the world would end this way (499). The next day he walked out on a glacier to examine its crevasses. The high snowfields around Mont Blanc seemed "horrible deserts," and the mountain itself alive, with glaciers as the "frozen blood" in its "stony veins" (500).

Although Shelley's note says that "Mont Blanc" (1817) was "composed under the immediate impression of the deep and powerful feelings excited by" its subject, those first impressions are shaped and intellectualized in both the A and B versions of the poem (1989, 534–7). Images from his letters reappear, often transmuted; "frozen blood" becomes the less-striking and original "frozen waves" (A, line 65) or "frozen floods" (B, line 64). What succeeds the stunned traveller is the Idealist, convinced that Mont Blanc has much to do with Mind and Power. Something beyond nature and us, but not called God, expresses itself in the visible and mental worlds. The Vale is an "awful scene, / Where Power in likeness of the Arve comes down / From the ice gulfs that guard his secret throne" (A, B, lines 15–17). This "Power dwells apart in its tranquillity, / Remote, serene, and inaccessible" (B, lines 96–7). In the final section, "The still and solemn power of many sights" abides; Mont Blanc is inhabited by "The secret Strength of things." And yet it is "the human mind's imaginings" that confer significance (B, lines 127–8, 139, 143).

Shelley has two principal ways of expressing the meaning of the scene. One is the image of the natural thinly covering the transcendental: the Arve "veils" power, the Alpine waterfall "some unsculptured image" (A, B, line 27), while in Mont Blanc the speaker sees "unfurled / The veil of life and death" (B, lines 53–4). Another approach is through the vocabulary of the Great, stripped of all theism. The "strange sleep" of the high regions "Wraps all in its own deep eternity," for though riven glaciers suggest earthquakes, "all seems eternal now" (B, lines 27, 29, 75). Beholding the ravine puts the speaker "in a trance sublime"; Mont Blanc "pierc[es] the infinite sky" (B, lines 35, 60). The idea that this is "the naked countenance of earth" (A, line 99; B, line 98), a common mountaineers' observation compatible with the image of a drawn veil, links the two modes. Shelley thus gives individual and *non-religious* expression to emotions that Addison and Burke associated with the Great. He would have many followers.

In the preface to *Laon and Cythna ... A Vision of the Nineteenth Century* (1818; revised as *The Revolt of Islam*), Shelley assists our inferences about how his travels through some of nature's great wilds might have contributed to his life and poetic development. First, they have been generally formative; familiarity with "mountains and lakes and the sea and the solitude of forests" is one component of his education. Second, these places (as we already know) have had specific influences on his work. "I have trodden the glaciers of the Alps and lived under the eye of Mont Blanc," he writes (1954, 317), and these memories are among the sources of *Laon and Cythna.*

The "traveller from an antique land" who told Shelley about Ozymandias may have been an historian, a travel writer, a friend, a conflation, or a fiction. What concerns us is how the famous sonnet (1818) sets its ancient moral, *vanitas vanitatum*, in the kind of Great landscape that was about to come into its own with travellers and intellectuals, at least. We can find examples of "Ozymandian" dismay in late-eighteenth-century art, for example in Piranesi (Thacker 1983, 203–4), but the shift from his vast palatial prisons to Shelley's "lone and level sands" is part of a trend generally apparent by the mid-nineteenth century. Shelley made the desert not an analogue of infinity, as Addison did, but an emblem of the futility of human effort and pride (the function of space in *Queen Mab*) simply by viewing the "colossal wreck" and boastful inscription of Ozymandias's statue in the context of the "boundless and bare" Egyptian wasteland. Behind the desolate landscape is a powerful sense of high antiquity and the wastes of time, a sense that grew with the geologists' findings about the earth's age. Shelley's ironic parable shaped and anticipated the perceptions of the next generation; David Roberts's famous series of prints of the Middle East (ca. 1840), for example, has the same free-floating melancholy over desert ruins as the sonnet.

In 1818 Shelley left England for good, travelled through Italy, and settled in Naples, where he wrote, "External nature" compensates for the "degradation of humanity" (quoted in Noyes 1956, 1,113). His exam-

ples included the Bay of Naples and Mount Vesuvius, which he and
Mary climbed with guides. It was a powerful experience for the one-time
experimenter with chemistry, who pronounced Vesuvius, "after the Glaciers, the most impressive exhibition of the energies of nature" he had
ever seen. Though lacking their "greatness" and "radiant beauty," it
possessed "all their character of tremendous and irresistible strength"
(cf. the "Power" of "Mont Blanc"). Hot lava crept onward "like the glacier"; cold lava presented an "image of the waves of the sea": both Great
phenomena. Amid the "horrible chaos" of the summit plain, "riven into
ghastly chasms," Shelley was in his element. Vesuvius was then "in a
slight state of eruption," emitting "volumes of smoke" or "enormous columns of impenetrable black bituminous vapour," and "fountains of liq-
uid fire"; "fiery stones" and "a black shower of ashes" fell "even on where
we sat." They stayed until dark, "surrounded by streams and cataracts of
the red and radiant fire," and "descended by torchlight" (in Noyes
1956, 1,114), Shelley living *Alastor.*

Prometheus Unbound (1820) sums up many themes in Shelley's career,
including his fascination with the Great. The preface says that the
"bright blue sky of Rome" was the poem's inspiration (P.B. Shelley 1965,
172). The maiden Asia, first seen in a "lovely Vale" and associated with
lush verdure, represents the redeemed nature of the millenium: the second Tempe at the end of the present age. Meanwhile, however, we live,
like Prometheus, in harsher conditions. The poem's first and principal
setting is "A Ravine of Icy Rocks in the Indian Caucasus" where
Prometheus is held and tortured until the overthrow of Jupiter. There is
no precedent in Aeschylus for this, nor for settings like "A Pinnacle of
Rock among Mountains" and "the Top of a snowy Mountain" (Nicolson
1963, 8). In this ravine, "crawling glaciers pierce [Prometheus] with the
spears / Of their moon-freezing crystals" (P.B. Shelley 1965, act 1, lines
31–2) and cold chains cut his flesh. It is a barren, painful setting –
again, there is no question of "liking" it there – but Prometheus suffers
on behalf of mankind, and Shelley handles the scene of his suffering
with the kind of respect usually given Calvary.

Shelley's interest in nature, as a traveller and as a reader, is visible
throughout the poem, though set now in a larger apocalyptic frame.
Earth refers to her "stony veins" (1.153), the phrase Shelley had applied
to Mont Blanc. She links her "earthquake-rifted mountains of bright
snow" (1.167) to the chaining of Prometheus; Burnet (whom Shelley
had read) connects mountains with original sin (Nicolson 1963, 375).
The "keen sky-cleaving mountains" of Asia's narrative, flinging the

radiance of dawn "From icy spires" (P.B. Shelley 1965, 2.3.28–9), are Shelley's Alps, while Demogorgon's cave, "Like a volcano's meteor-breathing chasm, / Whence the oracular vapour is hurled up" (2.3.2–4) is his Vesuvius, and since Demogorgon overthrows Jupiter, the image dramatizes Hutton's idea that volcanoes regenerate the earth (Matthews 1957, 227). Asia's claim that Prometheus "taught [mankind] the implicated orbits woven / Of the wide-wandering stars" (2.4.87–8) recalls the astronomical interests of *Queen Mab*, as does Earth's idea that the planets struggle fiercely "towards heaven's free wilderness" (4.399) against Jupiter the sun god's gravity.

The whole poem moves, and wants nature to move, from the hero's icy ravine to Asia's "lovely vale," itself once "desolate and frozen" (1.828). Yet at the end there is still room in Earth's mood of joyful redemption for "the caverns of my hollow mountains," "cloven fire-crags," "The oceans, and the deserts, and the abysses / Of the deep air's unmeasured wildernesses" (4.332–6). In Milton's time, some had held that the prelapsarian earth was smooth, but Shelley declines to complete the cycle this literally; the Alps will not be flattened at the millenium. The "plot" of *Prometheus Unbound* is that humanity is renewed through union with nature (Beach 1956, 213), and Shelley's vision of redeemed nature includes its great barren empty reaches, Hardy's Thule, as well as its verdant Tempes.

Hardy's underlinings in his pocket edition of Shelley were especially copious in *Prometheus Unbound*'s descriptions of nature, but he was also interested in a lesser-known poem of that year, "The Sensitive Plant" (Bartlett 1955, 16, 18, 23), whose plot moves in the opposite direction. It traces the plant (which somewhat resembles the poet) from its pure vernal "Paradise" through the "sweet season of summer tide," when it is tended by the Lady ("an Eve in this Eden"), to her death and then its own as the days shorten (Shelley 1965, lines 58, 173). If summer comes, it asks, can fall be far behind? The "blasts of the arctic zone" (line 271) mortify life, but the poem's true darkness is the way it subverts our belief in natural cycles:

> When winter had gone and spring came back
> The Sensitive Plant was a leafless wreck;
> But the mandrakes, and toadstools, and docks, and darnels,
> Rose like the dead from their ruined charnels.   (Lines 288–91)

Shelley's "wintriness" – a chilly, somewhat morbid barrenness – presages the next stage of evolution from Great to chastened sublime, and finds many echoes in nineteenth-century poetry.

The modernity of Shelley's vision of nature is underlined by Joyce's use of him in *Portrait of the Artist as a Young Man* (1916). While Stephen Dedalus is "drifting amid life like the barren shell of the moon," he recalls some lines of Shelley: "Art thou pale for weariness / Of climbing heaven and gazing on the earth, / Wandering companionless?" The fragment is oddly comforting: "Its alternation of sad human ineffectualness with vast inhuman cycles of activity chilled him, and he forgot his own human and ineffectual grieving" (Joyce 1976, 96). There is more hope, more spring, more balance in Shelley than the selective uses to which he has been put by later writers suggest, but their distortions of him tell us much about the country through which the next part of the road would be built. Shelley is said to have believed that nature was the "garment of the eternal" (in Noyes 1956, 964); the following generations would have more problems with that concept, more troubling questions about it, than did "the atheist Shelley."

"WILD SURMISE": JOHN KEATS

If Keats wrote less about the Great than did the other Romantics, it was owing to his short life, not to indifference. He often used skies and seas as metaphors of the transcendent, and responded enthusiastically to actual mountains in one brief encounter. His analogues of the excitement of "First Looking into Chapman's Homer" (1816) are an astronomer "When a new planet swims into his ken" and Cortez, "Silent, upon a peak," seeing the Pacific for the first time (Keats 1935, lines 10, 14). It is often noted that Balboa, not Cortez, "discovered" the Pacific, but Keats does not say that Cortez *discovered* it; his interest is quality of experience, not the history of exploration. Titian's painting of this moment may have brought Cortez to mind (Thorpe 1935, 45n.1): as in previous centuries, painters sometimes prepared poets and travellers to see and feel in a certain way.

The ocean is also used to calm. In "On the Sea" (1817), the "vex'd and tir'd" are invited to gaze upon "the wideness of the Sea" and hear its "eternal whisperings" as an antidote to the littleness of the world (Keats 1935, lines 9–10, 1); in "When I Have Fears" (1818), Keats combats his morbid self-concern by standing alone "on the shore / Of the wide world" and contemplating the Great until thoughts of self expire (lines 12–13).

In 1818 Keats (then 23, with less than three years to live) and Charles Brown toured the Lake District and the Highlands on foot, rising at five o'clock, carrying knapsacks, and walking up to 20 miles a day. They covered "642 miles in 42 days from Lancaster to Inverness via the Burns country, Loch Lomond ... Ben Nevis and Loch Ness ... Ben Nevis was quite a good effort [ascent] for the period. You can guess the weather from the lines Keats wrote about it: 'I will climb through the clouds and exist'" (Brown 1980, 83). Out of this trip came a journal, poems, and letters appreciative of mountains and lochs. "To Ailsa Rock" salutes the antiquity of a "craggy ocean-pyramid" off the west coast of Scotland that had been thrust up from the ocean floor by an earthquake's "mighty Power" (Keats 1935, lines 1, 5). Thus it represents "two dead eternities, / The last in air, the former in the deep! / First with the whales, last with the eagle-skies!" (lines 10–12). They also visited Fingal's Cave, whose basaltic composition Keats understood. "For solemnity and grandeur," he wrote to a friend (26 July 1818), the Cave "far surpasses the finest Cathedral" (265n.1; in the poem "Staffa" he calls it a "Cathedral of the Sea").

On 2 August they climbed Ben Nevis (at 4,406 feet, the highest peak in Great Britain) from sea level. Reaching the top after many hours, false summits, and snow-filled gullies, Keats admired the clouds "sailing about" like "large dome curtains" (573, letter, 3 August 1818). "Written Upon the Top of Ben Nevis" dwells on the "mists" there, and "in the world of thought." He found he had "an amazing partiality for mountains in the clouds" (564, Journal, 26 June 1818), and "although we did not see one vast wide extent of prospect all round we saw something perhaps finer – these cloudveils opening with a dissolving motion and showing us the mountainous region beneath as through a loophole" (574, 3 August 1818). What struck Keats as "the most new thing of all" was "the sudden leap of the eye from the extremity of what appears a plain [the flat top of Ben Nevis] into so vast a distance."

Keats had hoped that his journey would "identify finer scenes, load me with grander Mountains, and strengthen more my reach in Poetry" (570, letter, 18 July 1818). The "space" and "magnitude of mountains and waterfalls" he had imagined; what he was not prepared for was "the intellect, the countenance of such places," which "surpass every imagination" (565, Journal, 26 June 1818). "I shall learn poetry here," he predicted, "and shall henceforth write more than ever," hoping to add to "that mass of beauty which is harvested from these grand materials, by the finest spirits." His output in the next year or so – *Hyperion*, "The Eve of St Agnes," "La Belle Dame Sans Merci," all of the great odes – suggests that his exposure to Great natural forms did release some copious creative springs.

What is striking about Keats's contributions to the road is their general sunniness, compared to his contemporaries' work. Overall the Romantic legacy is fairly dark, especially in the second generation; Byron and Shelley deploy a "chastened" sublimity. Wordsworth and Coleridge are usually more positive, though "The Ancient Mariner" and the late Wordsworth, worrying about what tourists will do to the Lake District, exhibit a good deal of melancholy. Given Keats's delicate sensibilities and poor health (he had to curtail the walk on account of illness), we might reasonably expect to encounter more "mountain gloom" than we do. Instead of reflecting his doubts and problems, though, the Great was a source of strength and excitement that lifted him out of himself and the mundane. His recurrent images of lifting (Ailsa Rock, climbing Ben Nevis) are consonant with the original meaning of "sublime." Keats is thus a throwback to the ecstatic beginnings of English Romantic poetry – young Wordsworth in the Alps – or even in some respects to the eighteenth century.

Landscapes in Prose:
Fiction and Travel

While philosophers, scientists, and poets discussed the meaning of nature and our relationship to it, novelists and explorers responded imaginatively to the Great and earlier writings about it, or described "naïve" encounters with natural sublimity, unaffected by literature and philosophy. Whether continuing a tradition or operating independently, the fiction and travel writing of the Romantic period often had an impact on the tastes of later writers and explorers (Stafford 1976).

GOTHIC NOVELS

The kind of fiction that came to be called "Gothic" seems to have begun with Horace Walpole's *The Castle of Otranto* (1764), a flimsy pseudo-historical novel that resorts to supernatural events. Walpole's successors discovered that a backdrop of sublime, exotic scenery could enhance the effects they sought, and the considerable popularity of their work helped to promote interest in vast, wild, and barren landscapes, though they often had unpleasant associations in the books.

William Beckford was well constituted and situated to author exotic romances: a privileged life and a system of tutors allowed him to travel widely on the Continent and indulge his taste for Oriental literature before beginning to compose. He was even more ecstatic over the Alpine monastery of the Grande Chartreuse than Gray had been (Thacker 1983, 188). At the age of 22 he wrote *The History of Caliph Vathek* in French, publishing an English translation four years later. In *Vathek*, Beckford projected his enthusiasm for the Alps onto the Arabian Nights lands of which he loved to read (in translations provided by French orientalists early in the century), using barren landscapes to point a moral and adorn a tale. Vathek tries to heal his spiritual malaise in a mountain "paradise," a verdant summit plain with pure air (Beckford 1930, 203–4), but has to pursue a mysterious "Indian" across a plain and into a chasm in the mountains. Frequent verbal landscapes provide stage sets for Vathek's guilt and impiety. At first these are spectacular and exhilarating: the night storm among deep mountain gorges and the "perpendicular crags" among which Vathek navigates are backdrops from the Gothic melodramas that were beginning to thrill playgoers (226, 229).

But there is also a grim "plain of black sand," and the longer Vathek persists, the farther he is led into "dreary mountains," "barren wilds" and "deserts" (230–1). Byron and Shelley were fond of Gothic fiction, and their landscapes resemble Beckford's. The nocturnal apparition of lights on a mountain and the staged "afterlife" at a foggy tarn beneath bare cliffs are particularly striking. Vathek's final journey is across another plain towards the "dark summits of the mountains of Istakar" (266). The description of the palace of Eblis and its "Hell" was greatly admired: far down the stairs and through a dark portal, Vathek finds a roofed area so spacious that it seems "an immeasurable plain," upon which a multitude of damned souls, hands on fiery hearts, rush or wander, "as if alone on a desert" (270–1). Here, deep within the earth's subterranean recesses that fascinated Burnet and Coleridge, lie the treasures of "pre-Adamite sultans." (The theory of earlier creations that Byron took from Cuvier was a much older idea, revived by the speculations of eighteenth-century naturalists about the earth's antiquity.) The only sound is "the sullen roar of a cataract" (273), a sound that, for others, was often part of "mountain glory."

Painting and travel continued to interact. Beckford, like other touring gentlemen, brought along an artist, John Robert Cozens, when he went through the Tyrol in 1782 to Naples, where they stayed with Sir William Hamilton, returning via the Grande Chartreuse and Geneva. Cozens had earlier visited Europe with Richard Payne Knight, who was interested in the sublime. If Cozens's European landscapes are more spacious and brooding than those of his father Alexander (who taught Beckford), both of the Cozenses were students of sublime effects (Sloan 1986, 69–74). Oppé finds an anticipation of Turner in "Lago Maggiore," something "poignant" and Hardyesque about "Ruins in the Campagna" (whose subject is a "vast Desart"), and sublimity in "The Ravine" (1954, 145, 148, 151). J.R. Cozens, who probably read Bourrit (Sloan 1986, 118), influenced other artists, including Henry Fuseli and

John Constable, as well as writers and travellers. J.M.W. Turner, who admired Cozens's "Hannibal in His March over the Alps" (a subject that Gray wished Salvator Rosa had undertaken) in 1776, produced paintings of Wales, Scotland, and Switzerland that convey a "chastened sublime" (Adams 1981). Other influential Alpine painters included the Genevan J.A. Linck and the Lorys. Gabriel Lory, Jr, called the Simplon Pass "*grand et terrible*," comparing its effect on the imagination to Pergolesi's *Stabat Mater* and Haydn's *Creation* (Engel 1930, 140).

Of the early Gothic novelists, only Beckford shows any interest in deserts; mountains were the preferred source of sublimity. Ann Ward Radcliffe loved precipitous scenery, as her book on the Lake District (*A Journey ... to the Lakes*, 1795) shows, and this feeling pervades her novels, *Romance of the Forest* (1791) and *The Mysteries of Udolpho* (1794). Late in *Romance*, the heroine is escorted into Savoy. She first glimpses the "distant Alps, whose majestic heads ... filled her mind with sublime emotions," from the plain; coming nearer, she is "lost in admiration of the astonishing and tremendous scenery" (Radcliffe 1904, 277, 284). As she tires, the "gloomy grandeur ... awed her into terror," yet she is still drawn to the Alps (285). In the glacial valley of Montanvert, she feels as if her party "were walking over the ruins of the world, and were the only persons who had survived the wreck": possibly another echo of Burnet. La Luc's deist response is to lift his eyes to the "great Author" of these works in "silent adoration" (313). Other areas of the Great appear briefly: a storm engenders "dreadful sublimity," astronomy is called the most sublime study, leading us through awe to God, and the sea's "grandeur and immensity" produce sublimity and terror (314, 344–5).

Radcliffe's books are a mixture of what she had felt and what she believed one ought to feel. Her ideas of wild nature came from Shakespeare, books on travel and taste, and the paintings of Salvator Rosa, as well as from her own travels in England, Holland, and Germany. *Romance* portrays the Alps (where Radcliffe had never been) inaccurately (Engel 1930, 116–17), and *Udolpho*, well known to Romantic poets, also moves in realms of imagination. It opens with a studied contrast between pastoral Gascony and the "awful" Pyrenees that reflects the heroine's soul (Radcliffe 1963, 119). Emily is pleased by bucolic nature, but (like her creator) "loved more the wild wood-walks, that skirted the mountain; and still more the mountain's stupendous recesses, where the silence and grandeur of solitude impressed a sacred awe upon her heart, and lifted her thoughts to the GOD OF HEAVEN AND EARTH" (126). Wildness, silence, grandeur, solitude, awe, reverence: Radcliffe provided posterity with a veritable anthology of eighteenth-century responses to Great nature.

The chief limitation of *Udolpho* (which incurred Jane Austen's satire) is this tendency to present inherited clichés rather than original formulations. When Radcliffe describes a "romantic" glen in "barren" mountains, it not only *sounds* like a Salvator Rosa painting: it was, she tells us, "such a scene as *Salvator* might have chosen" (158). As Emily and her companions rode up into the Maritime Alps, "immense glaciers exhibited their frozen horrors, and eternal snow whitened the summits of the mountains. They often paused to contemplate these stupendous scenes" (176). Words such as "stupendous" and "sublime" are proffered as valid descriptive coin, along with terms like "vista" and "perspective" from the picturesque tradition popularized by William Gilpin in the 1770s. Radcliffe also preserves traditional distinctions and degrees in scenery: as the road descends, "features of beauty" begin to mingle with those of sublimity. And the Apennines, though "wild and romantic," have "far less of the sublime" than have the Alps; Emily knows better than to feel "awe" *there* (177, 191).

The Udolpho castle is a study in the architectural *sublime noir*. Emily is prepared by the "horrors" of the Apennines at twilight to feel "melancholy awe" at the sight of the castle, whose "gothic greatness" makes it a "gloomy and sublime object": "Silent, lonely," "more awful in obscurity" than in daytime, a desolation within "the desolation around them" (192–3). Inside Udolpho, they leave the sublime mode for that of mystery and horror. Sublimity requires spaciousness: it cannot live in dungeons and corridors. Radcliffe knew exactly what she was doing – her *Journey to the Lakes* shows her as a student of scenery who could classify each "prospect" according to a system – but her writing, with its bald deployment of sublime effects, is somewhat formulaic. We may not mind being emotionally manipulated if it is done skilfully, but we do not like to see the author working at it.

THE GREAT VOID: SÉNANCOUR

Another influential, though very different, Alpine novel, Étienne Pivert de Sénancour's *Oberman* (1804), connects eighteenth-century fiction of sensibility (Rousseau) with some of the darker existential literature of the nineteenth. Oberman, an extremely sensitive, depressed, and vague young man, has turned away from business and the world as uncongenial: "Je trouve partout le vide" ('I find emptiness everywhere'), he says, 'I feel surrounded by nothingness' ("le néant"; Sénancour 1984, 26). At

21 he has never known enjoyment and merely endures life. Oberman retreats to the Alps, seeking a refuge and drawn to the 'stern beauties of wild places' ("sévères beautés des sites naturels"; 30). Yet he cannot escape himself: reclining by a moonlit lake amidst grand nature, he realizes that sensibility such as his is both the 'charm and torment of our empty ["vaines"] years' (42). He decides to winter in the Rhone valley, which has 'the austerity of deserts,' partly *because of* the 'profound boredom' he feels there (53–4).

In September Oberman climbs well up the Dent du Midi, dismissing his guide after the first pitch lest anything 'mercenary adulterate his alpine freedom or a lowlander weaken the austerity of a wild place' (59). Having read de Saussure, Bourrit, and others, he recognizes some of the major peaks. In the pure air and isolation of his perch, he finds his thoughts more active, his consciousness less burdensome, than down below and concludes that society, not he, is in the wrong. Business calls him away to the cities and detains him for years, but he never forgets the mountains. Staying mostly in Lyon, where the Alps are visible on the horizon, Oberman feels miserable and considers suicide. His letters carry on a running philosophical debate with an invisible friend about life, happiness, religious doubt, nature, and so on. He comes to feel that 'there is no more happiness' ("il n'y a plus de bonheur"), at least for him; his is a 'settled despondency' ("habitude triste"), a 'temperamental antipathy to all that can be desired' ("humeur tranquille contre tout ce qu'on pourrait désirer"; 265, 285).

Still drawn to 'the simplicity of the mountains' (322), Oberman eventually, in the book's eighth year, builds a wooden 'hermitage' ("chartreuse") in the lower Alps. There, with only 'the dark pine, bare rock and infinite sky' above him, he seeks a separate peace, asserting the superiority of 'the life of the wretched Norwegian amidst his icy rocks to that of the petit bourgeois of the towns' (337, 345). But soon he realizes that all this too is futile; Self still cannot be placated, escaped, or changed: "je reste le même. Au mileu de ce que j'ai désiré, tout me manque" ('I remain the same. Surrounded by what I wanted, I still lack everything'; 353). Even in summer, a 'sterile wintriness' remains inside him (354). Once he thought that the Alps contained 'isolated traces' of the land of heart's desire (354–5); now he just feels 'extinguished' ("éteint"), a walking shadow (422). A friend comes to stay with him, but he sidesteps a possible romance with Fontalbe's sister. He is not made for love: he wants to write. *Oberman* ends with a fragment on a nearly fatal attempt to cross an Alpine pass alone on a snowy night.

In his hero, his tone, and his themes, Sénancour gets a running start on the nineteenth century. Before the Byronic hero, he created a protagonist more than halfway from the eighteenth-century sentimentalist (Goethe's Werther) to the Sartrean anti-hero in whom a "nausea" with life can well up at any time; Oberman heads the list of Robert Adams's venturers into the void in *Nil* (1966). But what makes the novel relevant here is Sénancour's use of the Great. That the Alps are unable to bring Oberman contentment is important; that this new kind of hero, with his constitutional *angst* and "ache of modernism," is persistently drawn to the Alps, whether or not they help, is even more so. There is some connection – no vaguer than the novel's other implications – between an inner void or "wintriness" and the barren landscapes of the Great. Sénancour's intuition was often ratified during his century: by French poets such as Théophile Gautier; by Matthew Arnold, saluting Sénancour and sometimes wearing the mask of Oberman; and by Hardy, declaring that the "chastened sublimity" of the Great suited the mood of the "more thinking" souls of his time.

MARY SHELLEY

Virtually the only Gothic novel whose popularity continues to grow is *Frankenstein* (1818), by Mary Shelley, whose mother, Mary Wollstonecraft, may have bequeathed her a penchant for scenic grandeur. In the summer of 1795 Wollstonecraft visited the Scandinavian coast, and – despite her attack on Burke's conception of sublimity (de Bruyn 1996, 206) – revealed a taste for beauty and sublimity, with a mind used to distinguishing between them. Generally, mountains are sublime or grand; meadows are "often beautiful; but seldom ... grand"; the coast's "ruder" nature seemed "the bones of the world" awaiting "beauty. Still it was sublime" (Wollstonecraft 1976, 112, 42). When the road emerges from pine groves, cliffs become "suddenly bare and sublime." The sea can exhibit both qualities; "little islands ... render the terrific ocean beautiful" (47, 73). She knew that "quick perception of the beautiful and sublime" can produce "misery" or "rapture," yet an all-night carriage-ride "sublimat[ed her] imagination" and lifted her soul "to its author" (58, 51). Susceptible to natural religion, then, Wollstonecraft took ecstatic pleasure in letting her soul diffuse into sky, mountain, and sea. Back on the German flatlands, she felt nostalgic for the peace and sublimity of the Swedish coast, complaining that "trade drags me back" (192).

Like Byron's *Manfred* and Percy Shelley's "Mont Blanc," *Frankenstein* emerged from the summer Mary Shelley spent with them in the Alps. Victor Frankenstein was born amid "the sublime shapes of the mountains" of "majestic and wondrous" Switzerland (Mary Shelley 1980, 36), but at a German university he fell into the occult studies that produced his famous monster and ruined his life. The first meeting of creator and creation after the latter's flight from his first murder takes place in the Alps, where Frankenstein has gone to seek consolation in "the magnificence, the eternity" of the "savage and enduring scenes" around Chamonix. Initially the power of the landscape lifts Frankenstein's mind to Omnipotence: the "mighty Alps" seem home to "another race of beings." Before Mont Blanc, in the "glorious presence-chamber of imperial Nature," he is both "elevated" and "tranquillised" (94–6). These reactions also occur in Mary Shelley's own Alpine journal.

But when Frankenstein (like most visitors) ascends the Montanvert valley, "a scene terrifically desolate," and walks out on its glacier (a "wonderful and stupendous scene"), his monster rushes up to confront him. No more than Byron, Manfred, or Oberman can Frankenstein escape himself, or his karma, by withdrawing to the glories of the Alps. The Great provides no innoculation against the troubles he is carrying, but does bring them out in the open, providing an *éclaircissement.* As in earlier Gothic novels, the outer desolation corresponds to an inner one. The monster demands that Frankenstein create a mate for him. Horrified but initially compliant, the scientist travels to a remote Orkney island, "hardly more than a rock," storm-beaten, barren, and poor. In this "desolate and appalling landscape" he starts to work, but eventually refuses to continue. Threatened with revenge, foreseeing catastrophe, Frankenstein says, "I desired that I might pass my life on that barren rock" (163, 164, 169). This wish (which is not carried out) expresses an Oberman-like yearning for isolation that a number of nineteenth-century intellectuals echoed.

In the framework to *Frankenstein*'s narrative, Robert Walton, an explorer, is sailing into the Arctic Ocean when he rescues the scientist (who is pursuing his creature northwards) from an ice floe. Frankenstein, seeing that he and Walton are two of a kind, ambitious intellectuals careless of society (Goldberg 1959, 33), and that his tale may be believed "in these wild and mysterious regions," tells it in order to be "useful" (Mary Shelley 1980, 30). After advising Walton to "seek happiness in tranquillity, and avoid ambition" (217), he dies. The monster then appears, orates over the corpse, and departs to immolate himself at the North Pole. Walton turns back.

This remarkably negative use of Great material supports the view that the novel is a critique of Romantic egoism and excess (Griffin 1979, 62–3). The Alps, Orkneys, and polar wastes are introduced not to expand the mind and spirit in Addisonian fashion, but as images of inner desolation wrought by crime, sin, and guilt. One could infer from Frankenstein's first and second days in the Alps that the Great is better seen at a distance, where it can inspire; to approach it is to court trouble. Like Dorothy Wordsworth, more interested in the humanity of the Alps and Highlands than in their landscapes, Mary Shelley makes kindness, humility, love, and piety her touchstones; mountains and glaciers are just scenery behind the actors. Frankenstein, "the Modern Prometheus," is not a hero in the sense of the ancient figure of myth or Percy Shelley's Prometheus; he is an overreacher, guilty of impiety and hubris.

As with Milton's Satan, however, Frankenstein and his settings are not necessarily felt as the author intended; the *frisson* of the glaciers and ice floes tends to linger, and may acquire an independent value. This was the case not only with *Frankenstein* but with other Gothic novels, which also did not praise or recommend their sublime scenery. The desert wastes of *Vathek* objectify the Caliph's damnation; the savage mountains in *The Mysteries of Udolpho* are ominous portents of Emily's trial by terror. In Mary Shelley's *The Last Man* (1826), a few survivors of "the last throes of time-worn nature" find brief consolation in the "Sublime grandeur" of the Alps, which is "in harmony with [their] desolation"; their misery takes its "colouring from the vast ruin," and this "solemn harmony of event and situation regulated [their] feelings" (1826, 9, 250). Soon, though, they decide that "vast and sublime" nature is "too destructive," and descend to the Italian plains to begin anew (257). Again the issue is not whether travellers or writers enjoy their immersion in the Great: it exists as a troubling power with transcendental overtones, vaguely fascinating to readers. No one is *bored* by the sublime, which made it valuable to novelists.

EXPLORATIONS: THE AMERICAS

Travel and exploration, which were crucial to the accumulation of knowledge about Great nature and hence to the formation of its aesthetics, played a larger role each century as the means of travel became more efficient instruments of the will. The adventurous, curious, or ambitious men who probed the planet's less-known regions at the turn of the nineteenth century could go farther and see more than their predecessors. Overland explorers opened vast areas of the New World to

European knowledge: Alexander Mackenzie reached both the western Arctic and Pacific coasts of Canada; Humboldt examined large areas of South America; Lewis and Clark explored the American Northwest; Simon Fraser traced his river through British Columbia; Pike, Long, and James marched to the Colorado Rockies. In the Alps, there were first ascents and a new generation of climbers. Navigators pushed deeper into the Arctic and Antarctic, Europeans into the Sahara. When we ask how these pioneers perceived the Great, however, we rarely find a clear answer. They were primarily men of action, not writers: though they were usually obliged to report to their backers, making texts was not their specialty, and aesthetic feeling was a luxury they could seldom indulge.

When Alexander Mackenzie left Alberta's Peace River and headed west in 1793, however, he seemed more appreciative of natural scenery than on his journey to the Arctic Ocean in 1789. But what he appreciated at first were pastoral, almost European beauties, not sublimities. Gently rising riverbank terraces, rich with trees and game, are termed "the most beautiful scenery I had ever beheld," a "magnificent theatre of nature" (Mackenzie 1911, 2:32). Other Mackenzian "beauties" (a word not used in the 1789 journal) are a broad reach of river, cliffs above colourful banks, verdant hills, a well-watered valley, and game plains near a river. The Rocky Mountains did not move him – their snowy summits were "a very agreeable object" because they appeared sooner than expected (45) – but Canada's Coast Range elicited the familiar Alpine vocabulary. From a pass still snowcovered in July, the next mountain looked "stupendous," and deep valleys added to the mountains' "awful elevation." On the return trip, Mackenzie pronounced the "rude and wild magnificence" of the Coast Range "astonishing and awful" (240–1, 317), still in the old sense of "filling with awe."

Alexander von Humboldt left a multivolume record of his rambles and research in South America, *Personal Narrative of Travels to the Equinoctial Regions of America during the Years 1799–1804* (1852). Translated into English in 1818–19 and widely disseminated in several languages, it reached most geologists and many general readers. Humboldt climbed the Teyde volcano on Teneriffe in the Canary Islands; later he wrote pages on its slope, mass, and geology, citing authorities (such as von Buch and Werner) and making extensive comparisons to other volcanoes in Europe and South America: a paradigm of his method. He insisted that scientists had to travel and compare, "viewing Nature in the universality of her relations" and "the globe as a great whole," in order to fathom geology's "regular laws" (Humboldt 1852, 1:104–5). In South

America, Humboldt climbed other volcanoes – enjoying their "grand scenes" (434) – studied atmospheric phenomena, and speculated on connections between widely spaced earthquakes and volcanoes.

Very much the *scientific* observer, Humboldt made few aesthetic remarks in this early work, showing more interest in geography and geology than in beauty or sublimity. One chapter compares and contrasts the features of various deserts, steppes, and savannahs around the world, likening them to oceans, but almost the only feeling expressed is that the South American steppe is "awful, as well as sad and gloomy," in its uniformity (2:85). There are few instances of the Great, to which Humboldt seems virtually oblivious here, yet his later books, discussed in the next chapter, do express emotional reactions to vast landscapes, and he was instrumental in raising the "land-consciousness" or broadening the horizons of many others, including Lyell and Darwin.

The report of Meriwether Lewis and William Clark on their expedition (1804–06) offers special problems. As presidential agents, they had to give a formal accounting, but what they provided were rough journals, as can be seen from the full texts (published in 1904 and 1986) or Bernard deVoto's selections (1953). Nicholas Biddle and Paul Allen prepared the journals for the "unabridged" edition of 1814, which was what most nineteenth-century readers saw. In this version, first-hand reactions are filtered, paraphrased, and supplemented; an awkward mix of "we" and "they" viewpoints makes it difficult to ascertain whose views are involved. Besides, Lewis and Clark had been given a specific pragmatic goal: to find new lands for settlement. River valleys were their highways, camps, and shooting grounds. A great barren to them was just a negative result; "this district affords many advantages to settlers" was the refrain they wanted to sing (Lewis and Clark 1814, 2:292). And they were hungry, tired, or sick as often as most explorers. But even allowing for all this, Lewis and Clark show much less non-utilitarian interest in the land than, for example, Major Powell floating the Colorado on another government expedition in the 1870s.

There are some aesthetic remarks in the 1814 text as the party traverses the often paradisean prairies, with their nearly "unbounded views" (Addison): the "infinite forms" of the aurora borealis (a dependable trigger) are "beautiful," the Great Falls of the Missouri River a "sublime spectacle," a "stupendous object which since the creation had been lavishing its magnificence upon the desert, unknown to civilization" (1:125, 260). But this is the voice of an editor in Philadelphia; Lewis's journal is more personal and less portentous here. He considers the falls "the grandest sight I ever beheld" and "majestically grand scenery," adding that he is "disgusted" with his "imperfect description" (1953, 137–8). Similarly, Lewis calls the striking cliffs that he named "the gates of the Rocky Mountains" the "most remarkable" he has seen (160); the editors inject the words "sublime" and "tremendous," reminiscent of Alpine travellers (1814, 1:310). Yet the distinction between the "wild irregular sublimity" of the Great Falls and the "elegance" of a lesser fall over a smooth ledge (263), which sounds suspiciously literary, *is* in Lewis's journal, where the lower fall is *"pleasingly beautifull"* and the higher "sublimely grand" (1986, 4:290).

The editors often term scenery "romantic," but Clark also used the word. At the mouth of the Columbia River, he found that the vista of ocean and cliffs had "a most romantic appearance," providing "the grandest and most pleasing prospects which my eyes ever surveyed" (6:182); the view from "Pompey's Pillar" on the Yellowstone River was of "high romantic clifts" (1904, 5:293). The term seems to jar with the scale and rawness of the American landmass at a time when, in England, it connoted Gilpin's picturesque or the new poetry; in Germany, Goethe or the Middle Ages. "Romantic" is a chameleon word, applied, often vaguely, to disparate artists, styles, phenomena, and periods in different lands: music and painting, and France, were not yet "romantic." It would have different meanings, and its vogue come later, in America. Europeans had been trying to describe their reactions to Great landscape for several centuries before Lewis and Clark; North Americans had to decide which of the old designations were appropriate for them, and which just excess baggage.

During the return march in 1806, Lewis, seeing many sites for the second time, was more appreciative of and analytical about the scenery. At the Great Falls, for example, he judged that with less water they "abated much of their grandure [*sic*]", yet were still "sublimely grand" (1953, 426; cf. 1814, 2:343). That is, though less grand than before, they still fell within the range deemed "sublime." He also observed that "the wide and level plains ... have somewhat the appearance of an ocean" (1953, 427): one of many independent verifications of Addison's premise that the psychological effect of a wide plain resembled that of the sea within the "Great" category of natural phenomena.

The Letters and Journals of Simon Fraser, 1806–08 are hurried fragments that offer as little aesthetic commentary as Lewis's and Clark's. Fraser's daunting assignment – to lead a party through the mountains of British Columbia via an unknown river canyon to the sea and report to his employers on the route's commercial utility – left little room for emotional or spiritual reactions. In the Fraser Canyon, though, surrounded by "precipices and mountains, that seemed at times to have no end," he gives vent to what amounts by his standards to an outburst: "I scarcely ever saw anything so dreary, and seldom so dangerous in any country; and at present while I am writing this, whatever way I turn, mountains upon mountains, whose summits are covered with eternal snows, close the gloomy scene" (Fraser 1960, 76–7). One could hardly imagine a better field description of "mountain gloom," in the period when the shift to "mountain glory" is supposed to be well underway (Nicolson 1959). But Fraser did not have Addison's "unbounded views": he was deep in a canyon, weighed down by responsibilities and uncertainties.

In his "Second Journal," Fraser interpolates a portion of his assistant's report on the same general area. Mr Stuart also found the landforms deeply impressive, but his reactions were more like an Alpine tourist's. A great cliff "resembling an immense pile [edifice] of natural architecture," but transcending human conceptions, "created a pleasing and awful sensation," leading him to "consider the superiority of Gods [*sic*] works over those formed by the hands of man." Where Fraser is gloomy, Stuart is momentarily deistic. "But to describe what I have often felt in these wild and romantic regions," he adds quickly, would far surpass his abilities; such a description would be a task "worthy of the greatest philosophers" (Fraser 1960, 154). For Stuart, the relationship between Great nature and the human spirit was a high mystery requiring the application of our best minds; further he could not go.

In the United States, two expeditions, one led by Zebulon M. Pike and the other by Stephen Long, probed Colorado's Rocky Mountains. The natural scientist Edwin James accompanied Long (1819–20) and left an interesting *Account of an Expedition from Pittsburgh to the Rocky Mountains* (1823). James analyzed rock formations, fossils, flora, and fauna, compared them to their counterparts in Europe and South America, and cited authorities such as Buffon, Werner, and Humboldt. While watching for valuable minerals that might be exploited, James also practised historical and speculative geology, noting the "reliquiae of the animals of a former world" in the sandstone outworks of the Rockies (1823, 2:1). His attempt to imagine the "remote" period when the "primeval ocean lashed the base" of the Rockies, depositing rocks and fossils, and the "catastrophe" that thrust up the great formations (2) makes him sound like a Neptunist and catastrophist; he takes no cognizance of the uniformitarian geology being developed by Hutton and Smith.

Like Lewis and Clark, James was looking for fertile lands favourable to settlement, but his report was discouraging; Long's expedition spent more time on the high plains, away from rivers and creeks, with their woods and grass. A minor key is established early, when artificial mounds on the prairie near St Louis evoke a Shelleyan outburst on the "insignificance and the want of permanence in every thing human." Standing on "these mouldering piles," reminiscent of the Egyptian pyramids, James has "an impression of sadness," and "cannot but compare their aspect of decay, with the freshness of the wide field of nature ...: their insignificance, with the majestic and imperishable features of the landscape" (1:66). Yet James has few good words for the prairies; the sadness of the mounds colours his passage of the Great Plains. At first the "woodless plains" are simply "not so good" for settlement and hard on travellers, but soon they become "barren, almost naked," signalling an approach to the "great Sandy Desert" (116–17, 136, 138). Wintering at Council Bluff, James noted the general aridity. "Forests attract rain," while "vast plains, and deserts" dissipate clouds (405).

James's reactions to the landscape in his second season were almost entirely negative. While "forests and grassy plains" in a river valley could be "extremely pleasing to the eye," and one's first reaction to the sweep of high prairie was "surprise and pleasure," the "uniformity" of the arid plains soon became "tedious" (417–19). Mirages and a lack of clues to size and distance rendered them deceptive, too. And "every step ... west brought us upon less fertile soil," until the plains of the upper Platte presented an "aspect of hopeless and irreclaimable sterility" (433, 459). Oppressed by deprivation and travail, James did not feel the vastness as Great, instead finding the "Monotony" of "vast unbroken plains" almost as tiresome as "the dreary solitude of the ocean" (460). "Dreary" rivals "barren" as the most characteristic adjective of James's account of the western plains, which are also described as "cheerless," "inhospitable," and "disgusting." They reminded him of what he had read about African and Asian deserts.

The only times James uses the words "beauty," "grandeur," or "romantic" are in connection with the Rocky Mountains. There he had a prepared category of feeling and an associated vocabulary, both of which he lacked in the "desert." He even calls the abrupt hills ("breaks") of the upper Platte and Missouri Rivers a miniature "transcript of Alpine scenery"; they can be understood best by analogy. Twice he does find the plains a pleasant contrast to what he has just gone through. After a few days in the "ruins" of Colorado's badlands, the formerly "monotonous" prairie seems "cheerful," and the "interminable … grassy desert" comes as a relief from several tough marches, but in both cases the reaction passes quickly as the essential enmity of the prairies reappears (2:19, 77). Any "smile" on the "stern features of Nature" is only "momentary" in this country (82). We do not expect travellers to appreciate the desert in 1820, yet within a few decades, explorers as hard pressed as James would find equally barren landscapes a source of aesthetic pleasure and spiritual uplift.

EXCELSIOR: THE ALPS

The exploration of Europe's mountains, hampered by the French Revolution and the Napoleonic Wars, never ceased altogether. Joseph Michaud climbed part way up Mont Blanc in 1791 and produced *Voyage littéraire au Mont Blanc* (1797), a sensitive impression sometimes quoted in modern mountaineering books. De Saussure, Ramond, and Bourrit published further "*voyages*" to various peaks and ranges. E.F. de Lantier created a popular tale, *Les Voyageurs en Suisse* (1803), by mining their works, and Rousseau's, and adding a plot (Engel 1930, 129–30). F.A.R. de Chateaubriand's "Voyage au Mont-Blanc" (1806), a casual, ill-tempered attack on mountains probably meant to counter Rousseau, grants them 'purity of line,' but counsels tourists to keep their distance: up close, the Alps offer only sensory deception, narrow views, and inconvenience (1948, 202–3). Familiar themes of the Great (such as purity) permeate Chateaubriand's grumblings, though. In 1811 there was a mountaineering achievement on a par with the "conquest" of Mont Blanc, but the first ascent of the remote Jungfrau lacked the dramatic build-up that de Saussure's prize had helped generate.

After 1814 the number of visitors increased, Byron and the Shelleys being in the first wave. The summer that they arrived (1816), Frances Winckley, Lady Shelley, made a tour inspired by Rousseau and Coxe. One of the few women to show an interest in the Great, she reacted much as the poets and some other men did. The "wildness," "grandeur," and "majesty" of the route to Salève and Servoz impressed her (Lady Shelley 1912, 1:232, 240). A first glimpse of Mont Blanc at sunset was "sublime indeed," its reappearance from behind clouds a "moment of ecstasy" (240, 243). This might be mistaken for gushing did Lady Shelley not scramble so enthusiastically to rough places in bad weather and react similarly. She rode up to Montanvert in the rain to see the Mer de Glace in its "fine desolation"; there she "felt the presence of God, and realised that state of chaos from which this lovely world has been formed." Walking on "that frozen sea," seeing crevasses and the "savage barrenness" of the rocks edging the glacier through a snowstorm, "was a sublime experience." She "never before felt so near Eternity," "never enjoyed anything more" (244–5), and speculated that a larger party and better weather would have lessened her enjoyment.

Reflecting this increased interest, the *Annals of Philosophy* published Col Mark Beaufoy's account of his 1787 climb of Mont Blanc in its February 1817 issue. The first Englishman to make the ascent, he was only a few days behind de Saussure. Beaufoy recalled his altitude sickness, "a sort of apathy which scarcely admitted the sense of joy" even on top, and a "confused impression of immensity," succeeded by a realization that the atmospheric clarity was tricking him into thinking that other mountains were closer than they actually were (1817, 101–2). Beaufoy represents his motives as chiefly scientific, though he does theorize that humans have a "natural" desire to reach the highest point of "remarkably elevated land" (97). He published other articles on mountains, and on the possibility of reaching the North Pole from Spitsbergen.

A party including Dorothy and William Wordsworth traversed the Alps in the summer of 1820. Dorothy's journal demonstrates a general interest in people and scenery, which she analyzes carefully. A vantage point between the Jura and the Alps affords her "grand" and "beautiful" views, arousing "joyful enthusiasm" (D. Wordsworth 1941, 2:96). Some passes, a deep gorge, and the Mer de Glace are also "grand" (190, 196, 285). The Jungfrau is "magnificent," and like some other mountains and passes leaves her "awe-struck" (101, 110, 184). "Sublime" is often conventionally applied to mountains, clefts, and river gorges, yet with thoughtful nuances. Mountains above a lake are "sublime in their steadiness," the Vale of Leventina is "sublime with simplicity," and Lake Chiavenna exhibits "melancholy sublimity," while in the higher Alps the sublime mingles with the fantastic (145, 198, 245, 104, 285). There is no systematic interest in the Great; other phenomena are as apt to claim her attention, and she passes up many opportunities for mountain rhapsodies.

The Chamonix region, famous and accessible, continued to attract most of the tourists and climbers, who for a while led charmed lives among half-understood perils. In August 1820, however, a few weeks before the Wordsworths passed by, three climbers died in an avalanche on Mont Blanc. This "first great Alpine tragedy" (Engel 1971, 62), the harbinger of a gloomier view of the Alps, led to the formation of the

Compagnie des Guides de Chamonix (1821) and the establishment of a safer climbing route. A panorama of the Swiss Alps exhibited in London (1825) drew good crowds, and in the next few years there was a spate of English books on the region, notably by Markham Sherwill, John Auldjo, William Hawes, and William Brockedon. People from many lands and walks of life visited the Alps during this period, one of the most important for nineteenth-century intellectual life being the geologist Charles Lyell (1818).

Victor Hugo, a pioneer of French Romanticism, is a fair representative of the reactions of literary travellers in the period. Some of his attitudes are familiar. In "Fragment d'un voyage aux Alpes," he portrays the passage from Sallanches to Chamonix as a difficult movement from the nature we know to a new and strangely moving one: 'solitudes of ice, granite and mists' (Hugo 1910, 3). Napoleon's crossing of the Alps may suggest that 'man is king of physical nature,' but all human works dwindle to insignificance in the shadow of this 'new revelation ["manifestation"] of God' (4, 8). The Alps have some darker tones, though; a stop at the 'lugubrious and desolate' Black Torrent reminds Hugo that the Mont Blanc range was once (and for some remained) "les Montagnes Maudits": the Cursed Mountains (6). For him, such legends complete "l'horrible beauté de ce site sauvage" (7). The oxymoron 'horrible beauty,' which, as we have seen, also occurs in some earlier writers, indicates an aesthetic system under stress, unable to describe in integrated terms what it sees.

But Hugo soon remembers that "sublime" is the word for such 'works of God' (8). No wonder the spirituality of the valley of Chamonix was recognized as early as the eleventh century and a priory built there, he says: as you climb, you look down to the hell of the river gorge and up to the heaven of the summits. It is a "paysage de merveilles" ('land of marvels'), full of optical illusions and hints of myth, dominated by the 'grandeur' and 'eternal presence' of Mont Blanc. The whole Chamonix region is both a 'divine laboratory' and a 'mysterious sanctuary' (13–14). The fragment breaks off there.

The growing stream of visitors had meaner consequences. An obscure pamphlet containing three accounts of the Grotto of Balme (Geneva, 1827) is a good weathervane. The first, de Saussure's, includes a guide's tale of 'fairy works,' an interview with an old treasure hunter, and his own careful examination of the grotto. The second, Bourrit's, emphasizing picturesque scenery and difficulty of access, mentions tossing a grenade down a natural well inside. The third, by J.F. Albanis Beaumont, says that all difficulties have now been removed: a road has been built, you can go far in on horseback, there are stairs and a café inside, and guides throw grenades down the well to regale visitors. Tourism had reached the Alps.

EXPLORATIONS II: THE POLAR REGIONS

In 1817 William Scoresby wrote Joseph Banks that changes in the Arctic's climate made exploration there more feasible than before. A new chapter in the annals of Thule opened as the Admiralty directed the Royal Navy to join the search for a Northwest Passage, a dream as old as Frobisher. In 1818 ships commanded by John Ross and William Parry reached Melville Bay and the entrance to Smith Sound, turning back from what would prove to be the actual passage. One of Parry's officers published his *Journal of a Voyage of Discovery to the Arctic Regions* (n.d.) anonymously. Evidently new to Arctic waters, he was more impressionable or less reticent than a captain could be. His first large iceberg, "an immense rock of white marble," presented "a magnificent spectacle," but Greenland looked "barren and dreary"; he was "appalled by the dismal aspect of snowy mountains, and black cliffs" (*Journal* 1964, 12, 17). On a clear evening at sea, "superbly grand" icebergs, "whiter than Parian marble" and infinitely various in form, crowned the "magnificence of this sublime prospect" (24). A windstorm, with moonlight and a "beautiful" aurora, made an "awful scene" (87): the crucial emotion of the Great arising from a vista Addison could scarcely have imagined.

Parry returned in 1819, crossed Lancaster Sound, and spent the winter in a harbour on Melville Island – the first deliberate Arctic wintering. His *Journal of a Voyage for the Discovery of a North-West Passage* (1821) affords glimpses of the experience, though Parry, writing the official account for the Admiralty, is more restrained than the chronicler of the 1818 voyage; he is above all the careful mariner, the responsible leader, the public servant. Completely surrounded by Great nature, he rarely makes an aesthetic remark, other than to note the beauty of a sunset or an aurora. Parry does consider the swell dashing loose ice against bergs, sending spray up a hundred feet, a "sublime and terrific" spectacle, and the starlit vista of an ice-covered gulf from a hill on Melville Island "grand and picturesque" (1968, 11, 198). Like Frederic Marten, he stresses the region's optical illusions: icebergs inverted by refraction, parhelia, or mock suns, and the deceptive sizes and distances of objects on the snowy plains of the island.

Parry occasionally touches on the darker side of the winter. Theatrical entertainments and a newspaper helped in "diverting the mind from the gloomy prospect which would sometimes obtrude itself on the stoutest heart," despite all the official cheeriness and a regular schedule (107). Parry does not pretend that he enjoyed the "dull and tedious monotony" of the landscape, to which his ships and men gave the only animation; it induced "melancholy" contemplations, and "the silence which reigned around [them]" was "the death-like stillness of the most dreary isolation" (125). On Melville Island, any piece of bare ground was an oasis in a desert (185). Yet the *Journal*'s evocation of vast spaces is said to have helped create the mystique that the Arctic possessed for the Victorians (Loomis 1977, 101). So great was the public interest that Parry reprinted the entire run of the ship's *North Georgia Gazette and Winter Chronicle* as an appendix. Only here, in some anonymous poems, is there a hint of religious response to the "frozen grandeur" and the aurora as wonders of God (54, 77, 83), and sombre engravings pique the imagination.

While Parry sought the Passage from the east, John Franklin – whose final expedition would be the great tragedy of the Victorians' Arctic endeavours – retraced Hearne's route down the Coppermine River and canoed east along the coast, looking for Parry and the Passage's western end. Franklin's *Narrative of a Journey to the Shores of the Polar Sea* (1823) reveals him as conventional in aesthetics and religion, with some interest in science. A devout man who held Divine Service every Sunday when not actually moving, Franklin had no deist leanings; he never talks of infinity or eternity in connection with the Great Barrens through which he moved. His tastes ran to the beauty of trees in autumn, mossy rocks, gentle hills and dales, the moon in winter, the aurora. He did admire Hill Gates, "a romantic defile" whose "grand and picturesque rapid" runs through "wild and majestic scenery" (Franklin 1969, 38–9). Generally, waterfalls and views from elevations are "romantic," "magnificent" or "majestic"; riverbank scenery is "beautiful."

Franklin never mentions the sublime, recognizes no kind of beauty except the European. On the tundra, the "uniformity of scenery" soon palled; the level Barrens in winter – a Canadian desert – were "cheerless" and "tedious" (37, 116, 120). The engravings, from sketches by expedition members, show vast spaces, but virtually the only feelings about them in the text (apart from those noted above) are negative: near the coast, Franklin feels "beset by naked mountains" on "every side"; the shoreline is "sterile and inhospitable"; Cape Barrow is "dreery" (341,

365, 367). Subsequent Arctic literature would prove that these are not the only possible reactions to such scenes. Franklin's responses reflect both his temperament and the conditions he encountered. Once they left the coast and headed south across the Barrens, there was no room for aesthetics, or anything but suffering and faith, as hunger and an early winter took seven lives.

At about the same time, a series of efforts finally surpassed the achievements of Captain Cook at the opposite end of the planet. William Smith, captain of an English trading brig and an Arctic veteran, sighted the South Shetland Islands (considered part of Antarctica) in 1819, and the mainland in 1820; Cook never claimed that he had seen the Antarctic mainland. The Russian circumnavigator Bellingshausen and an American sealer under Nathaniel Palmer also sighted the mainland that year. An American mariner, John Davis, likely made the first landing on Antarctica in 1821 (Cameron 1974; Jones 1982; Debenham 1959).

Of all this pioneering activity there are only the slightest written records, but in 1823 James Weddell reached 74°15' south latitude, a new record, and came back to write *A Voyage towards the South Pole.* As "Antarctic literature," it is preceded only by the material from Cook's voyages. Weddell had no more penchant for natural description than had Cook, and did not think he had found a continent, only a sea less icy than believed stretching towards the pole. Yet he does offer a few glimpses of the place and his feelings about it. The Antarctic, like the Arctic, was deceptive: his lookouts' "landfalls" proved "not land, but black ice[bergs]" (Weddell 1825, 32). He did not speculate on what material made them black, or its origin. Weddell sums up the region in a striking and economical (though inaccurate) phrase: a "cold, earthless land, with immense ice islands" (42). But these first tentative probes went largely undescribed; the great age of Antarctic exploration was still generations away.

The Arctic, so much nearer Europe, remained a stronger lure; Parry returned in 1821, 1824, and 1827. Even in his second and third *Journals ... for the Discovery of a North-West Passage,* he can still admire the grandeur of an aurora or a lone iceberg, the crystalline purity of the water and the diamondlike play of midwinter starlight. But often he sounds burnt out. Since accounts of Arctic winterings have lost their novelty, he decides to report only the differences from his previous experiences. After all, one Arctic winter is much like another: a "monotonous whiteness," an "inanimate stillness," and "the dreary solitude of this wintry desert" (Parry 1889, 27). Anyone coming from "more animated landscapes" must adjust to "prospects of utter barrenness and desolation" (1969, 6). Only after their summer release does he revive, calling the limestone formations of the Leopold Isles "picturesque and beautiful" (1889, 53), and the falls on the Barrow River "magnificent" and "sublime" (1969, 265). Such moments, however, are few: Parry's books are mostly scientific observation, flat description, or gloom; there is none of the spiritual or mystical response to the polar wastes found later in Nansen and Byrd.

While Parry (who established a new "farthest north" of 82°45′ in 1827) and others probed westward, ships of several nations followed the leads of Bering and Cook into the western Arctic. Franklin went down the Mackenzie River and followed the Canadian coast west (1825–27), while Captain Beechey (formerly Parry's lieutenant) sailed through Bering Strait and tried to link up with him (the parties never met). To Beechey, the northwest coast of Alaska seemed "desolate" and "dreary." The midnight sun and the aurora were beautiful, but the only northern landscape that impressed him was the "majestic array" and "magnificence" of Kamchatka's snow-covered mountains (Beechey 1831, 1:325–6). His reaction underscores the point made by Hearne, Mackenzie, Franklin, and others that the vertical Great inspired admiration long before its horizontal counterpart did.

Though the literary remains of these pioneers are meagre, they were necessary precursors to travel literature. More Great landscapes were known to and through them every year; aesthetic reactions would follow in the fullness of time, with more safety and leisure. Meanwhile, the hungry imagination could always pick up a Gothic novel: Frankenstein's monster had last been seen heading north.

THE SLEEPING DESERT

The period was not without major excursions into true desert: the first Europeans, Maj. Gordon Laing and René Caillé, reached the Saharan town of Timbuktu (1826, 1828), and John Lewis Burckhardt, a Swiss, travelled widely in Middle Eastern deserts. But there is little commentary on – let alone admiration for – the desert itself in their written remains. Burckhardt roved the Mideast from Syria to Nubia (1809–17) and wrote a number of learned volumes, published posthumously (1819–30). Yet *Travels in Nubia, Travels in Syria and the Holy Land, Travels in Arabia*, and *Notes on the Bedouins and Wahabis* record hardly any reaction to the desert *per se*. Natural description is minimal; Burckhardt was interested in anthropology and geography, not geology, and certainly not barren landscape.

When we add him to the explorers of North and South America, it begins to look as if Addison's "vast desarts" (in the modern sense) would *not* become part of the Great for travellers, despite occasional gleams of appreciation. It would have seemed ludicrous to predict, in 1830, that within a few decades some writers would be going to the desert for its own sake, and writing books about their feelings for it.

PART IV

Science and Sensibility: The Nineteenth Century

One of the few tenable generalizations about "the nineteenth-century European mind" is that it was unsettled. Established beliefs, old ways of feeling and writing, received definitions, and comfortable limitations were disturbed by the generations of scientists, scholars, and travellers born around and after 1800. And what began in science continued in literature. Hardy's Egdon Heath and predictions about Thule are the logical outcome of revisionist European thought about humanity, the earth, and the cosmos: ideas that began to take their modern shape about the time of his birth in 1840. His sensitivity to landscape and tendency to invest it with supra-material values are often prefigured in the previous half century.

The most compact example of the cultural impact of science in this period is *Essays and Reviews* (1859), which persuaded many intellectuals that some traditional attitudes were no longer viable. One of the essays, C.W. Goodwin's "The Mosaic Cosmogony," reviews the history of conflicts between science and religion from Copernicus to his own day, when the "growth of geology" has again brought up "the old question": six days and 6,000 years, or great antiquity? (Goodwin 1860, 210). Goodwin argues that the Bible provides good "religious instruction" but contains "erroneous views of nature," and that those who try to harmonize it with science do a disservice to both sides (211). Professedly no enemy to religion, he outlines the latest astronomical and geological theories of the universe, and the Higher Criticism of the Bible, noting the two creation accounts in Genesis, for example. Goodwin argues that the formation of the earth has been "the slowly continued work of ages," and that the "Mosaic" narrative, "at variance

with the facts," "has misled the world for centuries" (216, 231, 247).
Why would *God* do that? Genesis must therefore be "not an authentic
utterance of Divine knowledge, but a human utterance" (253), one
view among many.

"Go and See":
Lyell, Geology, and Belief

We have already seen that a greater awareness of and attention to physical nature formed part of the reverence that developed around the Great and contributed to it. The growth of a geological consciousness was also intimately involved in the "Thulean" sensibility that Hardy postulated (Dean 1981). It is as if early devotees did not quite understand what they were saying, or worshipping, but saw only a dark vision; as the nineteenth century comprehended the terrestrial Great better, the forms of homage changed without losing their intensity.

"NOT REST, BUT CHANGE": LYELL

The centre of Victorian England's keen sense of the earth was Charles Lyell's *Principles of Geology* (1830–34); an unbroken line of speculation, controversy, and assimilation connects that work to Darwin and Hardy. Lyell's evolutionary geology, whose major premise Darwin applied to anthropology, changed the course of science and European culture by showing that *creation was continuing*, linking past to present. The criticisms of Lyell one finds in scientific texts – that he distorted Werner or slighted Hutton, undervalued Continental work or merely synthesized others' ideas – are irrelevant to the question of his impact on his contemporaries' imaginations. Besides, many great scientific minds *have* been "synthetic." Wholly new ideas are rare; most breakthroughs involve putting together old data in new ways, seeing a significance that one's predecessors have missed. "We collect the data, and Lyell teaches us to comprehend the meaning of them," said A.C. Ramsay, a bit unfairly (Geikie 1897, 282). If Lyell's books were compendia, his lectures and papers, based on extensive field research, were original. And it is a gift, not a disgrace, to be able to interest a larger public in what has previously been a scientific preserve.

Lyell was well equipped to enunciate the *geo-logos* or discourse of the earth for his time. His father, an amateur of botany, Rousseau and de Saussure, had travelled in France, the Swiss Alps, the Lake District, and Ireland, where he examined rock formations; Lyell could always correspond with him about natural science. At the age of ten the future Sir Charles was breaking open "large chalk flints" to see which contained "crystals of chalcedony" and which "sparkling quartz" (in K. Lyell 1881, 1:9). Poets who observed nature closely – Milton, Thomson, Gray, Scott – were his favourites. Before he went to Oxford, Lyell had read Bakewell's *Introduction to Geology* (1813) and probably Playfair's *Illustrations of the Huttonian Theory* (1802); at Oxford he heard Buckland's exciting lectures on fossil geology. Though taught by a follower of William Smith, Buckland was then a disciple of the "diluvialist" Abraham Werner (Bailey 1962, 32–3, 37), so Lyell faced the great geological dilemma of the age early: is the present earth the product of ancient catastrophes, or of forces that are still observable?

Lyell "geologized" with Buckland and other members of the Geological Society, carrying an outline and map of British geology, observing the landforms, and trying to imagine what they had been and would be. On a ride through Scotland, Lyell discovered a taste for wild scenery. Loch Awe afforded "the finest mountain view [he] had ever seen"; a mass of unhewn red granite placed on a hill by ironworkers was the most moving monument to Lord Nelson he had encountered (in K. Lyell 1881, 1:49). Visiting the cave of Staffa, he called its height "magnificent," the columns "superb," and the roof "grand," then sailed to Iona, where "the finest aurora-borealis I ever witnessed was lighting up the east" (50). Lyell, then, was at once susceptible to Great scenery. Back at Oxford, he wrote a poem about Staffa, and expressed his impatience with studies that demanded "fanciful and laborious analysations & divisions of immaterial things which exist but in the mind" (in Wilson 1972, 56).

The Lyells spent the summer of 1818 touring Europe. Charles's letters are energetic, conveying interest in almost everything, but especially natural science. In Paris he visited Cuvier's lecture rooms and inspected his fossils. Between Paris and Geneva he noted flora, geological sites, and differences in climate from comparable altitudes in Scotland. At Chamonix, Charles climbed the Aiguille de Brevent (with a guide who said his father had accompanied de Saussure), walked up the

Mer de Glace to Le Jardin, and ascended Le Couvercle for a better view of Mont Blanc. He found the scene "sublime and terrible – bare rock, ice, snow, and sky, with a dead silence round" (in K. Lyell 1881, 1:73). The family proceeded to Lausanne – Charles cataloguing rocks, flowers, insects, and sites associated with Rousseau – and along the Rhine.

From Zurich, Lyell walked up the Righi, where he was amazed to see "a whole world at once" (81). He spent the night in the hut on top in order to view the Alps at sunrise. The scenery was "magnificent," "romantic," "grand," but geology remained a leitmotif. He considered the power of a cascade to move slate and alter its bed, wondered at (but could not then account for) "some extraordinary large bare planks of granite" below the glacier of the Rhone, and sought out the naturalist Wittenbach in Berne. Three times as much space is devoted to the causes and effects of the recent flood on the Dranse as to thoughts of Rousseau and Byron at Lake Geneva and the grandeur of the Dent du Midi. Before turning south to Italy, Lyell climbed to the Great St Bernard monastery, where the "wild and savage" scenery impressed him (97).

The family crossed the Simplon Pass and descended into Italy through "new, and very magnificent" scenery (98). Traversing the Apennines, Charles distinguished between the appearance of a sandstone landscape ("waste," "peculiar and extraordinary") and one whose foundation is limestone (109). Thereafter his journal is mainly devoted to art and history: "Geology was forgotten with all solid rocks hidden" under soil, vegetation, and buildings (Bailey 1962, 46). But the first experience of the Alps had been as crucial for Lyell as for eighteenth-century travellers, and his geological interests would necessarily bring him back to "exposures" – the bare landscapes characteristic of the Great – again and again.

After acquiring his BA, Lyell became a fellow of the Geological Society and toured the Lake District, where he was sometimes appreciative, sometimes unimpressed; there are no conditioned reflexes or required exclamations in his travel diaries and letters. In 1820 he began to study law, but an inflammation of his weak eyes that threatened to become permanent sent him on a second Continental tour instead. At Ravenna he observed the alluvial action of rivers, and evidence that the sea had retired five miles since Roman times. On his return, Lyell sought out a Sussex geologist, Gideon Mantell, a few years his senior. Their friendship soon ripened into a scientific cooperation that lasted until Mantell's death. After the publication of *Principles of Geology*, Lyell called

Mantell "one of the first of my twelve apostles" (in K. Lyell 1881, 1:329). The gift of a copy of Mantell's *Wonders of Geology* (1838) was one of the formative events of Thomas Hardy's young manhood.

Called to the bar in 1822, Lyell spent less time on law than on geology. He wrote a paper on limestone formations, became secretary of the Geological Society, and examined the Isle of Wight with Buckland. Surprised at "the hurried manner in which Buckland galloped over the ground," missing key elements, Lyell startled his old professor by showing him evidence supporting his theory of the structure of Sussex (120–1). That summer, carrying letters of introduction from Buckland and other scientists to Humboldt, Cuvier, and Brongniart, he went to Paris, improved his French, attended free lectures, and met the great geologists. Cuvier's "reflections on the former state of this planet" seemed "grand," though Humboldt was more impressive in person. Baron de Ferussac got him thinking about large questions such as climate change and cast doubt on Buckland's diluvialism, which Lyell still supported (137, 146, 139).

As secretary, Lyell edited the Geological Society's *Transactions*, and his geological work with Prévost (a student of Cuvier) and Buckland provided material for several papers. He also began to write for the *Quarterly Review*, which paid him (a serious concern at the time). In 1826 he reviewed the history of geology in the *Quarterly*, noting that Buckland's theory of ancient catastrophes forming the earth is "an assumption ... calculated to repress the ardour of enquiry" (in Wilson 1972, 157). Lyell ardently believed that creation was still taking place, and could be seen. He read Lamarck in 1827; though dubious about his view of species, he quite agreed with him on the earth's antiquity and vowed to convert readers of the *Quarterly* to that view. His first effort, a review of George Scrope's *The Geology ... of Central France* (1827), endorsed Scrope's main conclusions and extended them in space and time. Lyell also began to plan an elementary geology text, the germ of his *Principles*, jotting in his notebooks some broad guidelines, such as that "Nature is not repose, but war. It is not rest, but change" (180).

The year 1828 was devoted to planning the *Principles*, and to nine months of geologizing in Europe that carried over into 1829. First Lyell and the Murchisons went to France to see the volcanic Auvergne region of which Scrope had written so interestingly, and the equally volcanic Ardèche, "a country to make everyone desire to know something" (207). What they found – rivers cutting valleys through lava, and some previously unknown volcanoes – disproved Buckland's diluvian theories and enabled them to go beyond Scrope in some ways. Lyell's upcoming book was much on his mind. He wrote his father that his "great object" would be "*proving* the positive identity of the causes now operating with those of former times" (in K. Lyell 1881, 1:199): the doctrine of "uniformitarianism." The current perspectives on space and time were too narrow, he thought; to understand the present earth, we must view it *historically.*

Lyell headed for Sicily, inspecting examples of elevation and subsidence, and climbed Vesuvius and Etna, whose grandeur particularly impressed him; Etna could "give just and grand conceptions of Time to all in Europe," he thought (in Wilson 1972, 253). The evidence around Etna of great age and the huge volume of material that a volcano could produce confirmed his view that creation was a natural, continuing process. By January 1829 Lyell was exuding a sense of mission. "We must preach up travelling," he wrote Murchison, "as the first, second, and third requisites for a modern geologist." His book would try to "establish the *principle of reasoning*" in geology, using his fieldwork as support, the central idea being "that *no causes whatever*" have within observable time "ever acted, but those *now acting*," or even acted "with different degrees of energy from that which they now exert" (in K. Lyell 1881, 1:233–4).

Lyell stayed *au courant* with European work in his field, not only reading but seeking out naturalists wherever he went. In Italy he bought books that modified his account of the history of geology in the *Principles*. In Geneva he exchanged notes with Louis Albert Necker, de Saussure's grandson; in Paris he heard Prévost lecture, visited Cuvier, and arranged to support Deshayes, who was classifying fossil shells. He decided to visit Germany to find out if geologists there were ahead of the French or Italians, and began to learn German while writing the *Principles*. After his marriage, he spent most summers geologizing on the Continent (where his wife had relatives) and renewing his contacts with geologists there. And whenever he saw merit in their work he said so; in 1840 he quickly adopted Louis Agassiz's theory of glaciation.

LYELL'S *PRINCIPLES* AND *ELEMENTS*

What Lyell wanted to do in the *Principles*, he said, was to reach a wide audience and debate Bible-oriented critics of empirical science. He hoped to "make [his] sketch of the progress of Geology popular," despite his "anti-Mosaical conclusions" (in Wilson 1972, 267). When Scrope exhorted him, "you *have a science to create*," Lyell replied that it could not be done without "making war" on many of the public's "prepossessions" (271). He described himself as "a staunch advocate for absolute uniformity in the order of Nature," trying "to write for general readers" (in K. Lyell 1881, 1:260). His letter of 14 June 1830 to Scrope (who was going to review the *Principles*) says that it is time to "free the science from Moses" (i.e., Genesis), yet, believing that he is ahead of his time and wishing not to offend, he has said only half of what he could have (268–71). Scrope's review pleased Lyell, who thought it would help "sink the diluvialists" and other "theological sophists" (310).

Principles of Geology had a complex publishing history. The popularity of its three successive volumes created a demand for reissues even before the entire work had been published. Volume one appeared in 1830; volume two and a second edition of volume one in 1832; volume three and a second edition of volume two in 1833; a four-volume "third edition" in 1834, and so on. Lyell revised each edition to keep up with scientific progress and his own evolving ideas. The twelfth edition came out the year he died, 1875, and this only begins to hint at the extent of his influence. What began as the fourth volume of the *Principles* was soon separated and enlarged into an independent introduction to the subject of earth's *ancient* changes; published as *Elements of Geology* (1838), it reached a sixth revised edition in 1865. A *Student's Elements of Geology* appeared in 1871.

In the original *Principles* (the contents of later editions differ somewhat), the first chapters of volume one give a critical history of cosmogony and geology from ancient times to the 1820s. Lyell deals sharply with early theorists such as Burnet and Whiston; even Hutton, the father of uniformitarian theory, has his weaknesses scrutinized. Chapters five to nine define geology as a discipline and argue that "present causes" are adequate to explain the surface of the earth. A broad exposition of the aqueous and igneous agents of terrestrial change occupies the rest of the book. Volume two shows the effects of geography and climate on the distribution of species (later editions add more geology). In volume three Lyell answers critics of volume one by clarifying his philosophical position, but most of the book is a classification of strata from the Tertiary period. It also discusses unconformities, fossil geology, and volcanic action in a way that impressed many readers as clear and powerful.

Uniformitarianism, or "gradualism," was immediately recognized as Lyell's crucial doctrine, and he developed it throughout his life. Unlike diluvialists and catastrophists, who tried to reconcile geological evidence with the Creation and Flood narratives in Genesis, Lyell, following Hutton, argued that, given sufficient time, the natural processes presently operating could have created the earth as it is. Geologists have discovered, he wrote, that the earth's features "were not all produced in the beginning of things, in the state in which we now behold them, nor in an instant of time," but "gradually" (C. Lyell 1838, 2). Whereas the biblical creation (which conservatives dated to 4004 BC) was a *fait* long since *accompli,* the doctrine of "the adequacy of present causes" made creation both contemporary and inconceivably antique. "Give me but a *few* thousand centuries," Lyell begged Adam Sedgwick (in K. Lyell 1881, 1:459); for gradualism to work, "the earth must be ancient beyond human powers of comprehension" (in Albritton 1986, 140). The imaginative impact of a timespan approaching eternity has always been a part of Great aesthetics.

Lyell agreed with Hutton that geology found "no vestige of a beginning" of creation and no sign of an end. If to religious orthodoxy such views subverted the authority of the Bible and the Church, to Lyell the vastness of time and space posited by modern astronomers and geologists seemed rather to encourage a concept of creation more august than that of the literal readers of Genesis: a point that deists had been making for over a century. He told his audience at King's College in 1832 that a "system which does not find traces of a beginning ... is the most sublime" in its idea of divine power (in K. Lyell 1881, 1:382). In the *Elements,* he invites readers to consider the earth's crust, "vast and of magnificent extent in relation to man," yet only one four-hundredth of the radius of the earth, itself a mere speck in the heavens (C. Lyell 1838, 3): a trope reminiscent of Edward Young. Lyell's descriptions of the "extraordinary confusion" of those "stupendous monuments of mechanical violence," the Alps, also show the sense of grandeur typical of many encounters with the Great (518–19).

The central concept, endless creation, had other ramifications. One of Lyell's first reviewers, William Whewell, Cambridge don, clergyman, and no friend to uniformitarians, conceded that "the discontinuity which separated us from former creations is partly removed, and we are led by an intelligible road into those remote periods and states which at first appeared involved in darkness and disorder" (in Wilson 1972, 293). Lyell's term for Whewell's "discontinuity" was "discordance," to which he had a strong aversion: "Never was there a dogma more calculated to foster indolence and to blunt the keen edge of curiosity, than this assumption of the discordance between the former and the existing causes of change" (347). Lyell maintained that the history of the planet was a continuum, so "the present is the key to the past" (Geikie 1897, 281), as Buffon had said. Wordsworth wished his "days to be / Bound each to each by natural piety"; Lyell's geology taught that the ages were thus bound.

Whewell turned out to be an ally of sorts. As head tutor at Trinity, he may have facilitated the adoption of *Principles of Geology* as a text at Cambridge, and he coined the terms "uniformitarian" and "catastrophist" in reviewing the second volume. Lyell wrote to his sister, "Whewell of Cambridge has done me no small service by giving out at his University that I have discovered a new set of powers in Nature which might be termed 'Geological Dynamics'" (in K. Lyell 1881, 1:312). In uniformitarian geology, that is, the earth's surface was constantly changing, "dynamic." Lyell's proofs of the mutability of natural systems – for example, that London once had a tropical climate – were part of what prompted Tennyson to exclaim, "O earth, what changes hast thou seen!" (1971, *In Memoriam*, stanza 123), and his discovery that part of the Swedish coast had risen two feet in sixty-four years prompted the king of Sweden to ask him jocularly when he might begin building a railroad to England.

Lyell also provided a new incentive to travel to geologically interesting sites (mountains, beaches, cliffs, deserts) by showing that it was essential to "Go and see." Of course every geologist had done *some* fieldwork, but Lyell raised the standards, quantitatively and qualitatively. He thought that Werner's explorations had been too narrow, Buckland's too careless, for their conclusions to be valid; the uniformitarian must "examine with minute attention all the changes now in progress on the earth" and treat "every fact collected" as a clue in a mystery (in Wilson 1972, 291). French geologists, he felt, tend to "sit still, and buy shells, and work indoors, as much as we [English] travel" (in K. Lyell 1881, 1:303). The "grand secret" was "to revisit countries, and to compare them frequently, after thinking over what you see in the interval" (405). Not only other geologists but clergymen, professors, poets, ladies, and gentlemen followed his advice. In the next generation his writings drew men such as John Tyndall, Charles Doughty, and John Muir to the mountains and deserts of the world.

Lyell supplemented his fieldwork by reading travel literature, especially accounts of the high latitudes he was not likely to reach. In 1828 he carried a kettle up Mount Etna and "made a breakfast of hot tea" at the timberline, "following Captain Parry's advice" (217); a decade later, during a discussion of species, he brought up Parry's story of a dog/wolf mating. He met James Ross and discussed his Antarctic expedition with him. In *The Geological Evidences of the Antiquity of Man* (1863), in which he accepted Darwin's theory of evolution, Lyell cites Nordenskiöld on the glaciers of Greenland and Captain Cook on the ice sheet of South Georgia. The interest in ice stemmed from Agassiz's work on glaciers; Lyell agreed with him that Greenland gives some idea of Europe during the Ice Age (C. Lyell 1873, 279).

The importance of Lyell lies both in his ideas and in the extent of their diffusion among influential people. Charles Darwin became one of Lyell's first converts. The lectures that Lyell gave in London on the *Principles* in 1832 and 1833 were attended by a veritable Who's Who of the English intelligentsia: geologists such as Sedgwick, Buckland, Fitton, Murchison, and De la Beche, Babbage the father of the calculating machine, Daubeny the chemist, Henry Hallam the historian, Sotheby the auctioneer, Thomas Malthus, and others. When Carlyle asked Ruskin in 1865 for information on geology, Ruskin sent him the latest edition of the *Elements*. What J.S. Mill wrote in 1838 about Bentham and Coleridge being the "great seminal minds of England in their age" could easily have been extended to include Lyell a few years later.

For Lyell did not address himself only to geologists, but to the whole of science in its original sense: *scientia,* "knowledge." One of Hutton's limitations, he thought, was his mineralogical chauvinism; Smith, Cuvier, and Brongniart had made palaeontology (faunal succession) an essential part of geological method, to which Lyell added botany, climatology, and thermal chemistry. He corresponded with Babbage and with Herschel the astronomer, explained Faraday's experiments to Oersted in Copenhagen. Nor were Lyell's interests restricted to science: he was a cultured man who socialized with Sir Walter Scott, James Fenimore Cooper, Sir Robert Peel, Talleyrand, A.W. Kinglake, Prince Albert, and European royalty. Though Lyell waged a lifelong feud with religious conservatives, his concept of nature had a breadth and resonance that appealed to theologians, humanists, and most literate people. He was sufficiently confident of his theism to follow the evidence where it led.

Lyell's occasional religious images are interesting in this connection. In 1831 he wrote to Gideon Mantell ("one of the first of my twelve apostles") that a new volcano in the Mediterranean was the means by which "Nature … testified her approbation of the advocates of modern causes. Was the cross which Constantine saw in the heavens a more clear indication of the approaching conversion of a wavering world?" (in K. Lyell 1881, 1:329). This is playful, but the terms arise naturally from the kind of opposition he provoked. While writing the *Principles*, Lyell exclaimed in his journal, "I am grappling not with the ordinary arm of flesh, but with principalities and powers, with Sedgwick, Whewell [clergymen as well as professors], and others, for my rules of philosophising" (376). The usefulness of such critics to Lyell was constantly to remind him of the broader import of what he was saying.

"A POWER NOW IN ACTION": DARWIN

Lyell's willingness to learn from others is nowhere more evident than in his relations with Charles Darwin, twelve years his junior. Darwin read volume one of the *Principles* on the *Beagle* in 1831, first applying it in the Cape Verde Islands; at Montevideo he acquired volume two. Initially, then, Lyell was the teacher, Darwin the student, though the current began to alternate as soon as Darwin's letters reached England. Lyell (who provided some instructions for the *Beagle*'s captain) monitored the expedition closely, citing its findings in letters and addresses. "How I long for the return of Darwin!" he wrote Sedgwick (in K. Lyell 1881, 1:461). After the expedition Lyell and Darwin became friends, socializing and corresponding. Lyell was now the mentor, giving advice on papers and career management, and Darwin the protégé, accepting it gratefully. Yet Lyell abandoned his theory of the formation of coral atolls in favour of Darwin's ("though it costs me a pang": 2:12) in 1837, and years later allowed himself to be persuaded on the origin of species.

Charles Darwin's impact on his age is well known, but the extent to which his early scientific interests were *geological* deserves emphasis here, because that proclivity led him to the Great. At Cambridge (where he was supposedly studying divinity), Darwin encountered Professor Henslow, a botanist, who encouraged him to geologize with Sedgwick, serve as naturalist on the *Beagle,* and buy Lyell's book. Rarely has a professor done better by a student. Though Darwin's scientific credentials for the *Beagle* post were slight, he rose to the occasion magnificently, and the combination of the *Principles* and South America formed his mind and made his career. His scientific letters to Henslow, read or cited to the Geological Society by Sedgwick and Lyell, were printed. When he returned to England, Darwin said, he was "inclined for geology" by temperament, experience, and the warmth of the society's welcome (Wilson 1972, 433). He was immediately elected a Fellow, published his first papers in the society's *Proceedings*, and served as its secretary (1838–41).

Darwin's broad competence in the natural sciences was not generally known until the publication in 1839 of *Journal of Researches into the Geology and Natural History of the Various Countries Visited by HMS Beagle*, the official account of the expedition, though Darwin's part, often called *The Voyage of the Beagle*, was printed in 1837. Lyell praised it, and Darwin dedicated the second edition (1845) to him. A long, detailed record by an energetic and still healthy young man of how well he used the marvellous gift he had been given, it sold well and remains a classic of travel literature. Darwin had no time for introspection; the external world was too interesting. With unflagging curiosity, "Don Carlos" (as he was known in South America) ranged widely, examining everything: not only the Compleat Naturalist, versed in zoology, geology, botany, and meteorology, but a student of politics, anthropology, nutrition, and aesthetics. Here at last was a major scientist who wrote as engagingly as a popularizer – Hutton and Playfair in one package – and Darwin's concern with the interconnectedness of systems makes him one of our first ecologists.

Darwin maintained an interest in geology throughout the voyage of the *Beagle*. At their first stop, St Jago, he found that "the geology of this island is the most interesting part of its natural history" (Darwin 1972, 4). He examined the structures of Argentina's Sierra de la Ventana, of cliffs along the Rio de la Plata, of Patagonia's shingle beds and the mountains of the Falkland Islands, but all these were only a prelude to Chile. There he saw both relics and a demonstration of what earthquakes can do, as well as "the marvellous story" of upthrust and volcanic action in the Andes, which it "required little geological practice to interpret" (286). The Galápagos offered more vulcanism, the Pacific its puzzling coral atolls. On the final leg, in 1836, he "wandered over [Mauritius] from morning to night" for four days, "examin[ing] its geological history," and found Ascension Island's geology "in many respects interesting" (422, 428).

Nor was geology just an *early* interest of Darwin's, to be discarded when the question of species arose. He is the last of Geikie's "founders of geology," the two geological chapters in *The Origin of Species* (1859) having "produced the greatest revolution in geological thought which has occurred in my time" (Geikie 1897, 283). Neither chapter is geology for its own sake; they exist to remove objections to the theory of natural selection. "On the Imperfection of the Geological Record" shows the great gaps in knowledge that keep fossil collections from exhibiting "all the fine intermediate gradations" of species posited by evolutionary theory (Darwin 1962, 322). Geikie says that this demonstration "came as a kind of surprise and awakening" to many scientists, who "had never realized that the record was so fragmentary" (1897, 283), and credits

Darwin with teaching geologists how ancient the earth must be. The chapter "On the Geological Succession of Organic Beings" presents geological evidence for the theory that variation causes new species.

Of the unsettling ideas that Darwin promulgated or developed for the nineteenth century, then, several were rooted in geology. One was the "vast time scale" that Lyell persuaded him must be adopted to explain earth history (Greene 1982, 25). Darwin was staggered by the realization that the gravel beds of Patagonia extended from the Andes to the *east* coast, averaging two hundred miles wide and fifty feet thick:

When we consider that all these pebbles, countless as the grains of sand in the desert, have been derived from the slow-falling masses of rock on the old coastlines and banks of rivers; and that these fragments have been dashed into smaller pieces, and that each of them has since been slowly rolled, rounded, and far transported, the mind is stupified [*sic*] in thinking over the long, absolutely necessary, lapse of years. Yet all this gravel has been transported, and probably rounded, subsequently to the deposition of the white beds, and long subsequently to the underlying beds with the tertiary shells. (Darwin 1972, 147)

Time's vanishing perspectives were dizzying. In a river valley once occupied by an arm of the sea, he found that it made him "almost giddy to reflect on the number of years, century after century, which the tides, unaided by heavy surf, must have required to have corroded so vast an area and thickness of solid basaltic lava" (156).

Darwin's sensibility at such moments combines uniformitarian geology with Addison's description of how "stupendous works of nature" produce an "amazement in the soul" resembling "speculations of eternity or infinitude." Darwin's is an *educated* stupefaction caused by what he understands about the landscape, but he is still stunned by phenomena that move his imagination towards eternity. In the Andes he stands wondering beside a torrent carrying the mountains to the sea:

The roar which the Maypu made, as it rushed over the great rounded fragments, was like that of the sea. Amidst the din of rushing waters, the noise from the stones, as they rattled over one another, was most distinctly audible even from a distance ... The sound spoke eloquently to the geologist; the thousands and thousands of stones, which, striking against each other, made the one dull uniform sound, were all hurrying in one direction. It was like thinking on time, where the minute that now glides past is irrecoverable. So it was with these stones; the ocean is their eternity. (273)

Trying to comprehend the numbers of stones and years involved in the process of degradation, he feels like a savage "point[ing] to the hairs of his head" to signify "an innumerable multitude." On the beach he doubted that "present causes" could deposit such masses of alluvia; in the hills he wonders, "can any mountains, any continent, withstand such waste?" (273).

An idea often associated with the *duration* of nature, in Darwin and other geologists, is its *power.* Implicit in his examples of erosion, power is most clearly seen in the upheavals of mountains. A "great arched fragment, lying on its convex side" atop a range in the Falkland Islands, sets him imagining what "convulsion of nature" tossed about such "monuments" (170). In the valleys below, he finds that, "by a vibratory movement of overwhelming force, the fragments have been levelled into one continuous sheet." If we exclaim over small objects leaping a few inches in an earthquake, "what must we say to a movement which has caused fragments many tons in weight, to move onwards like so much sand on a vibrating board, and find their level?" For all the upthrust, broken strata that he later saw in the Andes, "never did any scene, like these 'streams of stones,' so forcibly convey to my mind the idea of a convulsion, of which in historical records we might in vain seek for any counterpart" (170). As aeons approached the idea of eternity, and a boundless universe that of infinity, proofs of stupendous natural forces suggested divine power by so far transcending the human scale.

Power acting over time produces change: Darwin's third theme flows from his first two as inevitably as the product of an equation, $P \times T = C$. Geology thrust earth's changes upon him. High up on the eastern side of the Andes, he found petrified fir trees embedded in volcanic sandstone that had once been seabed. Again, he was stunned:

I was at first so much astonished, that I could scarcely believe the plainest evidence. I saw the spot where a cluster of fine trees once waved their branches on the shores of the Atlantic, when that ocean (now driven back 700 miles) came to the foot of the Andes ... I now beheld the bed of that ocean, forming a chain of mountains more than seven thousand feet in height ... Vast, and scarcely comprehensible as such changes must ever appear, yet they have all occurred within a period, recent when compared with the history of the Cordillera; and the Cordillera itself is absolutely modern as compared with many of the fossiliferous strata of Europe and America. (286–7)

Unimaginable time, power, and change formed a Rule of Mutability he would later apply to the concept of species.

It is, then, "daily ... forced home on the mind of the geologist, that nothing, not even the wind that blows, is so unstable as the level of the crust of this earth" (277). In Chile, Darwin felt the earthquake of 1835 as a motion rather "like the movement of a vessel in a cross-ripple," or "skating over thin ice, which bends." He reflected, in a passage reminiscent of one in Humboldt's *Personal Narrative* (1852; see 1:349), that "a bad earthquake at once destroys our oldest associations: the earth, the very emblem of solidity, has moved beneath our feet like a thin crust over a fluid; – one second of time has created in the mind a strange idea of insecurity, which hours of reflection would not have produced" (Darwin 1972, 260). And it left behind emotional chaos: humiliation at seeing human works instantly overthrown, compassion for the victims, surprise at how suddenly the land could be changed, and withal deep interest in the phenomenon.

The Voyage of the Beagle combines science with travel and feeling. Darwin's aesthetic reactions to mountains and desert plains were nineteenth-century scientific versions of the emotions that Burnet, Gray, and Wordsworth felt in the Alps. On a climb at Tierra del Fuego, he and his companions attained an impressive vista: "To the south we had a scene of savage magnificence ... There was a degree of mysterious grandeur in mountain behind mountain" (182). Typically, he analyzes this mystery into its components: deep, thickly forested valleys between the peaks, and an atmosphere almost as thick and dark with storms. A familiar note is heard at the Strait of Magellan, where "the distant channels between the mountains appeared from their gloominess to lead beyond the confines of this world": the Great transcends the world the observer knows. Darwin finally embraced the barrenness of the Andes, pronouncing the "scene of desolation" around a high pass "grand" (289). Crossing a ridge that gave a "glorious view" of "wild broken forms" under a clear sky, "a scene no one could have imagined," he was glad to be alone: "It was like watching a thunderstorm, or hearing in full orchestra a chorus of the Messiah" (278).

The Andes also stirred him in other ways. On a summit, he found that his "pleasure" in the scenery was "heightened by the many reflections" he could by then make. "[W]ondering at the force which has upheaved these mountains, and even more so at the countless ages" required to wear them down, he remembered wondering in the shingle beds of Patagonia "how any mountain-chain could have supplied such masses, and not have been utterly obliterated." Here were the Andes, far from effaced, but he would "not now reverse the wonder, and doubt whether all-powerful time can grind down mountains – even the gigantic Cordillera – into gravel and mud" (221). Darwin supplied new examples of the power of time, one of the most venerable themes in English literature, examples beyond the ken of Shakespeare and Spenser.

In the Chonos Islands of Chile, Darwin makes a point often echoed in later accounts of mountain and desert travel. The mountains were "composed of grand, solid, abrupt masses of granite, which appeared as if they had been coeval with the beginning of the world" (244). Darwin is more articulate about the appeal of such a phenomenon than anyone except, perhaps, Goethe, whose "Essay on Granite" recognizes its 'dignity' as nature's oldest child. "Granite to the geologist is classic ground," Darwin explains. "We generally see it constituting the fundamental rock, ... the deepest layer in the crust of this globe to which man has penetrated. The limit of man's knowledge in any subject possesses a high interest, which is perhaps increased by its close neighbourhood to the realms of imagination" (244). The number of works by novelists – Poe, Cooper, Jules Verne – that extrapolate on data gathered by scientists and explorers makes his point; the whole genre of science fiction takes off from precisely the "limit of man's knowledge."

For all his voyaging, Darwin (who was prone to seasickness) has little to say about the ocean. The "immensity" of the Pacific reminds him "how infinitely small the proportion of dry land is to the water," and he finds "much grandeur" in the surf breaking over the windward side of a coral reef (360, 398). But when summing up his feelings at the end of the book, he asks, "What are the boasted glories of the illimitable ocean?" and answers: "A tedious waste, a desert of water, as the Arabian calls it" (435).

This does not mean that he necessarily dislikes deserts: Darwin's reactions to landscape are complex and unpredictable. In Patagonia he found "scarcely an animal or a bird. All was stillness and desolation. Yet in passing over these scenes, without one bright object near, an ill-defined but strong sense of pleasure is vividly excited" (144). At the book's end he tries to define this pleasure, because in retrospect "the plains of Patagonia frequently pass before my eyes; yet these plains are pronounced by all wretched and useless. They can be described only by negative characters; without habitations, without water, without trees, without mountains ... Why then, and the case is not peculiar to myself, have these arid wastes taken so firm a hold on my memory?" There is a difficulty here: if the plains are pronounced wretched "by all," how can Darwin's feelings be "not peculiar" to himself? Or does he too find them wretched? In fact, he is one of the first to record such sentiments. He "can scarcely analyze these feelings: but it must be partly owing to the free scope given to the imagination" by boundlessness, mystery, and an air of lasting unchanged from a remote past to a distant future (436–7). The appeal of the "arid wastes" resembles that of granite, then, and of the Great in Addison's analysis.

Yet Darwin was not a devotee of barrenness in general. In the deserts of northern Chile, a "sterile" and "uninteresting country," he felt "like a prisoner shut up in a gloomy court," while arid, volcanic Ascension Island struck him as "naked hideousness" (299, 427). And the book offers two paeans to the Brazilian rain forest, a "great, wild, untidy, luxuriant hothouse, made by Nature for herself" (431). Darwin has no set program, nor does he share Mrs Radcliffe's view that landscapes have intrinsic qualities; he presents any scene in all its variety, including the human mood or angle of vision. Cruising around Tierra del Fuego in a small boat, he feels chiefly its solemnity and remoteness; the next day, the scenery seems "grander," with "magnificent glaciers" (193). When the *Beagle* leaves Tierra del Fuego, a glimpse of Sarmiento Peak opens the Great stop; its "vast piles of snow, which never melt, and seem destined to last as long as the world holds together, present a noble and even sublime spectacle" (208). Yet he is glad to reach sunny, verdant central Chile, and so on, back and forth, as he looks for the truth of feeling about every scene.

Darwin's intellectual independence, his insistence on working things out for himself empirically, is almost Cartesian. In northern Chile, passing from a barren desert he found gloomy into arid mountains, Darwin liked them better – for awhile: "The scene on all sides showed desolation, brightened and made palpable by a clear, unclouded sky. For a time such scenery is sublime, but this feeling cannot last, and then it becomes uninteresting" (310). The New Zealand countryside made him examine his idea of desolation: "The whole scene, in spite of its green colour, had rather a desolate aspect. The sight of so much fern impresses the mind with an idea of sterility; this, however, is not correct" (367). Such hesitation suggests a fresh response, always welcome in a writer who we know read much travel literature. In discussing the clarity of the Chilean atmosphere he cited the eighteenth-century circumnavigator Admiral Anson, and in the Andes noted the "red snow, so well known from the accounts of the Arctic navigators" (220, 278). Many such works were in the *Beagle's* library.

Upon his return to England, Darwin joined Lyell as an advocate of "present causes," adding his own powerful examples. In 1838 he gave a paper showing the relation of volcanoes and earthquakes to the gradual elevation of the Andes. Darwin felt satisfied that "there is a power now in action, and which has been in action with the same average intensity ... since the remotest periods, not only sufficient to produce, but which almost inevitably must have produced, unequal elevation on the lines of fracture" (Wilson 1972, 455). This "power now in action," which the religious ascribed to God as First Cause but which was (also) demonstrably natural, was that of *continuing creation.* The exciting message of Lyell and Darwin was that anyone could "go and see" Creation at work. It was most plainly, easily, and dramatically viewed in bare landscapes that revealed the structure of the earth's crust, including the "vast uncultivated desert[s]," "huge heaps of mountains, high rocks and precipices" that Addison had called "the Great."

ASPECTS OF NATURE: HUMBOLDT, AGASSIZ, HAECKEL

Of the many important Continental geologists in this period, three must be at least mentioned. Alexander von Humboldt achieved great renown and influence during a long career that linked major figures of the eighteenth and nineteenth centuries. He studied under Abraham Werner (see chapter 6), but said that a meeting with George Forster, one of Cook's naturalists, formed his mind (Humboldt 1849b, 2:301). The empirical basis of his career was his fieldwork in the New World (1799–1804), after which he settled in Paris to oversee publication of his voluminous *Personal Narrative of Travels to the Equinoctial Regions of America* (see chapter 10). Lyell had read Humboldt by 1817, and when they met in 1823 he found him an approachable "hero," whose comparative method provided a "famous lesson" (in K. Lyell 1881, 1:125–6, 146). Humboldt's *Personal Narrative* helped persuade Darwin to sail on the *Beagle*; he himself convinced the king of Prussia to assist Louis Agassiz financially. In 1856 Lyell visited Humboldt, then eighty-seven, and found him absolutely up to date "in many departments," spending a hundred pounds a year on correspondence (2:225).

In Humboldt's extensive writings (many of them in multiple editions), which cover more than half a century, one naturally finds evolving interests and opinions. He began by trying to apply Werner's "quaint system" of mineralogy to South America, but outgrew it; Necker de Saussure believed that it was lapsed students like Humboldt who overthrew Werner's "neptunism" (Greene 1982, 35, 62). Humboldt formulated, then abandoned, a theory of the parallelism of European mountain ranges. In addition to scientific theorizing, however, Humboldt in his later works makes personal and aesthetic remarks that sometimes bear on our subject.

Aspects of Nature, in Different Lands and Different Climates (1849), for example, is among other things a travel book, some of which was written "in the presence of natural scenes of grandeur or of beauty" (Humboldt 1849b, 1:vii). An early essay "On the Rhodian Genius" (1795) describes the philosopher Epicharmus's daily excursions to a seaport to receive "the image of the boundless and the infinite" for which his spirit yearned (2:255). In the section on "Steppes and Deserts" (Humboldt had by then travelled in the Americas, Europe, Asia, and Africa) he observes that, "like the ocean, the steppe fills the mind with the feeling of infinity," though steppes are "dead and rigid, like the stony crust of a desolated planet" (1:2). Yet distinctions must be made, for each steppe is different, those of Africa being "grander and severer" than others (1:3). "On the Structure and Mode of Action of Volcanos" (1823) describes the memorable display by Vesuvius in October 1822, notes that only recently has the amount of travel necessary for accurate observations been performed, and calls volcanic eruptions "great phaenomena of deep-seated origin" (2:221).

Some of these themes recur in *Cosmos: A Sketch of a Physical Description of the Universe* (1849), a valediction that Humboldt said was the result of a lifelong desire to understand the connections between physical phenomena and to see "nature as one great whole" (1849a, ix). Standing "on an extensive plain or the ocean shore," we imbibe a "sense of the grandeur and vast expanse of nature," an "image of infinity" such as the stars provide (3). Sublimity, the emotion related to this sense, is felt in those places and on mountains (20). Humboldt shared with some eighteenth-century aestheticians the belief that scenes evoke specific emotions; thus quality of feeling depends to some extent on where you go. If by studying great natural phenomena we can feel their "vast sublimity," that is one of the "Incitements to the Study of Nature" (417). Humboldt closes by affirming that the progress from Mediterranean myths to European empiricism shows a "gradual development of the recognition of the unity of Nature" (569). *Quod erat demonstrandum.*

The other indispensable European geologist of these years, Switzerland's Louis Agassiz, began as a classifier of skeletons and fossils. When Lyell met him in 1832, Agassiz had obtained his doctorate, published a book, and, at twenty-five, inherited Cuvier's work; he then became professor of natural history at Neuchâtel. In 1836, soon after he received a medal from the Geological Society, two Swiss mining engineers, Ignace Venetz and Jean de Charpentier, showed Agassiz evidence that glaciers had carried "erratic" boulders across much of Switzerland: a notion suggested to them by the mountaineer Jean-Pierre Perraudin (Albritton 1986, 157–8) but adumbrated by Scheuchzer and Hutton. Developing their ideas, and connecting the movement of erratics with the striation of rockfaces near the glaciers, Agassiz proposed to the Helvetic Society in 1837 that much of Europe had been under glaciers during an "Ice Age" (Geikie 1897, 272). He was initially disbelieved: Humboldt advised him to go back to paleontology, and even de Charpentier was embarrassed by some of Agassiz's theories about *why* an ice age had occurred.

But Agassiz kept at his fieldwork on the Aar glacier, toned down his speculations, and in 1838 showed Buckland enough evidence to convert the former diluvialist to his glacial thesis (Bailey 1962, 136). 1840 was the pivotal year: Agassiz published *Études sur les glaciers de la Suisse*, went to Britain – finding more instances of glacial action in the Highlands – and read papers in Glasgow and London arguing that Europe had once looked like Greenland. Buckland quickly converted Lyell by showing him glacial moraines "within two miles of his father's house," and both spoke in support of Agassiz's theory (Wilson 1972, 501). A lectureship arranged by Lyell sent Agassiz to America in 1846; the revolution of 1848, which cut off his state funding, made Harvard a welcome home for the rest of his career. He discovered additional evidence for his theory in the glacial scouring of New England, the Great Lakes, and the West.

Agassiz's importance lay in identifying a new "geological dynamic," a "power now in action" though formerly more potent, and in showing how it operated. His energy and enthusiasm carried his theories over some rough spots (created partly by his enthusiasm) into general acceptance by the end of the century. He gave the venturesome a further incentive to explore mountains, with new objects of study when they got there, and provided new data on continuing creation. No one who has ever examined a glacier or its work will need to have the excitement of Agassiz's discovery explained. Numerous climbers for the rest of the century – Forbes, Tyndall, Muir, and others – went up with glaciation at the front of their minds. Fittingly, when Agassiz died, a boulder from a moraine of the Aar glacier was brought across the Atlantic as a headstone.

In 1868 Ernst Haeckel sent Lyell a copy of the first German edition of his *Naturalische Schöpfung* (translated as *The History of Creation, or the*

Development of the Earth and its Inhabitants by the Action of Natural Causes. An Exposition of the Doctrine of Evolution), containing a chapter on Lyell and Darwin. Lyell made grateful acknowledgment, as well he might: Haeckel expounded uniformitarianism for readers of German, and then the popular English version provided a European endorsement of "present causes." Haeckel credits Lyell and Darwin with reforming geology and biology by showing that existing agents, given sufficient time, can account for all known changes in nature. Since there is no reason to assume that long periods were *not* available – Haeckel states that the universe is eternal and infinite – Cuvier's "catastrophes" and "special creations" are supererogatory (1903, 1:129–34, 398). In Haeckel, uniformitarianism triumphs over catastrophism, over the Wernerians and Neptunists (whose school survived well into the nineteenth century in Germany), and over the "harmonizers" of science and scripture.

KEEPING THE FAITH: RUSKIN AND MILLER

Most nineteenth-century geologists were "amateurs" in some sense; only a few could (or had to) make their living from it. Outside the small circle of those who did regular fieldwork and published serious scholarship were many who were sufficiently interested in geology to read books and geologize, perhaps even to write something. The "satellite" geologists covered the same spectrum of attitudes as did the field's stars: while some were uniformitarians, others resisted Lyell's conclusions, making new science subserve old beliefs.

Nowhere is the impact of geological discovery on Victorian aesthetics better illustrated than in the career of John Ruskin. Late in life, Ruskin said that he had been naturally inclined towards the natural sciences – he was cataloguing minerals by age twelve – and had aspired to be president of the Royal Geological Society. Ruskin studied geology under Buckland at Oxford and did become a fellow of the society. He met Darwin in 1837, and ten years later Lyell was "glad ... to see more of Ruskin, who was Secretary of our Geological Section" at the British Association meeting, for "I like him very much" (in K. Lyell 1881, 2:131). Towards the end of his career, however, Ruskin complained that the Geological Society had neglected his writings in the field, which fill a six-hundred-page volume of his *Works*.

The centre of Ruskin's interest in geology was the Alps. For his fifteenth birthday, he requested and received a copy of de Saussure's *Voyages dans les Alpes*, which became his lifelong guide (Ruskin prompted Douglas

Freshfield to write de Saussure's life), along with James Forbes's *Travels through the Alps* (see chapter 15). After visiting the Alps Ruskin wrote a paper on "The Strata of Mont Blanc" (1834), his first prose publication, and composed "The Ascent of the St Bernard," a verse drama. He returned repeatedly: in 1864 Ruskin said that he had spent eleven summers and two winters studying the Alps' "external form" and "its mechanical causes," and these pilgrimages continued until 1876 (1906, xix). He lectured on them, discussed them in *Modern Painters* (1843–60) and *Deucalion* (1875–83), and authored papers such as "The Geology of Chamonix" (1858) and "On the Forms of the Stratified Alps of Savoy" (1863).

It was the *beauty* of the Alps, Ruskin said, that diverted him from geology to painting (1906, 89). This was probably an inevitable turn; for all his interest in geology, his love of nature was never satisfied with a scientific approach. As a young man he "devoted [himself] to pure, wild, solitary, natural scenery," especially that of mountain and sea, learning a "constant watchfulness" of nature "beneath the cloudless peace of the snows of Chamouni" (quoted in Cust n.d., viii–ix). Ruskin went to the Alps as he believed de Saussure had gone: "only to *look* at them, and describe them as they were, loving them heartily – loving them, the positive Alps, more than himself, or than science, or than any theories of science" (1906, xix). For him, the scientific and aesthetic approaches to mountains were complementary, not antithetical. In 1849 he made a "sun-portrait" of the Matterhorn (one of the first daguerreotypes) and measured the angles of various peaks in order to make his drawings and discussions in *Modern Painters* more accurate. In effect, Ruskin crossed the English Romantics' intense feelings for the Alps with de Saussure's thirst for knowledge about them.

The connections between Ruskin's geological, aesthetic, and spiritual interests are clearest in *Modern Painters*. The argument of volume one is summarized in the preface to the second edition (1844): early landscape painters (Claude, Salvator Rosa) paid too little attention to nature and too much to themselves, thus failing to achieve the goal of art, lifting our thoughts to God. Modern painters, especially Turner, annihilate their egos and praise God by reproducing grand nature as faithfully as possible; that is, they move from geology through aesthetics to God. Ruskin, who had a strict religious upbringing, retained a narrow Evangelical faith until the 1850s (Burd 1981, 10–12); both his geology and his aesthetics manifest his piety.

The section "Of Truth of Earth" includes chapters on "Central" and "Inferior Mountains" that use Ruskin's own observations of Alpine form.

Turner's "Alps at Daybreak" is judged admirably faithful to its subject ("It may not be beautiful ... but this *is* nature"; Ruskin 1903, 3:433), while Claude violates basic principles of aerial perspective and geologic structure. Most painters render Alpine snow poorly because they have not studied it, and the underlying landforms, closely enough. What we want, he insists, is "the pure and holy hills, treated as a link between heaven and earth" (449). Though startling after all the insistence on geological accuracy, this is simply another instance of natural religion; for Ruskin, geology had a spiritual dimension. Turner, his model of "truth to earth" and right worship, proves "the use of considering geological truths" (465). Turner's accuracy, however, has subsequently been questioned; Claire Engel argues that he is more impressionistic than Ruskin realized (1930, 201).

In the decade between the second and third volumes of *Modern Painters* (1846–56) Ruskin's faith weakened, owing partly to the impact of uniformitarian geology on literal readings of scripture. "If only the Geologists would let me alone," he wrote in 1851, "I could do very well, but those dreadful Hammers! I hear the clink of them at the end of every cadence of the Bible verses" (quoted in Cate 1982, 14). The clash between his two great loves was very painful to Ruskin, and the further the uniformitarians went the more disturbed and unsympathetic he became, as *Deucalion* shows. The chapter "Of the Novelty of Landscape" in volume three argues that what distinguishes modern landscapes is their focus on mountains, rather than humans, as in early painting. Modern humanity, says Ruskin, having lost its religious belief, takes more interest in this world. The latter, comprising both geology and aesthetics, is his chosen subject, but remains connected to the former.

The fourth volume of *Modern Painters* (also 1856), devoted to "Mountain Beauty," moves from Turner to geology to aesthetics. Ruskin, thinking it the "most valuable" part of the work, republished parts as *In Montibus Sanctis* (1884–85). There are chapters on the "Materials" of which mountains are made, on their "Sculpture" (erosion), and on the "Resulting Forms" (e.g., "Aiguilles," "Crests"). In 1900 the president of the Geological Society asserted that these chapters showed the importance of geology to scenery and "might be read with advantage by many geologists," giving Ruskin, post-mortem, some of the recognition he had craved (Ruskin 1906, xxiv). The aesthetic philosophy developed in the chapters on "Mountain Gloom" and "Mountain Glory" is discussed in chapter 12.

If Ruskin had lost much of his faith by about 1860, mainly from doubts about the text of the Bible (Burd 1981, 10–11), he never lost his capacity for religious feeling, only displacing some of it temporarily onto the mountains. In November 1861, depressed and self-exiled, he wrote Jane Carlyle from Lucerne that he had never seen anything "so entirely and solemnly *divine* as the calm winter days are, here ... the great Alps clear – sharp – all strength and splendour ... I'm just away tomorrow deeper into the Alps ... to see how the grimmest of them look in the snow" (in Cate 1982, 96). The more mountainous, the more godly, he says in *Modern Painters*, and the grimness of the range seems to attract him. Ruskin's editors believe that he always took a spiritual approach to geologizing; for him "the study of natural phenomena was part of the evidence of natural theology" (Ruskin 1906, xlvii). At a time when his faith in *scriptural* revelation was low, the importance of the "Book of Nature" was heightened.

Hugh Miller, a self-taught Scot who rose from quarry-boy to best-selling author, virtually defines the "spiritual (or Christian) geologist": all of his work was intended to show that geology could lead the soul to proper worship. Though careful to distinguish his ideas from those of the deists, who by then had a bad name, he shared with them the essence of natural religion. The titles of his books evoke writers such as Townsend, Paley, and Buckland earlier in the century: *Footprints of the Creator*; *The Two Records: The Mosaic and the Geological*; and *The Testimony of the Rocks; or, Geology in Its Bearings on the Two Theologies, Natural and Revealed*. Miller's position may have been antiquated, but he was a gifted writer, eloquent as well as pious. Geikie called him a "geological poet," Gillispie a "lyrical geologist," and his books outsold Lyell's and Darwin's (Gillispie 1959, 170, 172). Through them and his editorship of the journal of the Free Church he cofounded, he had more influence on nineteenth-century working-class readers than the better-known writers discussed above. He grew mentally unstable in his later years, however, finally killing himself.

Miller's career was built on *The Old Red Sandstone* (1841), which uses evidence from the fossils of that formation to refute the notion of evolutionary progress. Well before *The Origin of Species*, he attacked the idea that "apes have been transformed into human creatures," which he traced back to de Maillet. Miller argues that geological research does not support evolution, because "fish of the higher orders" do not evolve from the lower but "appear first ... There is no progression ... There is no getting rid of the miracle in the case ... The infidel substitutes progression for Deity; – Geology robs him of his God" (H. Miller 1857, 70). Every fossil manifests Divine Wisdom: for example, "Another and superior order of existences had sprung into being at the fiat of the Creator" (231).

In a note added to posthumous editions of *The Old Red Sandstone*, Miller's widow Lydia described him as a man whose life work it was to present "evidences drawn from geology in favour of *revealed* religion," so as to "meet the attacks of his infidel fellow-worker in the same field" (ix–x). She appended an address that Miller gave in 1852, titled "Geological Evidences in Favour of Revealed Religion," which claimed that geology can "acquaint us with God's doings" and reaffirm "the great First Cause" (288, 293). It was doubtless comforting to Victorian believers to find a writer on science who undertook to confirm, not disturb, their ideas.

Miller was more than tolerated by the inner circle of major geologists. T.H. Huxley, whom the Millers must have regarded as one of the "infidels," is said to have enjoyed *The Old Red Sandstone*; Louis Agassiz wrote a friendly introduction for the American edition of *Footprints of the Creator*. Lyell called Miller "one of our best writers" (though not for his geology), and when they met in 1855 found him "very just" in his "remarks on other geologists," and quite "willing to learn" (in K. Lyell 1881, 2:134, 205). Miller used Lyell selectively – as he did all scientific sources – in his books, for their positions on most major geological and palaeontological questions were quite different and kept diverging. Both were "consigned to perdition" by "clerical critics": Lyell for ignoring the Bible, and Miller for treating it as visionary, not literal, discourse (Gillispie 1959, 152, 178).

The Testimony of the Rocks (1857), a collection of lectures and essays, seeks to reconcile the Biblical and scientific timescales. Miller acknowledges that he once thought of the "days" of creation as *natural* days, but that field research has convinced him that they were "prophetic days," one of which "extended mayhap over milleniums of centuries" (1876, x–xi). That means a creation period of at least a million and a half years, far too long for biblical conservatives. In some respects Miller was a theological liberal by Victorian standards: he treated the six days of creation as visions (corresponding to geological periods) in a diorama that God showed Moses, admitted that Genesis could not be used to date the earth (since the geological record far outruns the Hebrew chronology), and viewed the Flood as an unmiraculous Caspian Sea affair (since geology does not support the idea of a universal deluge). Miller even exposes the "errors and nonsense" of misguided Christians who attack geology because it threatens their interpretation of Scripture. Yet the glossing of the "many long ages" of primitive animal life as mere "thousands of years" shows that Miller did not become a liberal *geologist*.

Miller did, however, manage to preserve the central idea of natural theology – that God can be seen and worshipped in the material creation – during the age of scientific geology. If his compromise did not please the zealots of either Christianity or science, it appealed strongly to a large centre of believers who did not want to ignore progress, and to scientists who did not wish to leave the moorings of traditional religion altogether. Both Miller and Ruskin show the pressure that geology put on belief in this period, increasing the spiritual valence of landscape, and different ways of relieving that pressure. Miller refused to take an "anti-geological" position (as Ruskin finally did) in order to preserve his beliefs, and was shrewder than Ruskin in coming to terms with the accumulating evidence. He said he found his geological rambles inspirational, and inspired others to believe that they could hear the teachings of the geologists without giving up their faith.

The writers discussed in this chapter cover a broad spectrum of progressiveness and importance. They teach a caution in generalizing about the beliefs that Victorian geologists held, and demonstrate that nineteenth-century geology was not only an empirical science but also a system of beliefs and values that involved soul and sensibility. The study of the land was usually an affair of passion, one way or the other; the emotions that Egdon Heath evoked in Hardy were no stronger than those exhibited by the geologists. Lyell felt that he was contending with "principalities and powers" in writing *Principles of Geology*, Ruskin that the geologists' hammers were knocking down his faith, Miller that his walks were following in the "footprints of the Creator." Their intensity infected their readers. Auden said that Yeats "became his admirers" after his death; the admirers of the giants of geology, not content to entomb their memories in themselves, attached their names to natural features across the New World. Humboldt "became" a great Pacific current, Lyell a mountain in California, Miller a noble inlet in Alaska: objects of contemplation and study in the natural world.

"What Is Nature?"
Some Influential Views, 1830–70

Although much of the writing about nature in the nineteenth century came from scientists, there were also attempts of the traditional, non-empirical kind to articulate a philosophy of nature. In Europe the legacy of Goethe remained potent. In the English-speaking world (where his influence was also felt), such efforts were dominated by four men acquainted with each other or each other's writings: Thomas Carlyle, Ralph Waldo Emerson, John Ruskin, and John Stuart Mill. Carlyle's correspondence with each of the others was sufficient to warrant publication in separate volumes. Mill met Carlyle in 1831 and gave Emerson a letter of introduction to him (1833). Carlyle and Ruskin began to correspond in 1851 and developed a close relationship, comparing views on many subjects. Ruskin said that, after Carlyle, Emerson was his best teacher, and Carlyle recommended that Emerson read Ruskin. This interconnectedness does not mean that they give us four statements of the same position, however; there are differences of substance as well as style between them.

SPIRITUAL NATURALISM: CARLYLE

For Victorian England, no set of statements about nature was more stirring than that delivered by Thomas Carlyle, another in the long series of eloquent Scots who have energized British literature. His main role was that of the angry prophet, denouncing scientific views of the universe and reasserting the older concept of nature as the visible expression of God. Both a Puritan and a Romantic in his penchant for personal religion, Carlyle was to England what Goethe was to Germany (Willey 1964, 111, 115), and continued Coleridge's work of transmitting Goethe and

German idealism to Anglo-American literary circles. When Emerson ventured some doubts about Goethe, Carlyle wrote back that he should learn German so as to understand Goethe better.

These (and many other) aspects of Carlyle are conspicuous in his first major work, the densely allusive *Sartor Resartus: The Life and Opinions of Herr Teufelsdroeckh* (serialized in *Fraser's Magazine*, 1833–34). The epigraph comes from Goethe. The protagonist, Diogenes (the first cynic) Teufelsdroeckh (roughly, 'Devil's dirt'), hails from Weissnichtwo ('I don't know where'): on one level, Edinburgh, but Socrates also played "I don't know." "Life and Opinions" calls to mind one eighteenth-century satirist, Laurence Sterne, author of *The Life and Opinions of Tristram Shandy* (1759–67), and as *Sartor Resartus* ('The Tailor Reclothed') unfolds, it often resembles *A Tale of a Tub* (1704), by Jonathan Swift, another darkly playful Christian from the imperial marches who used clothing as a metaphor of religious belief. In Carlyle, though, the deepest meaning of the image is that God wears nature as a garment. Teufelsdroeckh too is both Puritan and Romantic as he wanders, agonized, over some of Europe's most desolate landscapes in search of a religion more coherent than that offered by any established church.

Sartor Resartus offers a "spiritual Picture of Nature," Teufelsdroeckh's philosophy (Carlyle 1987, 41), whose crucial passages are given Great settings. The action begins when the "Sorrows of Teufelsdroeckh" send him on a pilgrimage into "the wilds of Nature." Among mountains and rocks "of that sort called Primitive by the mineralogists, which always arrange themselves in masses of a rugged gigantic character," the young misanthrope finds some cottages clustered by the "everlasting granite" (a bow to Goethe's essay), where "Beauty alternates with Grandeur" (116). But their peace is not for him: he must go deeper into the "huge mountain-mass," where there is "no trace of man." Here, in "a world of Mountains," at sunset, he has a remarkable epiphany. Hundreds of "savage peaks" glow in silent solitude, "like giant spirits of the wilderness." Teufelsdroeckh, gazing with wonder and desire, finds them "Beautiful, nay solemn": "never till this hour had he known Nature, that she was One, that she was his Mother and divine." A "murmur of Eternity and Immensity" steals through him as he sees the unity of all (117).

The passage seems earlier than 1833, with its echoes of Wordsworth and Byron (who is later rejected). The word "mineralogists" (instead of geologists) sounds quaint; not until the 1860s did Carlyle show an interest in geology. The vision of nature, more mystical than deist, owes something to Romanticism, but Carlyle distances himself from any fashionable pseudo-poetic gushing about mountains. Teufelsdroeckh assails "the epidemic ... of view hunting," and the Editor endorses the attack: "Never, as I compute, till after the *Sorrows of Werter* [*sic*], was there man found who would say: Come let us make a Description! Having drunk the liquor, come let us eat the glass!" (118). *Werther* is the one work by Goethe of which Carlyle speaks slightingly, but the satire is on the poet's abusers.

The perfidy of his friend and his beloved deepens the hero's misanthropy, and he staggers towards atheism in "The Everlasting No": "Doubt had darkened into Unbelief ...: Is there no God, then," he wonders, "but at best an absentee God?" (124). As this moral night deepens, he finds that his "once-fair world" is "all a grim Desert," but without any guiding pillars of cloud and fire (125). Seeing the universe as "one huge, dead, immeasurable Steam-engine, rolling on, in its dead indifference," Teufelsdroeckh is tempted by negation, the satanic No (127). But he summons the strength to utter his protest, "the most important transaction in Life," declaring his freedom and his hatred of Satan (129). This "grim" desert, then, is the scene of a crucial and ultimately positive spiritual crisis, after which Teufelsdroeckh "began to be a Man."

En route from the wilderness of negation to that of affirmation Teufelsdroeckh must pass through the "Centre of Indifference," a state of *contemptus mundi*. Again the Great provides the setting. The scene is "the solitude of the North Cape" (Nordkapp at the tip of Norway) on a June midnight. Teufelsdroeckh "stands there, on the World-promontory, looking over the infinite Brine," musing in the dusk; "behind him lies all Europe and Africa ... before him the silent Immensity, and Palace of the Eternal" (137). Solitude, silence, oceanic vastness, and eternity: it is difficult to find a short passage containing more of the standard attributes of Great aesthetics; even the vantage-point is Addisonian. At chapter's end, Teufelsdroeckh recalls that while gazing at the stars, which seem to pity the "little lot of man," he has thought, "What is this paltry little Dog-cage of an Earth"? (139). The use of the heavenly Great to dwarf human enterprise is at least as old as the cosmologists and poets of the Renaissance.

"The Everlasting Yea" begins with Teufelsdroeckh exclaiming, "Temptations in the wilderness! Have we not all to be tried with such?" In the Bible, Satan carried Jesus into "grim Solitudes" to tempt Him, but spiritual trial is a universal condition, and deserts come in different forms: "With or without visible Devil, whether in the natural Desart of rocks and sands, or in the populous, moral Desart of selfishness and baseness, – to such Temptation are we all called." The desert (as the Psalmist said) is a metaphor of life; "our Wilderness is the wide World in an Atheistic Century" (140). Abandoning this metaphor but not the Great, the hero recounts how "after weariest wanderings" he made his way onto "the higher sunlit slopes" of what sounds like Dante's Mount Purgatory: "that Mountain which has no summit, or whose summit is in Heaven only!" The Editor believes that Teufelsdroeckh's "healing sleep" before his spiritual rebirth took place in the "skyey Tent ... on the high table-land, in front of the Mountains" (141, 142).

Here Teufelsdroeckh realizes that nature is neither dead nor autonomous but "the Living Garment of God," to Whom the Everlasting Yea of Love must be said (143). This perception arises directly from his encounters with Great landscapes that Carlyle knew only from books. It is the sight of a "black Tempest" raging "round some Schreckhorn" that causes the protagonist to ask, "what is Nature?" His realization that nature lives seems "sweeter than Dayspring to the Shipwrecked in Nova Zembla": the classic mariner's nightmare since Barents came to grief there in 1596.

This vision of nature as inspirited by God is also the theme of "Natural Supernaturalism," where Time and Space, the materials of nature, are revealed as "Phantasms" veiling the "Holy of Holies," a "Living Garment" worn by the truth (193): an image derived from the Earth Spirit in Goethe's *Faust*. Scientists profess to understand and codify nature's laws, but "to the wisest man, ... Nature remains of quite infinite depth" (195): so much for the geologists and astronomers. Carlyle/Teufelsdroeckh (most commentators treat them as identical here) uses various metaphors for the relation of God and nature. Nature is a "Volume" whose author is God, or "the Time-vesture of God" that "reveals Him to the wise, hides Him from the foolish." But always the essential message is that "Time and Space are not God, but creations of God": mere "Forms of Thought" that conceal Him (195, 200, 198). To Carlyle, natural science was a branch of theology; whereas others lost the supernatural in the natural, he did the reverse.

These few chapters contain the gist of Carlyle's view of nature; elsewhere he mainly varies the images. "All visible things are emblems" of "some Idea," says Teufelsdroeckh, drawing on Plato and German idealism (56). Similarly with nature's temporal dimension: eternity looks in on us through time. Compared to nature, man is brief; "Nature alone is antique" (80). But here Carlyle's hostility to science trips him up, as he adds: "That idle crag thou sittest on is six-thousand years of age." And things had been going so well! Suddenly Carlyle looks not inspired but willfully blind; no respectable student of earth history had maintained such a thing for a century. The irony is that what geologists could have told him about nature's antiquity would have *strengthened* his point here.

Carlyle's description of a cascade invites comparison with the geological vision. "The Scaur Water," wrote Carlyle, "came brawling down, the voice of it like a lamentation among the winds, answering me as the voice of a brother wanderer and lamenter, wanderers like me through a certain portion of eternity and infinite space. Poor brook! yet it was nothing but drops of water" (quoted in Willey 1964, 133). The analogue that comes to mind is Darwin's meditation on the Maypu torrent in the Andes, rushing to its oceanic "eternity." To Darwin the brook speaks not sadly but eloquently; knowing the mechanisms of erosion, he is interested in what the Maypu can tell him about the world they share. Far from diminishing the brook to "drops of water," as Carlyle does, he marvels at what those drops have done and will do. Again Carlyle's lack of knowledge shuts him off from the excitement and full meaning of the scene.

Yet the literature of natural science was not entirely unknown to Carlyle, and decades later he grew interested in what geology had to say. In 1865 he wrote to Ruskin, offering to visit him and "take a serious Lecture from you on what you really know, and can give me some intelligible outline of about the Rocks, – *bones* of our poor old Mother; which have always been venerable and strange to me. Next to nothing of rational could I ever learn of the subject. That of a central fire, and a molten sea, on which all mountains, continents, and strata are spread floating like so many hides of leather, knocks in vain for admittance into me these forty years; who of mortals can really believe such a thing!" (quoted in Cate 1982, 108–9; spelling normalized). Ruskin replied encouragingly, recommending the tenth chapter of Lyell's *Elements of Geology.* The visit, which Carlyle said he enjoyed, took place within a month.

His friend John Tyndall, Alpinist and professor of science, persuaded the little-travelled Carlyle to winter on the French Riviera at the foot of the Maritime Alps in 1866–67. Carlyle was struck by the mountains' forms. Of course he despised the fad for "scenery," he wrote to Ruskin, "but I must own, these pinnacles … are the strangest and grandest things of the mountain kind I ever saw; bare-rocks, sharp as steeples, jagged as if hewn by lightning; most grim, perilous, cruel; 'sitting there,' I sometimes say, 'like so many witches of Endor, *naked* to the waist, but therefrom with the amplest petticoats of dark or bright green' … a really fine scene ... which I never yet raise my eyes to without something of surprise and recognition" (quoted in Cate, 126). This description, imaginative and observant of landscape, is most striking in how radically it differs from the philosophical view of nature in *Sartor Resartus*. Except for the biblical simile, the mountains are observed for themselves, not as a veil before the Infinite or the symbol of an Idea. We may wonder how different Carlyle's work might have been if he had seen such mountains earlier.

EMERSON'S BIFOCALS

Ralph Waldo Emerson may be "the most important writer and thinker [Americans] have had" (Adams 1954, 130), but the seeker after his views on nature will often need to remind himself that "a foolish consistency is the hobgoblin of little minds." Scholars have pointed out radical ambiguities in the traditions Emerson inherited and used. The conflicts between the pietistic and regulatory sides of Puritanism (Miller 1940) and between the dynamic and static aspects of the Romantics' organic metaphor (Adams) correspond roughly to the tension between his concepts of nature as idea and as fact. He left us not a settled statement but a series of observations spanning a quarter of a century. Still, the importance of Emerson to nineteenth-century thought, and of nature to him, requires that we follow his peregrinations.

In 1833 Emerson made his first trip to Europe, visiting Italy, Switzerland, France, and Britain. Armed with a letter of introduction from J.S. Mill, he went to see Carlyle, after which they began a correspondence that fills two volumes. That fall, Emerson commenced work on the "little book" called *Nature* (1836), his principal contribution to the question at hand. In the Jardin des Plantes in Paris he had been "moved by strange sympathies; I say continually, 'I will be a naturalist'" (Emerson 1957, 473). But what did this mean to him at the time? He read Carlyle, Coleridge, the mystic Emmanuel Swedenborg, and the Platonist Ralph Cudworth while he was composing. That in his first letter to Carlyle (1834) Emerson thanks him "for the brave stand you have made for Spiritualism" in *Sartor Resartus* (Norton 1883, 1:13) suggests that he was drawn to the concept of nature as a symbol of the immaterial, though external nature sounds real and meaningful when he writes to his fiancée (1835) that "a sunset, a forest, a snow-storm, a certain river-view, are more to me than many friends" (Emerson 1957, 19). This bifocal view of nature – as idea, and as fact – would characterize Emerson's thinking.

Nature begins with an epigraph from Plotinus – "Nature is but an image or imitation of wisdom" – yet the core of the introduction is empirical inquiry, and optimism about finding fresh answers to the question "To what end is nature?" First, says Emerson, we must define it. He anticipates "no confusion" in using both the "philosophical" sense – everything that is *not me* is nature – and the "common" meaning of "essences unchanged by man" (21–2). Despite his European travels, Emerson's nature was for the most part the New England woodlands variety, treated transcendentally, but he begins with the only area of the Great regularly available to him: the heavens. "The stars awaken a certain reverence," afford us "the perpetual presence of the sublime" (as Kant had realized), and furnish a sense of solitude: "If a man would be alone, let him look at the stars" (23). It is implied that, for the philosophical or poetic soul at least, "the world is too much with us"; nature offers an opportunity for spiritual withdrawal, as in a retreat.

Famous for its "transparent eyeball," "currents of the Universal Being," and transcendentalism, *Nature* has also had practical consequences for conservationist and environmental thought. If nature is understood as "the integrity of impression made [on us] by manifold natural objects" (a psychological, somewhat circular definition), then the woodcutter and the poet do not see the same tree, and no one "owns" the landscape, though the feeling perceiver has "a property in the horizon" (23). Nature also serves the human need for sensual, spiritual, and intellectual beauty ("The health of the eye seems to demand a horizon") and provides us with the materials of art and language. This applies not only to the conventionally pretty aspects of nature, but to the bleak and barren. "Crossing a bare common, in snow puddles, at twilight, under a clouded sky," Emerson "enjoyed a perfect exhilaration"; he was as pleased with "the graces of the winter scenery" as with those of summer, for "each moment of the year has its own beauty" (24, 28). From such a view of nature – similar to Thomson's – to the idea of declaring "national parks" was no great distance.

Interspersed with these statements, however, are others, less acceptable to environmentalists, expressing a simple optimism about humanity, and sometimes an arrogance about our place in nature. Despite the introduction's declaration of intellectual independence, much of this sounds like Blake, Coleridge, or Carlyle, as when Emerson writes that "Nature always wears the colors of the spirit," so that "The sky is less grand as it shuts down over less worth in the population," or that "Nature is the symbol of spirit" (25, 31). The idea that nature has a "ministry" to us, in which "all the parts incessantly work into each other's hands for the profit of man," belongs to a tradition of biblical exegesis that includes Pope's *Essay on Man* (25). In suggesting that a man looking at a far horizon "beholds somewhat as beautiful as his own nature," however, Emerson climbs out on a more fragile limb, which dips precariously as he claims that "the whole of nature is a metaphor of the human mind" (24, 35). This has some basis in Plotinus, but is a long way from either the *divine* Ideas that Carlyle saw embodied in nature or from Emerson's own epigram on America: "Great country, diminutive minds."

Emerson sent a copy of *Nature* to Carlyle, who praised it and lent it to friends. In 1840, however, he heard from Harriet Martineau that Emerson "was 'fallen into a very strange state in regard to External Nature'; taking it upon him, as I understood, to deny that poor old External Nature existed at all, 'other than relatively'; – a most questionable state in these times in these latitudes!" (Carlyle 1970, 228). Whatever this summary of Emerson's views was based on, it was not "The American Scholar" (1837), most of whose natural philosophy can be paralleled in Pope. Nature is viewed as the primary influence on the scholar's mind, a power "resembl[ing] his own spirit" yet "the opposite of the soul": the seal that makes the print. If nature gives our minds their laws, "Know thyself" and "Study nature" are the same counsel (Emerson 1957, 65–6). Perhaps Martineau (if not just paraphrasing conversation or *Nature*) was thinking of Emerson's Divinity School Address (1838), which holds that "when the mind opens and reveals the laws which traverse the universe ... then shrinks the great world at once into a mere illustration and fable of this mind" (101).

Emerson's poems, journals, and essays of those years look at nature in manifold ways. His journal entry of 6 November 1837 uses the wonders of the woods to refute the idea that "miracles have ceased" (1957, 84); intensely curious about nature's secrets, Emerson wishes geology and botany would give him more help. He had in fact begun to read Lyell in 1836 (Beach 1956, 338), and sounds like a uniformitarian when he calls sun, wind, and water "the forces that wrought then and work now" (Emerson 1957, 84). In the very year of the Divinity School Address he complains that "poets of nature" are not good naturalists, and marvels at how quickly a moonlit walk removes him from the human world. Far from shrinking to a mental fable, nature "grows over" him: "I become a moist, cold element" (88). Emerson's phrasing varied with the point he was arguing, and his views evolved. If we want to know his whole truth we have to stay for the whole picture.

In 1840, for example, he decided to "write a new chapter on Nature" as a "cipher" of universal religious history, asserted that "every natural fact is trivial until it becomes symbolical" (143), and published "Wood-Notes I," which speaks reverently of the devotion of a "forest seer" to the Maine woods. In the second part of the poem (1841), a pine tree chants in an ancient Ur-language of the "genesis of things," and of a "rushing metamorphosis" that melts "solid nature to a dream," though the principles endure (Emerson 1886, 33–4). Is this Lyell, or the view of which Martineau wrote to Carlyle? Nature's connotations remain benevolent and protective; to orphaned, exiled man, who thinks the horizon empty and nature foolish, she says, Come to me and be healed by the "primal mind" (37). Here man is a poor, small figure, not *supplying* a mind that comprehends and dissolves nature, but *needing* one.

Indeed, in the 1840s Emerson's views of nature seem to enlarge, while humanity shrinks. The "motto" for the essay "Experience" (1844) depicts "dear Nature" taking puzzled "little man" by the hand and reassuring him. "Mountains are great poets," writes Emerson; "Space is felt as a great thing. There is some pinch and narrowness to us, and we laugh and leap to see the world, and what amplitudes it has" (1957, 220). Part of the amplitude that dwarfs us is temporal: "Geology" has shown us the "secularity [antiquity] of Nature," he says in the 1844 essay on that subject (275). Emerson was by then feeling the impact of contemporary science: the 1845 journal entry "Metamorphosis is the law of the universe" (276) accords with other images of change in the 1840s; the 1849 edition of *Nature* replaces Plotinus with some lines on evolution. A journal entry in 1849 distinguishes three stages in the human apprehension of nature: Greek deification, Christian revilement, and the modern tendency to "marry mind to Nature" or "put Nature under the mind" (Emerson 1912, 8:78). His attitude towards this Idealistic tendency is not clear.

In 1850 Emerson formally recognized a division in his philosophy of nature in "The two Statements, or Bipolarity." "I affirm melioration," he wrote: the progressive tendency of natural selection. "I affirm also the self-equality of Nature": its universality or absoluteness. "But," he admitted, "I cannot reconcile these two statements" (Emerson 1957, 320), any more than we can reconcile his spiritual and physical ideas of nature. Later that year, he considered how views of nature had changed in his lifetime. In his "real or imagined" youth, those "who spoke to [him] of Nature were religious, and made it so, and made it deep: now it is to the young sentimentalists frippery, and a milliner's shop has as much reason and worth" (323). Whatever the full dynamics of this disillusion may have been, the immediate stimulus was some New England graffiti, a few months after his first glimpse of the Mississippi.

In the essay "Fate" (1852), Emerson looks at nature in a new way that reflects his accumulated reading and experience. "Nature," he has learned, "is no sentimentalist"; it is "what you may do," or "the tyrannous circumstance," that is, Fate (332, 336). This is a very different image from the guiding mother of the 1840s. The idea of evolution remained prominent. In "Works and Days" (1856) he considers the words in various languages for "the face of the world." The Latin *natura* contained a "delicate future tense," "*about to be born*," whereas the Greek *kosmos* (whose use by Humboldt he noted) expressed "that power which seems to work for beauty alone" (367). Science's emphasis on the antiquity of nature reappears in the poem "Seashore" (1856), where the sea speaks of its own great age and power.

"The Adirondacs" (1858), a verse journal of a camping trip in upstate New York, forms a strange coda to the drift of his statements about nature in the 1840s and 1850s. It is a straightforward tribute to physical nature as a stern but rewarding teacher, until the news that the transatlantic cable has reached America turns it into a paean to man's civilizing influence on nature. Suddenly the optimism of the 1830s reappears, stronger than ever. "We flee away from cities, but we bring / The best of cities with us," as when "From a log-cabin stream Beethoven's notes / On the piano, played with master's hand." Will we sacrifice our arts on the altar of nature, "Or count the Sioux a match for Agassiz? / O no, not we!" says Emerson. For the moment it seems possible to have the best of both worlds: in the wilderness, art will keep bear and snake, flood and fire, at bay. As the scholars head back to their libraries, Nature gives "Almost a smile," which Emerson may have misread (1886, 184–5).

Besides his own travels to Europe and the West – he reached California in 1871 – Emerson read travel literature. In reply to a request from Carlyle, he recommended Alexander Henry on Canada, F.A. Michaux on the South, and Frémont on the West. But he noted Thoreau's conviction of the "indifference of all places" in his elegy for his old friend (1862), recalling Thoreau's remark that he could see most of the phenomena Kane found in the Arctic, such as red snow, around Concord. This was not ignorance or xenophobia, Emerson believes; Thoreau thought "that the best place for each is where he stands" (1957, 387). Emerson does not offer his own view, but notes that while Thoreau was a keen observer of the natural world, "the meaning of Nature was never attempted to be defined by him" (388). He must have reflected how unlike his own career that was.

John Ruskin's troubled relationship with Victorian geology was discussed in chapter 11, but he is better known for the aesthetic philosophy that grew out of his scientific and religious interests. All of these strands are intertwined in *Modern Painters*.

Volume one (1843) treats briefly "Of the Sublime," hoping to correct earlier writers and simplify aesthetics by eliminating "the sublime" as a separate category. Sublimity, Ruskin argues, "is not a specific term ... Anything which elevates the mind is sublime, and elevation of mind is produced by the contemplation of greatness ... Sublimity is, therefore, only another word for the effect of greatness upon the feelings" (1903, 3:128), and "greatness" can take many forms: material, ideational, aesthetic, emotive. For example, the defiance of danger or death (not the fear of them) is sublime: Ruskin joins those uneasy with this aspect of Burke's *Enquiry*. The distinction between beauty and sublimity is discarded: they are "not distinct" qualities, but a continuum and a sector thereof. "The highest beauty is sublimity" (129–30). They are different but also continuous, then; there is no essential disagreement with Addison's *Spectator* essay (no. 412) on this point. Ruskin, engaged in a larger project than Addison – "investigations of the ideas of truth, beauty, and relation" – wants to treat sublimity as a "mode or manifestation" of beauty, not as an independent entity.

Part Two, "Of Truth," moves from general propositions to specific applications that Ruskin believes "are more important." His professed approach to nature is empirical and exact, yet "the duty of a painter is the same as that of a preacher": "Both are commentators on infinity" (157). Claude gives only a puny idea of the sea, Salvator of the mountains, because they did not revere physical detail: "There is no evidence of their ever having gone to nature with any thirst" (169). The love that is the prerequisite of great landscape painting is rooted in a precise knowledge of physical nature. Later sections discuss and demand "Truth of Space." The most important of these here is section four, "Of Truth of Earth," although the sections on skies and water (sections three and five) also have relevant material.

Ruskin wants landscape painters to give a "faithful representation of the facts and forms of the bare ground, considered as entirely divested of vegetation" (425). Some earlier commentators on the Great expressed interest in bareness, but Ruskin makes it an integral part of his aesthetics. Bare ground is the landscape painter's nude (vegetation, water and clouds being the clothes and hair), and "in all sublime compositions," this anatomy "must be seen in its naked purity" (425. Those who know the story of Ruskin's wedding night will see the irony here.). The "first grand principle of the truth of the earth" is that mountains are "muscular action," while plains are repose. Later he (like de Saussure and Mary Wollstonecraft) calls mountains the "bones of earth," but the general idea remains: they are fundamental structures within earth's flesh that form and move it (427).

Yet, says Ruskin, Turner's most sublime painting was of "the power, majesty, and deathfulness" of another area of the Great, "the open, deep, illimitable sea" in *The Slave Ship* (573). Perhaps this judgment – after all the emphasis on mountains – was what led Ruskin to generalize in the "Theoretic" section of volume two (1846) on the need for some approximation to infinity in art, in order to interest the soul in something better than the "miserable earth" (4:87; cf. Carlyle's "dog-cage"). The artist must transcend the material, lead us quasi-Platonically from earth to Truth by representing "the forms of all that we feel to be beautiful." For certain kinds of beauty are "types": earthly shadows of "moral perfections" (76). Infinity is a type of Divine Incomprehensibility, purity of Divine Energy, and so on. Mere vastness, a human measurement, is not accepted as implying infinity, but can produce sublimity. Though several of these relations are debatable, Ruskin provided new support for the deist view that contemplation of the natural world can unlock a spiritual dimension.

Volume four of *Modern Painters* (1856) concludes with the famous chapters on "Mountain Gloom" and "Mountain Glory" that Marjorie Nicolson turned into an historical progress of European attitudes towards mountains. "Mountain Gloom" might sound like a mere reconstruction of late-seventeenth-century attitudes, and "Mountain Glory" like a Romantic effusion, if both were not so deeply felt by Ruskin, so complex, and so clearly opposite sides of the coin of Creation. Mountains for Ruskin were radically ambivalent; he found in them a mirror not only of theology ("sermons in stones") but of psychology as well.

"The Mountain Gloom," for example, argues that although mountains were "calculated for the delight, the advantage, or the teaching of men," when we note "what actual effect upon the human race has been produced by the generosity, or the instruction of the hills," the illusions of von Haller, Rousseau, and Wordsworth are dispelled (Ruskin 1904, 6:385). The Alps' divine beauty looks down on "foulness," "torpor," "anguish" and "rocky gloom"; an English cottage "in the midst of its dull flat fields" is much happier (6:388–9). Mountain dwellers are "especially" subject to a "peculiarity of feeling," a "capability of enduring, or even delighting in, the contemplation of objects of terror" (393), for example grim religious art, or grotesqueness of any kind. This taste he blames on disease, Catholicism, "rudeness of life," and environmental influences. Mountain districts exhibit "sometimes the extreme of ugliness" in the "disorder" and "violence of the elements"; peasants who daily view "aspects of desolation" – floods, landslides, glaciers – easily accept cracked walls, dusty furniture and unsightly gardens as "natural" (409–10).

Ruskin says he has always found "a certain degree of inevitable melancholy" in Alpine districts, "nor could I ever escape from the feeling that here, where chiefly the beauty of God's working was manifested to men, warning was also given, and that to the full, of the enduring of His indignation against sin" (414). Like Aeneas bearing his father on his back from burning Troy, Ruskin has toted his cultural baggage to the wilds; suddenly Burnet and the seventeenth century seem close. Most men, Ruskin thinks, take a sunny view of nature and ignore its warnings, but "no good or lovely thing exists in this world without its correspondent darkness" (416); as Freud says, every brightly lit eminence has its dark shadow attached. We find the clearest images of heaven and hell in the mountains, for "where the beauty and wisdom of the Divine working are most manifested, there also are manifested most clearly the terror of God's wrath, and inevitableness of His power" (416).

For Ruskin, then, spiritual responses to great mountains are as natural as the spirituality of a sermon: mountains are texts for and about the soul. They promise, and they threaten. Here is one explanation of why some travellers find mountains, deserts, and polar wastes gloomy. Gothic novelists exploited this mood, which occurs as early as Deschamps's "Lay du desert d'Amours" (ca. 1500) in France. In the nineteenth century, however, European and North American writers made melancholy a theme of travel to Great landscapes, and this sombreness had some basis in the literature of exploration, at least from Cook's voyages onwards. In this sense, Nicolson's "gloom-to-glory" model is oversimplified. If one continues the story, beyond the Romantics and their mountains, gloom makes a comeback, although when the theological view that wild, tormented landscapes were reminders of the Fall lost ground, melancholy became a less-common response to the Great.

Having made his penance, Ruskin indulges his "excessive love" for mountains, "the beginning and the end of all natural scenery," in "Mountain Glory" (418). He enjoys low ("inferior") lands only insofar as they foreshadow mountains, and (though he knows that his own feelings are not "representative") believes it can be "proved" that the beauty of all landscape is proportionate to its mountainousness (420). Mountains are the "great cathedrals of the earth" and the schools under whose tutelage the Greeks and Italians achieved their "intellectual lead" in Europe; they have excited our purest religious emotions and given "inventive depth of feeling to art." Though mountains are *out of the way* of the masses of men," they are not irrelevant to humanity, or insalubrious (425–6, 435, 438).

If these (again) sound like seventeenth-century concerns, Ruskin's warning against infecting Swiss peasants with the "folly and vanity" of tourists is more contemporary, recalling Wordsworth's fears for the English Lake District (454). There may be good as well as evil in the process of modernization, he concedes, yet the greatest efforts of the human spirit have been associated with such aspects of "mountain gloom" as "a necessity for solitude" (457). Are we not, with our casinos in Alpine spas, setting up the moneychangers' tables in the "mountain temple"? Having lost our original "*awe* for the hills," we go to them now in an "experimental or exploring" or even "gymnastic" frame of mind (457–8) – all this, note, in the chapter on "Mountain Glory." His religious feelings now thoroughly aroused, Ruskin reviews the place of mountains in the Bible; the evocation of Aaron's death is particularly fine. The volume ends on this note of reasserting the holiness of mountains.

Ruskin's interest in Great landscapes – one could almost say in nature – always centred on the Alps, virtually ignoring other areas. One exception is "The Nature of Gothic" (1853), where he linked the "savageness" of Gothic art to its northern origins. Unlike Mediterranean art, that of the North is shadowed by the "wall of ice," "deathlike, its white teeth against us out of the polar twilight" where it was produced. There the workman's "fine finger-touch was chilled away by the frosty wind" and his eye "dimmed by the moor-mist," or "blinded by the sea-mist" (quoted in Unrau 1981, 37). From somewhere – perhaps accounts of the Franklin expedition – Ruskin had acquired strong feelings about polar wastes that were working on his imagination in ways analogous to the emotions of "Mountain Gloom."

Ruskin's views on nature, then, were more limited than those of the other writers discussed in this chapter – he presents a philosophy of mountains, not of nature – but we see his drift and can extrapolate. For him, as for Carlyle and Emerson, nature must be seen as the divine vestment, a symbol of the spirit, or it is dead, mechanical. Like them, he preached a return to an older view of nature, before rationalism sucked it dry of spirit. His version of this return was more radical than theirs, however, involving a fuller acceptance of the idea and implications of sinful, fallen nature than they envisioned. Ruskin contributed significantly to the darkening of Victorian natural philosophy; "Mountain Gloom" stands eternally confronting "Mountain Glory," as hell does heaven. It is not a question of passing through darkness on the way to light, as in Carlyle (or Nicolson): gloom and glory are equals, or equally true. Nevertheless, Ruskin made a strong case for viewing great mountains as messages of the utmost seriousness.

THE DANGEROUS GREAT: JOHN STUART MILL

Nature does not figure prominently in the writings of J.S. Mill, which concentrate on social questions; his one essay on nature appeared posthumously in *Three Essays on Religion* (1873). Yet he was more responsive to, and more deeply involved in evaluating, the natural world than his bibliography suggests. That he tinkered with "Nature" for much of the 1850s suggests that the subject was of more than passing concern, and the scant justice that the essay does to the role nature plays in his *Autobiography* (1924) arouses curiosity about whether his beliefs and feelings were in accord.

One of Mill's earliest memories (he would have been about seven) was of morning walks with his father in the meadows of Newington Green, during which he reported on his previous day's reading. Thus "with my earliest recollections of green fields and wild flowers, is mingled that of the account I gave him daily of what I had read the day before" (Mill 1944, 5). Among his favourite books at this time were Admiral Anson's account of his eighteenth-century circumnavigation, "a Collection (Hawkesworth's, I believe) of Voyages round the World, in four volumes, beginning with Drake and ending with Cook and Bougainville," *Robinson Crusoe* – all provided by James Mill as examples of resourceful men struggling against adversity – and the *Arabian Nights* (5–6). Mill remembered this as "a voluntary rather than a prescribed exercise," and believed that he acquired his love of rural nature on these walks. He was warned against natural religion, however, which his father had considered and rejected.

At the age of fourteen Mill spent a year in the south of France with the brother of his father's friend Jeremy Bentham. One of his most memorable adventures there was an expedition into the Pyrenees, during which he climbed the Pic du Midi de Bigorre. "This first introduction to the highest order of mountain scenery," Mill wrote, "made the deepest impression on me, and gave a colour to my tastes through life" (40). We might regard this statement as fashionably hyperbolic had wild nature not assisted later in restoring his mental and emotional health. He visited other European mountains during this stay and on later excursions to France, Germany, Switzerland, and Italy.

In his *Autobiography* Mill describes the nervous breakdown that he suffered at age 20 when he suddenly realized that not even the fulfillment of all his utopian projects would make him happy. Among other cures for depression he tried reading the Romantic poets. Byron did not help (Mill identified with the unhappiness of Harold and Manfred), but Wordsworth did. His poems "addressed themselves powerfully to one of the strongest of my pleasurable susceptibilities, the love of rural objects and natural scenery; to which I had been indebted not only for much of the pleasure of my life, but quite recently for relief from one of my longest relapses into depression. In this power of rural beauty over me, there was a foundation laid for taking pleasure in Wordsworth's poetry; the more so, as his scenery lies mostly among mountains, which, owing to my early Pyrenean excursion, were my ideal of natural beauty" (103–04). What helped Mill was not mere natural description, but Wordsworth's demonstration of how a love of nature could be "the very culture," the generative source, of pleasurable feeling, and a compensation for the loss of youthful freshness.

This personal narrative contrasts sharply with the formal statement of Mill's position in "Nature." Two busy decades intervened between reading Wordsworth and writing the essay: years that included his marriage, editorships, books, and meeting Carlyle and Emerson; another passed before he wrote the *Autobiography*, which therefore stands as his final statement on nature. The period during which he worked on "Nature" was a time when he was mainly concerned with the principles on which society should be organized: "The Enfranchisement of Women" and "On Liberty" were his principal publications in the 1850s.

The etymological, philosophical, and ethical speculations of "Nature" focus on whether nature is a proper guide to or "test of right and wrong" (Mill 1969, 13). We say "Follow Nature," yet, Mill notes, we everywhere alter it with bridges, ploughs, mines, buildings, lightning rods, breakwaters. Everyone approves such "triumphs of Art over Nature," in effect acknowledging that "the ways of Nature are to be conquered, not obeyed" (20). In fact, Mill argues, "the order of nature, in so far as un-modified by man, is such as no being, whose attributes are justice and benevolence, would have made, with the intention that his rational crea-tures should follow it as an example." *If* made by God, it was a "design-edly imperfect work," which man is to amend (25). Thus he finds the injunction to follow nature either unmeaning or immoral, since "the scheme of Nature ... cannot have had, for its sole or even principal ob-ject, the good of human or other sentient beings." We should not *follow* nature, then, but try to make it conform to "a high standard of justice and goodness" (65).

These were original conclusions for natural philosophy, yet they did not spring *ex nihilo*. Anyone who had been following the literature of ge-ology and paleontology since about 1830 – and Mill followed everything – had a basis for concluding that nature was "imperfect," that is, unfin-ished. The major achievement in English poetry of the 1850s, Tenny-son's "In Memoriam," which probably influenced Mill, shows how evolutionary science affected general attitudes towards nature and reli-gion (see chapter 18).

One of the inferences Mill drew from his reasonings was that human-ity must shake off certain "natural prejudices" founded on strong but ul-timately irrelevant feelings, such as "the astonishment, rising into awe, which is inspired ... by any of the greater natural phenomena" (26). His examples are storms, mountains, deserts, ocean, and sky – i.e., the Great – and the emotions mentioned are exactly those stipulated by Addison. For Mill the moral activist, the problem is that these phenomena dwarf humanity, making all our works seem insignificant and presumptuous. That is, the Great does not expand us; it shrinks us. "[W]hat makes these phenomena so impressive," Mill insists, "is simply their vastness." Mere size "constitutes their sublimity," a feeling "more allied to terror than to any moral emotion" (27). Accepting Burke's analysis, Mill uses it to make *his* point. Awe of the Great must, he says, be distinguished from "admiration of excellence," a moral attitude. Nature is amoral; the great natural phenomena exhibit a "perfect and absolute recklessness," obvi-ously a danger to society (28).

This is a significant darkening of the Victorian outlook on nature; evi-dently agnostics and Christians could share some ground on this ques-tion, though the shadow falls from quite a different direction than in Ruskin's "mountain gloom." Mill felt bound to point out to Carlyle that, friendship apart, they differed on many important philosophical matters, and Carlyle decided that Mill was not what he had thought. It is no surprise to learn that Thomas Hardy, who gave "chastened sublimity" the local habitation and name of Egdon Heath, was influenced by Mill's *Three Essays* (Rutland 1962, 67). The two men's paths crossed briefly in 1865 when Hardy saw Mill speaking in public and observed that "his vast pale brow ... sloped back like a stretching upland" (65).

It is not possible, then, to bring the natural philosophies of these four men into a single clear focus. Carlyle remained roughly faithful to Goethe's views, Emerson was at times a Kantian, at times something else, Ruskin moved back towards Christianity, and Mill insisted that we were finished with all that. As if to emphasize the chaotic state of the subject, T.H. Huxley, an advocate of Darwin, began his editorial in the first number of *Nature, A Weekly Illustrated Journal of Science* (4 November 1869), where one might have expected a manifesto of evolution, by quoting Goethe's aphorisms on nature (ca. 1780?). This "wonderful rhapsody," writes Huxley, "has been a delight to me from my youth up," and, despite some pantheism, its poetic vision "of the wonder and the mystery of Nature" remains valid (1870, 10–11). He could think of "no more fitting preface" for the new journal and in fact added little to Goethe, whose views resemble Shaftesbury's in some respects. The spectacle of this avant-garde Victorian endorsing Goethe's essentially eighteenth-century view of nature in a scientific context might puzzle the most enthusiastic advocate of "progress" or "schools" in western philosophies of nature.

13

Leaving Blanks:
American Novelists and the Great

By 1800 North America had become part of the aesthetic phenomenon that Hardy means Egdon Heath to represent: the supercession of ancient standards of beauty by something larger, grimmer, and stronger. The influence of Shaftesbury and Burke was felt in the colonies; William Bartram found some vastness and sublimity in the American southeast in the 1770s (Huth 1957, 10–11, 20–1). But the west was by its nature the true proving ground for the theories about reactions to Great landscape that originated when the spontaneous emotions of Alpine travellers were recollected in the tranquillity of England. Early explorers such as Lewis and Clark, Simon Fraser, and Alexander Mackenzie are therefore of as much interest here as Carlyle or Ruskin. Then, in the second third of the nineteenth century, American novelists began to work with both the theories and the accounts of exploration. Their popularity helped spread the ideas and attitudes that Hardy said would shape the itinerary of the tourist of the future.

FENIMORE COOPER AND NATURAL RELIGION

The first major American novelist was drawn to science and foreign travel in his youth. At Yale, Cooper studied chemistry with Professor Silliman (who later corresponded with Lyell) and astronomy, the latter interest being reinforced during his time in the navy (Clark 1959, 180, 198–9). These interests lasted: Cooper reviewed books by nautical explorers such as William Parry; in Europe he dined with Cuvier and Lyell in the 1820s. The introduction that Cooper wrote in 1832 for his popular novel *The Prairie* (1827) discusses "the geological formation" of the Great Plains, giving his references to the denudation of the land within the novel a firm grounding. In *Crater; or, Vulcan's Peak* (1847), another work with a Great setting, Cooper traces the precise operations and effects of volcanic action at one site in the Pacific Ocean. In *The Sea Lions* (1849), however, Cooper's penchant for seeing God in even the most realistic land- and seascapes takes over, and nature becomes a religious instructor.

Cooper wrote *The Prairie* without having visited the scenes it describes. His chief sources, the best and most recent available, were Biddle's edition of the Lewis and Clark journals, and Edwin James's account of Long's expedition, which were discussed in chapter 10. The two pictures were rather different: Lewis and Clark followed the fertile river bottoms, while Long traversed the high, dry country between drainages. It was this later, more arid portrait that suited Cooper's mood at the end of the Leatherstocking saga; his plot has various groups moving around the plains, depending on occasional springs for water. Cooper's introduction notes that whereas midwestern prairies tend to be fertile, the vast, bare plains west of the Mississippi "resemble the steppes of Tartary" and are "incapable of sustaining a dense population" (1985, 4). This "broad belt, of comparative desert," a "barrier" to Americans' westering ambitions, attracts Natty Bumppo in his last years.

Cooper reiterates the desertic character of the setting tirelessly. Like James, he is no lover of such a landscape, which he often describes as sterile and barren. For Cooper, though, the plains are not only a barrier to settlement but an historical and theological metaphor. Natty says that "the Lord has placed this barren belt of Prairie, behind the States, to warn men" of their folly in cutting down the eastern forests, turning the land into "a peopled desert" (24, 188). This oxymoron has even broader implications for the itinerant minister who preaches that the world is "no better than a desert" (87). Cooper also relates his "American desert" to those of the Middle East. The patriarch of the roving clan is Ishmael, who finds the lawlessness of these "endless wastes" congenial. Dr Battius notes that the "sandy deserts" of Egypt and Arabia "teem with the monuments" of departed glory, and Natty recalls hearing that the Holy Land was fertile until "the judgment" rendered it barren. Like Edwin James at the prairie mounds of Illinois, he wonders what civilization peopled these empty plains before the nomadic Sioux.

No answer is possible because Natty has no archaeological evidence, although to the narrator, too, these "wide and empty wastes" look like "an ancient country, incomprehensibly stripped" of population (355–6). What we have instead is a mood, an *Ortgeist*, or spirit of place, compounded of Cooper's reading and Natty's imagined lifetime of experience, expressed as qualities of landscape. The vast, "bleak plain" is "naked," "desolate," "monotonous," oceanic, deceptive. Natty and the prairie share "an appearance of induration" such as Hardy would give Egdon Heath (16); both, having declined from better days, stand as memorials to "the frailty of existence, and the fulfilment of time" (356). Cooper, without having seen a desert, empathized with the melancholy of some of those who had.

And yet his prairie is finally granted some of the qualities later attributed to real deserts by their most ardent admirers. Near the book's midpoint, the narrator suddenly announces that throughout the action "the Prairies had lain in the majesty of perfect solitude" (198). If that is a quality we were to assume, it is one that stands apart from the others – barrenness, sterility, dreariness – he has listed up to that point, and continues to chant. The other unexpected reaction to the prairie occurs when Natty explains his decision not to return to the "waste and wickedness" of the settlements: "If I live in a clearing, here it is one of the Lord's making" (370). So the western plains, for all their harshness, are godly in the eyes of the ageing hero; *their* bareness is a divine ordinance. This is a note heard in mid-nineteenth-century desert travellers – that it has an aura of spirituality, that one feels closer to God there – but not in James; Cooper, a long way from the prairies, added it to his principal source. Perhaps it was a leap of faith: that the desert might retain its biblical attribute of holiness.

From Cooper's years in Europe came several volumes of travel notes, among which *Gleanings* from Switzerland in 1828 contains some interesting responses to Great nature. For the most part, his reactions, emphasizing views and spiritual uplift, were what might be expected of a literary traveller to the Alps in his time. We hear enough of the "sublime" or "grand," the "beautiful" and the "picturesque" to see that Cooper knew these distinctions, though he treats them casually. The "thrill" of the Alps arises from their mystery, he says, and from the pleasure we take in objects that lead us to contemplate the invisible (1980, 13). Their pure "new world" affords us "a glimpse, through the windows of heaven," so that we regard them with "religious awe" (22–3, 41); Cooper's almost eighteenth-century penchant for natural religion had surfaced. For him, the Swiss Alps were a "vast natural altar to God" (98), with signs of spirituality everywhere: crosses, shrines, chapels, pilgrims. Moved by the Alps' "chastened grandeur," he often "wonders" at the deceptive scale of the mountains and glaciers (41, 56), finding there both "frightful beauties" and "magnificent solitudes" (213, 233).

Occasionally a more individual touch appears among the familiar epithets. Cooper could experience a climb up the Righi Staffel as a chapter out of *Pilgrim's Progress*, then try to explain the origin and movement of glaciers scientifically, or parallel the Alps' sublimity with that of Niagara Falls. The separate remarks are not unusual, but before Ruskin the combination of religion, science, and aesthetics in one writer is. Cooper is most surprising when he surveys an Alpine plateau, "treeless and almost shrubless," and concedes it an "exquisite nakedness" (93). His tour of the cantons stretched from summer into fall, however, and as the weather changed so did the mountains and his feelings about them. One gloomy October day the Alps looked "stormy and grim. I did not like to examine them in that state, for they had the air of friends whose faces had become cold" (261. It is amusing to hear Cooper, an easterner, agreeing with an English couple about the lamentable lack of mountains and "grand scenery" in America; 70).

Several components of *The Prairie* reappear in *The Crater; or, Vulcan's Peak*, with different emphases. Again there is a geological base, now more prominent in the text and more central to the action, set mostly on an active volcanic formation in the Pacific. Since his studies in natural science at Yale, Cooper had read Humboldt and Lyell (Scudder 1947; Clark 1959). Apparently he used the fourth edition (1835) of Lyell's *Principles of Geology* as his guide to volcanic phenomena (Clark 1960, 273). Again the setting is one of "utter nakedness," "dreariness," and "desolation" (Cooper 1962, 59), but this time we are quickly shown the spiritual concomitants of such a landscape. In one of many echoes of Defoe, Mark and Bob, shipwrecked on a barren reef, turn to God in their need. Indeed, *The Crater* may be seen as *Robinson Crusoe* rewritten with a Lyellian consciousness. When a storm carries off Bob, leaving Mark "with none between him and his God," he kneels "on the naked rock" and prays (125). His solitude in the great ocean under the vault of heaven leads Mark to meditate deistically on the "vast and beneficent design" of the universe (139).

When earthquakes promote his reef into an archipelago and new volcanoes rise into mountains, Mark reveres this "exhibition of the power of nature" and decides to stay rather than attempt escape, for "amid such scenes" one feels "nearer to the arm of God" (167). More devout now, he sails his dinghy towards the "sublime" island-mountain that he names Vulcan's Peak, feeling "secret awe" at the "dread majesty" of the scene (175, 179): standard Great aesthetics. Atop the peak he finds a veritable Garden of Eden. Later, after Bob reappears, they make contact with the outside world and establish a colony in the archipelago. At this point the parallel with Adam and Eve becomes explicit, and the novel turns into a social fable. What is striking here is that the characters are happiest at first when they are a few people engaged in reclaiming barren land. As barrenness yields to lush verdure, as desert becomes jungle, happiness is replaced by various kinds of social rot – sectarian strife, corruption, litigiousness, journalism – which Cooper finally sinks in the Pacific.

Just two years before his death, Cooper used the Great to teach another young man religion. Roswell Gardiner, the hero of *The Sea Lions* and a rationalist in spiritual matters, will not be accepted by his pious sweetheart until he accepts the full mystery of Christianity. To achieve this Cooper sends him on a sealing ship to the Antarctic; the ocean, after all, possesses "many of the aspects of eternity" (Cooper 1849, 1:119). Cooper portrays Tierra del Fuego, gateway to the region, as a strikingly desolate snow-covered mass of rock, in an ocean like a "rolling prairie" (182). Gardiner climbs Cape Horn, America's "Ultima Thule," to view the "grand spectacle" of three oceans meeting (187); Cooper liked to give his readers mountain vistas (Huth 1957, 33). In the ice pack, the bergs are as "glorious" and "sublime" as the Alps, signalling God's "might and honour" in that "seeming void" (Cooper, 194, 197), and the volcanic island where the seals gather is "majestic," "barren," and "grand" (199): defining attributes of the Great. In this region of sterile "grandeur," Gardiner will learn humility and true religion (2:17).

He and two companions climb the volcano, finding "sublimity" and "beauty" in its "vastness" and wildness, which they think "incline one to worship God" as much as any qualities could (22). That inclination increases when they try to escape north through a dangerous icefield by moonlight, a "scene of natural grandeur" they regard with "awe," compounded of "admiration" and "dread" (53). Gardiner becomes more religious during the sufferings of an enforced winter on the island, and while sailing past an active volcano on the way out. Cooper's conclusion, that Gardiner acquired true religion by learning "his own insignificance" in the whole scheme of creation, mirrors his preface, where he attacks human indifference to "sublime natural phenomena" that manifest God (1:iii), and calls the roll of explorers – Hudson, Parry, Ross, Franklin – who have brought His polar wonders to our attention. Cooper, then, uses the Great to promote a conservative Christian outlook, the opposite of Mill's position. While *The Sea Lions* is not compelling as theological argument (how does Antarctica lead Gardiner not just to

God but to Jesus?), it draws its impressive homiletic scenery from the narratives of polar navigators.

Cooper's development shows a rough curve from scientific to religious views of nature, with some attempt to combine them. What remains constant is an interest in Great phenomena: desert plains, the ocean, mountains, the Antarctic. Cooper was certain that they were important, and that they pointed to a transcendental truth.

WASHINGTON IRVING'S EXPANSIVENESS

When the aristocrat of American letters returned home in 1832 after a seventeen-year absence, he wanted to see the West while it was "still in a state of pristine wildness" (Nash 1982, 72–3). In Europe he had made his name by setting European folktales in the eastern United States. Now, with critics encouraging him to be more *American*, he wanted to break out of the Atlantic literary world. What began as a tour of the Northeast with two European friends grew by chance into a trek westwards as far as Oklahoma, where Irving, used to salons and polished company, acquitted himself well. His journal contains extensive notes on flora and fauna, as well as on people and scenes. He described a Missouri hill as "limestone rock and stones full of shells and miniature basalt like giant causeway – boundless view of silent Praries [*sic*]" (Irving 1986, 5:78), revealing an amateur interest in geology and a knowledge of the Giant's Causeway in Ireland, an object of scientific study since the eighteenth century. On this expedition, a "turning point" in Irving's career, he was sufficiently "struck" by "the great West" to want to portray "the boundless and the sublime in western nature" for readers (1964, xvi; 1961, viii, x).

Irving made extensive "Notes concerning the Far West," drawing heavily on Lewis and Clark, to enrich *A Tour on the Prairies*; many of his journal entries, revised and expanded, are also recognizable. Though more interested in events and anecdotes about colourful people than in landscape, Irving, like his companions, was impressed by the plains. A "grand prairie" he described as an "immense extent" of rolling grassland with a few scattered groves of trees like distant ships, "the landscape deriving sublimity from its vastness and simplicity" (Irving 1967, 107). The "Great Prairie," "vast and beautiful," elicited a broad aesthetic generalization: "There is always an expansion of feeling in looking upon these boundless and fertile wastes" (183). While "and fertile" reminds us that he never reached the barrens, we have no reason to think that

Addison's "vast Desarts" had to be barren as well as unpopulated; the point is that boundless vistas expand our spirits.

Other areas of the Great figure in Irving's *Tour.* He and his friends (like other observers) repeatedly noted how much the prairie resembled an ocean, especially during a tempest. "A thunder-storm on a prairie, as upon the ocean," Irving noted, "derives grandeur and sublimity from the wild and boundless waste over which it rages and bellows" (103). Addison thought that we are more pleased by the Great when some beauty or novelty – such as a sky "adorned with stars and meteors" – is joined with it; this held true for Irving, who especially recalled the "fine starlight, with shooting meteors" on one calm night. "It is delightful," he says, "in thus bivouacking on the prairies, to lie awake and gaze at the stars; it is like watching them from the deck of a ship at sea, when at one view we have the whole cope of heaven." But this particular night, without knowing why, he felt "unusually affected by the solemn magnificence of the firmament; and seemed … to inhale with the pure untainted air an exhilarating buoyancy of spirit, and, as it were, an ecstasy of mind" (216, 217), which sounds like a quasi-religious experience.

Two of Irving's companions also published accounts of the trip, and a third, the count de Pourtales, left letters and a journal of the trip (in French) that were published in translation over a century later. The count appears to have felt some of the same emotions as Irving about the landscape. Ten days out, on the Missouri-Kansas border, he describes the prairies as "the steppes of the New World," "oceans of enamelled greenery" with a "flowing, expansive, monotonous grandeur" (34). Three weeks later, the prairies seemed "eternal and majestic," and the view from a hill "stretched to infinity" (53).

Irving went on to write two books on the Far West, which he had not seen: a popular history of the fur trade on the Pacific coast, and a biography of Captain Bonneville, an explorer. John Jacob Astor, an old friend, suggested the first project (for obvious motives), supplied Irving with manuscript records of his firm, and provided a place to write: his own house, where Irving met Bonneville. Astor's collection of reports and letters from traders and explorers supplemented published travel narratives and Irving's own knowledge. His tour of the prairies had taught him one essential emphasis. In planning the work, he wrote himself a memo: "Everything on a large scale, talk of distance" (Irving 1961, 1:x). Only a small part of *Astoria* (titled after the trading settlement Astor had founded on the Oregon coast), then, represents first-hand experience; west of Oklahoma Irving relied on secondary sources.

Chapter 22, on "the great American desert," combines accounts of early expeditions with extrapolations from Irving's own time on the prairies. He begins with a familiar analogy, enlivened by contemporary science: the western plains are "a region almost as vast and trackless as the ocean," whose "ancient floor" it is "supposed by geologists" to have been (Irving 1964, 210). Eureka! The cliché turns out to have been carrying a concealed truth all along. Irving, who had evidently been reading travel books as well as geology, then gives this simile a social analogue. Much of the West is and will probably remain "a lawless interval between the abodes of civilized man, like the wastes of the ocean or the deserts of Arabia" (211), the haunts of pirates and Ishmaelites, as in Cooper. Both comparisons are repeated. He also likens the western plains to "the immeasurable steppes of Asia" (as Pourtales does), and the badlands to "the ruins of a world": Burnet's response to the Alps.

But what kind of a land is it *essentially*? The competing visions of the American West as desert and as garden have been well chronicled; Irving assigns each its place. The "immense tract" between the Mississippi and the Rockies includes both "undulating and treeless plains" – the verdant prairies he had seen – and "desolate sandy wastes": the desert he had not (210). His remarks about lawlessness apply to the latter regions, away from the rivers and "vast pastoral tracts" that may be habitable (211). Of course it was all "desert" in the older sense, "a land where no man permanently abides," with occasional scarcities of food and moisture (210–11). Irving had, then, from his sources and experience, at least the beginnings of an ecological grasp of the West.

The Rockies represented for Irving "the limits ... of the Atlantic world" geologically and ideologically (211), the mountains beyond the Great Plains having inspired systems of belief not in the European lexicon. Various tribes made the Rockies the abode of the Supreme Being, Wacondah, or the location of paradise, the "happy hunting-grounds" (242–3). The religion is different, but once again high mountains are a spiritual realm. Although by this time *Astoria* has moved well beyond Irving's personal experience, his popularity made his portrait of the West influential.

EDGAR ALLEN POE: THE POWER OF WHITENESS

Poe's appetite for Gothic fiction such as Beckford's *Vathek* and for travel literature was what led him to write about the Great. His reviews of *Robinson Crusoe*, Irving's *Astoria*, J.L. Stephens's *Incidents of Travel in Egypt*, and J.N. Reynolds's account of Antarctic exploration signal the kind of interest in mountains, deserts, the sea and the poles that made something like *The Narrative of Arthur Gordon Pym of Nantucket* (1837) almost inevitable. In discussing Cooper's work he suggested that the theme of "life in the Wilderness" or "upon the ocean" has an "intrinsic and universal interest" (Poe 1975, 19). Add his love of sailing, his fascination with J.C. Symmes's theory of polar openings into the hollow earth, and the fact that the United States, having dispatched one Antarctic expedition in 1829, was preparing another for 1838, and the groundwork is complete.

In 1840 Poe dismissed his *Narrative* as "silly," and in some ways it is. The prefatory ruse – Pym, fearing that his own report would be disbelieved, says he allowed Poe to turn his facts into fiction – is flimsy; the narrative of Pym's voyage towards the South Pole is often careless; and the truncated ending, wherein Pym apparently disappears in Antarctica, leaves open the question of how he managed to reappear in America. But as usual Poe was operating proficiently at the level of dreams and images. French writers, at least, understood this: Charles Baudelaire translated the book in 1857 and Jules Verne wrote a sequel, *Le Sphinx des glaces* (1897). Running obsessively through Poe's *Narrative* are two themes: one of them, desolation, already established in accounts of Great landscape, the other, whiteness, about to become so. At the outset, Pym's friend Augustus's face, "paler than any marble," foreshadows the ending, in which white is piled on white (Poe 1975, 49). Poe's feel for the peculiar power of whiteness is one of the ways in which he anticipates Melville and Frost.

The full manifestation of that power is, however, withheld until blankness has been given a meaning, which can be found only within those who seek it. Pym, like Robinson Crusoe, longs for the sea despite an early misadventure, but there the resemblance ends. Crusoe dreams of profit; Pym, a post-Byronic sailor, is "most strongly" attracted to the "suffering and despair" of castaways. "My visions were of shipwreck and famine ... of a lifetime dragged out in sorrow and tears, upon some gray and desolate rock, in an ocean unapproachable and unknown" (57). To Defoe these yearnings would have appeared senseless, but not to readers of Crusoe's and others' adventures in 1840. "Such visions or desires – for they amounted to desires – are common," Pym has "since been assured, to the whole numerous race of the melancholy among men" (57). They did indeed become widespread among nineteenth-century literary characters. Pym describes his own temperament as "enthusiastic" and his imagination as "somewhat gloomy although glowing": a typical Poevian hero.

Pym's visionary side develops while he is stowed away. After reading an account of the Lewis and Clark expedition he falls asleep, awakes confused, then lapses into a "stupor" during which he has "terrific" dreams of "limitless," "forlorn and awe-inspiring" deserts where tall, grey, leafless tree trunks extend to the horizon (65). This Daliesque landscape yields to a more typical desert: Pym seems to stand, "naked and alone, amid the burning sand plains of Zahara [*sic*]" (66). Throughout the book Poe parallels desert travellers with mariners exploring high latitudes. Pym's ship visits Desolation Island, "one of the most dreary and utterly barren countries in the world," and Tristan d'Acunha, also barren, in the South Atlantic (165, 170–1). As the ship heads south, Pym offers a brief history of Antarctic exploration out of Cook, Reynolds, and Benjamin Morrell's *Narrative of Four Voyages* (1832), an important American source. They negotiate the pack ice and enter the warm, open polar sea of Symmes's and Poe's imaginings, where a gentle current sets towards the South Pole.

At 84° South (a latitude that would actually be *on* Antarctica in most longitudes) they discover Tsalal Island, a curious blend of Middle Eastern culture and landscape, Swiftian satire, real and imaginary Pacific islands, mountain-climbing adventures, and racial parable. Everything about it is black: the natives, their teeth, the stones, the fauna – even the nearby sea. The wealthier natives live in black tents like biblical patriarchs or modern Bedu. Most of the crew perish in an avalanche at the bottom of a narrow ravine reminiscent of the Siq at Petra, of which Poe had read in Stephens's *Incidents of Travel*. Pym and Dirk survive in an even narrower one. By cutting steps in the soft stone with knives, they manage to get out; later, Antarctic mountaineers, they climb down a sheer cliff, using pegs as pitons, handkerchiefs and shirts for belaying, to reach a place of "singular wildness" whose "huge tumuli," scorpions, and lava remind Pym of descriptions of the "dreary regions" around "degraded Babylon" (230). Poe is geologically precise about the types of black minerals encountered: granite, slate, marl, soapstone.

Pym and Dirk escape without realizing the meaning of the oddly shaped chasms and inscriptions they have found, but a postscript tells us that the former denoted the Ethiopian verb "to be shady," the latter, "to be white" in Arabic (241). Why those cultures came to express themselves thus in this place remains a mystery. Traces of Hebrew and Polynesian have been detected in the natives' speech. Interpretations of this whole remarkable section have ranged from Marie Bonaparte's rebirth image and Leslie Fiedler's homosexual consummation to Harold Beaver's parable of apartheid, but what is important here is the contrast between the dark, intestinal landscape of the island and the "wide and desolate Antarctic Ocean" onto which Pym and Dirk launch their canoe (234). They drift south, through showers of "fine white powder" that sounds like volcanic ashfall but induces numbness and "dreaminess of sensation," towards a mysterious curtain of grey vapour that gradually whitens to a "limitless cataract" falling silently from the heavens into the sea (237–8).

The "region of novelty and wonder" (236) into which they disappear is the area explored by Robert M. Adams in *Nil: Episodes in the Literary Conquest of the Void in the Nineteenth Century* (1966), though any "conquest" is the author's, not the characters'. As they enter the "white curtain" and white birds fly about, a cataract rushes them into an opening chasm, and the narrative ends with the appearance of a white shrouded giant in their path (238–9). Obviously this leaves a few questions open, but the lure of mystery is Poe's real subject here; his inscrutable Antarctica is, like Egdon Heath, a land of obscurity and nightmares. Though he knew no more of what was really at the Pole than did his readers, Poe transformed that ignorance into a strength by imaging it, as cartographers do, or did, with a white blank, "*blanc*-ness." White has begun to shift from its traditional western association with purity to its more typically modern connection with death, horror, or mystery, as in Frost's "Design." The whiteness of the veil connotes nullity, annihilation, absence, not bridal innocence. Nor is Pym's "white and deathly" vision an anomaly in Poe's world; many of his protagonists share it.

"The Journal of Julius Rodman" (1840), supposedly recounting "the First Passage of the Rocky Mountains" by a European in 1792 (Poe 1902, 9), is another vicarious foray into the Great. It is a less artistic fragment than *Arthur Gordon Pym*, which had the excuse of Antarctica's being *terra incognita* for breaking off mysteriously; Poe's lack of interest, or the constraints of *Burton's Gentleman's Magazine*, in which it was published, cut short Rodman's tale. Again Poe is the "editor" of papers inherited from the protagonist, whose motives he analyzes in the introduction. What drew Rodman to the West's vastness? A desire for the peace he could not find among men: Rodman, who "fled to the desert as to a friend" and traversed an "immense and often terrible wilderness" with "evident rapture," is another of the century's post-Byronic misanthropes (11, 13). His "morbid sensibility" and taste for the "dreary and savage aspects" of nature recall Pym and Roderick Usher, other seekers of the Poevian barren. Rodman sets off up the Missouri River into the "voluptuous beauty" of the prairies with an old voyageur as his guide (41–2), but the "Journal" breaks off with an account of a bear's attack in mountainous country still east of the Continental Divide; Rodman's Rockies, like Pym's Antarctic, remain a strategic blank.

The rest is silence, the quality on which Poe's other excursions into the Great focus. In his 1857 *Works* are two undated pieces called "Silence." One is a short poem about two kinds of silence, which are compared to "Body and soul" (Poe 1857, 39). One, named "No More," "dwells in lonely places," but we "Dread him not." The other type, which also "haunteth the lone regions where hath trod / No foot of man," casts a "shadow" that elicits the warning, "commend thyself to God!" In "Silence, – a Fable," a demon tells the speaker about "a dreary region in Libya, by the borders of the river Zaire." The scenery, as exotic as the geography is vague, resembles that of Pym's dream in the *Narrative*. By the river is a grey rock engraved with the word "Desolation"; on it sits a man whose features indicate "deity," "disgust with mankind," and "a longing after solitude": another superior misanthrope (295, 296). Nothing the demon can conjure up fazes the speaker, however, until he makes everything silent in the "vast illimitable desert" and engraves on the rock the word "Silence." The terrified speaker flees. Silence was often noted by early travellers to Great landscapes as one of their distinguishing qualities.

Poe's 1838 review of Stephens's *Incidents of Travel* shows that he read widely in the desert travellers early in his career. Of the older writers, he knew not only the standard authorities, Shaw and Pococke, but obscure writers such as Joseph Pitts and Henry Maundrell; of more recent ones, Karsten Niebuhr the Arabian explorer, John Jacob Burckhardt (who located Petra in 1812), the French scholar Volney, Chateaubriand, Lamartine, and the lighter, more popular James Morier. On their authority, he is able to twit Stephens for some topographical inaccuracies. This Poe, the well-read stickler for fact, is barely recognizable in the fiction, whose creator is never content until he has converted the explorers' laborious details into a vague, shifting dreamscape inhabited or traversed by a tortured soul.

EXPLORING BLANKNESS: HERMAN MELVILLE

Herman Melville is, of course, an important writer on the symbolic meanings of the sea, but even without that dimension he would figure here through his fascination with barren landscapes and his meta-phorical use of them. Like Poe, he was fascinated by the writings of John Stephens (see chapter 14), whom he mentions in *Redburn* (1849). Melville several times combines different areas of the Great to a degree that suggests the category was now fully developed, typically achieving this fusion by the way in which he uses white, the "colorless all-color" of Moby Dick and of the desert.

The characteristics that we consider "Melvillean" first coalesce in *Mardi* (1849), where the narrator jumps ship in the middle of the Pa-cific Ocean ("so much blankness to be sailed over") and enters a realm of romance and symbolism (Melville n.d., 1:10). In a small boat Taji reaches the Mardi archipelago and spends the rest of the novel sailing around it. Mardi turns out to be the planet with all its states and citizens: to voyage through Mardi is to think about the world (Feidelson 1959, 166–7). In Marvell's "The Garden" (1681) the mind is an ocean; Melville reverses the equation. This mind-sea, especially in its pale white, phosphorescent state, signifies "the infinite possibilities of the world" (Grenberg 1989, 31), but eventually "the world" fades: in "Sail-ing on," the narrator admits "It is the world of mind" he voyages (Melville n.d., 2:207).

The book also explores Great settings and conflates their various as-pects. When he first takes to his boat, Taji feels what most such venturers have felt, an "awful loneliness" on the "ocean moors of the Pacific," but his skiff is also "a goat among the Alps" (1:27, 34, 33). The narrator dreams of "prairies like rounded eternities," with Alps and Andes on the horizon, oceans all around, and far south the Antarctic: "Deathful, deso-late dominions" where the "bleak" sea, filled with warring iceberg navies, beats at the base of the ice barrier (2:33). The dreamer sails the "boundless expanses" of the heavens along with Homer, Shakespeare, and other great writers. Here, and in later meditations on the universe, Melville sounds like an early aesthetic philosopher – Lucretius or Fon-tenelle – but his rapture is disciplined by modern science. When the voyagers land on the Isle of Fossils, Babbalanja gives them a geological lecture on its volcanic origins.

Melville's predilection for white, two years before *Moby Dick* (1851), is interesting. Neither the "blankness" of the Pacific (blank=*blanc*=white; 1849, chapter 3), the "ghastly White Shark" (chapter 13), nor the "pal-lid white" ocean (chapter 38) has the benignity of traditional associa-tions of white; as in Poe, they connote mystery, and the terror of a *tabula rasa* that contains (or is) a vague message on which choices must be based. Enough of *dark* omens: the modern omen, more frightening still, is white. What was Good is no longer sure, or helpful. In *Mardi*, the ideal bride and quest-object, Yillah, is white, but so are curses, murderers, and troubled seas, which is disturbing. "Yillah, like the whale, is white, and with the same fundamental meaning," Feidelson argues (1959, 170). Yillah, the Absence made of many presences, is the question that Taji sails over the novel's horizon still trying to answer.

Whitejacket: The World in a Man-of-War (1850; the frigate is a microcosm of the good ship earth sailing through space) carries the obsession with white as the colour of ambiguity even farther. The narrator is named for his most distinctive piece of clothing; isolated, portless, Whitejacket seems to identify with his jacket, "white as a shroud" (1850, chapter 1). He punningly considers dyeing it to escape its blankness ("You must hie to the dyers and be dyed, that I may live": chapter 19) but does not do so. The mast-head is his "Pisgah-top" (the mountain in Jordan from which Moses glimpsed the Promised Land); when he falls thence into the ocean, he rips open his jacket "as if I were ripping open myself" (Melville 1850, 369). The jacket's whiteness suggests both the "infinite potentialities" of Moby Dick, and Whitejacket's "fear of annihilation" (Feidelson 1959, 181).

Although some aspects of *Mardi* and *Whitejacket* foreshadow Melville's *chef d'oeuvre*, in *Moby Dick* the shadows are deeper. The novel opens with a tribute to the power of pools and oceans to attract the human spirit, throughout history and myth. But the novel is no Addisonian hymn to the lure of the infinite: to Ishmael (the desert-wanderer of Genesis 16) a sea voyage is a substitute for suicide ("Cato throws himself upon his sword; I quietly take to the ship"; Melville 1991, 3), and one of the myths cited is that of Narcissus, who drowned in a pool seeking his own image. What drives Ishmael to sea is spiritual grimness ("November in my soul"); what *pulls* him is the wondrous idea of the great whales. And not just any whale, but (even before he hears of Moby Dick) "one grand hooded phantom, like a snow hill in the air" (7). Thus begins the story of one of the most disastrous attempts to enter the Great.

It takes awhile for disaster to ripen, but there are ample portents *en route*. In "The Mast-Head" chapter, Ishmael compares his mast-top meditations to those of the "old astronomers" who "were wont to mount to the apex" of the Egyptian pyramids "and sing out for new stars," and of St Simon Stylites, "who built him a lofty stone pillar in the desert" (155). It is a general vista of the Great: sky, desert, and "the infinite series of the sea" contemplated from an artificial mountain (156). But the first attempt to make a mast-head was the ill-fated Tower of Babel, and "now-adays" many of the lookouts are "romantic, melancholy, and absent-minded young men." Such a character may "[lose] his identity; [take] the mystic ocean at his feet for the visible image of that deep, blue, bottomless soul, pervading mankind and nature," and plunge to a Nar-cissean end (158–9). Here the sea is a "visible image" of Emerson's All-Soul, but the activity of trying to harmonize with a pantheistic world is revealed as not only dangerous but bathetic (falling): the very opposite of the traditional sublime (lifted up).

When Ishmael tries to explain why "The Whiteness of the Whale" ap-palls him (chapter 42), he moves from the kind of catalogue that he es-sayed in "The Mast-Head" into deeper waters. Initially he refers to an "elusive something" that makes the polar bear and the white shark terri-ble, the albatross impressive, the albino repellent, and so on. He recalls the pallor of corpses, shrouds, and Death's horse, but still wonders *why* the White Tower of London, milky seas, Antarctic frosts and other pale phenomena are so horrifying. And why should white be the colour of both holy purity and of death? Ishmael suggests two possibilities. Per-haps the "indefiniteness" of white "shadows forth the heartless voids and immensities of the universe, and thus stabs us from behind with the thought of annihilation," which sounds like the *frisson* of seventeenth-century astronomy. Or, because white is paradoxically both "the visible absence of color, and at the same time the concrete of all colors," we find "a dumb blankness, full of meaning, in a wide landscape of snows – a colorless, all-color of atheism from which we shrink" (195).

Interpretations of this resonant chapter have been legion. For John Parke, the whale's whiteness is "the neutrality of nature" (1959, 88). To Robert M. Adams it connotes just that "nil" or "void" that is his subject (1966, 143–7). Harry Levin suggests in *The Power of Blackness* that "Ish-mael's whiteness, by virtue of a culminating paradox, is blackness in per-versely baffling disguises" (1958, 221). But the most useful point here is Feidelson's: that the mystery of whiteness is associated with that of the sea, through shared qualities (e.g., ambiguity), and images such as the "white surf" and "creamy pool" in which the *Pequod* finally sinks (1959, 30, 33). The "meaning" of the whale's whiteness, then, is the meaning of the natural Great; in a later chapter, the antiquity of whale fossils gives Ishmael "shuddering glimpses" of the "Polar eternities" of the Ice Age (Melville 1991, 457).

John Parke observes that Melville operates "completely outside the Christian frame of reference" (1959, 93); we can add, "outside a *religious* frame of reference." Ishmael calls white the colour of atheism in the context of the "dumb blankness" of "a wide landscape of snows" (Melville 1991, 195), but white is most often associated with the sea in the novel: Moby Dick himself, the silvery "Spirit-spout" that reveals him, the great white squid that they mistake for him. Thus in *Moby Dick*, as in *Mardi*, the oceanic Great has atheistic connotations. Apropos, Parke describes Ahab's struggle as one between inner and outer "chaos" (1959, 95–6). "Chaos" was a word that unscientific travellers applied to parts of the Great whose dynamics they did not understand (e.g., glaciers). Along the road to Egdon Heath, Ahab is one of those (Frankenstein is another) whose encounters with sublimity are more than they can bear, because it sets up a sympathetic vibration with their own problems. Ahab dies trying to get at the heart of its meaning.

As we have seen, Melville tended to give wild nature a metaphorical reading. *The Piazza Tales* (1856) include ten sketches of the arid, volcanic Galápagos Islands off the coast of Ecuador, "five-and-twenty heaps of cinders," which he calls by their Spanish name, "The Encantadas, or Enchanted Isles." This is not the lyrical epithet of tourist brochures but an irony: any "enchantment" is baneful. What served Darwin as a laboratory for species theory Melville finds a wasteland with parallels to the human condition, an earthly piece of Dante's Hell or Purgatory (Chase 1950, xii-xiii). The first sketch stresses three qualities of the islands often sensed by visitors to Great landscapes: desolation, melancholy, and solitude. Melancholy he associates with the Dead Sea (as described by Stephens and others), solitude with northern forests, expanses of ocean, and Arctic icefields. The "special curse" that makes the Encantadas so desolate is their unchanging fixity: there are no seasons and "rain never falls" (Melville 1950, 231). That this is not actually true supports the idea voiced by many commentators that the Galápagos are a device to convey "the metaphorical truth of humanity's fallen world" (Grenberg 1989, 153).

"The Encantadas" is both surrealistic and impressionistic; Melville typically works outward from a core of literal truth to how the thing seems to him. Ashes abound near the islands' cinder cones, which in the author's vision become "sackcloth and ashes" (Melville 1950, 235). He gives a series of religious metaphors: the Encantadas "are a most Plutonian sight. In no world but a fallen one could such lands exist"; they are "apples of Sodom" (232–3), and so on. But if the islands suggest metaphysical verities, they are still real objects that one can go and see. The Rock Redondo, which reminds Richard Chase of Dante's Mount

Purgatory, is a 250-foot "dead desert rock" that the narrator climbs for its "Pisgah view" of the "eternal ocean" (241, 243, 244). This is one of Melville's composite Great scenes, a desert mountain in the sea; from it, Massafuero Island seems "a vast iceberg" (245), while Abington looks "solitary, remote, and blank": a "No-Man's Land" in an "archipelago of aridities" (249, 250).

These islands are inhabited by fugitive sailors, pirates, and great tortoises that, "strangely self-condemned," drag themselves stubbornly through a "woe-begone landscape," looking grotesquely alien yet eerily familiar. Examining their scarred, mossy shells like "an antiquary of a geologist," the narrator feels their "dateless, indefinite endurance" deeply (234, 237). The more he describes the denizens of this environment, the more symbolic they seem. Like the pirate who saw in one particular isle a "meditative image of himself," Melville perceives the minimal existences of outcasts on barren strands in "a vast and silent sea" as images of our own lives (250, 253). The Galápagos are both "a vision of the world's end" and a "not too distorted mirror" of our present condition (Grenberg 1989, 153). The "intolerable thirst" that the islands provoke, "for which no running stream offers its kind relief," and the stake-and-bottle "post-offices" that rot and fall before anyone comes to collect their messages, have a Beckettian resonance (Melville 1950, 285, 286). "The Encantadas" is determined to find the coded meaning of this barren landscape.

Melville's travels in the Levant (1856–57) did not cheer him up, as friends and family hoped; he was depressed throughout the trip, especially in Egypt and Palestine (Horsford 1955, 24–5). Like some earlier visitors to the region, he was struck by its air of geological exhaustion. From Istanbul, "Asia looked a sort of used up – superannuated" (Melville 1955, 75). In the Cyclades, stony, ruin-covered Delos, "barren" and "sterile," led him to exclaim that the Greek islands had lost their virginity, were "worn," "meagre," dry and bleak compared to the pristine freshness of Polynesia (109–10). It is difficult to say how much of Melville's depression arose from the landscapes and how much came with him. He looked up Hawthorne in England on the way out, and the two walked on the beach, talking of faith and doubt. Hawthorne described Melville as "wandering to-and-fro over [metaphysical] deserts, as dismal and monotonous as the sand hills amid which we were sitting" (quoted in Ra'ad 1991, 207). Melville's account of the meeting is much more positive: "An agreeable day. Took a long walk by the sea. Sands and grass. Wild and desolate. A strong wind. Good talk" (Melville 1955, 63).

The Pyramids made a deep impression on Melville. From Cairo, "nipped between two deserts," he rode out to Gizeh, where the Pyramids sat on "a great ridge of sand," like a wave fixed "in act of breaking, upon the verdure of Egypt" (Melville 1955, 117, 119). In form, the Pyramids suggested the Alps; in their colour, the desert. Yet "nothing in Nature," he thought, "gives such an idea of vastness" (117). Melville's "awe and terror" of the Pyramids' "massiveness and mystery" arose partly from their religious associations: "I shudder at idea of ancient Egyptians. It was in these pyramids that was conceived the idea of Jehovah" (i.e., the culture that produced them also schooled Moses; 118). He was most impressed by their air of tremendous antiquity and duration. They seemed "vast, undefiled, incomprehensible, and awful," but he also noted that the desert was "more fearful to look at than ocean" (119). He kept trying to express his sense of the Pyramids' huge simplicity, comparing their effect on the imagination to that of the sea, yet in the final analysis they seemed neither natural nor of man; "It was that supernatural creature, the priest," who invented both them and theology, "for no holy purpose" (123–4).

Much of the Holy Land proved oppressively barren, and Melville responded with images of death. The old enemy, white, appeared in the wilderness of Judaea as "whitish mildew pervading whole tracts of landscape – bleached – leprosy"; here, he said, "you see the anatomy – compares with ordinary regions as skeleton with living and rosy man" (137). Richard Burton, Freya Stark, and other writers on deserts have made similar remarks. Jerusalem from a distance looked like "arid rocks" (139). Even without its "historic associations," Melville noted, the city's "extraordinary physical aspect" would "evoke peculiar emotion"; he had "little doubt" that "the diabolical landscapes [of a] great part of Judea must have suggested to the Jewish prophets, their ghastly theology." Jerusalem was grey, Judaea stony, and "Everything look[ed] old" compared to Europe and America. It was a country that would "quickly dissipate romantic expectations," he concluded, wondering, "Is the desolation of the land the result of the fatal embrace of the Deity?" (151, 153, 154).

A connection between barrenness and holiness is often asserted by nineteenth-century writers on the desert, but none took barren scenes more personally or read deeper significance into them than did Melville. Viewing the isle of Patmos, reputed home to St John the Evangelist, he felt the full burden of modern scepticism. "When my eye rested on arid heigth [*sic*]," he jotted, "spirit partook of the barreness [*sic*]. – Heartily wish Niebuhr and Strauss to the dogs. – The deuce take their penetration and acumen. They have robbed us of the bloom. If they have undeceived anyone – no thanks to them" (166–7). This outburst against the German Higher Criticism while the writer is gripped by inner and outer barrenness is modern in feeling, thought and scene; Melville sees as clearly as Hardy that bleak settings are appropriate to the unslaked thirst and unread messages of post-Christian *angst*; he would explore these ideas further in *Clarel* (1876, chapter 19). If "Melville and Poe are both crises" in the existential "dislocation of man" (Davidson 1959, 81), they are also milestones along the road to Hardy's sombre moor in Wessex, "at present a place perfectly accordant with man's nature."

14

The Naked Truth:
Desert Travel, 1830–70

Turn and tell of Deserts lonely; lying pathless, deep, and vast,
Where in utter silence ever Time seems slowly breathing past;
Silence only broken when the sun is flecked with cloudy bars,
Or when tropic squalls come hurtling underneath the sultry stars!
Henry Kendall, "The Fate of the Explorers" (1861)

Hardy's "heaths" and "moors" were the aesthetic equivalent of Addison's
"vast desarts," but by the middle of the nineteenth century more travellers were seeking out the genuine article. The deserts of choice were in
the Middle East, whose biblical associations gave it deep cultural interest, and which political developments were making more accessible.
The Ottoman Empire's long, slow decline and its interest in western
science opened many doors, first to those with means and connections,
such as the earl of Sandwich, who included the Levant in his Grand
Tour (1738–39), later to ordinary tourists. English readers had a large
appetite for accounts of exotic locales (especially those mentioned in
scripture), and travel writers, always willing, were gradually more able to
oblige. We have already met some of them: Thomas Shaw, Richard
Pococke, who travelled throughout the Mideast and described it exhaus-
tively (1743) before visiting Chamonix, and Robert Wood, who published illustrations of the ruins of Palmyra in the Syrian desert (1753).
Some important travellers whetted those appetites further in the
next few generations, without producing distinguished writing on the
desert. In 1772 a German surveyor and astronomer, Karsten Niebuhr,
only survivor of the Danish expedition to Arabia (1761–67), published
an account of his trials that was translated into French in 1773 and English in 1792. Niebuhr, Pococke, Wood, and Thomas Shaw were among

the sources of C.F. Volney's massive, scholarly *Voyage en Égypte et en Syrie* (1787), which offers glimpses of the Suez and Gaza deserts. Volney's work became a standard source for scientific accounts – such as the multivolume *Description de l'Égypte* (1809–28) that came out of Napoleon's campaign – and for travel literature, including Chateaubriand's *Itinéraire de Paris à Jérusalem* (1811) and Lamartine's *Voyage en Orient* (1835). J.L. Burckhardt's "discovery" of Petra in the trans-Jordanian wilderness (1812) piqued many imaginations, and the well-publicized travels of Lady Hester Stanhope (Pitt's niece) in the Mideast stimulated further interest; Lamartine made a point of visiting her in Lebanon.

Another of Lady Hester's visitors was a young Englishman, Alexander William Kinglake, who stopped by during his travels of 1834–35. Kinglake wrote a high-spirited account of his journey, *Eothen* (1844; the title means "from the East"), which remained popular in England into this century and is still reprinted. Yet the same qualities that make the book delightful – self-mockery, ironic human comedy, playful allusiveness, and emphasis on imagination – obscure Kinglake's attitudes towards nature. The purport of a reference to "the mysterious 'Desert'" between Tiberias and Baghdad, for example, is unclear, evaporating in oblique references; the passage is more about verbal association than about deserts (Kinglake 1961, 94).

Kinglake travelled through real desert twice: from Gaza to Egypt, and from Cairo to Suez. On the first passage, he "used to walk away" from camp "towards the East," so that he "could better know and feel the loneliness of the Desert" (144). But his chief emotion was a "childish exultation" in his "self-sufficiency," no sooner announced than undercut. After eight days he entered the Nile Delta with intense relief. On his second trip, Kinglake charged on ahead of his servants until he found himself alone in the "arid waste" without food or water. He surveyed ("not without a sensation of awe") "the vacant round of the horizon," yet "this very awe gave tone and zest to the exultation with which I felt myself launched" (184–5): "exultation" again, and not, on this trip, undercut. Kinglake completed the ride to Suez on his own. There are no dark or cosmic undertones here, and the only spiritual notes come from the biblical resonance of the Red Sea. Kinglake compares the desert to the ocean, but when he mentions the "sublimity" of oceans and mountains he does not add "and of deserts" (162). Comedy does not seek the serious expression of emotions associated with Great phenomena, so we cannot finally say what Kinglake felt; he does not want us to know.

The biblical theme, muted in Kinglake, is played *forte* in the work of an American, John Lloyd Stephens, whose *Incidents of Travel in Egypt, Arabia Petraea, and the Holy Land* (1837) stirred Poe and Melville. Despite his no-nonsense Yankee persona, Stephens wrote "sacred geography": a pious tour through scenes hallowed or cursed by scripture. But though his responses were governed by the Bible, he covered a lot of ground, and some of his reactions are interesting. Struck by the immensity of the Great Pyramid, he compares it to the volcanic cones of Etna and Vesuvius, which he had climbed. His first sortie into the desert west of the Nile, devoid of biblical meaning, produces no emotional reaction, but when Stephens heads east into the desert of Suez, he notes that he is in the track of the Hebrew tribes and (Yankee or not) is glad there is no railroad (1991, 149, 152–3). Like several of his predecessors, he observes that the desert's barrenness affects perception, giving significance to the smallest object (155).

The Sinai Peninsula becomes more spiritual for Stephens as he approaches the Mount of the Ten Commandments. At first it is just a desolate land whose mountains are "striking" principally because of their great age (169). But later a deep ravine with "torn" rocks makes a "scene wild to sublimity," and emerging from it he first glimpses "the holy mountain of Sinai" standing in "awful grandeur," rich in Mosaic associations and "the majesty of nature" (177). From the monastery of St Catherine, Stephens explored Mount Sinai. Ensconced on its peak, he asks himself if this "naked rock" could be the place where Moses spoke with God. The clear, immediate answer is that "of Sinai there is no doubt": no natural site could be "more fitted for the exhibition of Almighty power." Etna and Vesuvius now seem "nothing compared with the terrific solitudes and bleak majesty of Sinai," from whose summit one sees "the wildest and most dreary, the most terrific and desolate picture that imagination can conceive" (188). Stephens's "soul cleaved to the scene around [him]"; he left convinced that Sinai, now bare and still, had "been shaken by an Almighty hand" (189, 213).

Balancing hallowed Sinai is cursed Edom (Arabia Petraea), whose "barren waste" seems to fulfil the denunciations of Jeremiah, Isaiah, and Ezekiel (234). Anxious to be the first American to reach Burckhardt's find, the Nabataean cliff-city of Petra, Stephens rode up El Ghor, the valley connecting the Dead and Red Seas, and climbed into Petra from the west. "All was bare, dreary, and desolate," he recalled, "eternal barrenness and desolation," albeit with "pure air" and marvellous weather (237–8, 244). Near Petra, the mountains grew "more wild and rugged" and eventually "rose to grandeur and sublimity," though Petra and Mount Hor are said to confirm biblical prophecies against the Edomites (246). It never occurs to Stephens that the prophets might have been explaining rather than predicting a wilderness; he shows no awareness of origin myths, the Higher Criticism, or geology's latest time-scales.

Stephens claims that he travelled "as a geologist" and read the "book of Nature," but Edom is finally just a chaotic proof of the Bible, and the "grandeur" of Judaea's "Mountains of Desolation" is predictably "gloomy" (292, 383). He remembers his "pilgrimage" in the desert as "long and dreary," yet notes that his experiences there increased his self-confidence and awareness of his powers (289, 313). It is interesting to see the original meaning of "desert" expiring in Stephens. At the so-called Desert of St John in the hills of Judaea, he found "no appearance of desert ... except solitude" (382), a remark that would have startled Addison, for whom a "desert" was precisely "a deserted place." As western travellers broadened their acquaintance with deserts, the word began to acquire topographic and climatic – as opposed to demographic – meanings.

William Bartlett also presents himself as a "sacred geographer" for whom every step in "the Holy Land" is an act of piety. After writing a guide to biblical "Walks" in and around Jerusalem, he spent *Forty Days in the Desert on the Track of the Israelites* (1845): "the earliest ground hallowed by Biblical history – the Desert 'of the Wandering'" (Bartlett n.d., preface). Whatever one thinks of Bartlett's attitudes towards religion or Arabs, he was a susceptible desert traveller. Between Cairo and Suez he felt "the terrible and triumphant power of the sun upon this wide region of sterility and death" (10); in the "terrible" wilderness of Sinai he acknowledged a "feeling of utter weariness" and solitude (50–1). From the top of Serbal, the 'Mount of God,' he looked out upon "eternal barrenness" and "desolate sublimity" with mixed feelings, though, and by the time he reached the monastery of St Catherine he was longing for the freedom of the desert: "I had become half a Bedouin" (65, 73, 82). Still, riding up to Aqaba, "it was impossible to shake off the infectious melancholy inspired by this desolate region" (94).

With all Bartlett's emphasis on the Bible, there is a solid core of what seems a genuine aesthetic response to landscape; not *all* of his emotions have a biblical function, and they often resemble those reported by less pious travellers. Like Stephens, he made his way to Edom, a region "fallen" into "utter ruin," yet Petra's temples, cut into sandstone cliffs, had "all the strange, wild, magical beauty of those fantastic combinations which, in dreams, seem to transcend ordinary reality" (129–30,

142). In Egypt, he found the Pyramids "sublime" and the Sphinx "almost awful." Surveying an "ocean of sand" from atop the Great Pyramid, he was struck by the "vastness" of both the natural and temporal components of the scene (193–5). At the end, when Bartlett asserts that his purpose has been to describe scenes and impressions, not to offer religious speculation, one is inclined to believe him. His feelings are not too predictable to be credited; he was drawn to as well as repelled by the "awful sublimity" of the desert.

One of the most popular Victorian books on the Mideast (17 editions in less than two decades) was Eliot Warburton's *The Crescent and the Cross. Romance and Realities of Eastern Travel* (1845). Warburton, who liked to pose as a modern Crusader, has little to say about deserts, but the differences between the biblical and non-biblical ones are interesting. In Egypt he calls the Pyramids "vast" and "awful" without commenting on the surrounding desert; in Nubia, the "trackless, monotonous desert" is the "wildest, loneliest, and dreariest" he has ever seen (Warburton n.d., 177, 129). Though the superlatives suggest interest, the "weary eye" sweeping a "circle of blank desert and unclouded sky" sounds fatigued. Later, the "wide, wild desolate waste" is "utterly blank and mournful" (133).

In sharp contrast, the landscape around Jerusalem, "so blank to the eye," is "full of meaning to the heart" (247). *Here* the "sterility of all around," the intense "silence and desolation," interest Warburton because of their sacred associations (247, 249). Even the Jordan valley and Dead Sea – for many travellers a fearful waste – seem to Warburton not "gloomy or curse-stricken" but "*riante,*" or laughing (279, 176). Examining the nomads' "romantic ... mode of life," he notes their "love of the desert," which is not all "barren sand and naked rock": there are fertile savannahs with some game, and the desert-sailors steer from one of these "isles of verdure" to the next (290). This glimpse of the Bedu (often seen as analogues of the Hebrew patriarchs) in their element was just a prelude to more thorough investigations by better-qualified writers, but helped bring more western travellers to the area.

Robert Curzon's search for old manuscripts took him to the Coptic monasteries of the Natron region in the Egyptian desert in 1837. As he recalled in *Visits to Monasteries in the Levant* (1849), the "dusty plains" extended "in hot and dreary loneliness to the horizon." "Yet although parched and dreary in the extreme from their vastness and openness, there is something grand and sublime in the silence and loneliness of these burning plains," Curzon felt (1955, 111–12). He also noted the pure air and healthy nomads, free from the cares of city dwellers. In the Holy Land he said little about the landscape, other than to grant the Judaean hills a "wild grandeur" (179). Like most European visitors he saw the region through biblical lenses: "Almost every step [was] rendered interesting by its connection with the events of Holy Writ" (159).

Curzon apologizes for burdening the public with "another book of travels in the East, when it is already overwhelmed with little volumes about palm-trees and camels, and reflections on the Pyramids" (19); Mediterranean tourism and travel literature were burgeoning. Of the various literary styles employed, "sacred geography" was preponderant, as either an occasional inflection or the *raison d'être* of the whole volume. Although relatively unimportant in Curzon's book, W.M. Thackeray's *From Cornhill to Gran Cairo* (1846), or Mark Twain's *The Innocents Abroad* (1869), sacred geography was the chosen genre of popular midcentury clerical writers such as Arthur Stanley, William Thomson, and George Sandie, who viewed the entire Middle East, including its deserts, as a confirmation of "the Book."

In the prefatory material to *Sinai and Palestine* (1856), Arthur P. Stanley, an Anglican dean, poses the question whether, or how, the geography of Palestine and the character of the Hebrew nation are related (Stanley 1863, vii-viii). The "Advertisement" added in 1864 describes the book as an attempt to demonstrate the effect of "Holy Land" on "Holy History." This frame of reference leads Stanley both to howlers, such as the assertion that Egypt had no history until Moses, and to landscape metaphors: the journey from Egypt to Jerusalem, for example, is parabolic of that through "the wilderness" of life. Stanley's vision is clearest where biblical associations are fewest. Arabia Petraea is accursed Edom, but also "the Alps unclothed" and "an ocean of lava," full of grandeur and silent desolation (13–14).

The most popular sacred geographer was the American missionary William Thomson; sales of *The Land and the Book* (1859) rivalled that of the Bible itself in late-nineteenth-century England and America. Its success is not mysterious. By the time of its composition Thomson had been living and travelling in the Levant for a quarter of a century, and knew both the land and the Book well. He presents his detailed research intimately, as if he were the reader's personal guide. The introduction, a classic of its type, begins, "The land where the Word made-flesh dwelt with men is, and must ever be, an integral part of the Divine Revelation" (Thomson 1880, xvi); the landscape is part of the Message. And he indicates immediately what kinds of revelations we can expect: "Mournful deserts ... rebuke the pride of man and vindicate the truth of God," while "yawning gulfs" such as that of the Dead Sea "warn the wicked, and prophesy of coming wrath" (xvi).

For Thomson, every ruin and badland fulfilled biblical prophecy. The Judaean wilderness was "the Creator's own conception of desolation absolute," the Dead Sea a "type" of the burning lake of Hell and "fit symbol of that great dead sea of depravity and corruption which nothing human can heal!" (625, 615, 662). But Thomson, like the Hebrew prophets, balanced doom with hope: "*supernatural* streams of divine mercy" can give new life to that "dead sea," so "Let the world-wide desert rejoice" (662). Thomson recalls seventeenth-century clerics in his determination to apply the divine metaphors encoded in landscape to moral life; a phrase such as "the wild Arabs of the Mohammedan desolation" (21) functions on both the moral and topographical levels. Thomson's geology was also archaic: he thought that the Jordan River had never reached the Gulf of Akaba because human history was too brief for such great changes (624). His only guide to the antiquity of the globe and the species was the Bible.

Rev. George Sandie hoped "to supply additional proof of the historical accuracy of the [biblical] narrative" in *Horeb and Jerusalem* (1864, xii), but he also testifies to the power of desert landscape. East of Cairo "lay the DESERT, in all its sternness and utter desolation," which at first seems "dreary"; soon, however, Sandie understands the meaning of the biblical phrase "the great and terrible wilderness" (70, 100). Beyond Suez, the "silent barrenness" of Sinai and the fixity of what looks like a "tumultuous sea" deepen "the feeling of the desolation and terror of the Desert." "What confusion! ... What a deathlike stillness!" he exclaims (105, 109). Yet wandering here was good for the Israelites: scenic grandeur and "physical terror" trained them, strengthening character and soul. The appalling landscape made them "connect these aspects of the great and terrible wilderness with the greatness and majesty of Him" (227–8). No one else had explained the spirituality of the desert more succinctly (Melville would suggest that the desert *generated* the Hebrew concept of God).

Most sacred geographers who saw the desert struggled with the feelings it produced, like early Alpine travellers. John Gadsby's *My Wanderings* (1860–61), which tries to contain the author's strong responses to vast, barren landscapes within a biblical framework, reveals his aesthetic confusion. Though his typical reaction to Mideastern deserts is that they are "dreary," there is another side to the coin. The sandy wilderness of

Sinai, "for natural grandeur, exceeded conception, but it was as dreadful as it was grand," while "a vast expanse of sand and barren rocks" is "terrifically grand" (Gadsby 1867, 420, 424). The grandeur is never reconciled with the dreariness. From the wilderness of Judaea he had an "almost boundless" view, "wild to sublimity," of the "vast plains" of the Jordan valley (494). The shore of the Dead Sea was "desolate" and "deathlike," yet so "lovely" and "*unmatchable*" that he was sorry to leave (508). Thus Gadsby wavers between sacred geography and Great aesthetics.

Turning from these scripture-soaked accounts of the Mideastern Great to reports on non-biblical deserts, we find responses to the landscape *per se*, not to its historical associations. Edward John Eyre, for example, an English parson's son who emigrated to Australia in his teens, wanted to be the first European to explore its arid interior; between 1836 and 1841 he hiked large stretches of the enormous antipodal desert. Young and not well read when he travelled, only thirty when he published his *Journals of Expeditions of Discovery into Central Australia* (1845), Eyre is valuable as an untainted, independent informant. Still, he has his angle: like Lewis and Clark, he was seeking good lands for settlement. But Eyre was usually disappointed; his routes are strewn with place names such as Lake Disappointment, Cape Arid, Mounts Hopeless and Deception. Most of the back country proved "sterile and worthless" for ranching or farming, yet "singular and interesting" (Eyre 1964, 1:vi).

Eyre's journals, especially those covering his attempt to reach central Australia from the south, record a series of failures. From the top of what became Mount Eyre, he saw a range of mountains and, apparently, a distant lake; when he went there, however, he found the countryside "barren in the extreme" and the "lake" a dry salt pan that he could not even cross. Eyre saw this "desolate and forbidding" landscape, a "dismal prospect," with "feelings of chagrin and gloom" (56, 58, 59): a scene and emotions often reiterated in the journals. Mirages were frequent: during his western journey, Eyre found the effects of refraction on the "vast plains" to be "singular and deceptive" (324). Disappointed by the "wretched arid-looking country" around Mount Barren, he declared the whole route of his 1840–41 wanderings "sterile and desolate" (2:97, 113). The title of his Australian biography is *Waterless Horizons* (Uren and Stephens, 1941).

Eyre did not love deserts, though he made his reputation exploring them; he always hoped to find something else. Virtually his only positive reactions are to heights. The tall cliffs along the Frome River in the

Flinders Range had a "gloomy grandeur" that, "in unison with the sublimity of the scene around," Eyre found "imposing" (1:123). Later he was "struck ... with admiration" at the "grandeur and sublimity" of the cliffs of the Great Australian Bight, whose "massy battlements of masonry, supported by huge buttresses," seemed "romantic" and "beautiful even amidst the dangers and anxieties" of his situation: the cliffs denied him access to water (327).

These occasional aesthetic responses led one of Eyre's biographers to style him "always basically a romantic" (Dutton 1967, 94), which is misleading unless taken to refer to the disillusioned personae of Shelley and Byron. But Eyre's readers are unlikely to agree on any single category for this restless, ambitious man who would stagger home from one exhausting expedition only to volunteer for another. Eyre rarely discussed his own motives, which remain shadowy. Uren and Stephens suggest that he was driven by the "urge to see new country," pointing out that he went west along the Bight against urgent advice after he had given up all hopes of a "practical opening" for settlers to the northwest (1941, 93, 142). Certainly he had a kind of wanderlust, and sought a place in the history of Australian exploration.

Until about 1850, travellers were still apt to neglect or dislike deserts. Though Dr Charles Meryon crossed the Syrian desert to Palmyra, his account in *Travels of Lady Hester Stanhope* (1846) is vague (he was writing about his employer, not for himself, and long after the fact). He met Burckhardt and read other eastern travellers, but other than telling us that the desert is barren, with varied topography, and that the term denotes an absence of villages and water, not a sandy waste, Meryon has little to add (n.d., 2:102–3). Similarly, Francis Parkman says less about landscape in *The Oregon Trail* (1849) and his western journals than we might wish. He considered "love of wilds and hatred of cities" as "natural" emotions, chose epigraphs from Byron and Shelley, and could be pleased by mountains, but most of Parkman's epithets for the Great Plains were negative (1991, 16). The oceanlike swells of Kansas seemed "monotonous," the Wyoming badlands a "curse" of "dreary and forlorn barrenness" (40, 158). Meryon and Parkman are useful reminders that the emotions Hardy thought Egdon Heath could evoke were not always or universally felt, especially by those in travail; there is plenty of chastening but little sublimity in Parkman, except for thunderstorms and mountain ranges.

Richard Burton's *Personal Narrative of a Pilgrimage to Al-Madinah and Meccah* (1855), however, makes up for any number of negative results.

Burton, a formidable scholar, linguist, and traveller of Satanic energy – "the Devil drives," he noted wrily – came to know the Egyptian and Arabian deserts well, and wrote copiously about them. He was also forthright about his motives. Never really at home in England after a childhood and young manhood spent abroad, Burton was by 1853 "thoroughly tired of 'progress' and of 'civilisation,' " of Europe and "European politics," and since travel as far as Cairo had become tame and trite, he would press on beyond (1964, 1:2, 35, 7, 29).

While preparing for the *hajj* (pilgrimage), Burton liked to walk out from Cairo at night and, seated on "some mound of ruins," breathe "the fine air of the Desert" (84–5). There were, he felt, "certain scenes" that remain in memory all one's life: "a thunder-cloud bursting upon the Alps, a night of stormy darkness off the Cape, an African tornado, and, perhaps, most awful of all, a solitary journey over the sandy Desert" (88). Except for the omission of the polar wastes (and the addition of a night stroll through the streets of old Cairo), it is a complete catalogue of Great sites. Burton chafed in the city like a prizefighter in training camp, longing to test his "powers of endurance" against the desert after four years of "European effeminacy" (141). Deserts, he thought, erase social and racial distinctions so that "man meets man," and larger adversaries: "Man's heart bounds in his breast at the thought of measuring his puny force with Nature's might, and of emerging triumphant from the trial" (148, 149). Other travellers speak of struggling against nature; Burton thinks he can win.

In the desert, which many found monotonous, Burton felt exuberance, an "effect of continued excitement on the mind," a quickening of soul and sense. "What can be more exciting? what more sublime?" he asks. In many particulars Burton's portrait of the desert is familiar, though unusually complete. Its capacity to heighten awareness is confirmed ("Every slight modification of form or colour rivets observation: the senses are sharpened, and the perceptive faculties ... act vigorously when excited by the capability of embracing each detail"), as are its dangers, the purity of its air, and its revelation of earth's nakedness: "flayed rocks, the very skeletons of mountains." It is not in the sensory data, then, but in his emotional reactions that Burton differs from other venturers into the desert. Between Cairo and Suez he neither complains of discomfort nor constructs a sacred geography, but eulogizes the "wildness and sublimity" of "the glorious desert" where "Nature returns to man." There, he assures us, we will find "tranquillity," and afterwards "suffer real pain in returning to the turmoil of civilisation" (148–51).

Burton has no single aesthetic attitude towards the desert; it varies with the time and the locale. His set piece on a summer day in Arabia shows that the sun is the enemy and under its rule the desert is ugly, yet dawn and sunset have a "delicious" beauty that beggars description (207–9). A morning haze can "beautif[y] even the face of Desolation," and the "hideousness" of midday enhances the "charms" of evening (154, 158). Beauty also depends on the kind of landscape in question. The desert mountains of the Red Sea coastline have a "barbarous splendor" and "savage gorgeousness," while the "barren" scenery behind Yambu' is "dismal"; in general Burton does not respond to the extreme barrenness that "disfigure[s]" Arabian nature (196, 226, 251–2).

Yet even the most barren desert is (for non-aesthetic reasons) "dear" to him, as the place where one can live most healthily, freely and honourably (244, 390; 2:10, 19). Besides these socio-biological recommendations, Burton, the scientist and sceptic not inclined to prattle about his beliefs, lets slip a spiritual remark after six hundred pages. Marching towards Mecca through a silent desert that seems "peculiarly Arabia," he traverses "a wilderness where, to use my companion's phrase, there is nothing but He." Having at most endorsed the Arab's observation, Burton quickly sidesteps to a footnote that quotes and explains it (" 'La Siwa Hu,' i.e., where there is none but Allah"), then reverts to his earlier rhetoric: "Nature scalped, flayed, discovered all her skeleton to the gazer's eye" (2:131). The two remarks are not unrelated – He lives even where nature seems dead – but if you blink you could miss the hypothesis of transcendental presence. The sense of cosmic import with which Hardy endows Egdon Heath, the feeling that something about this waste matters deeply, is implicit in Burton's treatment of deserts.

There is even less of Scripture, and even more enthusiasm, in Eugène Fromentin's reaction to the Sahara. By the mid-nineteenth century European writers and artists, as well as adventurers, could travel to African deserts (while English and North American travellers preferred the Bible lands, Europeans were equally likely to head for central and western North Africa). A British-financed German, Henry Barth, explored large tracts of the Sahara in 1850–55, Henri Duveyrier studied the Tuaregs and their country (1859–61), and Dr Nachtigal reached the Tibesti Mountains in 1863. France established a "sphere of influence" in the region; French troops began the conquest of Algeria in 1830, occupying parts of the Sahara.

Fromentin, a painter, had no desire to influence Algeria; he just loved the land, particularly the desertic South. Stimulated by his first visit in

1848, he returned to spend the summer of 1853 in the Sahara. In *Un Été dans le Sahara* (1857?) he looks back with intense nostalgia to the sensations of that time, 'burning' to return to the 'cloudless sky and shadowless desert' ("Il y a deux choses que je brûle de revoir: le ciel sans nuages, au-dessus du désert sans ombre"; Fromentin 1938, 10). In language as pellucid as the desert sky, Fromentin embraces all that the Sahara has to offer, especially what some would call its worst: "D'autres reculeraient devant la nudité d'un semblable itinéraire; je t'avoue que c'est précisément cette nudité qui m'encourage" (10).[1] There is something of the minimalist in Fromentin, as there must be in those who love the desert; its appreciation predates minimalism as an artistic movement, but not the minimalist cast of mind.

Still, Fromentin's total acceptance did not come easily; it had to be achieved. At his first bivouac in the Sahara after passing through a 'naked, desolate' landscape, he seems puzzled, even depressed, by the nullity of the desert. "C'était une grande chose sans forme, presque sans couleur, le rien, le vide et comme un oubli du bon Dieu" (45)[2]: a touch of Robert Adams's literary "Nil," though here the only void seems to be the outer one. A desert mountain, Fromentin finds, is powerful, not beautiful ("Ce n'est pas beau, c'est formidable"; 58). Soon, though, he is professing to enjoy the sun, solitude, warm wind, vast horizons, and silence. In a passage still quoted by the *Guide Bleu* to Algeria, Fromentin asserts that "Le silence est un des charmes les plus subtils de ce pays solitaire et vide" (66),[3] and his explanation sounds familiar. In this great space, silence becomes "une sorte de transparence aérienne, qui rend les perceptions plus claires, nous ouvre le monde ignoré des infiniment petits bruits et nous révèle une étendue d'inexprimables jouissances" (67).[4] This is the auditory counterpart of the visual phenomenon noted by Burton and others: in the desert you pay more attention to less.

Fromentin's theme is that in the desert life is reduced to essentials, a mode he finds profoundly attractive. Because 'bareness is the Sahara's true face' ("c'est par la nudité que le Sahara reprend sa véritable physionomie"), he is glad to pass beyond the limits of vegetation, and hopes

---

1. 'Others may recoil from the bareness of such an itinerary; I affirm that it is precisely that bareness that attracts me.' All translations are my own.

2. 'It is a great, formless, almost colourless thing, a nothingness, a void, as if forgotten by God.'

3. 'Silence is one of the most subtle charms of this lonely, empty country.'

4. '... a sort of aerial transparency that clarifies our perceptions, opens an unknown world of infinitely small sounds and reveals an expanse of ineffable delights to us.'

to see not a tree more: "ce qui me plaît dans le lieu où nous sommes campés, c'est surtout son aspect stérile" (69).[5] It is little minds, he decides, that are drawn to details; what the great masters learn from nature is simplicity. Far from the Louvre, the desert teaches Fromentin to see things 'simply, to find their true great form' ("par le côté simple, pour en obtenir la forme vraie et grand"; 70–71). A verdant section of the Sahara thus comes as a 'disagreeable surprise' because it obscures the 'true form' under a mass of superficial detail (81). This taste for the simple, unitary effect, which may also underlie his love of the desert sky's 'pure cobalt blue' (103), stayed with Fromentin. The diary he kept while travelling in Egypt in 1869 has stark word-paintings of the Nile valley and western desert that manifest the same aesthetic: "Un mimosa tout seul au milieu d'une plaine ... . Ce n'est rien, c'est délicieux" (Fromentin 1935, 74).[6]

As his Saharan journey continued, Fromentin kept learning. First, he decided that the hardships of desert travel were not sensations to avoid; 'slowness and extreme fatigue' were essential to the experience (1938, 101). This insight arose from a certain 'seriousness' or 'severity' that he sensed in the landscape around Laghouat, an oasis in an arid ocean, where he realized how powerfully the country had gripped his imagination. Fromentin described the vista of mountain and desert from a height of the town: "Tout cela est très grave, plein de grandeur et d'une forme et d'un aspect qui ne permettent pas d'oublier qu'on touche au pays de la soif et qu'on est sur la limite du grand désert" (313).[7] "Grandeur" and a sense of danger are frequent responses to the Great. He notes that the Sahara does not "charm"; rather "il est aussi capable d'émouvoir fortement que n'importe quelle contrée du monde. C'est une terre sans grâce, sans douceurs, mais sévère, ce qui n'est pas un tort, et dont la première influence est de rendre sérieux" (178).[8] A 'severity that is not wrong' is an inspired leap at the contribution not only of the desert but of the natural Great to the human spirit and its aesthetic spectrum.

5. 'What pleases me about the place where we have camped is precisely its sterility.'

6. 'A mimosa, alone in the middle of a plain ... It is nothing; it is delightful.'

7. 'All is very serious, full of grandeur, and of a form and appearance that do not let us forget that we have reached the country of thirst and are at the boundary of the great desert.'

8. '... it is as capable of arousing strong emotion as any landscape in the world. It is a land without grace or gentleness, but with a severity that is not wrong, and whose primary influence is to make one serious.'

At Laghouat, a 'lost city, surrounded by solitude' in the northern Sahara, Fromentin moves into an almost mystical space; he can feel "la fixité un peu morne du beau temps, enfin une sorte d'impassibilité qui du ciel semble être descendue dans les choses, et des choses avoir passé dans les visages" (178, 179).[9] This 'slightly gloomy fixity' is not depressing, however, once the eye becomes accustomed 'to the grandeur of line, the emptiness of space, the bareness of the earth' (179). His best moments are spent on the heights above Laghouat, "en face de cet énorme horizon libre de toutes parts" ('facing this enormous horizon, free in every direction': 180); again "a spacious horizon is an image of liberty." There Fromentin remains through the hot *midi* to observe the changing light, wondering "quel peut être ce pays silencieux, revêtu d'un ton douteux qui semble la couleur du vide; d'où personne ne vient, où personne ne s'en va" (185).[10] Readers who suspect incipient sunstroke receive some support; after chronicling such a day he admits to experiencing "une certaine ivresse" ('a certain intoxication') due to the quantity of light absorbed and entering a spiritual state, "une sorte de clarté intérieure" ('a kind of internal light') closely ressembling fever (187–8).

Fromentin gradually gives up trying to define the appeal of the desert, but never wavers in his advocacy. During a night march under starry skies, he can sense a "murmure indéfinissable" ('undefinable murmur') issuing from the heavens, almost a music of the spheres (220). As in Charles Doughty, there is a vertical as well as a horizontal dimension of movement and consciousness. Despite the Saharan heat, a 'shower of fire,' he asserts that 'there is something incomparable in this country that makes me cherish it' ("il y a dans ce pays je ne sais quoi d'incomparable qui me le fait chérir"), and regrets 'bitterly' that he has to leave "le Pays de la soif" ('the Land of Thirst'; 279).

But he did leave, "vaincu … par cette soif mortelle" ('overcome by that mortal thirst'), he wrote in *Une Année dans le Sahel* (1909, 201). At Blida, a verdant spa in the coastal hills where he had previously stayed, however, Fromentin found that his feelings and perceptions had been altered. The coast had a different beauty, a softer heat, a less menacing aridity than the Sahara's, and the great desert had spoiled Blida for him,

9. '… the slightly gloomy fixity of fine weather, finally a sort of impassibility that seems to descend from the heavens into things, and from them to pass into faces.'

10. '… what this silent country can be, clothed in a doubtful tint that seems the colour of void; where no one comes or goes.'

making it seem merely "joli" and "petit" ('pretty' and 'small'; 207). Every morning he woke up, comfortable and secure, and felt a 'bizarre regret' that he was not in the Sahara; he saw the bland days pass with indifference (208–9). He informed a friend who inquired about his travels that he had 'seen summer in his kingdom,' and told a surprised native of the Sahara that "ton pays est le plus beau du monde" ('your land is the finest in the world'; 204).

The opening of the Suez Canal in 1869 (which would shift the bulk of travel through the Middle East from land to sea) brought a flotilla of foreign visitors, including Fromentin. In poor health, he made a quick tour, but his *Journal de voyage en Haute-Égypte* (1881) shows that he had not lost his feeling for desert landscape: as he approached Cairo on the train, the eastern and western deserts seemed to him to join, nullifying the Nile Valley (Fromentin 1935, 47). But up the Nile he steamed, all the way to Aswan, initially marvelling at the play of light and colour, then gradually adopting a vocabulary of desolation and austerity as the landscape became drier and stonier. Three days up the Nile, the aridity was 'complete and terrible'; a day later the vertical emphasis reappears: "Au-dessus, le ciel blanc, au-dessous, le Nil immobile" ('Above, the white sky; below, the motionless Nile'; 67, 73). Fromentin soon rediscovered his taste for this minimal palette. At Abydos, he could pronounce the sweep of arid mountains and desert "très beau" (85).

Fromentin also rode the new train across the eastern desert from Cairo to Suez. The run was made at night, and he thought that this, too, was "très beau": desert, moonlight, "une solitude absolue" (120). Back at Cairo, he walked out to the silent, deserted Valley of the Mamlouks to see the 'superb' Mokattam escarpment trailing off into the desert: "L'étendue de l'horizon est immense" ('The sweep of the horizon is immense'), he wrote, and the line of colour where earth meets sky "donne une première idée charmante de cette chose grave, solennelle, monotone souvent, redoutable quelquefois, jamais ennuyeuse, qu'on appelle le désert."[11] Thus it always appears, he reflected: "aplati, infini et n'ayant d'autre couleur que la couleur idéale de la distance, de la solitude et de la lumière" (139).[12] This would be a difficult hue to locate on

---

11. '... gives a first idea of that serious, solemn thing, often monotonous, sometimes fearful, never boring, called the desert.'
12. '... flattened, infinite, and having no colour but the ideal colour of distance, solitude and light.'

a colour wheel; Fromentin's desert transcends the senses and ordinary language to partake of the infinite and the ideal.

Fromentin was not an explorer, barely even an adventurer by the standards of his time; he went no farther than towns on the edge of deserts. But as an appreciator of desert landscape he was unsurpassed until Doughty. Without the stimulus of sacred geography, without even a goal in mind, he loved the desert itself, the *Ding an sich*. The desert was Fromentin's Mecca, a marvellous mystery the sight and feel of which were attainment enough. 'A serious, solemn thing, often monotonous but never boring,' the desert moved him deeply, intoxicated him, simultaneously attracted and freed him. With his abiding interests in landscape, vastness, immobility, silence, and durability, Fromentin was ripe for the Sahara. His ardent embrace of it set a new standard for venturers to the desert.

15

Mighty Fortresses:
The Meanings of Mountains, 1830–70

High mountains were the only area of the Great widely seen as "sublime" before 1830: de Saussure and Mont Blanc, Rousseau and the Romantics had accomplished that. In England, these feelings were institutionalized during Victoria's reign. The Alpine Club, formed in 1857, published accounts of its members' outings in *Peaks, Passes and Glaciers* (1859, 1862), which was superseded by the *Alpine Journal* (1863–). More adventurers, scientists, and tourists than ever climbed higher in the Alps, which became "the playground of Europe," in Leslie Stephen's words (1871). But the Alps were taken more seriously than his phrase implies; they (and some other mountains) were approached with various motives, ranging from the scientific to the religious, aesthetic, and moral.

Victor Hugo's "Alpes" (1839) restates several themes of his 1825 "Fragment d'un voyage aux Alpes" (see chapter 10): mountains are spiritual entities that blend contradictory phenomena, produce sublime sunsets, etc. Usually, he feels, Switzerland's "grandes montagnes rendent religieux" ('great mountains seem religious'; Hugo 1910, 196). It is easy to locate the source of this feeling: a cliff wrinkled like an anxious brow is "un ensemble prodigieux de choses harmonieuses et magnifiques pleines de la grandeur de Dieu" ('a prodigious collection of harmonious and magnificent elements full of God's grandeur'; 197). A "prodigy" being a freak of nature, a "prodigious" yet "harmonious" ensemble is an oxymoron, like the summit of Mount Pilatus, "horrible et … beau tout à la fois" ('at once horrible and beautiful'; 198), a response with a long history. The Alps' "waves of granite" seemed almost as unlikely to Hugo as they did to Conrad Gesner in 1550.

The main difference between the 1825 and 1839 accounts is a glimmering of scientific consciousness in the latter. The Righi and the Rossberg have no 'geological connection' ("rapport géologique") with the Alps, Hugo notes; they consist of different stone (178). A high cliff reveals 'the Alps' colossal bone-structure' ("l'ostéologie colossale des Alpes"; 197). The remark is metaphorical, and has parallels in earlier reports, but perhaps something of Cuvier and the Auvergne had reached Hugo. A few years later in the coastal Pyrenees, however, it is again all spirit. The mountain summits are 'unknown worlds,' God is near and the soul rises joyously to meet Him (1910, 336, 352). Almost every day he revisits natural settings that are no less transcendental, perhaps even more so, for being desolate. Sitting on the end of a headland, hundreds of feet above the sea, he exclaims, "Magnifique et éternel spectacle!" (358). Hugo's emotions in the settings Addison called "Great" are those described in number 412 of the *Spectator.*

Hugo belonged to the old world in being a scene-collector, not a climber. William Brockedon, who wrote guidebooks to Alpine travel in the 1820s, was a more active walker and more conventional thinker than Hugo. His *Journals of Excursions in the Alps* (1824) and *Passes of the Alps* (1828) preserve the era's standard aesthetic distinctions and responses to high mountains. Mont Blanc, seen from a distance, represents "beauty and vastness"; the Mer de Glace "oppresses" a perceiver actually on it, yet close to the Glacier of Bossons, you realize "the grandeur of these magnificent masses" (Brockedon 1833, 16, 19, 18). His party enjoyed a "sublime" dark storm-cloud as they would an eruption of Vesuvius, but were "appalled" by the "wildness and danger" of the steep gorges (20, 26–7). Brockedon was impressed by the silence, purity, solitude, and severity of the Alps, and the way their scale deceived his judgment of height and distance. A natural amphitheatre was both "dreary" and so "grand" that "the *mind* was overwhelmed"; like Hugo, he approved the French epithet for the Alps, "les belles horreurs" (224, 165). Brockedon is a repository of the period's clichés about the Alps, but his were based on first-hand experience.

Brockedon's books show that the lower Alps were by then a tourist's playground: the main routes had been marked, the correct reactions suggested ("glorious" Monte Rosa, "sublime and beautiful" St Bernard pass), and the Chamonix guides were well organized. He himself worked on Murray's guidebooks. Alpine panoramas were exhibited in major European cities, where the Alps were part of popular culture. In 1832 Alexandre Dumas *père*'s "Notes de Voyages. Suisse" in the *Revue des*

Deux Mondes created the 'Alpine serial novel,' and Rodolphe Töpffer sat-
irized the excesses of Alpine literature in his *Voyages en zig-zag. Excursions
dans les Alpes* (Engel 1930b, 178, 182–4).

From the 1830s on, increasing numbers of scientists and other "mountaineers" went to the higher Alps to escape the crowds and find what they
had come for. Robert Shuttleworth, a botanist, found "one of the first
high-altitude bivouacs" in 1835 "not entirely disagreeable," owing to its
"novelty" and uncanniness (Engel 1971, 81). Some of Europe's most important geologists, such as Léonce Élie de Beaumont and Louis Agassiz,
became "*Alpinistes*" to conduct their research. During the summers of
1838–41, Agassiz's party camped by the Unteraar glacier and walked
over that and others, gathering evidence on glacial flow and an "Ice
Age." His *Études sur les glaciers* (1840) made many converts and added
new interest to mountains (see chapter 11). Agassiz also climbed the
Jungfrau in 1841, an experience he reportedly found moving (87–8).

THE HIGH VICTORIANS

Another important scientific mountaineer was Dr James Forbes, now
best known from Ruskin's admiring references. Forbes studied glaciers
and ascended the Jungfrau with Agassiz, pioneered several high routes
in Dauphiny with guides such as Couttet and Balmat, whose local fame
he spread, and recounted his adventures and findings in a series of
books aimed at the general public: chiefly *Travels through the Alps of Savoy*
(1843), *A Physician's Holiday* (1850), and *Norway and Its Glaciers* (1853).
Forbes influenced the next generation of climbers both through his
own books and through the selections from them that Brockedon in-
serted in Murray's popular series of Alpine guides.

Ostensibly, Forbes was drawn to mountains by science, particularly
glaciology – almost half of *Travels through the Alps* is devoted to "Observations on the Phenomena of Glaciers" – though he also studied Alpine
geography and geology. He often cited de Saussure, many of whose
routes he retraced, as his model, and corrected contemporary geologists
(including Agassiz and Lyell) on points of science or professional conduct. Though he saw himself as a minor explorer, Forbes asked where
the Parrys and Franklins of Europe and the Alps were to be be found (in
the case of Franklin, the question soon became ironic). When Forbes
discusses his motives, he reveals still broader interests. Travel "seems to
expand" human life, he notes, and the Alps especially "convey to the
imagination the fullest sense of the sublime" in nature (Forbes 1845,

11). The principal Alpine pleasures he stipulated were intellectual stimulation, reading nature's philosophy, health, and invigoration.

Great nature, then, always had more than scientific interest for Forbes. Of his time with Agassiz he later wrote, "I shall never forget the charm of those savage scenes" (1853, 297); on the summit of the Jungfrau he recited a speech from Byron's *Manfred*, and his books contain dozens of aesthetic episodes. Forbes habitually calls the Alps "majestic," "vast," and "wild"; the Mer de Glace is "wildly grand" and full of "sublimity" (1845, 58, 74). Other recurrent themes of *Travels through the Alps* are isolation, beauty, danger, and desolation. When his party found a corpse in the snow on Mont Collon in 1842, Forbes felt "personal danger" and "a stronger sense of sublimity" amid the surrounding "desolation," of "loneliness with nature and, as it were, the more immediate presence of God," than ever before (280–1). The Alps stirred him emotionally and spiritually, setting the high standard by which he judged other landscapes in Scandinavia and Britain.

Few foreign climbers knew much of Norway when Forbes went there in 1851. While the vastness of the mountains tricked his sense of scale, he initially found the scenery "grand" rather than "sublime" in the Alpine sense (1853, 2, 8). North of Trondheim he acknowledged some sublimity, though his most frequent verdict was "desolate grandeur" (47, 57). Gradually, however, his antipathy to the barren plateaux gave way to admiration of the "solemn and glorious" vistas farther north (52). From Bergen, Forbes was rowed up several fjords, through "some of the sternest and wildest scenery in Norway": "Majestic mountains," waterfalls like beautiful drapery (he cites Ruskin's *Modern Painters*), and at their source, huge glaciers, to which he often climbed. Forbes still writes as a scientist, citing de Saussure and Agassiz on glaciers, von Buch (no one newer) on geology, yet remains open to emotional impressions. Rowing in the "deep black" waters of the "desolate and even terrific" Sognefjord, between bare, vertical cliffs, under low, dripping clouds, he felt an "overwhelming ... sense of solitude and isolation" (146).

Forbes's appeal to John Ruskin is easy to understand: he had an ample poetic and spiritual dimension along with his empirical curiosity. To give a sense of the high country where he found the body, Forbes quotes Alexandre Dumas: "le domaine des glaces et des neiges, le palais d'hiver, le royaume de la mort" ('the realm of ice and snow, winter's palace, death's kingdom'; 1845, 273). He concludes *Travels through the Alps* by explaining why a glacier is a better image of human life than a river;

"heaven descended," urged on by fate, it gradually acquires character, is scarred by struggle and dies, but is reborn (387–8). Forbes was another of those for whom great mountains are a moral exemplar.

In the 1850s "Alpinism" began to reach mania proportions among healthy, high-minded English university men on their summer holidays. Alfred Wills's books, *Wanderings among the High Alps* (1856) and *The Eagle's Nest* (1860), which caught (and furthered) this wave just as the Alpine Club was formed, combine science, aesthetics, and high adventure. Wills does not just climb cliffs or scramble over boulders; he negotiates "schistaceous gneiss." Yet he also believes that no picture can possibly convey the "grandeur and sublimity" of Alpine nature (1858, ix). Despite his frequent use of "sublime" (not always clearly distinguished from "beautiful"), Wills is analytical about scenes and his feelings towards them. The Glacier du Géant, for example, is a "bare and desolate region," a "desert of ice," yet a scene of "beauty" withal (16–18). He fell partway into one of its "awful" crevasses and glimpsed a "strange scene of fantastic magnificence" below the treacherous snow-bridge before his guides hauled him out (19–20). At the Col du Géant, they found bits of straw from de Saussure's cabin, marvellously preserved by the frost (22): the familiar note of the Great having power over time. Wills was "astonished" by the "potent and awful forces of nature" there (27).

The centrepiece of Wills's "wanderings" was his climb of the Wetterhorn, compared to which Mont Blanc was a "bagatelle." *En route,* his party spent the night in a cave amid cliffs and glaciers, "a splendid wild scene" (272). After they doused their lanterns and retired, the Swiss guides sang a German hymn in three-part harmony. For Wills, the scene was epic, Miltonic: "The effect, in that strange place, in 'darkness visible,' ... beneath the shadows of the eternal mountains, was inexpressibly solemn" (275). Too excited to sleep, he went outside at 2:00 A.M. to the most "beautiful ... nocturnal view" he had ever seen: stars shining like fire, glaciers sparkling; in sheer exhilaration, he stripped and bathed in an ice-cold torrent (277). On the climb, they struggled up a steep glacier to where an ice-and-snow cornice of "marvellous beauty" overhung them like a wave crest or "enchanted fortress" (285). Cutting through it, they moved in a step from a "blank wall of ice" to the "boundless expanse" of a summit vista. Though "appalled" by their "awful" position, Wills experienced "profound" emotion arising from the "sublime and wonderful prospect"; in this "majestic, but desolate" place, "we felt as in the more immediate presence of Him who had reared this tremendous pinnacle" (287, 290).

In his valuable essay on the small fraternity of Victorian Alpinists, David Robertson suggests that members of the Alpine Club (which Wills helped found) had a "tendency" to treat any "transcendental experiences" as "private"; religious outbursts came from non-members (1977, 125–6). But the exceptions he admits – Wills, John Tyndall, and Leslie Stephen – were and are the club's best-known climber-writers. Rare such passages may be (as rare as the moments that inspire them), but they appear in a wide spectrum of articles and books by members and non-members alike. The capacity of high mountains to induce reverence in those who approached them was as great as ever, and at intense moments the vocabulary was still apt to become metaphysical, if not specifically religious. What I find striking is the amount of spiritual and emotional agreement that the Alps could elicit from three such different men as Wills, a Unitarian lawyer, Tyndall, a professor of physics, and the anti-scientific Leslie Stephen, *littérateur.*

Tyndall initially adopts a scientific posture, dedicating *Glaciers of the Alps* (1860) to Michael Faraday and explaining in the introduction that he became interested in glaciers from reading Sedgwick and Forbes, the latter at the suggestion of his fellow climber T.H. Huxley. Several chapters discuss the physics of glaciers quite technically (Tyndall differed with Forbes on this subject, which turned Ruskin into his bitter enemy). But "the scientist" is only part of Tyndall: he was also a gifted stylist whose books went into Everyman's Library in the next century, and a lover of poetry who supplied epigraphs from Tennyson and Emerson, quoted Byron's "Cain" on a foggy glacier, and, inspired by Coleridge, lingered at Chamonix to view the sunrise. A sensitive perceiver of mountains' moods, Tyndall often hailed the Alps' beauty, grandeur, intimations of spirit or transcendence, purity, and silence.

Most of these qualities occur in virtually every one of Tyndall's narratives. In the Oberland he admires the "pure white cone" of the Silberhorn against the dawn sky and feels "awe" amid the loneliness and "savage magnificence" of its glacier (Tyndall 1906, 11–12). He declares that once the laws underlying the apparent confusion of a glacier are known, its "order and beauty" are perceived (13). Glaciers were usually seen as "chaotic" until scientists, especially Agassiz, were able to show that their order could be apprehended. The breadth of Tyndall's sensibility becomes apparent when, crossing the Grimsel Pass on a Sunday, he observes that "the scene was itself a Sabbath" in its stillness (20): spirituality is inherent in the natural scene. Another climber called Tyndall a "reverent agnostic"; he certainly revered Mont Blanc. On his first climb (1857), the party commenced walking at 2:00 A.M. in "an atmosphere of perfect purity"; moonlight on the snow made a scene "wild, grand, and beautiful," in which the mighty glacier dwarfed the humans (65–6). On the summit, Tyndall's dominant impression was of "magnitude": the essence of the Great (73).

No reader could miss Tyndall's intense enjoyment of his climbs, his sense of strength and exultation. For him, the "wild beauty and desolation" around the Strahleck Pass possessed "exceeding magnificence" (87), as did many other scenes. Staying with friends at a high cabin to do research on glaciers, he doubted whether anyone ever was or could be happier than they, healthy and busy in such surroundings, gathering before the fire each evening to compare notes. Such joyful passages, however, alternate with more hushed tones. At dusk on the Finsteraarhorn, Tyndall found the "deep and solemn silence" and the "beauty" of the "glorious mountains" worthy of "adoration" (94–5). At dawn, his impression of the "magnificent corridor" between the Oberland's highest peaks was "not that of vastness or sublimity but of loveliness not to be described" (Tyndall rarely used the word sublime). "There was something saintly in the scene" while the "holy light shone forth," but the religion that Tyndall thought of there was Buddhism, whose "essence" is inactivity and "immortal calm" (97). After devoting one clause to "the repression of all action," though, his restless spirit moves on.

One of Tyndall's themes, perhaps related to his scientific vocation, is that actual "Nature often transcends the human imagination" (180). That is apropos of a glacier, and atop the Finsteraarhorn he insists that "imagination" could not exceed the "reality" of such a view's "grandeur" (102). Yet Tyndall was not a materialist; his Nature is a bountiful and ancient goddess, worthy of adoration by her inferior, man. During his winter expedition to the Mer de Glace, "prodigal Nature rained down beauty [six-rayed snowflakes like 'Frozen flowers'], and had done so here for ages unseen by man. And yet some flatter themselves with the idea that this world was planned with strict reference to human use" (187). Like a latter-day Swift or Voltaire, Tyndall inveighs against anthropocentricity, using as his weapon the overwhelming antiquity often felt (and then being shown) in Great landscapes. Yet nature is not his ultimate frame of reference. Watching a "supernatural" dawn sky that "baffled analysis," Tyndall thinks of Tennyson's line, "God made himself an awful rose of dawn," and leaves it at that (183).

Tyndall resigned from and stopped writing for the Alpine Club in 1862, feeling that his empirical approach was unwelcome. That same year he published *Mountaineering in 1861,* which partly confirms, partly broadens the Tyndall of *Glaciers of the Alps.* Imagination has a larger role, especially in regard to Agassiz's Ice Age theory, which was gaining ground. Trying to imagine how Switzerland must have looked when covered by the glaciers that polished its boulders, Tyndall suggests "an icy sea dotted with dreary islands" (a fair description of the Arctic Ocean, then being explored with much publicity), and decides that the "unspeakable desolation" of all Europe "encased in frozen armour" must have been less grand than the present reality (1906, 210–12). The most scientific chapter, "Reflections," which follows, returns to the theme of order. Primitive man ascribed the grander phenomena of the Alps to the "personal agency" of gods, but "time ... chasten[ed] the emotions" and allowed the intellectual faculty to apprehend the natural laws underlying these phenomena (221–2). For Hardy, the emotion that time had chastened was sublimity.

In the next chapter the pendulum swings again; Tyndall's ecstasy atop the Weisshorn is his most metaphysical, Emersonian passage: "An influence seemed to proceed from [the panorama of peaks and valleys] direct to the soul; the delight and exultation experienced were not those of Reason or of Knowledge, but of BEING: – I was part of it and it of me, and in the transcendent glory of Nature I entirely forgot myself as man" (239). Suddenly it seems relevant that he had studied in Germany and could still recite Schiller. Tyndall soon desists from making "observations," there being "something incongruous, if not profane, in allowing the scientific faculty to interfere where silent worship was the 'reasonable service'" (240). If this, or his reconnaissance of the Matterhorn – where he relishes his self-reliant solitude and feels "irresistible fascination" with "the mystic pinnacle" (257) – cannot lay the ghost of "Tyndall the scientific mountaineer," nothing will. Climbing Monte Rosa alone, in his shirtsleeves, with his tea and ham sandwich, Tyndall is more like John Muir than any of his predecessors: going lightly, lovingly, and with irresistible energy to the mountain temple.

The Alpine writings of Leslie Stephen were more ephemeral than Tyndall's in these years, but he was as ardent a climber and a more graceful and prolific writer. Even among Victorian Alpinists, where the pool of literary talent was impressively deep, Stephen stood out as an *éminence littéraire.* He married Thackeray's daughter, became an influential author, scholar, and editor, befriended Hardy, and sired Virginia Woolf. Stephen, who began climbing the year the Alpine Club was formed, later became president of the club; no less a mountaineer than

Edward Whymper called him the fleetist of Alpinists. He is hailed in Claire Engel's *Mountaineering in the Alps* (1950) for his climbs, his informed love of Europe's mountains, and his research on the history of climbing: "We realize with a shock that the author of the *History of English Thought in the Eighteenth Century* and of the *History of Criticism*, the editor of ... the *Dictionary of National Biography*, was also the man who climbed for the first time the Shreckhorn, the Zinal Rothhorn, the Mont Mallet, the Bietschhorn, the Disgrazia, the Blumlisalp ... and found new routes up many peaks" (Engel 1971, 116). No other important Alpinist could be called a focus of Victorian letters, or vice versa.

Soon after making his first notable ascent, the Allalinhorn, Stephen began to publish accounts of his climbs, mostly in the club's *Peaks, Passes, and Glaciers*, then in its *Alpine Journal* (which he edited from 1868 to 1872), or in *Cornhill* and *Fraser's* magazines. Eventually he collected and revised many of these pieces in *The Playground of Europe* (1871; see chapter 19), pondering the meanings of mountains and mountaineering there and in *Hours in a Library* (1874–79). Yet his own convictions emerge less clearly than do those of more straightforward men such as Wills and Tyndall or more earnest ones such as Hugo; Stephen was playful, self-protective, a Sterne or Kinglake of the Alps. His sophisticated humour and light ironies give his narratives an obliquity that leaves the author in half shadow (the revised versions in *Playground* are more oblique yet).

"Ascent of the Shreckhorn" is a good example of his technique. The original 1862 version "By the Reverend Leslie Stephen, MA" is a stylish, mostly lighthearted account of a difficult climb in a mountain wilderness by a man who at times seems horrified by his surroundings. From a ridge "in the very centre of the regions of frost and desolation," he looks out across "dreary wastes of snow" to a "grim circle" of summits, but distances the horror with a joke: "It is melancholy to observe the shockingly bad state of repair of the higher peaks" (*Peaks* 1862, 2:9–10). Stephen's avoidance of the kind of passionate outburst that the Alps had evoked from some early writers (Burnet, Dennis) is said to have been rooted in his dislike of Ruskin's rhetorical style (Engel 1971, 115). There is no sign of the "immortal being" passage that commentators like to quote; that was added during the 1871 revision.

It is precisely Stephen's religious attitudes that are so elusive. In "The Eiger Joch," he terms the mountain known as the Mönch a "hoary pillar of the mid-aerial church" (*Peaks* 1862, 2:15). Is this just a play on "the monk"? Or does it suggest that the Alps served him as a kind of religion?

He is usually described as non-believing, and later renounced holy orders. The rest of the account is secular enough. On the descent his party had to bivouac on the Aletsch glacier. Stephen says that he "really enjoyed" the excitement, beauty, "perfect stillness," and "absolute solitude," then turns to his discomfort and hunger. The next morning the glacier seemed "extremely ugly"; he regarded the Matterhorn and Weisshorn "with utter indifference, and thought what I should order for breakfast. Bodily fatigue and appreciation of natural scenery are simply incompatible" (51). At a perfect place for sublimity, we get debunking, *Realpolitik*: the "mid-aerial church" seems to have been deconsecrated. Yet one could not call this deflationary pragmatism "typical" of Stephen, who clearly enjoyed the Alps as keenly in his wry way as Tyndall did. Among Hardy's contemporaries, the man most likely to have prompted the idea that *modern* minds are attracted to barrenness was Leslie Stephen.

PEAKS, PASSES, AND GLACIERS

The publications of the Alpine Club offer much more than Tyndall's and Stephen's narratives; they record the broad, energetic curiosity for which Victorian intellectuals and explorers are known. The second series of *Peaks, Passes, and Glaciers* (whose preface mentions the doubling of the club's membership in three years) contains accounts of climbs in the Alps, the Pyrenees, Norway, and Iceland, as well as scientific papers and tables. Only one writer besides Stephen disclaims scientific interests, while five espouse them, and most carried equipment to measure elevation, so Tyndall had company. Endurance was a virtue much in demand. E.T. Holland's "Itineraries in Iceland" portrays a strange northern waste with cold, dark, wet weather, a half-savage place of few rewards or saving graces. Yet he persisted in a two-month circumambulation, riding horseback for hours in driving sleet and climbing onto icefields. Holland notes that the "noble meeting-place" – a meadow amidst lava fields – of Iceland's ancient democratic assembly, the Althing, had a "stern savageness," which he thought elicited the "severe and unyielding energies of the lawgivers" (*Peaks* 1862, 1:8).

Largely because of Holland's long narrative, the aesthetic keynote of these volumes is "barren desolation," which, however, fascinates rather than repels most writers. The next most common reactions – "sublimity," "beauty," and "grandeur" – are widespread among the sixteen mountaineers, who often express their pleasure in climbing. E.S. Kennedy, the volumes' editor, recounts his ascent of the Pizzo Bernina in exuberant prose mounting to a "JOYOUS CONCLUSION" (183). J.G. Dodson, MP, asserts that the Alps are better than oceans or deserts at imparting "health and vigour," and hails the "naked purity" of mountains (190, 192). Asking himself "*cui bono*?" (i.e., 'why bother?') on the summit of the Aletschhorn, F.F. Tuckett answers, for the "joy" and satisfaction of it (2:58). F.W. Jacomb, a frequent contributor, says that the "pleasure" of climbing increases his "enjoyment" of the "splendid scene" from a summit; a dawn walk up an Alpine valley gives him a sense of "mountain glory," joy, health, and reverence for "the great Giver of all this good" (1:313, 319–20). For him, lunch on a glacier in full view of the Matterhorn is "high festival, under the blue vault of heaven" (338).

The spiritual overtones of Jacomb's narrative pervade other writers as well. William Brinton, MD, says that a "tall peak" is "another world," where one "wonders and reveres" like a barbarian in the Roman senate, and understands why primitive man "worshipped in high places" (439). Charles Packe remarks that mountain summits lead our thoughts to the infinite (2:115; Addison said that *views* of mountains do this). William Matthews felt exalted by the "sense of solitude and isolation from mankind" at night on Monte Viso. The "solemn silence" and "wonderful canopy of heaven," inconceivable to lowlanders, made it seem almost "the portal of another world," bringing to mind Wordsworth's lines on the "starry sky" and "lonely hills" (160). Other writers were equally moved in secular ways. During his night on the Aletschhorn, Tuckett felt that he was in a great theatre; the moonlit glacier, peaks, and ridges had an "unearthly beauty, suggestive of scenic change or magic transformation" (50). Edward Schweitzer responded to the *freedom* of the Alps, choosing as the epigraph for his narrative a German poem beginning, "Auf den Bergen ist Freiheit!" A spacious horizon was indeed for him "an image of liberty."

Peaks, Passes, and Glaciers gives a heady sense of the dawn of modern mountaineering, when there were first ascents and new routes to be attempted on every hand, the maps had blank spaces to be filled and errors to be corrected, and climbers formed friendships with each other and with their guides that outlasted their climbing days. It also confirms abundantly that Europe's Great landscapes were valued as providing spiritual and imaginative sustenance of a high quality.

And this is to skim only the high points of the mid-century mountaineering literature. Although some of it does have literary pretensions (such as A. Bainbridge's *Alpine Lyrics*, 1852), most efforts were humbler.

"Blackwell's Mountaineering Library" includes, for example, along with more familiar names, A.W. Moore's *The Alps in 1864*. Moore wrote for himself and a few friends – his "journal" was privately printed in 1902 – so his claim to be more interested in "minuteness of topographical detail" than in elegant expression is credible (1939, 1:xix); the narratives are so exact that they could be used as a climber's guide. Aesthetic observations are rare, but Moore occasionally acknowledges "rugged" or "ravishing grandeur" (54, 67). Once when he was camped on a moraine, the clouds parted at sunset to reveal a peak of Les Écrins, and he was "electrified by the glory" of "so sublime a scene" (66–7). Mont Blanc's ice cliffs also seemed "sublime," though dwarfed by the vastness of their surroundings. Moore is probably more representative of Victorian mountaineers than either Tyndall or Stephen.

CONTINENTAL VOICES

The Victorians led all nineteenth-century interpreters of the Alps. Their Alpine Club preceded those of Italy and Switzerland (1863), Austria and Germany (1869), and France (1874). The guides were Swiss and many of the climbers were European, but the major climber-writers were English. The Alpine Club's publications had no counterpart on the Continent; France, which showed little interest in England's mountain literature, produced a relatively weak one of its own (Engel 1930b, 231, 240, 248). The French rarely tried to combine mountaineering with literature, as *Peaks, Passes, and Glaciers* did. The French Alpine Club's *Revue* was narrow and technical, as if 'mountaineering had killed the mountains' ("l'alpinisme a tué la montagne," 250).

French authors and climbers usually inhabited different worlds. Hugo wrote feelingly but made no ascents; Lamartine, who wanted to be 'the poet of the Alps,' kept them in the background except in his verse-novel *Jocelyn* (1836), and there he imports details from the Apennines. His pseudo-Alps are intellectual and Christianized: "Jehovah … a consacré les cimes" ('consecrated the summits'), he believes, and they remain vague objects of veneration (in Engel 1930b, 166–73). Flaubert enjoyed riding into the Pyrenees one day in 1841 and looking down on France. He produced an appreciative sentence – "Si vous voulez du grand et du beau, il faut sortir de l'église et gagner la montagne, vous élever des vallées et monter vers la région des neiges" ('If you want the great and the beautiful, leave the church and go to the mountains, lift yourself above the valleys and climb to the snows') – but rarely climbed; he was drawn to deserts (Flaubert 1910, 385). Taine's *Voyage aux Pyrénées* (1855) concentrates on the history, legends, and libraries of the region; the peaks, which he did not know, are cloaked in mist.

Continental climbers' narratives, especially ascents of Mont Blanc, continued to appear but were generally without literary pretensions. One exception is Édouard Desors, who climbed and studied glaciers with Agassiz, and does give a vivid sense of high mountains in his books (1840, 1841). He held 'geological communion' with the Alps, asserting that their 'new world' somehow 'effaced' the individual ego (Engel 1930b, 194). Another interesting mountaineer-author is E. Rambert, who in 1866 tried to define "le plaisir du grimpeur" ('the climber's pleasure'), and called views of and from high peaks "agrandissant" ('enlarging'; 241–3).

A modest revival of French Alpine literature began with several articles by Théophile Gautier (collected in *Vacances de lundi*, 1869). "Vues de Savoie et de Suisse" (1862) is a remarkable appreciation of mountains. Living in cities and on plains, we tend to forget that we are whirling through space, says Gautier, because our terrestrial vehicle is covered by human artifacts. Great mountains remind us that we are on an ancient planet where life may be only a temporary accident that could be ended by a 'Neptunian or Plutonian' cataclysm; they retain the image of primitive chaos and record the earth's search for its final form (Gautier 1881, 49–50). Standing in lonely silence, they have seen centuries glide by like avalanches, civilizations vanish like bubbles.

So far, any geologist might agree, but then Gautier asserts that the Alps have not changed since prehistoric times and will not change until some cataclysm overthrows them. No Alpine Club member of the 1860s was this geologically illiterate, and the idea that blood oozes from the pores at high altitude, or that one could not contemplate Alpine panoramas for more than a few minutes 'without dying,' would have drawn a smile from Stephen or Tyndall. Yet Gautier's *feelings* for the Alps are impressive. No poet, not even Byron, he says, can adequately depict this region where the earth retains its original 'starry beauty, elsewhere spoiled by man' ("sa beauté d'astre, défiguré par l'homme"); mountains transcend us to approach 'the eternal, the infinite, the domain of God' (52–3). He writes so sensitively of a group leaving 'the human zone' of the Grands Mulets to climb Mont Blanc ("Quelle solitude, quel silence, quelle désolation!") and toiling through the 'horrible chaos' where glaciers meet, like some 'ossuary of primitive creations,' that it is a shock to be reminded that he is not describing his climb but reacting to photographic "Vues" by Messrs Bisson *frères* (54–5). Cameras had arrived in the Alps.

"Le Mont Blanc" (1868) is a light description of a tourist's Alpine excursion – until a sudden glimpse of the mountain produces 'a dazzle ["un éblouissement"] of admiration.' It is so 'splendidly magnificent,' like some lunar fragment fallen to earth, that it seems to 'open the dreamgates' leading to a spiritual realm. The peak's 'ideal, absolute white' recalls Gauthier's poem "Symphonie en blanc majeur" (1852; chap. 17); clouds drift along the mountain like angels on Jacob's Ladder. Revealed for a moment from behind a cloud-curtain, the 'King of the Alps' produces an aesthetic glut, giving Gautier a 'complete sensation of the beautiful, the grand and the sublime' (153–4). At dawn, Mont Blanc appears in its 'sublime nudity,' free of all cloud, resembling a rough-hewn block of Carrara marble in its 'admirable purity' (157). Gautier feels small: the 'colossal masses' of the Alps dwarf Chamonix and all human works (165).

A love of natural history brought Jules Michelet to the Alps and Pyrenees. "La Montagne" (1868), a remarkably impressionistic, self-regarding effort for a scientist, is also strikingly dark hued. Michelet first sees the Grindelwald glacier through his hotel window not as an illustration of Agassiz but as a 'luminous chaos' that produces 'astonishment and horror' (Michelet 1930, 191). A bunch of wildflowers preserved in the ice is an image of death, not of time's defeat; the chamois hunters who made the first ascents are said to have been *seeking* danger (193). Michelet imagines someone's first 'terrible' glimpse, long ago, of Mont Blanc, noting that it has been seen as the 'debris of a dead star' or a 'sepulchral planet' (194). Yet, though he stresses the ominous side of the white mountain – it should be seen during bad weather – the Alps are also the 'altar' (200) and reservoir of Europe. Michelet took a broad view of the Great: he fantasizes about the North Pole, which reminds him of those 'intermediate poles,' the Alps and Andes, when flaming peaks thrust up through the ice (213).

FARTHER AFIELD

In 1868 A.W. Moore (see above), a pioneer of winter mountaineering, went on one of the first English expeditions to the Caucasus, but most of the reports on great mountains outside Europe in this period come from the Americas. Francis Parkman's brushes with the Rocky Mountains, recounted in his journal and *The Oregon Trail*, impressed him more than did the vast plains; whereas the "Great American Desert" was "dreary and monotonous," the Rockies were "sublime," requiring a quotation from *Childe Harold* (1991, 64, 270–1). John Wesley Powell began to explore the Rockies in 1867 and John Muir the Sierra Nevada in 1868, though their written accounts belong to later decades.

One such report comes from Friedrich Hassaurek, an Austrian-American diplomat who travelled widely in the Andes. Throughout *Four Years among the Ecuadorians* (1867), Hassaurek seems to care little for the Andean peaks and *altiplano*; if mentioned at all they are "dreary," "melancholy," and barren. Only in the final paragraph, as he is quitting the country forever, does he suddenly confess the hold on his imagination of the mountains' "grave majesty," a "beautiful dream" that "will live forever in my recollection" (Hassaurek 1967, 195). Whence has this come? No aesthetician, Hassaurek can only testify to the impact of space and height on sense and feeling: "No scenery has ever made such a lasting and intense impression on my mind as the highlands of the Andes .... I shall treasure it up as one of the fondest reminiscences of my life" (196).

What brought people to the mountains in this period? Robertson (1977) lists the motives actually given by Victorian climbers as pleasure, science, moral and physical improvement, quasi-military adventure, and camaraderie. Treating the question more generally, Engel thinks that "keener minds" sensed the harmony of a "higher order" in the Alps, and that an "unconscious asceticism" brought many (1971, 13–14). Climbers are always primarily adventurers, she says, but otherwise hardly any two climb for the same reasons. They may love beauty, nature, quiet, solitude, or independence; may be misanthropists, geologists, masochists, primitivists; may seek the eternal and infinite, a loss of self, triumph, danger, the unknown (178–81). The question is too complex to admit of a single answer, but the two lists do overlap. Engel, herself a climber, is more apt than Robertson to admit aesthetic and spiritual appeals. If she is right – and I think she is – Victorian mountaineers did respond to incentives described by Addison and other writers discussed here, as well as to moral and social motives.

In 1865 an accident during the first ascent of the Matterhorn took the lives of four climbers out of a party of seven. It was nearly the Alpine equivalent of the loss of the Franklin expedition for Arctic exploration; the public was shocked to be reminded that not all ascents were merely successes or failures: these grand adventures could end fatally. The Matterhorn incident gave a darker cast to the idea of conquering peaks, and reinjected some gloom into the mountain glory.

16

The Arctic Saga:
Polar Exploration, 1830–67

Ah, for just one time I would take the Northwest Passage
To find the hand of Franklin reaching for the Beaufort Sea,
Tracing one warm line through a land so wide and savage,
And make a Northwest Passage to the sea.

Stan Rogers (1981)

The idea of the Arctic piqued sensitive imaginations long before the late balladeer Stan Rogers turned Franklin's tragic epic into a metaphor of his own odyssey. On a rainy November day, Charlotte Brontë's Jane Eyre sat down to read Bewick's *History of British Birds*, which fascinated her with accounts of "solitary rocks and promontories" inhabited only by seabirds, and of the coast of Norway, island-studded from Lindeness to North Cape:

Where the Northern Ocean, in vast whirls,
Boils round the naked, melancholy isles
Of farthest Thule; and the Atlantic surge
Pours in among the stormy Hebrides.

Nor could I [she recalls, having quoted Thomson's "Autumn"] pass unnoticed the suggestion of the bleak shores of Lapland, Siberia, Spitzbergen, Nova Zembla, Iceland, Greenland, with "the vast sweep of the Arctic Zone, and those forlorn regions of dreary space, – that reservoir of frost and snow, where firm fields of ice, the accumulation of centuries of winters, glazed in Alpine heights above heights, surround the pole, and concentre the multiplied rigors of extreme cold." Of these death-white realms I formed an idea of my own: shadowy ... but strangely impressive (C. Brontë, n.d., 2).

There are no tales of warmth at the Pole here: scene and mood harmonize with Jane's own desolate situation.

This passage suggests that Charlotte Brontë had been reading the literature of polar travel with some attention, and (like her sister Emily, Coleridge, Mary Shelley, Poe, Baudelaire, and other writers) had been stirred by it. She would have known some of the authors discussed in earlier chapters – Cook and Parry, perhaps Weddell, Franklin, or Beechey – and exploration was continuing in her own day. John Ross's second Arctic voyage (1829–33) discovered the Northern Magnetic Pole while "frozen in." The Royal Geographical Society's *Geographical Journal* began to publish reports of polar voyages in 1832. One of Ross's officers, his nephew James Clark Ross, went to the other extreme, sailing through pack ice into what is now the Ross Sea, reaching 78°11′ South latitude, sighting the Antarctic mainland, and naming Mount Erebus (1839–43). And the Franklin expedition in quest of the Northwest Passage, which was to crown all of England's efforts, departed in 1845 – never to return. It was missing, and the Great Search was about to start, when *Jane Eyre* appeared.

The loss of the entire Franklin expedition was the darkest chapter of the nineteenth-century Arctic saga, chastening the polar sublime considerably in the public imagination, which had tended to romanticize northern voyages (Loomis 1977, 106–8). The first tragedy of scale in Arctic exploration, it shocked England even more than would the Matterhorn deaths or Scott's Antarctic disaster later, especially when evidence was found of scurvy, starvation, and cannibalism among Franklin's men. The story unfolded in slow motion, but inexorably, from the first traces found in 1850, to the public disclosure in 1854 of the expedition's fate, to the discovery of bodies, relics, and a message in 1858. The Hakluyt Society published Gerrit de Veer's record of *Barent's Three Voyages* in 1853, as if to remind readers that polar voyages had *always* been dangerous.

Yet, ironically, the search for Franklin opened a new phase in Arctic exploration that produced solid achievements and eventually metamorphosed into the quest for the North Pole. In their expedition of 1850–54, Capt. Robert Le Mesurier M'Clure and his crew finally discovered a way through the long-desired Northwest Passage while seeking the lost expedition, though they could not bring *HMS Investigator* through it. The Royal Navy functioned as the Arctic's Alpine Club, sponsoring and coordinating most of the relief voyages and publishing their reports; whalers and American ships also participated. Among those searching for Franklin were men who were interested in the Pole and later became popular writers on the Arctic: the U.S. (Grinnell) expedition included Elisha Kane, who brought Isaac Hayes on his second trip.

Just how all of this activity affected the development of a "Thulean aesthetic" is, of course, the question here. Most official accounts of expeditions offered no more emotional and imaginative sustenance than in Captain Cook's time; the *leaders* did not create the "Arctic sublime" (Loomis 1977) or "Arctic Grail" (Berton 1988) that fascinated the public. People, especially literary people, were stimulated by the idea and images of the Arctic rather than by Admiralty narratives. Charles Dickens wrote a defence of the Franklin expedition for *Household Words* ("The Lost Arctic Voyagers," December 1854), and collaborated with Wilkie Collins on a sympathetic play, *The Frozen Deep* (Loomis 1977, 108–9). Charles Baudelaire translated Poe's *Arthur Gordon Pym* (which used the myth of a warm polar sea) in 1857. Years later Tennyson wrote an epitaph for the memorial to his uncle-in-law, Sir John Franklin, in Westminster Abbey:

> Not here! the white North has thy bones; and thou,
> Heroic sailor soul,
> Art passing on thine happier voyage now
> Toward no earthly pole.

His sympathies were requited to the extent that Elisha Kane named a stone pillar on Greenland's coast for Tennyson.

We infer the reasons for the public fascination with the polar regions after Cook, then, from the responses of those who stayed behind. To some extent it was doubtless the mystery of what was up or down there, added to the powerful appeal of Great landscape to the imagination. The most emotive appreciations were visual, pointing to the central role of the imaging or imagining faculty. The first hasty efforts of illustrators with Cook's and later expeditions, touched up by professional artists at home, became engravings that appeared as plates in the official account and/or in periodicals such as *The Illustrated London News*. Significantly, when that paper used "Alpine" language to portray the Arctic in 1850 – "awful majesty," "sublime severity" – it was describing not the thing itself but Burford's *Panorama of the Polar Regions* (Loomis 1977, 107). The final stage was paintings such as Caspar David Friedrich's *Arctic Shipwreck* (ca. 1824, sometimes confused with his lost *Wreck of the Hope*), Frederic Church's *The Icebergs* (1861) and Edwin

Landseer's *Man Proposes, God Disposes* (1864), beside whose emotional content almost all the explorers' narratives seem flat (103, 110; Lopez 1986, 246).

Much of John Ross's 1835 *Narrative of a Second Voyage* [1829–33] *in Search of a North-West Passage*, for example, is merely a log, with some pontificating about the role of Providence in Arctic navigation and the movement of icebergs. Ross, an able though unamiable commander (Berton 1989, 111–13), rarely comments on scenery, and the only terrain he approves is mountains: Greenland's are "magnificent," Disko Island's "stupendous"; Cape Byam Martin has "grandeur" (John Ross 1969, 50, 80, 88). For the most part, though, rocky islets, "barren and repulsive," dot the winter landscape, a "dreary, heart-sinking, monotonous, waste ... the very mind is paralyzed [by the] uniformity and silence and death" (139, 191). After this outburst he seldom looks at the "miserable country" again, except to call the "rugged mountains and islands" of Boothia Felix (named for his gin-producing patron) "considerably picturesque" (208, 382).

While John Ross did not admire the Arctic version of the Great, it moved him as a formidable enemy who proved too strong. The "impressive" sight of seamen cheering their arrival at the "western sea" in the still of night, after a long sledge journey amid a "dreary waste of ice and snow" – the Arctic here providing a foil to the human spirit – is almost the last cheerful moment until their rescue (403). After two winters, his ship remained imprisoned in a "vacuum of wide-spread ice and snow" (462). Ross swears that the landscape is uninteresting, yet some of the engravings are striking, and he suddenly breaks out in passionate denunciation of ice. It is all very well for English skaters to enjoy it, and even he has found icebergs "sublime," but on a long expedition ice and snow became a "plague," a "torment," an "evil" that he "hated," and the hatred has remained (601–3). His bitterest moment was abandoning his ship to "this melancholy desert" (643). Ross would not sentimentalize the Arctic in retrospect, nor did he feel its spirituality, as others did. His own religion ran in narrow channels of conventional and rather dour piety; he did not admit that the text "The world was good" applied to the Arctic.

His nephew and second-in-command, James Clark Ross, a more likeable figure than his uncle both to the crew and in his prose memorials, charted most of the new territory, located the Northern Magnetic Pole, and when given his own command in the Antarctic accomplished as much with a great deal less suffering. He too was pious, especially about the Sabbath and close brushes with icebergs (as were most mariners who essayed polar sailing). James Ross occasionally indulges a moment of natural religion: he could not see the "stupendous and magnificent" mountains of Antarctica without "adoration of the Author, and Maker ... of all" (James Ross 1969, 1:198). Thus the "grandeur" that he typically perceives in bergs and peaks has a religious basis, though it does not surface often. After an "awful" storm in the ice pack, Ross thanks God for showing them the "wonders of the great deep," His power, and their weakness (2:169, 175), but usually he admires the "eternal snow" of the Admiralty Range, the "wonderful" Ice Barrier, or the "wildness and beauty" of Hermite Island without preaching.

One reason for the modest number of devotional passages may have been the scientific foundation of the voyage: the British Association's desire to obtain data on terrestrial magnetism in high southern latitudes. The committee that set Ross's agenda included the astronomer Sir John Herschel and William Whewell (who had reviewed Lyell's *Principles*); Joseph Hooker, who went on to write *Flora Antarctica* (1847?), was his assistant surgeon and naturalist. A number of islands, capes, and mountains were named for scientists (Herschel, Whewell, Lyell, Darwin, etc.). Ross's geological analyses, Hooker's botanical descriptions, and numerous tables and appendices give the *Voyage of Discovery and Research in the Southern and Antarctic Regions* (1847) a strong empirical base.

It is probably not its science but the plan and luck of the expedition that make James Ross's text more cheerful and exciting than his uncle's. By retreating to New Zealand or the Falklands at the end of each season, the *Erebus* and *Terror* avoided wintering in Antarctica, so while the crews had plenty of discomfort and peril, they escaped the long periods of darkness and inactivity. The only dull notes are struck in relatively low latitudes: Kerguelen Island's extraordinary barrenness is "dreary" (John Ross's favourite adjective for the Arctic), while Hooker found Hermite Island near Cape Horn "gloomy" (1:94; 2:289). Further south, no one had occasion to be bored. Within the Antarctic Circle, James Ross frequently found scenes he considered "grand," "sublime," or "wonderful."

Still, it is a relief to turn from these official accounts to Elisha Kent Kane's *Arctic Explorations in the Years 1853, '54, '55* (1856), for a time the most popular travel book in the United States. Trained in medicine and natural science, Kane served as doctor for shipping magnate Henry Grinnell's American Relief Expedition (1850), and observed the discovery of the first Franklin relics. He returned in 1853 as head of "the Second Grinnell Expedition in Search of Sir John Franklin," but was at least equally interested in the theory of a warm, open sea near the pole (Villarejo 1965, 16, 46; Berton 1988, 241–3). Partly because of this multilayered agenda, Kane was neither a competent captain nor a successful explorer, making a number of mistakes that eventually split his crew, but his clear, simple, dignified, general-interest writing about the sensations of being in the Arctic made his book popular. Despite his misadventures, and the ill health that led to an early death, Kane conveyed the beauty and grandeur of the Arctic, and its power over the religious sensibilities, more feelingly than had any of his predecessors.

Although he rarely missed an opportunity for geological analysis of the landscape, Kane was always open to the aesthetic appeal of his surroundings as well. He introduces his themes early, evoking the "gorgeous spectacle" as the midnight sun appears over a "great berg, … kindling variously-colored fires on every part of its surface, and making the ice around us one great resplendency of gemwork, blazing carbuncles, and rubies and molten gold" (Kane 1971, 1:37). The idea of vast scale ("great berg") is repeated in the "grandeur" of cliffs, bays, and other scenery, the "immense" blocks of "belt-ice," the "boundless" icefield feeding the mighty glacier he named for Humboldt, and so on. Ice is often "pure and beautiful" (92, 397). The image of "gemwork" recurs near the end, as the survivors retreat southwards along the west coast of Greenland. By climbing a hill, Kane obtains a "sublime prospect" of the central icecap, "a vast undulating plain of purple-tinted ice, … gemming the horizon with the varied glitter of sun-tipped crystal" (2:271). Like the earliest navigators, Kane found a strange richness in Thule.

Kane's Arctic is a study in synaesthesia: glacial "oceans" of "picturesque sublimity" lie in a wide "desert" whose oases are the return of spring (1:220, 236, 244). It is a land of "blank whiteness" with "noble sections and scenes of splendid wildness and desolation" (222; 2:80) where he and his men suffer greatly, yet where the laws of existence are admirably simple. Towards the end of the book, Kane grows metaphysical. The Arctic winter night fills him with awe; a "grander scene than our bay by moonlight can hardly be conceived. It is more dream-like and supernatural than … earthly" (2:56). When the sun returns after their second winter, he virtually hails it as a deity: "Blessed be the Great Author of Light! I have once more looked upon the sun"; running towards it "was a Sunday act of worship" (52–3). Rising behind the "black portals" of the "Delectable Mountains" (named from Bunyan's *Pilgrim's Progress*), the sun makes them seem a "celestial gate" (85). As the body weakens, the spirit flares; more and more the men seem to inhabit "a landscape such as Dante or Milton might imagine, – inorganic, desolate, mysterious." In his darkest mood, Kane felt that he had reached "a world unfinished by the hand of its Creator" (57).

Kane's *Explorations* contains virtually all the glorious and gloomy elements that Loomis (1977) says existed in the popular Victorian perception of the Arctic: fascination with the vast and mysterious, beautiful and terrible landscape; intense awareness of its dangers after Franklin's disaster; and a theological dimension, including doubts about the nature of the Arctic creation. As in most polar narratives, the text is less emotional than the illustrations, which are mostly from Kane's sketches or descriptions and often make dramatic use of chiaroscuro to depict cloud, land, moonlight, and starlight (as in *Tennyson's Monument* and *Starting to Hunt*, for example, where J.M.W. Turner's influence seems probable). Chiaroscuro, the sharp juxtaposition of dark and bright masses, is the visual counterpart of the ideas of gloom and glory. In perilous situations the illustrations become melodramatic (*Parting Hawsers Off Godsend Ledge*). Often it must have been such pictures, more than the text, that worked their way into readers' minds.

Isaac Hayes, the doctor on Kane's expedition, returned in 1860–61 to survey the coasts of Greenland and "Grinnell Land," reaching almost 82° north latitude. With the books closed on Franklin, Hayes felt free to proclaim an agenda that is only implicit in Kane: *The Open Polar Sea. A Narrative of a Voyage of Discovery towards the North Pole* (1867). An unwary reader might assume from this title, or even from the text, that Hayes had actually *found* the body of temperate water that some theorists posited at the poles. Having long yearned for this "mystic" goal, Hayes states that he saw "open polar sea" near Mount Parry during a spring sledging journey (1867, 295, 315–17). This equivocation – a classic instance of the *idée fixe* – is his low point, however; as a rule, Hayes is as trustworthy as most Arctic explorers, and unusually impressionable and articulate.

If Hayes were a poet, his aesthetic paradoxes would be called modernistic; his vast Arctic desert has the "terrible beauty" of Yeats's "Easter 1916." When the fog first lifts off Greenland, it reveals "a land of enchantment": icebergs "like castles in a fairy tale," "noble mountains," a coast of "austere magnificence" and "frowning desolation" (23). Having "come of [their] own free will into a region of stern realities" that is also Valhalla, "seat eternal of the gods," they find bright sky and warm air at midnight, bergs like precious stones, pure clear water of a rich green. Drifting among great icebergs, conscious of both their "terrible aspects" and their "wondrous beauties," Hayes quotes Coleridge: "And ice, mast-high, came floating by" (46–7). Some of these motifs recur thematically:

magnificent desolation, divine severity, beautiful dangers. Surprisingly, Hayes's enthusiasm survives the halcyon summer weather, though it darkens and deepens towards awe as winter approaches. A terrific gale gives "a most wonderful exhibition," making a scene as "magnificent" and "wild" as Shakespeare or Dante might have imagined (69–70).

The sense of being "alone … in the Arctic desert" after the sun disappears in October provokes a series of references to solitude and desertic qualities, with the ship as an oasis (90). Yet Hayes does not become gloomy, as John Ross had done; his desert is "drear" only when a comrade must be buried (248). An arduous autumnal journey over a Greenland glacier ends at a camp "as sublime as it was dangerous," far inland and high up, "in the midst of a vast frozen sahara, immeasurable to the human eye" (120). Images of sublimity and vastness dominate the later chapters without displacing the early themes. Hayes sees a "matchless beauty" in icebergs that may be older than Eden – the familiar note of antiquity marvellously preserved – while the Arctic winter is at once "a terror," "rugged and severe," and "sublime and beautiful" (131, 201–2). The long winter night and increasing privations affect his perceptions, moving him, like Kane, towards the metaphysical. Objects stand isolated, unrelated to one another, his "mind … wanders into space," and silence becomes an almost unendurable entity (202–4).

Hayes's Arctic becomes analogous not only to the desert but to other Great environments during his painful last months. The route of their retreat up Smith's Sound lay through a mountainous wilderness of ice blocks, often described in Alpine terms. For three weeks the snow-blind men made only three miles a day across this surface, through cold and storms. "Human nature cannot stand it," Hayes thought, yet they negotiated the "vast ice-jungle" and survived (285–6). Although oppressed by the scale, the "dreariness and desolation" of the Arctic (312), Hayes regained a feeling for its charm and beauty on his way south that summer. By early May the "vast sea of whiteness" had a "stern, quiet sublimity" at midnight (295). The Arctic still seemed, as it had from the first, a divine abode, best evoked by Romantic poetry. In his last descriptive passage, Hayes called the Tyndall Glacier "impressive evidence of the greatness and power of the Almighty hand," and thought of Byron's lines on the "cold sublimity" of the Alps (393).

The polar wastes, like the desert, moved from the theoretical to the actual, experiential Great more slowly than did other areas mainly because they were less accessible. Getting to know them entailed more time, more planning, greater resources, and usually greater suffering than did climbing, star-gazing or warm-water sailing. The nineteenth century succeeded in establishing modes of transport that brought enough observers to high latitudes and back to allow them to rough out the beginnings of an aesthetic consensus, though it was the middle of the century before this happened. As we have to wait for Burton and Fromentin in the 1850s to see the desert embraced for itself, it is not until Kane and Hayes in the 1850s and 1860s that the Arctic is firmly apprehended as belonging to Great nature and evoking sublimity. And still, compared to Nansen, Amundsen, Scott, Shackleton, and later polar explorers, it is only, so to speak, the tip of the iceberg.

17

Desert Souls:
The Great and Barren in
European Literature, 1830–66

The road from the Great to Egdon Heath was never just an English lane:
Burnet, Addison, and their successors tried to speak universally, and had
Continental sources, allies, and analogues. Even in this study, which fo-
cuses on English-language writing, names such as Petrarch, Giordano
Bruno, Fontenelle, Buffon, Bashō, von Haller, Rousseau, de Saussure,
Goethe, Kant, Humboldt, Agassiz, Hugo, and Fromentin suggest a phenomenon of some cultural breadth. An extension into other national
literatures would be a logical next step. How have South American writers responded to the Andes, the Arabs and the Chinese to their deserts,
the Russians to their steppes? Do the aesthetics of other cultures exhibit
historical patterns of development similar to Europe's? Do generalizations based mainly on England, France, Switzerland, and North America
hold for Scandinavia, Chile, Asia, and Africa? In this chapter, however,
which discusses how mid-nineteenth-century European writing dealt
with the natural Great, I can only point to some of the larger straws signalling the wind's changes in that area.

The shift that Hardy claimed to have observed, from an aesthetics of
beauty (Tempe) to one of "chastened sublimity" (Thule) "in keeping
with the moods of the more thinking among mankind," is visible in
some of nineteenth-century Europe's best-known poems and novels. Often the idea is that the great barrens of the world – deserts, polar wastes,
and sea more often than mountains, with their sublime connotations –
reflect the speaker's or character's soul, providing an "objective correla-
tive" of its isolation and melancholy. The predominantly dark cast of the
Continental literature allies it with late English Romantic and Victorian
poetry and with Hardy, rather than with the observations of most scientists and travellers.

FICTION AND DRAMA

Some of the earliest and most extended examples occur in major novels. Honoré de Balzac, for example, begins *Eugénie Grandet* (1833) by observing that certain provincial houses "inspire une mélancholie égale à celle que provoquent les cloîtres les plus sombres, les landes les plus ternes, ou les ruines les plus tristes" ('instill a sadness like that induced by the gloomiest cloisters, the dullest heaths, or the saddest ruins'; 1972, 5). Balzac compares the melancholy of such houses to the 'aridity of waste lands' and the 'boniness' of ruins. One such dwelling is the 'pale, cold, silent' house (built of volcanic tufa) where the heroine spends her life (23). Its main entrance resembles 'the porch of a jail,' which, Hardy remarked of Egdon's appeal, often has more dignity than the facade of a palace (23–4). Moreover, Eugénie's home, with its imprisoning function, bare upper floors, perpetual cold shade and melancholy, is "l'image de sa vie," the 'image of her life' (269). In its primacy and tonal centrality, the house is Balzac's equivalent of Egdon Heath: the inanimate thing that establishes the context for human actions.

It would be interesting to know exactly what "landes ternes" meant to Balzac in 1833. He stayed in France most of his life (travelling to Russia in 1847), never visiting a desert except in his reading, yet deserts keep appearing in his novels and stories. The desires of Lady Arabella Dudley (in *Le Lys dans la vallée*, 1836) are compared to a desert windstorm, and her eyes to its vastness. In the short story "A Passion in the Desert," a Provençal soldier has a strange encounter with a panther at an oasis. "In the desert," concludes the old soldier, "there is everything, and nothing ... it is God without mankind" (Balzac 1985, 26), which sounds like an analogue of the Arabic proverb that Burton cites: "In the desert there is only He." Whatever their source, Balzac's feelings about desert lands ran strong and deep.

In *Dead Souls* (1842) Nikolai Gogol uses empty landscape more directly – without the intermediate term of a house – to evoke the idle, "lonely lives" of the characters (1961, 126). The scraggly, marginal Russian plain is a good setting for Manilov, in whom there is "always something missing," something "not yet ready," while the "wasteland" in which Plewshkin lives is both run-down real estate and his avarice made visible (32, 127). Virtually the only land that the narrator enjoys is the neglected garden, "beautiful in its spectacular wildness," that "blended into the open fields" behind Plewshkin's house (128). That combination intrigues the narrator: "It was wild, and somehow beautiful and desolate at the same time." This approaches the aesthetic formulation that Shaftesbury had given the Augustans, though the narrator's assertion that such an effect "could not have been contrived by Nature or by Art alone," only by their "combined efforts," would probably not have been made in England after the early eighteenth century (129).

Gogol's use of symbolic emptiness, however, is very much of the nineteenth century. *Dead Souls* is one of Robert Adams's prize exhibits in *Nil. Episodes in the Literary Conquest of Void*, but, again, the *characters* do not "conquer" anything. The "flat emptiness" of the fields and the surrounding steppe is also, from first to last, the spiritual condition of Chichikov, Nozdrev, and the others (Gogol 1961, 105), who might be said to have been "conquered" *by* the wilderness around them, if they did not indeed *project* it. The only conqueror is the narrator/author, who comprehends the bleak truth that emptiness prevails, within and without. Here, then, is how one Russian author used waste lands: as a mirror.

Another writer drawn to inner and outer barrens was Gustave Flaubert, who was fascinated by deserts from his youth. One form that this attraction took was probably conceived, in 1845, the day he saw Breughel's tableau *The Temptation of Saint Anthony*, the desert hermit (AD 250–356). Flaubert's journal describes the painting in some detail: in the foreground St Anthony is caressed by three nude temptresses, while two devils' heads, "moitié vivants, moitié montagnes" ('half living, half mountains'), look on from the distance (1908, ii). In 1848–49 Flaubert wrote a long play, *La Tentation dè Saint Antoine*, then left for Egypt. With a sensibility steeped in Byron, Hugo, and *The Arabian Nights* (Steegmuller 1972, 9–11), he was well equipped to help invent "orientalism" (Saïd 1978, chap. 2, sec. 4). He climbed the Great Pyramid at dawn (seeing the desert as petrified ocean) and cruised up the Nile, sampling its brothels and scenery. The "orientalisme épique" of his novel *Salammbô* (1862) was probably inspired by the temples of Karnak, which seemed to Flaubert "une demeure de géants" ('a dwelling of giants'; Carré 1956, 2:116–17).

At Aswan, however, he felt like the land – "very empty, very flat, very sterile" – a complaint repeated in his journals and letters with regard to himself and to modern life in general (Steegmuller 1972, 126). Flaubert crossed the eastern desert, through a sandstorm, to Koseir on the Red Sea, observing the desert in some detail, though his responses, ungoverned by any consistent attitude, do not coalesce into a unified portrait. His reaction to a walk in the desert highlights a quality often mentioned favourably by nineteenth-century European visitors to Great landscapes: "Silence. Silence. Silence." The absence of man, the noisy animal, made it possible to hear Nothing. Flaubert also had a glimpse of Nubia, where he struck another familiar note. "La nature est tout autre" ('Nature is wholly different') here, he wrote (Carré, 2:112): Great forms constitute virtually another world. The experiences of these months in Egypt would turn up repeatedly as mood and details of setting in his literary prose (Carré 1956, 2:128–9; Steegmuller 1972, 7).

In 1856 Flaubert completed a revision of *La Tentation de Saint Antoine*, but, alarmed by the hostility that *Madame Bovary* had aroused, did not try to publish his "drama," believing that its religious scepticism might injure his reputation further. As he had written to Louise Colet, serious writers in their time and place were isolated: "On n'a ni base ni écho; on se trouve plus seul qu'un Bédouin dans le désert, car le Bédouin au moins connaît les sources cachées sous le sable; il a l'immensité tout autour de lui et les aigles volant au-dessus."[1] If he could not identify with the nomad, he could envy his greater compensations for solitude.

The 1849–56 version of *Saint Antoine* (published in 1908) makes interesting use of both Breughel's painting and Egyptian nature. As in Shelley's *Prometheus Unbound*, the opening scene direction sets a stark context for the struggle: "Le soir, sur une montagne. À l'horizon, le désert" ('Evening, on a mountain. A desert horizon'). The landscape serves throughout as a projection of Anthony's dessicated soul; when some grasses burn, for example, he exclaims, "ma chair brûle!" ('my flesh burns!'; 1908, 129). Before this scene sits the bored and weary hermit, subject to every temptation from Logic to the Queen of Sheba. Flaubert was the first of many to see that there was a lot of himself in his troubled saint (Unwin 1979, 18). Louis Bertrand noted Anthony's conscious embrace of "le vide sans fond" ('the bottomless void'); and the Devil's remark to Anthony, that "la désolation roule dans ta tête" ('the wasteland is in your mind'), sounds like Flaubert's sensation of emptiness and sterility at Aswan (Flaubert 1908, xxi, 245).

At the beginning of Part Three, the Devil carries Anthony into space, much as he carried Byron's Cain (Flaubert admired Byron: "Quel poète!"). The hermit's reaction to the Void – "Je flotte éperdu dans des immensités froides" ('I float bewildered in cold vastnesses') – is stronger than to the desert, which has become simply an extension of his weary soul (164). The frigid immensities that bewilder Anthony represent in

1. 'One finds neither a foundation nor an echo, but is more solitary than a nomad, who at least knows of hidden springs under the sand; he has vastness all around him and eagles flying above' (Flaubert 1927, 4:39). All translations here are my own.

physical terms the moral relativism and Spinozan ethics with which the Devil tempts him (Unwin 1979, 21–2). Anthony's distracted attempts to pray are punctuated by the Devil's laughter; the drama's last words are the Tempter's "Hah! Hah! Hah!"

Flaubert knew that this dénouement would not be acceptable to the reading public and shelved *Saint Antoine* until the 1870s (see chapter 19). But he was still interested in deserts, visiting Algeria and Tunisia in 1858 and finishing a novel about ancient Carthage, *Salammbô*. Most critics think that Egypt, not Tunisia, was the paramount influence on *Salammbô*'s topography, although the novel's florid scenery and long descriptive passages may owe as much to nineteenth-century opera as to scenes of travel. Flaubert's landscape is full of extremes. Now it is as redolent of Venus as his Nile orgies: the barbarians marching across a sandy plain bordered by mountains like swelling breasts feel "un accablement ... plein de délices" ('an oppression full of delights'; 1953, 31); now fields as empty as deserts stretch to a horizon dotted with burned villages. Descriptions of the countryside and of Carthage, its people, and their gods do not aim at visual accuracy but at truth of feeling. We cannot recognize temperate Carthage and its fertile hinterland – ancient or modern, peaceful or war-torn – in this dreamscape; as in *Saint Antoine*, setting expresses a spiritual condition.

Virtually every image and setting in the novel symbolizes the moral bankruptcy of the culture. A "waste land deeper than the deserts of Carthage" exists in the character of Schahabarim, while a "spiritual-sensual thirst" paralleling a physical one plagues the barbarian mercenaries (Adams 1966, 81, 79). There is also a desert within the Ancients of Carthage, "savants dans les disciplines religieuses, experts en stratagèmes, impitoyables et riches" ('expert celebrants and strategists, pitiless and rich'); the iron icon of their god Moloch has a gaping hole where his heart should be (Flaubert 1953, 127). The "effroyable ['frightful'] solitude" that surrounds the ravaging Punic army (188) and "l'aridité" ('the dessication') that Salammbô sees (203) are not topographical features of Tunisia, but spiritual characteristics projected by a nineteenth-century soul onto the third century BC. In Flaubert as in Robert Frost, the most fearful deserts are within.

POETRY

French lyric poetry of this period offers more concentrated examples of "chastened sublimity." The early poems of Théophile Gautier, for example, exhibit the kind of spiritual sereness found in Hardy's "Neutral Tones." Gautier's bleak "Pensées d'Automne" has none of Keats's mellow fruitfulness but plenty of mist; it is *late* autumn, and the sky is "terne" (1932, 1:38), Balzac's adjective for dull heaths. The last leaf of summer trembles in his heart as well as in the woodland. This mood is first expressed via Great nature in the sonnet "La Caravane" (from *La Comédie de la mort*, 1838). We are all a 'human caravan' dragging our burning feet through the "Sahara du monde," the 'world-Sahara' (2:145). Sweat provides our only drink, a vulture the only shade, and a grave the only oasis in this 'temporal waste' ("désert du temps"). The grim and powerful symbols of this poem anticipate those twentieth-century climatologists who believe that our world will end as desert; that the desert is our future.

Gautier found metaphorical deserts more meaningful than real mountains at this time. In "Montée sur le Brocken" ('Climb of the Brocken'), Gautier, perhaps with a sceptical glance at Goethe's epiphany on that peak ("Harzreise im Winter"; see chapter 6), insists that he felt like a 'ridiculous Titan' up there, belonging to neither heaven nor earth (173). But in the 1840s Spain's Sierra Nevada stirred him; the snowy ranges seemed a stormy ocean, Chaos awaiting the Creator's word, or an immense cemetery of bygone races: Behemoth, Leviathan, Titan ("J'Étais monté plus haut," from *Poésies nouvelles*, 289). Now Gautier loves the proud, sublime mountains madly ("J'aime d'un fol amour"), though they have no plants, no use, nothing of human concerns: just the free, pure air, and beauty ("Dans la Sierra," 291). He prefers them to fertile fields (too far from God) partly because their barrenness accords with his own. "In Deserto," his first attempt to treat mountains and deserts as a "unified field," declares that they are less dry and dead to vegetation than his stony heart is to feeling ("moins secs et moins morts aux végétations / Que le roc de mon coeur ne l'est aux passions"; 281). If only some Moses could make a spring gush from his heart!

Gautier's controversial orientalism dates from *Une Nuit de Cléopâtre* (1838), before his visits to Turkey (1852) and Egypt (1869); his was initially a literary affinity, based on reading Champollion, Lamartine, Gérard de Nerval, later Flaubert, and others (Carré 1956, 2:135–209). This obsession – expressed in prose, in verse ("Gazhel," "Sultan Mahmoud"), even in ballet – united with his sense of the desert as symbol in "Nostalgies D'Obélisques" (1851). After contemplating the Egyptian obelisk in Paris, he evokes that of Luxor, sitting "Dans la solitude éternelle, / En face de l'immensité" ('In eternal solitude, /Facing vastness'). Immensity then takes over the poem:

> À l'horizon que rien ne borne,
> Stérile, muet, infini,
> Le désert sous le soleil morne,
> Déroule son linceul jauni.[2]

Above, the cloudless sky is another desert, 'implacably pure.' The obelisk, trapped in a grim desert so different from Fromentin's, oppressed by history, wishes it could find a home in Paris too.

Émaux et Camées also contains the remarkable "Symphonie en blanc majeur" (1852). An icy white evocation of the mythical and symbolic North, it fulfils Gautier's early symptoms of a wintry spirit and stands as the polar counterpart of "La Caravane." After all, if the world does not end as desert, we are told, it will end in ice. The climax of Gautier's extensive boreal iconography is the apparition of a northern Madonna:

> Est-ce la Madone des neiges,
> Un sphinx blanc que l'hiver sculpta,
>
> Sphinx enterré par l'avalanche,
> Gardien des glaciers étoilés,
> Et qui, sous sa poitrine blanche,
> Cache de blancs secrets gelés?[3]

'Our Lady of the Snows' is cognate with the Sphinx of avalanches and glaciers that inter unlucky Alpinists; Gautier understood the full range of possible meanings available in the key of 'White Major' at about the same time as Poe and Melville.

Suggestive, allusive, interrogative, and full of dissolves, "Symphonie en blanc majeur" is difficult to paraphrase, but clearly indicates Gautier's interest in the pictorial and imaginative qualities of the Arctic (probably stimulated by his association with Baudelaire). "Oh! qui pourra mettre un ton rose / Dans cette implacable blancheur!" he

2. 'Out to the limitless horizon, / Barren, silent, infinite, / The desert spreads its yellow shroud / Under the gloomy sun' (Gautier 1932, 3:43).

3. 'Is it the Madonna of the Snows, / A white Sphinx, sculpted by winter, / Buried by the avalanche, / Guardian of starry glaciers, / And who hides white frozen secrets / In her white breast?' (Gautier 1932, 3:24)

exclaims at the end ('Who could give this implacable whiteness a rosy hue!'). This 'implacability,' along with images of white "debaucheries," 'great white battles,' and the polar night, suggests a response to the disappearance of the Franklin expedition. Borealist and orientalist, drawn to mountains, polar wastes, and deserts, Gautier made a broad poetic application of the images and possible meanings of the natural Great, based on his own travels and a sensitive reading of those who had been there.

Given Charles Baudelaire's penchant for translating Edgar Allen Poe (including *Arthur Gordon Pym*) and his dedication of *Les Fleurs du mal* to Théophile Gautier, "maître et ami," his use of Great nature to express emotion in poetry is not surprising. Oceans, polar wastes, and space serve him as analogues of certain kinds of experience. Of these, only the sea has a positive or cheering value (as a young man he voyaged to Mauritius). In "L'Homme et la mer" (1861, sec. 14), ocean 'mirrors' the free man ("Homme libre"), who sees his own soul in the 'infinite rolling' ("déroulement infini") of its waves (Baudelaire 1975, 1:19). Addison wrote, "A spacious horizon is an image of liberty"; Baudelaire adds, "for the liberated soul." The appeal of swimming in the ocean is that of plunging into one's own image, embracing it, and knowing the sea for an entity as secret, deep, and combative as oneself. In "Obsession" (1861, sec. 79), though, he hates a *stormy* ocean as a reminder of self.

Baudelaire also discusses the appeal of the sea in section thirty of "Mon Coeur mis à nu" (from Poe's idea that one could revolutionize the intellectual world by writing a book called *My Heart Laid Bare*) in his *Journaux intimes* (1887). Why, he asks (in prose), is a view of the ocean so eternally pleasing? This was Addison's question, and Baudelaire's answer is not so different. The sea gives us the ideas of immensity and of movement simultaneously; as little as six or seven leagues (say forty miles) of it represent a 'gleam' ("rayon") of infinity that can suggest the whole idea ("l'infini total"; 1975, 1:696). A circle twice that size affords us the highest idea of earthly beauty. Baudelaire is less categorical than Addison – he has 'the highest idea of beauty' rather than the Great or sublime – but the nineteenth-century trend was away from the precise aesthetic distinctions of the eighteenth, and they agree that the pleasure has something to do with infinity and is eternal. One can read a great deal of Baudelaire without finding anything that pleased him as much as the sea.

His typical metaphorical use of nature first surfaces in "De Profundis Clamavi" (*Les Fleurs du mal*, 1861, sec. 30). From his private depths, the speaker views "un univers morne à l'horizon plombé" ('a gloomy universe with a leaden horizon'), a *mis en scène* consonant with those of Balzac, Gogol, and Gautier. But Baudelaire adds imagery appropriate to the translator of Poe, in the aftermath of the search for Franklin:

> Un soleil sans chaleur plane au-dessus six mois,
> Et les six autres mois la nuit couvre la terre;
> C'est un pays plus nu que la terre polaire[4]

The inner exploration is as terrible as the Northwest Passage:

> ... il n'est pas d'horreur au monde qui surpasse
> La froide cruauté de ce soleil de glace
> Et cette immense nuit semblable au vieux Chaos[5]

Cold is cruel, and a winter is a long night: the imagery of Arctic exploration suggests the subjective landscape.

Polar and wintry images inform several of Baudelaire's other 'flowers of evil.' His "Chant d'automne" (1861, sec. 56) makes Paul Verlaine's better-known "Chanson d'Automne," with its sobbing violins, seem a sentimental and self-indulgent pose. Baudelaire's autumn, like Théophile Gautier's, is advanced, his mood wintry: 'Deep winter will return to my soul' ("Tout l'hiver va rentrer dans mon être"; 1:57). And then, like the sun in its 'polar hell,' his heart will be nothing but 'a red block of ice' ("Et, comme le soleil dans son enfer polaire, / Mon coeur ne sera plus qu'un bloc rouge et glacé"; 1:57).

In "Le Goût du Néant" ("The Inclination to Nothingness": 1861, sec. 80; 1:76), the imagery is Alpine. The speaker feels "le Temps m'engloutit minute par minute," which Adams renders as "slow engulfment by the snows of Time" (1966, 117), with "le Temps" doubling as 'time' and 'weather.' (The 1859 *Revue française* version reads, "Le Temps descend sur moi": 'Time/ Weather descends on me.') The "engulfment" occurs tangibly, "Comme la neige immense un corps pris de roideur" ('as a great snow [covers] a stiffening corpse'). That Baudelaire is referring to mountaineering accidents seems more likely when he closes

---

4. 'A sun without heat hovers overhead for six months, / And night prevails for the other six; / This is a country barer than the polar lands' (Baudelaire 1975, 1:32).

5. 'No horror in the world exceeds / The cold cruelty of this icy sun / And this vast night, resembling the ancient Chaos' (Baudelaire 1975, 1:33).

with, "Avalanche, veux-tu m'emporter dans ta chute?" ('Will you carry me off in your plunge?') The title reminds us that the persona has a taste ("Goût") for these images and ideas.

Other poems reach out to the void of space for their images of *le néant*. In "Obsession," the poet is best pleased with a starless night, "Car je cherche le vide, et le noir, et le nu!" ('For I seek emptiness, and blackness, and bareness!'; Baudelaire 1861, 1:75). "Le Gouffre" (from *Nouvelles fleurs du mal*, 1868) goes farther into blackness, and ambiguity. Beginning with a reference to Pascal's *Pensée* on the terrors of infinite space, the speaker exclaims, 'Alas! *All* is abyss' ("Hélas! *tout* est abîme"; 142; my emphasis). Silence and deep gulfs of space are everywhere; he fears sleep as he would a huge hole. Through 'every window' he sees only the infinite, and his soul ("mon esprit") is "Jalouse du néant l'insensibilité." If this means that he desires (or envies) the insensibility of nothingness, then why the attitude implied by "Hélas," the fear of space, of sleep, of infinity? What he says he wants seems to be all around him, and within. Adams notes that everywhere else in *Les Fleurs du mal* "l'infini" is an ideal, a desired escape (1966, 120); only here is it terrible. Perhaps the emphasis should fall on the wish for insensibility; his tragedy is that he can feel.

Another possibility is that there is more than one void. In the abyss one would *not* be, but non-being may also occur here. "Le Goût de l'infini" (part of "Le Poème du Hachisch" in *Les Paradis artificiels*) discusses the kind of infinity that resides in a drug-induced abduction from self and world. But Baudelaire's ambiguity about *le néant* is too radical to be resolved. In a passage from his *Journaux intimes*, thought to be the basis of "Le Gouffre," he asserts that he has always had "la sensation du gouffre," and has 'cultivated his hysteria with joy and terror' ("J'ai cultivé mon hystérie avec jouissance et terreur"; 1862, 1:668). The references to a lifelong sense of solitude in "Mon coeur mis à nu" suggest that solipsism was Baudelaire's "gulf." Even in love, he says, "Le gouffre infranchissable, qui fait l'incommunicabilité, reste infranchi" ('the insurmountable gulf of non-communication remains unbridged'; 696). An early existentialist with a severe case of Sartrean nausea, Baudelaire distinguished between areas of the Great. He rejoiced in the sea, but found his inner void mirrored in the *néant* of deserts, the Arctic, and space.

Charles-Marie-René Leconte de Lisle, who was born on the island of Réunion in the Indian Ocean, came to France in 1837 but lived on Réunion again in 1843–45, also wrote of vast and gloomy solitudes: space, empty beaches, deserts, the polar ocean. The attitudes of his early poems towards these voids are shifting and uncertain. In *Poèmes antiques* (1852), he strikes various ancient and mythological poses. "Midi" (1852) says that the meaning of an 'immense extent' of sun-struck fields depends on what you bring to them: one who feels for humanity will find that "la Nature est vide" ('empty') and flee, but a disillusioned soul, a Keatsian seeker after melancholy who would 'taste the highest of dark pleasures' ("Goûter une suprême et morne volupté"), should linger. He will find that the sun 'speaks a sublime language' ("parle en paroles sublimes"), and, his heart tempered in 'the Divine Nothingness' ("le Néant divin"), will be reluctant to return to the city (Leconte de Lisle 1974, 1:292–3).

"Midi" is said to have been Flaubert's favourite poem, although several pieces in *Poèmes barbares* (1862) seem more Flaubertian. "Le Désert," for example, envisions a dreaming nomad in another 'immense extent,' this time specifically Middle Eastern. Perhaps Flaubert admired the balance of different outlooks in "Midi"; the *Poèmes barbares* are less provisional, albeit graphic. "Les Hurleurs" describes a pack of emaciated dogs, howling at the moon on an arid, bone-strewn beach in Africa. It is a remarkable night: there are no stars, yet a 'pale' moon swings sadly through the heavens like a gloomy lamp ("Comme une morne lampe oscillait tristement"). Why gloomy? The poet's response to astronomical data is morbid but spacious:

> Monde muet, marqué d'un signe de colère,
> Débris d'un globe mort au hasard dispersé,
> Elle laissait tomber de son orbe glacé
> Un reflet sepulchral sur l'océan polaire.[6]

Imagination traces the light back from the tropical to the polar ocean. After wondering what 'unknown anguish' makes the dogs bay, the speaker says that he has learned to understand their despairing cries "du fond de mon passé confus" ('from the depths of my obscure past'). Between him and these howlers at a dead world there is, after all, some relation.

In "Les Éléphants," on the other hand, the human does not figure at all. No one is driving the caravan of elephants over the desert towards

---

6. 'Silent world, marked with a sign of anger, / Debris of a dead world scattered at random, / It sends down from its icy sphere [or orbit] / A sepulchral reflection on the polar sea' (Leconte de Lisle 1974, 2:171).

their home; men and women live somewhere else. These 'huge pilgrims' ("pèlerins massifs") following their patriarch slowly across the red sands are impressive, but Leconte de Lisle's emphasis is first and last on the landscape (183). At the beginning, the desert is "une mer sans limite" ('a boundless sea'), and at the end "sable illimité" ('endless sand'). There is "Nulle vie et nul bruit" ('No life and no sound'); everything sleeps in these vast and "mornes ['gloomy'] solitudes." Even the elephants finally disappear over the poem's horizon, "Et le désert reprend son immobilité": the desert 'resumes its fixity.' This and other poems suggest that Leconte de Lisle was a writer "preoccupied with Nothing" (Robert Adams 1966, 124). Though he campaigned against Romantic excesses, his visionary landscapes share a lot of ground with Byron and Shelley; Leconte de Lisle used the Great as gloomily and nihilistically as they ever did, and with less glory.

There are other metaphorical uses of the barren and Great in the work of Leconte de Lisle and of Stephane Mallarmé, another of Adams's dwellers in the void, "haunted by ... emptiness" (155), and, like Baudelaire, an admiring translator of Poe. In "L'Azur" (1864, from *Le Parnasse contemporain*), the 'powerless' or 'impotent' ("impuissant") poet, overwhelmed by the 'serene irony' of the sky's 'eternal blue,' curses his own talent as he crosses a 'sterile desert of griefs' ("un désert stérile des Douleurs"; Mallarmé 1945, 37, 1,431). Only then, wrote Mallarmé, does he himself enter the poem (1,430), fleeing with closed eyes and 'empty soul' ("Mon âme vide"). The speaker is passionately, almost incoherently unhappy with what common folk call splendid weather; he wants the clear azure sky obscured by smoke, fog, anything that will hide it. For "Le Ciel est mort" ('Heaven/the sky is dead'), and he rushes to the oblivion of matter. But the gesture of escape is futile; the azure that haunts him triumphs, and he concludes by chanting its Name.

Thus Mallarmé finds in broad daylight the fearful sense of void that the night sky gave some earlier writers. If *Hérodiade* is the earliest expression of "the full Mallarmé cosmos of ... lofty glaciers, remote stars, silences, refusals, absences" (Robert Adams 1966, 157), "L'Azur" represents at least a fair start on it. Mallarmé's remark in a letter of 1866 that in composing *Hérodiade* he had fallen into two "néants," an inner and an outer, seems capable of wider application to his work, and sometimes the outer nothingness was an aspect of Great nature. Along with Théophile Gautier, Baudelaire, and Leconte de Lisle, Mallarmé shows that all of the areas outlined by Addison and his successors were employed by nineteenth-century French poets in imaging their emotional states, whether or not they had experienced the physical reality.

SCIENCE FICTION: JULES VERNE

Verne stands apart from the other major nineteenth-century European constructors of an aesthetics of Thule in his scientific optimism and humbler status as a popular writer. He is one of those authors – with Defoe, Swift, Lewis Carroll – whom we read as children (often in juvenile editions), and whose full meaning we discover only when, as adults, we are ready for it. Verne uses Great settings, as backgrounds or as subject, in ways that are imaginative, even poetic. Untrammelled by any strict realist program, he let his emotions and speculative faculty play freely over the material gathered by scientists and travellers. Charles F. Horne, who edited Verne, noted the careful research and scientific plausibility of his subject's series of *Voyages extraordinaires*, but acknowledged that the demands of "romance" sometimes led Verne to employ "extravagant means" to get his explorers safely home (Verne 1911a, 2:1–2). Verne's plain expository style and the wide adoption of his books by Anglophone readers make it feasible to examine them in English.

Verne's interests included oceans, mountains, volcanoes, polar lands, the interior of the earth, and their associated sciences. In *A Trip to the Centre of the Earth* (1864), the narrator emphasizes the geological research that sent him and his uncle on their expedition. When they find evidence that an early Icelandic alchemist went to the earth's centre, they decide, like good geologists, to "go and see" for themselves (20). As they travel to Snaefell, a dormant volcano in Iceland and the alchemist's reputed point of entry, Verne works in both his extensive reading on northern exploration and Vergil's Aeneas, who also visited the underworld. There may be an echo of Thomas Burnet in the description of the volcanic region's "terrible chaos" as "nature's ruins" (39), by 1864 a standard image. The area proves geologically interesting, and while climbing over rock and ice to Snaefell's summit, they "admire the awful grandeur" of the "magnificent spectacle": midnight sun, distant ocean, valleys, glaciers, and "snowy summits" (resembling a stormy sea), all of which gives the narrator a "sense of lofty sublimity" (50, 55).

Here Verne is simulating Alpine literature, but once the expedition reaches the crater and descends into the volcano, he is on ground previously worked only by Athanasius Kircher, Burnet, Coleridge, and a very few others. The adventurers walk down a large tunnel by electric torchlight, making geological observations and admiring lava and quartz crystals. As the days pass, whole strata are revealed, from granite and Silurian sedimentaries, through old red sandstone, marble, and fossils "ascending the scale of animal life," to a great cavern of coal, and so on (76). In a "vast and magnificent hall" fifty miles beneath the Atlantic Ocean, they argue about the composition of the earth's crust, the temperature of its interior and other scientific questions (96). A hundred miles below Scotland they discover a "vast and apparently limitless sea," lit by an aurora-like phenomenon and bordered with primitive flora, under a tremendous vault that dwarfs all human efforts (131). Clouds float over this Central Sea, a scene of "awful grandeur" greater than anything Humboldt saw (119).

To this point Verne plays mainly on the scientific imagination, but henceforth he moves, as Parke warns, into romance. After various adventures on a raft – including a terrific electrical storm of the Alpine sort – and on land, they surmise that the way to the earth's centre lies down a narrow tunnel. When they blast away the boulder blocking its entrance, however, the whole sea and the raft go down into the abyss at a hundred miles an hour. For a moment it looks like a parable of hubristic science chastised, but this is no *Frankenstein*. The raft shoots back up a shaft, the water becomes lava, and they erupt from a side crater of Stromboli, an Italian island, none the worse for wear and seemingly careless of the changes they made below. Yet Verne's *Trip* finally moves to re-establish its scientific frame: the survivors publish their results and solve the mystery of an erratic compass.

The Adventures of Captain Hatteras (1864) is a two-part fantasy on themes of Parry and Kane. Part One, "The English at the North Pole," launches a fictional expedition into northern waters. Verne had been reading the explorers (many of whom are cited), and his purpose was to develop those episodes of their voyages with strong imaginative appeal. So the ice pack in Davis Strait "acts powerfully on the imagination" and plays tricks on the senses (1911a, 2:247, 250), as in actual accounts of Great landscapes. The "peculiar effects of refraction" in the "vast icefields" deceive the sailors' eyes, mirages produce inverted doubles of objects' images, and eerie parhelia make the very sun other-worldly (265): all phenomena reported by Parry.

The familiar motifs of gloom and glory are intertwined. "Picturesque mountain scenery" at the Arctic Circle gives way to "a widespread heap of desolation": an icefield like "the ruins of some mighty city, with its fallen obelisks and overturned towers and palaces. It was a veritable chaos" (257, 266). The Devil's Thumb, a "weird, fantastic" peak in "dreary, desolate surroundings" (glaciers and "vast encircling icebergs"), is a "dismal spot" of "peculiar gloom" (270). Then the pendulum swings back: the white peaks and glaciers of Mount Rawlinson are a "splendid spectacle," and a storm on Melville Bay achieves "grandeur" (304, 306). It suits the aesthetics of the place that icefields under a beautiful night sky seem as grand as "some vast cemetery" (351).

When Hatteras looks at the "blank white space" on the map, he imagines the "open polar sea" of Elijah Kane and others (321): the theme of Part Two of his *Adventures*, "The Ice Desert." Its incidents, including the mutiny and departure of half the crew, are based on Kane's voyage, but Verne tells us what *should* have happened. Hatteras and his band of loyalists march north over a "level plain of ice," a "vast, monotonous desert" (such as the South Polar Plateau would prove to be), and eventually reach the "open polar sea" indicated on Kane's map, where they launch their sloop (3:17). The "wonderful transparency" of this "marvellous ocean" exhibits its denizens like "a vast aquarium," while the "strange supernatural purity" of the air exhilarates them to the point of intoxication, as in Poe's *Narrative* (103), both purity and strangeness being common responses to the natural Great. After various trials – storm, fog, volcanic eruption, whirlpool – the mile-high volcano at the North Pole rises "in all its grandeur" amid a vista of "incomparable majesty" (109–10). Despite its eruptions, they land and begin to climb. Hatteras alone reaches the top, but goes insane or has a stroke. At the end he is living quietly in an asylum, "victim of a sublime passion" (130): luckier than Ahab, but chastised.

Another pair of Verne's tales, *A Trip from the Earth to the Moon* (1865) and *A Tour of the Moon* (1865), explores the emotions that might accompany a human venture into space, unaided by Satan. The aesthetic responses of Verne's astronauts approximate those sketched by Addison and confirmed by many travellers. During a close orbit of the moon's barren surface, Mount Copernicus appears "radiant with beauty," and Mount Tycho, one of a vast "group of Mont Blancs" in a "never ending Switzerland and Norway," evokes "silent ... admiration," though Michel Ardan rather oddly suggests locating a town for misanthropes there (Verne 1911b, 314, 344). The "desolate world" below "captivates" them by its "strangeness," and the starscapes on the dark side move the narrator to remark that "imagination loses itself in this sublime Infinity," despite Barbicane's admonition that "we are astronomers; and this projectile is a room in the Cambridge University, carried into space. Let us make our observations!" (341, 327, 312). They theorize that the moon aged more quickly than earth, which will likewise cool, dry, lose its air, and die. The moon, like the desert or the poles, may be earth's future.

This sobering note is unusual in Verne, whose work generally affords some relief from the grimness and free-floating melancholy of the poets and novelists discussed above. Where Flaubert and Baudelaire saw desert or void as depressing analogues of self, Verne usually saw opportunities for scientific exploration, and felt some of the old uplift of the eighteenth century ("this sublime Infinity"). In the mansion of Great nature were, after all, many rooms, and more than one kind of aesthetic response.

18

On the Beach:
Victorian Writers by the Sea of Doubt

Since Thomas Hardy was himself a Victorian poet, we should expect to find in Victorian poetry occasional glimpses of the territory which, following him, I have styled "Egdon Heath." The remainder of the road there is short and relatively direct, for a broad range of nineteenth-century English poets, major and minor, sensed the attractions or perils of science, the natural Great, and/or "chastened sublimity." Collectively these writers show that Hardy was not isolated in his view that a major shift of aesthetic feeling about nature had begun in western culture, but that responses to that shift covered a wide spectrum.

"EMBLEMS OF INFINITY": TENNYSON AND BROWNING

Two of the period's major poets, while aware, to different degrees, of recent developments in science, generally maintained their allegiance to traditional modes of belief. John Heath-Stubbs somewhat harshly called the extent to which Tennyson and Browning allowed their sensibilities to split into intellectual and imaginative compartments (so as to accommodate conflicting data) "dishonest" (1950, 99). They saw the "darkling plain" of doubt, he contends, but would not venture upon it. Yet, though they are not to be grouped with Arnold or Hardy, neither poet just refused to budge; both admitted emotions that Addison, Wordsworth, and Coleridge would have recognized as belonging to the highest order of encounters with nature.

Alfred Tennyson wrote about Great nature throughout his career. One of his first published poems, "On Sublimity" (1827), written in his mid-teens, shows that he was already familiar with the tradition of literary sublimity – the epigraph is Burke's "The sublime always dwells on great objects and terrible" – and desired to join it. It is an aesthetic manifesto whose taste in landscape recalls Shaftesbury's: "O tell me not of vales in tenderest green, / ... Give me the wild cascade, the rugged scene" (Alfred Tennyson 1987, lines 1, 3). Tennyson's sublimity here is a compound of Milton, Georgian graveyard melancholy, Burke's psychology, Keatsian mediaevalism, and images from nature and travel literature.

The speaker moves from a cathedral where "more than mortal music" sounds among "vast columns" at midnight (lines 23, 26) to the natural sublime: the night sky over a loch, a stormy night at sea. No purist, young Tennyson could find sublimity on a "blasted heath" or "dizzy height," but also in a ruin, a grave, a "secret wood" (lines 56–9). The defining characteristic of this sublime is Burkean "obscurity" (line 61), involving a transcendental mystery of some kind, though most of the natural examples – Niagara Falls ("Immense, sublime, magnificent, profound!"), hurricanes, desert sandstorms, volcanoes – were staples of travel and scientific writing. Tennyson was fascinated by caves (including Fingal's), springs, and whirlpools, "the terrible Maelstrom." In short, whatever could "freeze the blood, / Yet charm the awe-struck soul which doats on solitude" (lines 99–100), a kind of delightful fear, was sublime for the budding laureate.

Among Tennyson's juvenilia are three poems on the subject of memory. One of these, the "Ode to Memory" (1830), shows that bare expanses of land were prominent in the poet's recollections of his youth. These include "the high field on the bushless Pike" (i.e., peak; 1987, line 96), but evidently the most memorable tract was the marsh-and-dune country by the North Sea near Mablethorpe where the Tennysons spent summers. The poem refers to "a sand-built ridge / Of heaped hills" (lines 97–8), of which, according to his son, Tennyson said, "I used to stand on this sand-built ridge ... and think that it was the spine-bone of the world" (Hallam Tennyson 1897, 1:20). In the ode this feeling of enlargement comes as the poet contemplates

> Stretched wide and wild the waste enormous marsh,
> Where from the frequent bridge,
> Like emblems of infinity,
> The trenched waters run from sky to sky.
>
> (Alfred Tennyson 1987, lines 101–4)

"Ode to Memory" is a derivative poem with few of Tennyson's mature verbal harmonies, but it does indicate his early susceptibility to the Great.

Hallam Tennyson prints a fragment about Mablethorpe that he says his father wrote in 1837 (1897, 1:161). As a child, the speaker "took delight in this fair strand and free," where "stood the infant Ilion of the mind," but as an adult he returns to find only "The drain-cut level of the marshy lea, / Gray sand-banks, and pale sunsets, dreary wind, / Dim shores, dense rains, and heavy-clouded sea." This is perhaps less a repudiation of Mablethorpe or his earlier feelings about it than a confession, much in Wordsworth's manner, of a loss of youthful sensitivity, an inability to feel what he once did. The fragment does not go on, however, as Wordsworth does, to explore the bases of the loss and possible compensations for it.

Tennyson began *In Memoriam A.H.H.* (1850) in 1833, soon after the sudden death of his close friend and brother-in-law-to-be, Arthur Henry Hallam, made "a desert in [his] mind" (1987, sec. 66, line 6). Expanded and revised during the 1830s and 1840s, it grew from another memory-poem into a meditation on the period's great issues: not only his but the Victorians' central poem. One of these issues (along with religion and philosophy) was natural science; Tennyson first loved and later studied nature. At Cambridge his tutor was William Whewell, who wrote an important review of Lyell's *Principles of Geology*. Tennyson himself read Lyell in 1837, was troubled by him, and in 1844 asked a friend for a copy of Robert Chambers's *Vestiges of the Natural History of Creation*, which reassured him somewhat about Providence (H. Tennyson 1897, 1:222–3; Langbaum 1970, 59). In 1848 a Miss Rundle heard him exclaim over palaeontology: " 'What an era of the world that must have been, great lizards, marshes, gigantic ferns!' Fancied, standing by a railway at night, the engine must be like some great Ichthysaurus. I replied how beautiful Hugh Miller's descriptions of that time are: he thought so too" (H. Tennyson 1897, 1:277).

Another early interest was astronomy. As a boy Tennyson exhorted his older brother (worried about a dinner party) to "think of Herschel's great star-patches," and at Cambridge he wrote a fragment imagining how it would look and feel to be on the moon (20, 40). He read theories on the formation and structure of the universe by Lucretius, Laplace, Herschel, Chambers, and others.

Meditations on science or cosmology recur often throughout *In Memoriam.* Tennyson's thoughts on the relation of human life to geology in section thirty-five (1987, lines 9–12), where he hears

> The moanings of the homeless sea,
>   The sound of streams that swift or slow
>   Draw down Æonian [ancient] hills, and sow
> The dust of continents to be

are "clearly indebted to" Lyell's *Principles* (Hill, in A. Tennyson 1971, 138n.8). "Æonian music measuring out / The steps of Time" (A. Tennyson 1987, sec. 95, lines 41–2), where the "moanings" of section thirty-five become dance music for orderly change, probably alludes to debates over the age of the earth and the universe, material that both fascinated and disturbed Tennyson. Sections fifty-five and fifty-six are an anguished recapitulation of the subject of section thirty-five: "Are God and Nature then at strife," he wonders, the latter being "So careless of the single life"? (sec. 55, lines 5, 8). But the full truth is even more shocking; fossil geology has shown nature, "red in tooth and claw," to be equally careless of the *type*, the species (sec. 56, line 15). Shall even man, then, who loved and trusted God, "Be blown about the desert dust, / Or sealed within the iron hills" (lines 19–20), after all his achievements and aspirations merely another fossil?

Tennyson was not "a Lyellian," but (again) the question is intensity of response rather than allegiance. The poet's reaction to the new science was like Darwin's to the Chilean earthquake: what had previously appeared fixed was revealed to be contingent, transitional. "They say," he wrote,

> The solid earth whereon we tread
>
> In tracts of fluent heat began,
>   And grew to seeming-random forms,
>   The seeming prey of cyclic storms ...
>   (Sec. 118, lines 7–11)

"They" included Lyell and Laplace (whose nebular hypothesis reappears in sec. 89, lines 47–8: Hill, in A. Tennyson 1971, 185n.1). Lyell's theory is also the subject of section 123, an imaginative embodiment of geology's findings comparable to Coleridge's re-creation of the navigators' voyages in "The Ancient Mariner":

> There rolls the deep where grew the tree,
> O earth, what changes hast thou seen!
> There where the long street roars, hath been
> The stillness of the central sea.   (Lines 1–4)

Lyell himself never provides such a lucid evocation of the emotional impact of uniformitarianism.

For Tennyson, the problem is the loss of a traditionally assumed solidity. The hills are *not* eternal:

> The hills are shadows, and they flow
>   From form to form, and nothing stands;
>   They melt like mist, the solid lands,
> Like clouds they shape themselves and go.   (Lines 5–8)

If this is "perhaps the most beautiful rendition in English poetry of a modern scientific theory" (Langbaum 1970, 71), it is also part of a profoundly troubled and divided passage. While Tennyson's mind cannot rebut the scientists, his soul cannot assent: "But in my spirit will I dwell, / And dream my dream, and hold it true" (A. Tennyson 1987, sec. 123, lines 9–10). *In Memoriam* begins and ends with a credo, but here spiritual belief is a "dream" that the poet chooses to accept. No moment in the poem is more "representative" of Tennyson and of the Victorians than this, though it is such passages that made Heath-Stubbs and Graham Hough (1947) question the unity of Tennyson's thought.

Tennyson evidently spoke to and for many Victorians in this poem. Hallam Tennyson claims that important scientists, including Herschel and Tyndall, regarded him as "a champion of Science" for his "love of Nature" and "trust in truth," adding, "Science indeed in his opinion was one of the main forces tending to disperse the superstition that still darkens the world" (H. Tennyson 1897, 1:298–9). In a letter describing the impact that *In Memoriam* had on him and his contemporaries (despite its religious tenets), Henry Sidgwick recalls that the journal *Nature* eulogized Tennyson as "preëminently the Poet of Science" (302). A writer for the *Saturday Review* (who wished that Lyell had been a poet) found one exception to the "mere wordy inflation" of most scientific verse: Tennyson, whose ear and understanding of science could give "in a few perfect lines the whole pith of a well-digested theory," its troubling problems included ("Lyell and Tennyson," 22 June 1861, 11:631–2). And the American explorer E.K. Kane named a greenstone turret in the Arctic for Tennyson (see chapter 16).

In Memoriam was the high point of Tennyson's poetic engagement with evolutionary thought, but not his last encounter with the Great or use of its aesthetics. Images from the 1830 Pyrenees trip with Arthur Hallam appear in "Œnone" (1832) and "In the Valley of Cauteretz" (1861). Tennyson toured Switzerland in 1846, spending a night atop the Righi and climbing the Wengern Alp. Although he wrote Edward Fitzgerald that "great mountains disappointed me," he recorded in his journal that views of the Bernese Alps and from the Wengern Alp were "the best things in the tour" (H. Tennyson 1897, 1:233–4). Nor do the parts of *The Princess* that he wrote while travelling sound "disappointed." His son states that "Come down, O maid, from yonder mountain height," a lyric "descriptive of the waste Alpine heights and gorges, and of the sweet, rich valleys below," was composed in Switzerland; other passages in that poem use images from a climb of Mount Snowden (252). He also toured the Highlands and the Irish sea-cliffs before his marriage.

In "The Daisy" (1855), Tennyson recalls scenes from a tour of Italy with his wife Emily in 1851; prominent among these are images of the Alps, recollected in tranquillity. Crossing dry torrent-beds where olean-ders bloomed, "we saw the glisten / Of ice, far up on a mountain head" (A. Tennyson 1987, lines 35–6). Later, at Milan, the poet went up on the roof at dawn: "Sun-smitten Alps before me lay," and he remembers "How faintly-flush'd, how phantom-fair, / Was Monte Rosa, hanging there" (lines 62, 65–6). He does not specify how the Alps affected him, though their beauty is implied, but while climbing to a pass he picked the daisy that, pressed and rediscovered, evoked this most Wordswor-thian of Tennyson's lyrics.

Tennyson's interest in large-scale natural wonders continued through-out the 1850s and 1860s. His house at Farringford on the tip of the Isle of Wight gave extensive views over the downs and the Solent, and in the summers he toured wild places – Wales, Cornwall, the Scilly Isles, the Au-vergne, the Pyrenees (again) – climbing mountains, taking long walks on the beaches, and geologizing. He sailed to Norway (1858) through seas "like a mountainous country" (H. Tennyson 1897, 1:428), arranged to use the telescope at Oxford, and continued to read cosmology, puzzling over his old tutor Whewell's *Plurality of Worlds* (which picks up on Fontenelle's title): "It is inconceivable that the whole Universe was merely created for us who live in this third-rate planet of a third-rate sun" (379). That observation – which could send readers in a number of different directions – reveals both Tennyson's intellectual candour and the challenges that science posed for him and other pious Victorians.

"Lucretius" (1868), virtually "a condensation of *De Rerum Natura*," forms part of a "general resurgence of interest in Lucretius" at that time (Hill, in A. Tennyson 1971, 275n.5). Tennyson's Lucretius is appropriately cosmic in his ramblings: thunderstorms during the night have given him dreams of creation and apocalypse, which naturally lead him to wonder about the aloof deities "who haunt / The lucid interspace of world and world" (A. Tennyson 1971, lines 104–5). The feeling for grand nature that informs the poem is contrasted with the sordid tale of a jealous wife and a poisonous love potion. Lucretius' cosmological speculations appealed to the Tennyson of "The Higher Pantheism" (1869), one of many Victorian attempts to reconcile science with Christianity. The poem asks a series of questions designed to portray physical nature as "the Vision of Him who reigns," though also as "sign and symbol of [our] division from Him" (A. Tennyson 1971, lines 2, 6). Tennyson had more to say about evolutionary thought and the relation of nature to deity in his old age, but *In Memoriam*, with its precarious balance and prolonged tension between his readings in science and his Christian piety, remains his major statement on these issues.

Robert Browning, only three years Tennyson's junior and as precocious a poet, did not contribute material of relevance here until the mid-1840s, when he could write of Italy. Browning was less interested than Tennyson in natural science and evolution. While other English writers were reading Lyell, he was exploring the Continent; where other Victorians found their faith shaken, Browning remained thoroughly religious. But his responses to Europe's mountains, and a brief literary excursion into the desert, gave him a small part in the development of Great aesthetics.

In "The Englishman in Italy" (1845), the speaker recalls riding up to a ridge overlooking the plain of Sorrento. Picking his way through "rock-chasms and piles of loose stones / Like the loose broken teeth / Of some monster which climbed there to die / From the ocean beneath" – which a geologist could have told him was not entirely fanciful

– he achieves "the top of Calvano," the structural centre and climax of
the poem, where "God's own profound / Was above me, and round me
the mountains, / And under, the sea" (Browning 1970, lines 153–6,
172–4). The speaker's reaction to this scene on a clear evening is
intense:

> Oh, heaven and the terrible crystal!
> No rampart excludes
> Your eye from the life to be lived
> In the blue solitudes.
> Oh, those mountains, their infinite movement!
>
> (Lines 177–81)

This is an older, but to Browning obviously not obsolete, reaction to
mountains: that their spiritual power is related to that of Heaven. Seeing
that the "soft plains" below have only a "sensual and timorous beauty,"
"fair" but slavish (lines 189, 195–6), he concentrates on the sea – the
other manifestation of the Great – until he descends.

Men and Women (1855) contains two other poems that give heightened meaning to mountain climbs. In "By the Fire-Side," the speaker
foresees that in years to come he will sit with his love and reminisce
about the Italian outing that first revealed their affection. They ascended to a ruined chapel "Halfway up in the Alpine gorge" and found
themselves "in the heart of things": a torrent threaded over the rocks,
and, above the forest, "see, in the evening-glow, / How sharp the silver
spear-heads charge / When Alp meets heaven in snow!" (lines 32, 36,
43–5). After examining the chapel, known as "John in the Desert," they
were able to speak of their love; "a bar was broken" and "we were mixed
at last" (lines 233–4). That their *éclaircissement* occurred in this setting
was no accident: "The forests had done it; there they stood; / We caught
for a moment the powers at play: / They had mingled us so" (lines 236–
8). Browning feels no urge to reach a peak, but senses that within sight
of where "Alp meets heaven," "we stand in the heart of things."

"The Grammarian's Funeral" shows even more clearly that Browning's are "sacred ascents." The poem is chanted by mourners bearing
the corpse of a Renaissance scholar to his grave on the "top-peak" of
"a tall mountain" (lines 137, 15). The mountain, "citied to the top, /
Crowded with culture," would not interest Alpinists, but they would understand the meaning given it: "wind we up the heights," exhorts a
voice, "Our low life was the level's and the night's; / He's for the morn-

ing" (lines 15–16, 21–4). "This high man," a Browning hero who "ventured neck or nothing" in order "not to Live but Know," earned highest honours by the intensity of his commitment: "here's his place, where meteors shoot, clouds form, / Lightnings are loosened" (lines 119, 109, 139, 141–2). "The Grammarian's Funeral" uses one of the oldest connotations of mountains – nearness to God – without any irony or sense of cliché, as if it were a Renaissance, not a Victorian, poem. "Loftily lying, / Leave him," they sing, "still loftier than the world suspects" (lines 146–7).

"Prospice" (from *Dramatis Personae*, 1864) is a speech such as any Browning hero, or Tennyson's Ulysses, might utter. "I will drink / Life to the lees," vowed Ulysses in 1842; "let me taste the whole of it," says Browning's voice (line 17). "Look forward" to life, the poem urges. Its imagery is drawn from mountaineering, though Browning's own struggle was with the death of his wife in 1861. "Fear death?" asks the speaker (line 1).

> Where he stands, the Arch Fear in a visible form,
>   Yet the strong man must go:
> For the journey is done and the summit attained,
>   And the barriers fall,
> Though a battle's to fight ere the guerdon be gained,
>   The reward of it all.
> I was ever a fighter, so – one fight more,
>   The best and the last!   (Lines 7–14)

Inspiring words for Victorians, and for later adventurers. A garbled version of the lines beginning "I was ever a fighter" was found on a piece of paper at the grave of three members of Ernest Shackleton's Antarctic expedition of 1915–17; it was probably penned from memory by Shackleton himself, a lover of Browning's poetry (Quartermain 1963, 84).

St John the Evangelist (the "John in the Desert" of "By the Fire-Side") is another striver in an allegorical landscape. Throughout "A Death in the Desert" (1864) he is trying to make sense of his life at its end, "Feeling for foot-hold through a blank profound" (Browning 1970, line 193): a "white depth," as in Poe and Melville. That his "desert" is a cave on the isle of Patmos – the old sense of desert(ed) – emphasizes Browning's metaphorical use of empty lands to express John's sense of living in a time of barren materialism when his message will not flourish. Some older critics attacked this poem for its didacticism, or for being "academic" and "dishonest" (Stevenson 1932, 157; Heath-Stubbs 1950, 98–9). While the first of these charges (at least) is difficult to refute, John's conviction that his sufferings are an integral part of the spiritual value of his efforts was shared by many real and fictional explorers. As he puts it, "When pain ends, gain ends too" (line 207). If this sounds like masochism, to a good number of Victorian climbers and other voyagers into the Great it stated an obvious and important truth.

"VAST EDGES DREAR": MATTHEW ARNOLD

Recent attacks on Arnold's critical positions and deconstructions of his persona notwithstanding, there have been many testimonials to his stature as a Victorian author. Basil Willey accepted Arnold's own claim in 1869 that his "poems represent ... the main movement of mind of the last quarter of a century" in Europe, rating him "the most intelligent" Victorian writer in his comprehension of his age (1964, 261). John Heath-Stubbs called him one who, more honest than Tennyson or Browning, "set out across the Darkling Plain" of Victorian *Angst* towards us (1950, 99). And he is central here: Arnold's darkling plain and Hardy's Egdon Heath are contiguous if not synonymous (Harvey Webster titled his 1947 study of Hardy *On a Darkling Plain*), and Arnold often used mountains as symbolic settings or as metaphors for states of the soul. Like Hardy, he was a bright young man who lost his faith early and was drawn to the "chastened sublimity" of the Great in its stead.

Half a generation younger than Tennyson, Arnold as a youth met Wordsworth, read Carlyle and Emerson; he grew up breathing the atmosphere of Lyell and the Higher Criticism. His first book of poetry, *A Strayed Reveller* (1849), shows him struggling with the meaning of nature in his twenties. The sonnet "In Harmony with Nature" denounces a preacher's facile advocacy of the old partnership: "Know, man hath all which Nature hath, but more, / And in that *more* lie all his hopes of good" (Arnold 1979, lines 5–6). Whereas nature is cruel, fickle, and unforgiving, man tries to be otherwise. "Man must begin, know this, where Nature ends; / Nature and man can never be fast friends" (lines 12–13). But Arnold's dogmatic stridency and view of nature here contrast with the tone of another sonnet, "Quiet Work," in the same collection. The "quiet work" is nature's, and we can learn from its combination of toil and tranquillity, which "shall not fail, when man is gone" (line 14). If Arnold's natural philosophy in the two poems is at some level reconcilable, their emphases are quite distinct and yield different natural aesthetics.

"Empedocles on Etna, a Dramatic Poem" (1852) caused Arnold considerable anguish. He omitted it from his 1853 *Poems* because, he said, while "interesting" as a portrait of a Greek philosopher who exhibited the "modern problems" typical of Faust and Hamlet, it failed to provide the "charm" and "delight" that poetry should (Arnold 1979, "Preface," 654–5). A work in which "suffering finds no vent in action," where "mental distress" goes unrelieved and there is "nothing to be done," Arnold declares, gives pain, not joy (656). Whatever the general truth of this proposition, it is a very odd description of "Empedocles on Etna," at whose conclusion the philosopher ends his sufferings by leaping into the active "vent" of Mount Etna; Arnold writes as if this climax did not exist. We should set aside this strained application of Schiller's theory of poetic joy to "Empedocles" and take the poem for what it is: the prelude to a suicide and the beginning of Arnold's poetic engagement with mountains.

As a dramatic poem about a mighty soul struggling with the meaning of life and pain in a high, bare setting, "Empedocles on Etna" resembles *Prometheus Unbound*, but Arnold can neither share Shelley's optimism as to the outcome nor identify so completely with his protagonist. Though Empedocles occupies the poem's centre, it opens and closes with the harpist Callicles, who represents the beauty and consolation of Apollonian art. Critics have interpreted these two characters as the warring sides of Arnold's own nature – philosopher/scholar versus poet (Heath-Stubbs 1950, 100–2; Miyoshi 1969, 185, 195–8) – but their locations on the famous Sicilian volcano show that they are also "Thule" and "Tempe." Callicles, who sings feelingly of the mountain's beauty, stays in the forests of its middle zone where his pastoral mode is viable; he never meets Empedocles, seen only on the barren upper slopes. Empedocles, "the first evolutionist" (Stevenson 1932, 46), is given the nineteenth century's feeling for the significance of volcanoes (and glaciers) as superhuman agents of change. He hears and admires Callicles' songs rising from below, but there is no indication that the Arcadian poet ever hears the philosopher.

Callicles pays conventional tribute to nature as apprehended through Greek myth, much like William Collins in the 1740s. In the second scene, Empedocles interrupts his climb to listen to Callicles, and then chants a long philosophical hymn, the intellectual centre of the poem. Here Arnold's model is not Shelley but Pope's *Essay on Man*, also considerably darkened. Given that

> The Gods laugh in their sleeve
> To watch man doubt and fear
> Who knows not what to believe
> Since he sees nothing clear,
>
> (Arnold 1979, act 1, sc. 2, lines 87–90)

the only sensible philosophy is "Know thyself." But Empedocles is tired, life is short and the world is old. He begins to sound like Ecclesiastes: "Our wants have all been felt, our errors made before" (line 211). In "a world so vast," amid a nature so indifferent, man feels lost, and "peopl[es] the void air" with gods (lines 213, 278). Instead of dreaming, we should "moderate desire" and "Nurse no extravagant hope" (lines 386, 425). He then sends his friend Pausanias away, saying, "I must be alone."

And indeed, at the beginning of the second and final act, set that evening, Empedocles is seen at the summit of Etna

> Alone! –
> On this charred, blackened, melancholy waste,
> Crowned by the awful peak, Etna's great mouth,
> Round which the sullen vapour rolls – alone!   (2.1.1–4)

Here Etna is both symbol and allegory: a real place standing for a broader reality, *and* the visible expression of an inner state. Whether Arnold is paraphrasing Pindar or expressing the "science-inspired fatalism" of "nineteenth-century rationalists" (Stevenson 1932, 164, 46) here matters little for our purposes; the point is that he employs Great aesthetics to express Empedocles' frame of mind as, weary of life in a miserable world, he turns to the elements. At the smoking crater's edge he hears Callicles singing that art can help, but Empedocles dislikes artistic solitude. Finding no satisfactory middle ground between that and the too-busy world, however, and feeling the loss of youthful freshness, he addresses the stars. At first he projects his own sadness onto them, but then realizes that while *he* is dead, all nature is alive.

Throughout his climactic epiphany Empedocles is extremely sensitive to the natural elements that he perceives as "brimm[ing] with life" (Arnold 1979, 2.1.308). Moving gradually from sight to imagination, he apostrophizes the starry night sky, the fires of "this terrible mount / Upon whose charred and quaking crust I stand," the "sea of cloud" below, and "that other fainter sea, far down," the Mediterranean, "O'er whose lit floor a road of moonbeams leads / To Etna's Liparean sister-fires," the island-volcanoes of Lipari, "And the long dusky line of Italy" (lines 306–7, 311–14). Yearning to join this vastness –

> Oh, that I could glow like this mountain!
> Oh, that my heart bounded with the swell of the sea!
> Oh, that my soul were full of light as the stars!
> Oh, that it brooded over the world like the air!   (Lines 323–6)

– he dives into the crater. From below, Callicles, looking up to the cone, says that that is not Apollo's (art's) realm; presumably Dionysus is the patron deity of Etna. But Arnold's art, Apollonian *and* Dionysian, comprises Thule as well as Tempe. He ends by having Callicles hymn the silent night and calm stars, which is the way Apollo likes to see them; Empedocles hailed their light and life.

Several poems about the Swiss Alps in the 1853 collection help to explain the mood of "Empedocles on Etna": six "Marguerite" lyrics that went into "Switzerland," plus the first of the "Obermann" poems, all written in 1849–50. They are closely linked, "étroitement unis," as Louis Bonnerot said (quoted by Allott in Arnold 1979, 122). If Sénancour's *Oberman* (see chapter 10) first drew Arnold to Switzerland in 1848, it was "Marguerite" who gave the tour piquancy and drew him back in 1849. Both works record saddening experiences – in "Switzerland," a feeling of romantic loss and personal isolation; in "Obermann," a conviction that the culture has failed to meet the individual's deepest needs – and both use the Alps to express the speaker's mood of despair, estrangement, and disillusion. For Arnold, Switzerland came to represent "emotional freedom and the poetic life" (Allott, in Arnold 1979, 122) that seemed increasingly remote as the years passed. He revised and supplemented both poems for decades.

Not all of "Switzerland" is relevant here, but "Parting" (the second in the final sequence) employs images of Great nature to convey the poet's conflicting feelings about Marguerite. It alternates between requests to ride the "storm-winds of Autumn" to the Alps' "cold, distant barrier, / The vast range of snow" (Arnold 1979, lines 1, 11–12), and lyrical evocations of Marguerite and pastoral England. *She* would be his first choice:

> In the void air, towards thee,
>   My stretched arms are cast;
> But a sea rolls between us –
>   Our different past!   (Lines 63–6)

Arnold uses the oceanic Great to evoke the gulf between souls: an image developed in subsequent poems. Here, however, the Alps dominate. The pains of loving and losing Marguerite make him yearn for still white peaks and "vast seas of snow" (line 28). Only wild nature can "calm" and "restore" him, up on the "high mountain-platforms" where "white mists" drift "In the stir of the forces / Whence issued the world" (lines 83, 85, 87, 89–90). Whiteness and primordial antiquity, both frequent nineteenth-century reactions to the Great, are what the Alps offer him.

The rest of "Switzerland" turns to other areas of the Great. The speaker of "A Farewell" (number three), resigned to parting from Marguerite, imagines that someday, "life past," they will "greet across infinity" (lines 53, 76):

> How sweet, unreached by earthly jars,
> My sister! to maintain with thee
> The hush among the shining stars,
> The calm upon the moonlit sea!   (Lines 77–80)

Whereas Pascal's 'man without God' was terrified by interstellar abysses, Arnold's speaker, finding no support in his culture, seeks comfort in the thought of (again) the "calm" of the void, used to image a metaphysical state.

But this mood is rare in Arnold, for whom the consolation of a beatific life after death is a fragile construct. Typically the sea divides us, or expresses our isolation, a word rooted in "island" (*isola*). In "To Marguerite – Continued" (number five), which the novelist John Fowles calls the Victorians' noblest lyric, every soul is an island in the "watery wild" (line 3). Feeling the "enclasping flow" of the ocean, we know that in theory our "bounds" are "endless" (lines 5–6), but what we *feel* is separation, enislement. Where "once ... we were / Parts of a single continent" (as John Donne and his age believed), now we are divided by "The unplumbed, salt, estranging sea" (lines 15–16, 24).

Similarly in "Absence" (number six), life away from Marguerite is imaged as "time's barren, stormy flow" (line 19): presumably the ocean, now tempestuous, although some Victorian climbers applied such language to lava and to glaciers. Finally, in "The Terrace at Berne" (1863), a retrospective on Marguerite added to "Switzerland" in 1869, the main emphasis is again on the ocean as an allegory of human existence.

> Like driftwood spars, which meet and pass
> Upon the boundless ocean-plain,
> So on the sea of life, alas!
> Man meets man – meets, and quits again.   (Lines 45–8)

This is a significant variant on "ships that pass in the night"; we are mere flotsam, not organized into vessels. Thus the end of "Switzerland" is dominated by images of the sea. The Alps appear in the distance at the beginning of "The Terrace at Berne" – "The Jungfrau snows look faint and far" (line 6) – and at the end: "The mists are on the mountain hung, / And Marguerite I shall see no more" (lines 51–2). The relation is unexplained; we have to recall the earlier poems, chiefly "Parting," where the speaker yearns for the Alps' mists and primordial forces when he cannot be with Marguerite, to understand the connection.

In "Stanzas in Memory of the Author of 'Obermann,' " Arnold uses the Alps differently. Here he is actually *in* the mountains, where "the awful Alpine track / Crawls up its rocky stair" (lines 1–2), and everything reminds him of Sénancour. In a note to the sequel, "Obermann Once More" (1867), Arnold identifies Sénancour's appeal as "profound inwardness," "austere sincerity," a "delicate feeling for nature," more "gravity and severity" than Rousseau, and "perfect" isolation (quoted by Allott in Arnold 1979, 135); "Stanzas" praises his ability to depict both Alpine beauty and the "fever" of "human agony," ranking him with Wordsworth and Goethe as seers in a "troubled day" (Arnold 1979, lines 21, 36, 46). But we modern poets, says Arnold, "reared in hours / Of change, alarm, surprise," we "Have a worse course to steer" (lines 69–70, 64). Arnold's "melancholy fatalistic mood" here and in "Dover Beach" arose both from the "depressing" aspects of evolutionary theory (Stevenson 1932, 46) and from the findings of biblical scholarship, which were also challenging traditional beliefs.

Arnold sees Sénancour, a "sadder sage" than Wordsworth or Goethe (1979, line 81), as a kindred spirit whose life and work manifested the "two desires" that disturbed Empedocles and

> toss about
> The poet's feverish blood.
> One drives him to the world without,
> And one to solitude.   (Lines 93–6)

One alternative to "the world" is the Alps, a place to which an artist may withdraw to find peace. Though Arnold decides that he cannot choose them – "I in the world must live" (line 137) – his farewells are half-hearted: "I go, fate drives me; but I leave / Half of my life with you" (lines 131–2). What he is saying farewell to, his editors think, is not only Sénancour but his own "unstrung will" and "broken heart" (line 183), his "youth, insouciance and Marguerite – and also, in the long run, to the writing of poetry" (Allott, in Arnold 1979, 144n.). However that may be, the poem is deeply autobiographical, and Arnold's return to Obermann and the Alps nearly twenty years later in a different mood shows that the subject did not cease to resonate for him.

"Stanzas from the Grande Chartreuse" (1855), like "Parting" and "Obermann," moves from the Alps to the human problems that they raise for Arnold. "Stanzas" is by far the most descriptive of the three: it takes him thirty lines to narrate his journey to "the Carthusians' world-famed home" (Arnold 1979, line 30), the monastery that had impressed Gray, Beckford, and many others. Seeing the "bare / And white uplifted faces" of "the Brotherhood austere" at their "stern and naked prayer" (lines 40–1, 65, 38) causes the speaker to ask himself what *he* is doing there in an Alpine eyrie, poised between the established churches and schools of the lowlands, and "the high, white star of Truth" to which they bid him aspire (line 69). His famous answer comes as a surprise, perhaps even to himself:

> Wandering between two worlds, one dead,
> The other powerless to be born,
> With nowhere yet to rest my head,
> Like these, on earth I wait forlorn.   (Lines 85–8)

What at first seemed Other ("Cowled forms") is recognized as Kin, requiring sympathy if not belief. Confronted with the old and new modes, "He hangs between; in doubt," as Pope said.

The resolution is less striking than this poignant image of the dilemma. Arnold chooses sides, moving quickly from "they" to "Like these" to asking the monks to "hide me in your gloom profound." His actual stay was brief: he was honeymooning and soon returned to the world. In the poem, however, the speaker identifies with the Carthusians, repudiates Byron, Shelley, and even Obermann as mockers or wailers who could not help the suffering they described, and calls himself a lost child, hiding from the modern world of faithless thrivers.

Something in the monks' minimalism – "naked," "austere," "bare," "white" – appeals powerfully to him, and he empathizes with their plea to society: "leave our desert to its peace!" (line 210). This Alpine "desert" (in the old sense of "unpopulated") foreshadows the imagery of "Dover Beach" and "Sohrab and Rustum"; Arnold had virtually finished with the Alps.

Though not published until 1867, "Dover Beach" was written during or shortly after the Arnolds' wedding trip in 1851. The poem's centrality to Victorian thought has long been granted, and not only by literary critics. Before John Heath-Stubbs and Harvey Webster took their titles from it, Alfred North Whitehead in *Science and the Modern World* (1925) treated "Dover Beach" as an "emblem" of "the divided mind of the time" (Miyoshi 1969, ix). It is also a classic study in the Great as described by Addison and chastened by the nineteenth century. From atop Dover's cliffs, the speaker contemplates a vista of sea and coast by moonlight, and is prompted to "speculations of eternity." But, though "the moon lies fair / Upon the straits" (Arnold 1979, lines 2–3) and he calls his love to the window to enjoy the air, there is nothing "pleasing" or "delightful" in *his* meditation. The "tremulous cadence" of waves moving pebbles on the beach brings "The eternal note of sadness in" (lines 13, 14), evoking Sophocles and the whole history of religious belief. The scene is a study in black and white: the moon "blanches" sea and land; a lighthouse in France gleams briefly; the English cliffs stand "Glimmering and vast" (line 5).

The rest of the poem develops several resonant metaphors from the spacious images of the opening passage. The English Channel dissolves into the Sea of Faith, whose tide, "once ... at the full," is now "Retreating" with a "melancholy, long, withdrawing roar," ebbing "down the vast edges drear / And naked shingles of the world" (lines 22, 25–8). Underneath the Miltonic phrasing is a geological allusion: along the "edges" of upturned strata and on the "naked shingles" of raised beaches, geologists and palaeontologists – Hutton, Cuvier, Lyell – had found evidence of an earth history that traditional interpretations of scripture could not accept or explain. The speaker, after warning his "love" that the world "Hath really neither joy, nor love, nor light, / Nor certitude, nor peace," closes with a vision of humanity on a "darkling plain" overrun by "confused" and "ignorant armies" (lines 33–7). Though this image may have come from Thucydides, it was still apposite to Victorian issues; Newman had used "night battle" as a metaphor for "Controversy" in a sermon in 1839 (Allott, in Arnold 1979, 257n.). By the end of "Dover Beach," then, the initial values of "sea," "night," and "beach" have been transmuted: the sea is sad and ebbing, the night moonless, and the "pale" beach a dark plain of dubious battle.

"Dover Beach" has become Arnold's most famous poem, but *his* favourite, for awhile at least, was "Sohrab and Rustum" (1853). In Arnold's land-conscious retelling, the Persian tragedy of the father who kills his incognito son in single combat is framed by and measured against the Oxus River's descent from the Pamir Mountains to the Aral Sea. The poem begins as "the fog rose out of the Oxus stream" (Arnold 1979, line 2), unfolds beside the river, and closes with an evocation of its course reminiscent of Shelley's "Alastor." Rustum mourns,

> But the majestic river floated on,
> Out of the mist and hum of that low land,
> Into the frosty starlight, and there moved,
> Rejoicing, through the hushed Chorasmian waste,
> Under the solitary moon; he flowed
> Right for the polar star.   (Lines 875–80)

Rustum, Sohrab, and all that are left behind; as in the first chapter of *The Return of the Native,* nothing human is allowed to intrude on the image of desert waste beneath dark heavens. For a time the river almost loses itself, dividing into many channels among reeds and sandbars,

> forgetting the bright speed he had
> In his high mountain-cradle in Pamere,
> A foiled circuitous wanderer – till at last
> The longed-for dash of waves is heard, and wide
> His luminous home of waters opens, bright
> And tranquil, from whose floor the new-bathed stars
> Emerge, and shine upon the Aral Sea.   (Lines 886–92)

Life flows to its natural end; Sohrab has already compared us to swimmers whom the ocean may carry up on land or "Back out to sea, to the deep waves of death" (line 395).

Arnold's view of life as a passage from mountains through deserts to the sea under cold, distant heavens – four aspects of the Great – is rich in specific details provided by orientalist translators and travellers to the Middle East. Besides his principal literary sources, Saint-Beuve's "Le

Livre des rois, par Firdousi" (1850) and James Atkinson's *The Shah Nameh of the Persian Poet Firdousi* (1832), which includes Firdousi's *Soohrab,* Arnold drew on Sir John Malcolm's *History of Persia* (1815) and Alexander Burnes's *Travels into Bokhara* (1834), which he also used in other poems (Allott, in Arnold 1979, 319–20): a clear instance of travel literature passing into *belles lettres* and shaping its aesthetics. Arnold was stimulated by the euphony of the names and the scale of the scenery in his sources – the broad yellow Oxus in the "glittering sands," the "Indian Caucasus, / That vast sky-neighbouring mountain of milk snow" (Arnold 1979, "Sohrab and Rustum," lines 105, 161–2) – as well as by the pathos of the narrative. Perhaps he saw the Oxus's career from mountains to sea as parallel with his own.

Most of Arnold's major poetry (the important exception is "Thyrsis," 1866) was written between the mid-1840s and 1860, but twice in the 1860s he paused to review his youthful passion for the Alps: once in "The Terrace at Berne" (see above), and again in "Obermann Once More" (1867). Back in the Alps after twenty years, Arnold naturally thinks of Obermann, "master of my wandering youth" and still meaningful (1979, line 39). This time the novelist appears in a vision, speaks to the poet about history, especially the development of Christian belief, and asks, "Perceiv'st thou not the change of day?" (line 81). Following Europe's revolutions, humans live on "Blocks of the past, like icebergs high," "Poor fragments of a broken world" (lines 211, 217). Burnet's image of the ancient earth collapsing to form the Alps (applied to the Antarctic by Forster) here describes the modern spiritual condition. The poem uses other scientific or quasi-scientific ideas metaphorically as well: the faith that "ebbed" in "Dover Beach" is now the ancient "central fire" of earth that burned low, bringing on an ice age (lines 221–8n.).

Obermann once "fled" to the "wilderness" of "Alpine snows" (as Arnold's youthful persona had yearned to do) and his assessment of the nineteenth century is virtually that of Arnold at the Grande Chartreuse: "the old is out of date, / The new is not yet born" (lines 249–50; 245–6). But then, expanding on line eighty-one, Obermann says that things have now changed for the better:

> Despair not thou as I despaired,
> Nor be cold gloom thy prison!
> Forward the gracious hours have fared,
> And see! the sun is risen! (Lines 281–4)

With "green, new earth" appearing from under the ice, Arnold is too joyless for a mid-Victorian bard; he should "tell / Hope to a world new-made!" (lines 311–12). The poet then awakes and sees dawn break over the Alps. The Arnold of critical tradition – a melancholy agnostic, unable to affirm religion, science, or nature – yields here to the visionary optimist, determined, as he was in the 1853 preface, that poetry should bring joy. Whether or not Arnold's "new serenity" (Miyoshi 1969, 199) was justified or is convincing, the extent to which he kept expressing his vision in terms of Great time and space (mountains, deserts, icebergs, theories of earth history, the heavens) is remarkable.

OTHER VOICES

The work of the less-central Victorian poets contains a number of metaphorical uses of the deserts that nineteenth-century travellers were exploring and describing as never before (see chapter 14). Coventry Patmore's "Sahara," for example (Canto 9, Book 1 of *The Angel in the House*, 1854), locates the desert *here*, in "The Wife's Tragedy" of unrequited marital love, or in a familiar, holy environment ("The Close") when his love is absent. For Patmore, the desert is clearly a barrenness to be avoided. But as the century progressed and deserts gained currency in literature, they refused to be confined to a single meaning. "I desire the wilderness," says the disillusioned speaker of Gerard Manley Hopkins's "The Alchemist in the City" (1865): "free and kind the wilderness."

The widespread idea of desert wilderness as a place of escape from a world too much with us, begot religious asceticism, is the founding premise of Edward Fitzgerald's popular translation of *The Rubáiyát of Omar Khayyám* (1859; revised in 1868 and 1879). A blatant piece of orientalism and part of the Victorians' "turn toward the past" (Miyoshi 1969, 233), Fitzgerald's poem also expressed the "science-inspired fatalism" and "pessimistic hedonism that so many people drew from evolution" (Stevenson 1932, 48, 164). The speaker is an agnostic who, sure of only *this* life, counsels *carpe diem*: "Ah, take the Cash, and let the Credit go!" (Fitzgerald 1879, quatrain 13). *The Rubáiyát* uses the desert as setting and metaphor, refuge and mirror; beginning as a place the hedonist would gladly run to, it ends as *la condition humaine*.

Fitzgerald's speaker desires to escape with his love to "the strip of herbage ... / That just divides the desert from the sown" (quatrain 11). In the famous stanza

A Book of Verses underneath the Bough,
A Jug of Wine, a Loaf of Bread – and Thou
  Beside me singing in the Wilderness –
Oh, Wilderness were Paradise enow! (Quatrain 12)

we see that Omar's "wilderness" is as convenient as Robinson Crusoe's island, with its adjacent general store: the lovers are supplied with food, drink, and a shade tree. Fitzgerald just wants them to be able to look out over the desert and contemplate its meanings. The transience of "Worldly Hope" is likened to "Snow upon the Desert's dusty Face" (quatrain 16); life is imaged as a "batter'd Caravanserai" (quatrain 17), a "Wind along the Waste" (quatrain 29), and a caravan:

A Moment's Halt – a momentary taste
Of BEING from the Well amid the Waste –
  And Lo! – the phantom Caravan has reach'd
The NOTHING it set out from – Oh, make haste! (Quatrain 48)

In Fitzgerald's desert of life – the poem's pervasive metaphor – all we can hope for is to enjoy our stops at the oases.

A volcanic desert figures prominently but ambiguously in Christina Rossetti's verse fable "The Prince's Progress" (1866). While the princess waits in "one white room," the prince awaits the full moon before starting, dallies with a milkmaid, and stays with a hermit seeking youth in a desert "Of rugged blackness": "A lifeless land, a loveless land," a "Tedious land for a social Prince" (Rossetti 1979, lines 23, 128, 133, 152). He keeps pausing, delaying, lingering. Years pass; the princess grows old and dies before he arrives. Rossetti does not qualify the desert other than in the quotations above, but those and the plot suggest that this desert symbolizes a wasted life, one that misses love and finds only tedium. That at least would be the princess's perspective: but how would the prince explain his conduct? Was there something in him that was not "social," something that responded to the hermit's or the desert's simplicity, and was the land therefore not *merely* "tedious"? Rossetti does not say; we are told only that he tarried there, as if it met an obscure need, at a time when actual travellers were spending longer in the desert than their friends at home could understand.

When Thomas Hardy began to publish verse as dark as Arnold's that same year, critics blamed modern science. With Hardy, there seems some basis to the charge: he was given Gideon Mantell's *Wonders of*

Geology in 1858, read Lyell and Darwin early, studied astronomy and saw
humanity's insignificance in the cosmic scheme; by 1864 he was doing
less Bible-reading and churchgoing (Millgate 1982, 68, 90–1; Webster
1964, 46). The evidence that he became a "scientific determinist"
(Beach 1956, 509) begins with "In Vision I Roamed" (1866), oppressed
by the interstellar void in the French manner. The speaker's imagination carries him so far "through ghast heights of sky" into "the flashing
Firmament" that "any spot on our own Earth seemed Home" (Hardy
1982, lines 1, 5, 8). And then, he says, my "sick grief that you were far
away" yielded to gratitude "that you were near" in planetary terms, not
on "some foreign Sphere," in which case he might have "lived unaware,
uncaring all that lay / Locked in that Universe trackless, distant, drear."
So, despite his cosmic *angst*, the speaker is deeply involved with another
human being, and it appears that what he knows of astronomy has finally comforted him.

Besides its scientific dimension, the sonnet offers a scenario similar to
those of Byron's *Cain* and Shelley's *Queen Mab*, Shelley being one of
Hardy's favourite poets. Hardy was an avid reader of Thomson, Crabbe,
Wordsworth, Browning, and other poets discussed here, of the Bible
and the classics (including Lucretius), and of non-fictional prose, including Carlyle, the notorious *Essays and Reviews* (like Mantell's book a
gift from his mentor Horace Moule), geology, and astronomy. We also
glimpse here and in "Neutral Tones" (1867) some of Hardy's private
stresses: resentment at not being able to qualify for university or the
ministry, and the tension of unconsummated attraction to several young
women, one of whom may have rejected his marriage proposal (Millgate
1982, 55, 72–3).

The breaking of his long engagement to Eliza Nicholls is the likely
background of "Neutral Tones," a remarkably stark portrait with Hardy's
characteristic juxtaposition of inner and outer barrennesses. As in Verlaine's "Colloque sentimentale" (1869), a bleak winter scene – "a pond
edged with grayish leaves," the white, "God-curst sun" – reflects the characters' dead romance (Hardy 1982, lines 15–16). While the speaker
and his companion discuss "which lost the more by our love," her smile
is "the deadest thing / Alive enough to have strength to die." Hardy
would, in a decade, apply this sere technique to Great landscape, arguing the "congruity" and "harmony" of Egdon Heath's "sombreness" not
only for himself, but for modern humanity.

In the early Victorian period the Irish Catholic poet Aubrey De Vere
published copious amounts of religious nature poetry, employing many

kinds of landscape. In one of his sonnets, "The Sea-Cliffs of Kilkee" from
A Song of Faith (1842), De Vere sounds like an eighteenth-century deist
hailing the supernatural in nature: "Awfully beautiful are thou, O sea! /
View'd from the vantage of those giant rocks / That vast in air lift their
primeval blocks" (1875, lines 1–3). The speaker feels that he has wandered into a Miltonic scene:

> I scan the dread abyss ...
> ... the eternal shocks
> Of billows rolling from infinity
> Disturb my brain ...

What disturbs him is the realization of human insignificance: "Here
Man, alone, is nought; Nature supreme, / Where all is simply great that
meets the eye – / The precipice, the ocean, and the sky." Much of what
earlier writers on the Great had felt – awe of vastness, fear, intimations
of eternity and infinity, the sheer simplicity of it – is intimated in these
few lines.

FICTION

The rich field of mid-Victorian fiction contains fewer instances of Great
aesthetics than one might expect to find. While an interest in Darwin
cannot be equated with an approach to Egdon Heath, there was some
common ground, so it seems significant that Lionel Stevenson's *Darwin
among the Poets* (1932) covers all the major Victorian poets, whereas Leo
Henkin's *Darwinism in the English Novel* (1940) and George Levine's *Darwin and the Novelists* (1988) offer little of relevance here. The novel, with
its primarily social concerns, took some interest in evolutionary biology;
poetry was a broader forum in which the new geology could also be discussed. Thus with the Victorians as with the Georgians, Great themes appear earlier and more extensively in verse than in the novel. This was an
English phenomenon, however; European and American novelists –
Balzac, Flaubert, Poe, Melville – were as apt to employ the chastened
Great as were their poetic colleagues. In England such material tended
to occur in non-fiction (Carlyle, Ruskin, Kinglake, Tyndall) or in verse.

There are, of course, exceptions to this generalization; most areas of
the Great are mentioned in Victorian fiction. Emily Brontë's *Wuthering
Heights* (1847) makes the effects of topography on character central,
contrasting the wild, rugged folk of the heights with the soft types down

at the Grange. *Jane Eyre* shows that Charlotte Brontë had been reading the northern voyagers (see chapter 16) and that they (and Thomson) had stimulated her imagination; probably no generation of English writers since the Renaissance has been without a few who were stirred by the tales of the navigators. The ocean has a different symbolic function in James A. Froude's story "The Lieutenant's Daughter" in *Shadows of the Clouds* (1847). The narrator offers two versions of the plot and then asks rhetorically which ending is true. The only answer forthcoming is the "cool sea breeze" and the "wide sheet of the Atlantic," representing (we suppose) the enigma of human existence in an indifferent universe (Froude 1847, 287).

Renaissance Europeans drew most of their data about the nature of the universe from astronomy, and in the nineteenth century there were novels in which the night skies are still viewed with the old *frisson*, either of sublimity or alienation. In Dickens's *Great Expectations* (1860), young Pip, thinking of the escaped convict Magwitch out on the moors, "looked at the stars, and considered how awful it would be for a man to turn his face up to them as he froze to death, and see no help or pity in all the glittering multitude" (1953, 46). This may be a reminiscence of the Franklin expedition, which stirred Dickens, combined with his awareness of the Herschels' and other astronomers' researches into the vastness of the cosmos. Still, these exceptions prove the rule: there are relatively few such episodes in early Victorian novels. Until about 1870, it was mostly poets, led by Arnold, who were on the road to Egdon Heath. But the novelists were about to join the march.

19

On the Heath:
The 1870s

In the decade of the 1870s, what had previously been a fairly loose body of data on human responses to Great nature began to coalesce. Diverse writers gathered up themes and ideas from many sources and gave them enough coherence so that, before its end, Thomas Hardy thought he could discern the shape of a new, "modern" aesthetics of nature emerging from the mass of commentary. Looking at the amount of evidence and the momentum it acquired, we may be surprised that the phenomenon was not remarked earlier, and feel that Hardy – far from being a lonely, eccentric prophet – was riding a wave.

EXPLORINGS

The 1870s were, among other things, a decade of exploration. Scientific or adventurous travel to the world's great barrens flourished, furnishing abundant new evidence of the growing appeal of Great landscapes as phenomena to be known and understood. In the Arctic, a German sledging expedition, the first of several probes towards the Pole in the decade, reached 77° north latitude in 1870. A year later the American explorer Charles F. Hall died in northern Greenland from natural arsenic poisoning, the latest casualty in the quest for Ultima Thule. The Weyprecht-Payer expedition (1872–74) sought new lands and higher latitudes than their predecessors; Franz Josef Land was discovered at 80° north in 1873. As Weyprecht and Payer returned from their "farthest north" of 82°5′, George Nares took his ship across the Antarctic Circle in 1874 and rekindled public interest in the possibility of a southern continent. An Arctic expedition under Nares and Clements Markham reached 83°20′ north and established the insularity of

Greenland in 1875–76. And in 1878–79 a Swedish expedition traversed the Northeast Passage over the top of the Eurasian landmass.

Knowledge of deserts was also increasing – a French expedition to Timbuktu (1873–74) was wiped out, but Charles Doughty survived two years of travel in Arabia, living with the nomads (1876–78) – and mountains were as popular as ever: in 1874 the French formed a Club Alpin Français, and A.W. Moore (see chapter 15) made a second climbing expedition to the Caucasus. In America, the areas that came to be known as Yellowstone and the Grand Canyon were explored around 1870.

The Doane-Washburn expedition to the Yellowstone region (1870) discussed the idea of setting aside some land there as "a great National Park" (Langford 1972, 118). If this notion was not quite unprecedented, it was relatively novel in the New World, and reveals an evolving concept of the relationship between humanity and great tracts of "empty" land. Nathaniel Langford's memoir shows that members of the expedition felt some familiar emotions when they reached the Grand Canyon and falls of the Yellowstone River: "We are all overwhelmed with astonishment and wonder at what we have seen, and we feel that we have been near the very presence of the Almighty. General Washburn has just quoted from the psalm: 'When I behold the work of Thy hands, what is man that Thou art mindful of him?' " (29). To plain men, the venerable idea of natural religion was still viable.

Major John Wesley Powell spent four years surveying the Colorado River basin (1869–72); his report, *Exploration of the Colorado River of the West and Its Tributaries* (1875), describes the first known penetration of the Grand Canyon. Powell undertook this expedition despite the warnings of native people, who told him that a god had made the canyon as a trail through the mountains to heaven, but added the river to prevent humans from going there at will (1875, 7). He could find no one who had gone far enough into the canyon to be able to tell him what to expect; Powell essentially launched his party's four wooden rowboats into a myth.

An impressive figure whose hard, biblical, midwestern upbringing resembled John Muir's, Powell was a professor of Geology and an army officer (he lost an arm at Shiloh). In 1867 he went to the Rockies, climbed Pike's Peak, explored the Grand River (headwaters of the Colorado), lectured on the long time-span required by geology, and lobbied government for funds to obtain a "geological section" of the continent (Darrah 1951, 92). Powell returned to Colorado in 1868, climbed Long's Peak, studied the effects of altitude, and planned his expedition.

Historians of the West have praised Powell's role in replacing misconceptions with facts about the area (Stegner 1954, viii, xvi, 7), but our business is with his impressions of landscapes that he was among the first Europeans to see. A career and a topography so different from Hardy's should provide a good test of the validity of the novelist's generalizations.

Exploration of the Colorado is at once scientific record, adventure narrative, and aesthetic appreciation; Powell was as apt to report the "roseate flashes" and "iridescent gleams" of a "landscape revel[ling] in the sunshine" as points of geology or geography (1875, 15). He realized, however, that "sublime" had become a cliché. Many of the engravings, such as the view of towering crags from the bottom of Grand Canyon (fig. 1) and the "Island Monument in Glen Canyon," a shrouded form with the sun behind it (fig. 24) are in the sublime style, but he avoids using the word. The qualities Powell most admires are "beauty" (applied both to verdure and to bare rock) and "grandeur" (his equivalent of the Great). So Lodore Canyon, "a chapter of disasters and toils" for his party, yet told "a story of beauty and grandeur that I hear yet – and shall hear" (30). Neither hardship nor the prevailing nakedness of the land made it ugly in his eyes; the Green River Badlands are a "barren desolation ... yet there is a beauty in the scene" (9). Neil Armstrong would describe the moon thus a century later.

Powell's scientific pursuits and interest in the prospects for settlement never interfered with his sensitivity to spiritual qualities in the landscape. He gave poetic names to striking features (Trin-Alcove Bend), and would use the word "glory" in a religious sense, as in "The cañon opens, like a beautiful portal, to a region of glory" (21). But Powell's is a balanced presentation; the same canyon at dusk seems "a dark portal to a region of gloom – the gateway through which we are to enter on our voyage of exploration tomorrow. What shall we find?" He knew as he wrote that the answer was hardship, danger, and, for some, death, as well as great beauty, so his text is laced with darker hues, fore-shadowings, from the outset. Powell noted, for example, how the desert's heat waves made mountains seem to float in a trembling sea, giving the "impression of an unstable land" (51).

Powell's typical responses are first united in "beautiful" Labyrinth Canyon, "grandly arched," where reflections of cliffs in quiet water trick the eye, suggesting "profound depths," yet there is "exquisite charm." The butte country above is "naked, solid rock – a beautiful red sandstone" (54); bareness remains consonant with beauty. He names one

formation the Butte of the Cross, illustrated with a solar halo (fig. 19).
They "glide along, through a strange, weird, grand region ... a whole
land of naked rock ... cañon walls that shrink the river into insignificance, with vast, hollow domes ... never moss-covered; but bare," or walk
over "terraces paved with jasper" (55). This complex sensory matrix –
beautiful, grand, deceptive, bare, spiritual, rich – also occurs in some of
our earliest accounts of deserts and northern seas, but Powell adds a
personal touch. At the junction of the Grand and Green Rivers (the beginning of the Colorado) he climbs to a summit whence he can survey
canyons, cliffs, and "ledges from which the gods might quarry mountains" (58). Twice he calls such landforms "Titanic."

These notes continue to be heard as Powell travels, with fear and admiration, through the gods' country. This "curious" land of natural am-
phitheatres, pyramids, "stairways," and "royal arches" often leads his
thoughts beyond ordinary physical life. "What a chamber for a resting
place," he remarks ambiguously of one side canyon (61). Another is
named the Music Temple, and delicately fluted cliffs seem "carved with
a purpose" into architectural forms (70). The Grand Canyon itself, "a
vast wilderness of rocks," intensifies the narrative's chiaroscuro; a mile
deep in its "grand, gloomy depths," he marvels both at the canyon and
at the play of cloud and shadow that seems to "lift" the rocks to "the region above," that is, "the heavens" (83, 86). Powell divides his experiences during those "grand and awful months" into the "deep, gloomy
solitudes" of the narrow canyon and the spacious "vision of glory" above
(114, 132), but reminds us that the canyon revealed the region's "geological records" (89). At the end he added two chapters on geology, calling the Grand Canyon "the stony leaves of one great book" for "the
library of the gods," telling "the story of creation" (193–4). His uniformitarian conclusion, "Thus ever the land and sea are changing" (214),
would have pleased Lyell.

MOUNTAINS AND MOUNTAINEERING

Mountains continued to be the favourite point of contact between adventurous souls and Great landscapes. A straw in the breeze, A.G.
Girdlestone's *The High Alps without Guides* (1870) indicated the direction mountaineering would take; more and more amateurs imbued with
an experiential ethic wanted to climb on their own, without a commercial buffer between them and the mountains.

For Alpinists, 1871 was an *annus mirabilis*, with a cluster of books by old and new hands. Leslie Stephen (see chapter 15) collected some of his climbing narratives from various magazines in *The Playground of Europe*, prefacing them with two new chapters on the history of European attitudes towards mountains. "The Old School" and "The New School" commence modern study of the history of European taste in mountainous landscape. Starting from Archbishop King's comment in *De origine mali* ('The Origin of Evil,' 1702) that "we complain of the mountains as rubbish," "disfiguring ... the earth," though they produce water and weather useful to farmers, Stephen chronicles the Alps' low repute in the eighteenth century. Even Rousseau, among their first admirers, "had not learnt our modern admiration for barrenness on its own account," and so did not feel "the modern sympathy with savage scenery" (1894, 7). Stephen does not wonder at their "simple-minded abhorrence of mountains," but rather asks, "Why do we love them?" (9, 11). He answers that they possess scientific and aesthetic interest, and wonders if the eighteenth-century demonizing of mountains was not "merely expressing" our awe "in another way" (21).

"The New School" dates the enthusiasm for mountains to Rousseau and de Saussure, with a prelude by von Haller. For Stephen this change stemmed from social developments: along with the rights of man and the ideas of the *philosophes* came praise of the Alps for protecting peasants from "corrupt civilisation" (46). He emphasizes flight from society as a motive for climbing, finding a precedent in de Saussure's realization, on an Alpine summit, of "the pettiness of man" (52). And, like Thomas Hardy (whom he edited and befriended in 1871), Stephen ventures a prediction: "We may turn with greater eagerness than ever from the increasing crowds of respectable human beings to savage rock and glacier, and the uncontaminated air of the High Alps" (48). His summation returns to this note: "Life, we shall soon be saying, would be tolerable if it were not for our fellow-creatures. They come about us like bees, and as we cannot well destroy them, we are driven to fly to some safe asylum. The Alps, as yet, remain" (68). In the annals of travel to Great landscape, there is perhaps no more forthright expression of misanthropy, and it comes from the patron of one major modernist author (Hardy) and the father of another (Virginia Woolf).

Also in 1871 a veteran Alpinist of a different stripe, John Tyndall, published a collection of his own accounts of climbs spanning the years 1857–69 (some of them reprinted from *Mountaineering in 1861*), characteristically called *Hours of Exercise in the Alps.* Tyndall's enjoyment of Alpine scenery and enthusiasm for climbing had not diminished; he still "scampers" or "gallops" across glaciers, then lies for an hour watching the clouds or measures glacial movement. When he feels weak in London, says Tyndall, he goes to the Alps for his cure. So a tough climb on the Lauwinen-Thor restores his health, and "subsequent exercise made both brain and muscles firmer" (Tyndall 1899, 16). He describes himself as "a lover of natural knowledge and of natural scenery," and his book as "a record ... of strong and joyous hours" (v). Tyndall, who endorsed the theory that we have a pleasurable collective memory of early barbarian experience with mountains, is the prototypical adventurer, drawn to Great landscape because he finds its challenges exciting and is happiest when meeting them; his responses to the Great are virtually the opposite of Hardy's.

Tyndall has other dimensions besides this unflagging energy, though. His aesthetic sense is as stimulated by "the majestic architecture of the Alps" as his scientific side is by the story of their formation (4), so he devotes a chapter to "Alpine Sculpture." Tyndall finds in the Alps grandeur, beauty, and drama: during a storm, mighty clouds appear almost to overpower the "colossal," "Titanic" mountains (88); seen from a ledge on the Matterhorn, "grand" cloud banners inspire "awe" (121). In calmer times, an Alpine sunset can be "unspeakably grand" and a lingering dusk "sublime" (94–5).

Behind the adventurous, sensitive scientist is a believer of sorts. On the approach to the Weisshorn, he sees the stars "shining with a pure spiritual radiance" (96). At times Tyndall climbed alone so as to "contract a closer friendship for the universe" (117). Yet, though he sometimes uses religious language ("temple," "communion," "consecrated," "adoration") and admits that even an agnostic might feel "religious awe" on a solo climb of the Matterhorn (280), Tyndall shies away from religion *per se.* When he asks himself on the summit of the Jungfrau who formed "this colossal work," his unexpected answer is "the sun" (190). His is not the deist view that God is seen through nature, but the existentialist's, that there is "morality in the oxygen of the mountains" (155). They constitute an ethical system; "the Alps improve us *totally,* and we return from their precipices wiser as well as stronger men" (156). That wisdom and strength can be derived from Great landscapes was becoming an article of faith among adventurers. Their wisdom might be sobering, though: on a later climb he felt "saddened" by the "inexorable decay" of the mountain, "hacked and hurt by time" (291).

A new Alpine voice was heard that year. Edward Whymper had gained fame as a mountaineer during the 1860s, especially for his costly conquest of the Matterhorn in 1865. Whymper may have grown from a "cold-blooded and cynical" youth who devoured books about the Arctic and took forty-five-mile walks into an unhappy and unpleasant man: repressed, misogynic, "lonely and self-centred" (Smythe 1940, 69, 315). Yet the clarity and honesty of *Scrambles amongst the Alps* (1871) made it popular, lessening the prejudice against mountaineering that grew after four of Whymper's companions fell to their deaths on the Matterhorn. True, next to Tyndall's books *Scrambles* is not emotionally expressive. Whymper does have feelings about mountains – the Matterhorn is grand, the Weisshorn noble, and Mont Pelvoux sublime – but they are conventional, and held in check until the end. A gifted artist who had been hired by the Alpine Club to illustrate its volumes, Whymper says that he "dealt sparingly in descriptions, and ... employed illustrations freely" (1981, 4). His engravings sometimes supply the passion lacking in the narrative and should be considered part of the book's rhetoric.

Another oblique way in which emotion enters the book is through poetic citation. On Mont Pelvoux, Whymper quotes from John Greenleaf Whittier's "Snowbound," beginning at "The ranges stood / Transfigured in the silver flood" (23); on the summit of the Matterhorn, he spends "one crowded hour of glorious life," again quoting (155). Speaking for himself, Whymper is most apt to be moved by isolation. Atop Mont Pelvoux he is struck both by the immense panorama and by the absence of any "human habitation": "all was rock, snow or ice" (25). Sleeping out alone in a hollow by a streamside cliff, he loves the elemental simplicity of it all: "Nothing could be more perfect – rock, hole, wood and water" (28). Like Tyndall, but perhaps more like Stephen's misanthropic Alpinist, Whymper climbed alone when possible. In 1861 he made a "solitary scramble" to above thirteen thousand feet on the Matterhorn, where the view, "when seen alone and undisturbed, had ... strength and charm." He resolved to spend the night and was rewarded: at dusk, "while the summits shone with unnatural brightness, ... the earth seemed to become less earthly and almost sublime: the world seemed dead, and I its sole inhabitant" (50).

Scientist as well as minimalist (or solipsist), Whymper was conversant with uniformitarian geology. Some hoodoo pillars with capstones are "remarkable examples of the potent effects produced by the long-continued action of quiet-working forces"; on the "desolate, ruined and shattered ridge" of the Matterhorn, he is impressed by the "tremendous effects" of frost and "the long-continued action of forces whose individual effects are imperceptible" (29, 53). If "Professor Ruskin" finds "no aspect of destruction" on the Matterhorn, he is too distant: seen up close, its cliffs are ruins (64). Attitudes of reverence are left to professors and guides – until the end of the book.

Shortly after the Matterhorn fatalities, "lo! a mighty arch appeared" in the mists, an "unearthly apparition" of "two vast crosses" (157). In a footnote, Whymper coolly adopts the Arctic explorer William Parry's term "fog-bow" for this phenomenon, but in the text these "spectral forms" (which his guides connect with the accident) are "a fearful and wonderful sight, unique in my experience, and impressive beyond description, coming at such a moment." The episode seems to unlock something in Whymper. Thinking of his comrades "buried in snow at the base of the grandest cliff of the most majestic mountain of the Alps" (159), he tries to express what mountaineering has meant to him: glory in one's strength and resourcefulness, exultation in scenic grandeur, the awakening of dormant faculties. Finally he is moved: "There have been joys too great to be described," and "griefs upon which I have not dared to dwell" (162). His last words admonish climbers, "Look well to each step, and from the beginning think what may be the end"; his last three engravings depict the broken ends of two ropes and the body of a dead climber sprawled on a cliff ledge. Whymper's dark, emotional eloquence comes late, but is the more impressive for his long restraint.

Literature continued to celebrate mountains. The American regional poet Cincinnatus "Joaquin" Miller's *Songs of the Sierras* (1871) are actually poetic tributes not only to California's mountains but to the spirituality of grand nature in the Far West generally. In "Californian," an ocean beach is

> not a place for mirthfulness
> But meditation deep, and prayer,
> And kneelings on the salted sod,
> Where man must own his littleness
> And know the mightiness of God.   (Miller 1872, 68)

The distant Sierra Nevadas seem "A fringe of heaven" (69), and in "Tale of the Tall Alcalde," the Indian God Yopitone has his "snowy throne" atop Mount Shasta (208). In a preface to "Even So," Miller pays tribute to the "eternal" Sierras and claims credit for having made them well known to European readers (278).

Miller's verse drama "Ina" ranges from Mexico to Oregon. To woman-troubled Don Carlos, the moonlit "white buttes" around Popocatepetl flash "Like silver tents pitch'd in the field of heaven"; the high peaks with their "snows everlasting" are "Like milestones that lead to the city eternal" (131). They are "so purely" arrayed, he thinks, "Because of their nearness to the temple eternal," yet they cannot comfort him (132). He joins the misanthropic mountain man Lamonte on Mount Hood and accepts his invitation to live there in order to escape humanity. Don Carlos sees nature as violent (a view associated with Darwin), but others keep a more benign, traditional idea; for Lamonte, snow-covered volcanoes are nature's breasts, filled with inspiration. Though Miller's verse is limited by poetic diction, local colour, and even doggerel, he connects European notions of the holiness of mountains and the ocean firmly to the American West.

RUSKIN'S REACTION

John Ruskin's sprawling *Deucalion* (some parts first given as lectures in 1874–77 and 1880, chapters and half-chapters published in 1875–83, the title page dated 1879) grew out of his lectures on glaciology and Alpine rambles. Ruskin's early passions had hardened into a hatred of much of contemporary thought and culture. He rejects evolutionary science, attacks other writers on the Alps, deplores modern industrial society, and frequently professes his own (recently recovered) Christian faith (Burd 1981, 10–12). *Deucalion* is a jumbled, idiosyncratic, multidisciplinary text, at times exhibiting symptoms of mental and emotional disturbance. In the introduction (1875), Ruskin attacks Darwin and other "materialists" as "*half* wits" whose theories are less true than pagan myths (1906, 99).

"The Alps and Jura" (1875) advocates studying Alpine geology with a walking stick and knapsack, not a guide and alpenstock (i.e., no mountaineeering), and attacks Leslie Stephen for saying that the Alpine Club "has taught us for the first time really to see the mountains." For Ruskin, "our modern enthusiasm" seems "vulgar," "shallow," and "childish" beside the work of Hesiod, Pindar, Vergil, Scott, and Swiss artists, who also "had eyes for" mountains (103). In "The Three Aeras" (1875), he regrets Lyell's recent death and proclaims himself "his scholar," yet calls his "great theorem" only partly proved, broadly "disputable," and "entirely false" in its "broadest bearings" (117). Ruskin then gives his own version of earth history. The "forms" of the first era are unknowable; in the second (pre-biblical) era, the mountains we know were formed; in the third, they are being degraded: there is no creation now. Landforms are virtually unchanged since "the Fathers." Have you, he asks, noticed any changes in your lives? By the standards of the 1870s, the level of argument is pathetic.

In "Of Ice-Cream" (1875), which concerns glacial flow, Ruskin attacks the glaciology of John Tyndall. It is a nastier, more personal assault than that on Stephen or Lyell, quite disproportionate, one might think, to the question whether glaciers flow impulsively or inductively, cut their beds or fill them up. Disproportionate, that is, unless behind the scientific question lurks a theological one: whether creation is past (biblical) or present (uniformitarian). Ruskin's secular Bible is still James Forbes's *Travels in the Alps* (1843); Forbes's proof that glaciers flow like fluids is good enough for Ruskin, who reverently recalls meeting Forbes at Simplon in 1844.

"The Valley of Cluse" (1875) puts Ruskin's concerns in a different, though not contradictory, light. Using the placid Cluse valley as an ideal foil to the contemporary Babel, he declares his hatred of modern society's noise, as he does in *Fors Clavigera* (1871–74). Ruskin is part of a larger movement here: some nineteenth-century travellers did consider the absence of civilization and other humans part of the appeal of Great landscapes, as we have seen, and this kind of misanthropy has grown in the twentieth century. Ruskin (like Swift) loved some individuals, detested others, but came to dislike the masses intensely, especially when they insisted on touring places he loved, creating pressure for a railroad through a quiet valley.

Ruskin's geology had been reasonably *au courant* in the 1840s, but he could never accept evolutionary science. His accumulating rejection of Lyell is elaborated in "Yewdale and Its Streamlets" (1878), where he complains that geologists deal only with the remote past (which was not true), argues that "present causes" cannot account for present landforms, and refutes uniformitarianism with table-top demonstrations of glacial flow. It is not necessary to "go and see," he insists: "You have no business to seek knowledge far afield, when you can get it at your doors ... You have no business to go outside your doors for it, when you can get it in your parlour" (Ruskin 1906, 258). In dismissing not only the work of Lyell but the whole empirical thrust of modern geology, Ruskin is out of his depth. His response to the threat is ostrichlike: he will stay home with his apparatus for demonstrating erosion and glacial flow; he will *not* go and see, any more than he would join the Alpine Club on the high peaks. In the humanities and in the sciences, Ruskin grew sentimental about modes of life and thought that he valued, alternately denying and deploring that things had changed.

The literature of deserts ranged from "sacred geography" through science to dark meditation. E.H. Palmer described *The Desert of the Exodus* with the professed aim of determining the "Scriptural topography" of the region (1871, 1: vii). In the Sinai, he asserts, nature is beautiful though barren, and "God is nigh" (27, 33–4). Mount Sinai, "stately" and "awful-looking," illustrates the "universal harmony of the Moral and the Physical": its primitive rocks suit the laws proclaimed there (53–4), as Holland said of Iceland. The "desolation of Horeb," he insists, "does not oppress the soul" but engenders feelings of "wonder and awe" (104). At other times, though, faced with the "awful wilderness" or "alone with the barren rocks," he gives no such assurance (125, 196). The "barren wilderness" beside the "sterile" Red Sea is an "utter and oppressive desolation," yet this is "where God was pleased to manifest himself to man" (207–8, 245). And so it goes, back and forth, depending on the topography, its scriptural value (or lack thereof), and his moods. The desert's bareness is terrible, but here, sometimes, holy; another desert would be different.

In France, Gustave Flaubert's *La Tentation de Saint Antoine*, which he had put aside in 1856 (see chapter 17), was finally published in 1874. Hoping to make this third version acceptable to the public, Flaubert compromised with prevailing tastes and social norms in some respects, especially at the end, but the continuities outweigh the changes. A long scene direction at the beginning still evokes a small platform in the desert mountains of Egypt; in the centre, "immenses ondulations" of desert roll away to the Libyan range on the horizon (Flaubert 1936, 1). A bored Saint Anthony still paces his rocky enclosure, wondering why he stays with 'nothing to do!' (14). He remains a recognizable version of Flaubert, with some touches of Goethe's Faust. Once more the Devil flies him through space, like Byron's Cain. The desert is again a spiritual state as well as a landscape: 'My heart is drier than a rock!' ("J'ai le coeur plus sec qu'un rocher!"; 246).

Édouard Maynial says that the one vital book Flaubert read between the early and final versions of *Saint Antoine* was Haeckel's *Natural*

Creation, and that the doubts and temptations of science and rationalism are embodied in the character of Hilarion (in Flaubert 1936, xv–xvi). While it is interesting to know that the new science touched Flaubert, there is no fundamental change in how nature is represented in the final version; Haeckel's influence simply confirmed an existing outlook. Mountains, desert, and space still form the parameters of Anthony's struggle to understand the purpose of existence, and may mirror that struggle. But the 1874 ending, with its revelation of God-in-nature, is not what most observers would call a "scientific" conclusion. Anthony delights in a vision of the birth of minute life, desires a mystical union with the material world, sees the face of Christ in the sun-disk, makes the sign of the cross and prays, untroubled by diabolic laughter. While it is easy to imagine theological objections to this, the irreverent, have-at-you mockery of 1849–56 is gone. Thus toned down, but still a potent image of spiritual quest in the desert, *La Tentation de Saint Antoine* at last came before the public.

Twenty years after his voyage to the Levant (1856–57), Herman Melville published *Clarel. A Poem and Pilgrimage in the Holy Land*, exploring issues that his experiences there raised for him. The two volumes are not easy going – at times clarity and grammar are cut to the Procrustean bed of his iambic tetrameters, whose rhymes and archaisms can be ludicrous – but *Clarel* has some redeeming features. One is the way Melville's own memories combine with his reading in travel literature to produce a remarkable concatenation of topographies associated with the Great. The desert is oceanlike, and Time a "vast sea" whose reefs are bookish thoughts (Melville 1963, pt. I, sec. i). The "blank towers" of Jerusalem are "Like the ice-bastions round the Pole," the whole city looks like a house on a moor, and its Jews resemble penguins on a Patagonian beach (I.i, xxxiii). The number of polar allusions in this desert poem is surprising: the "Crag of Agonies" in the Wilderness of the Temptation recalls an iceberg off Labrador, the glassy Dead Sea suggests polar ice, and one character's face resembles Mount Hecla in Iceland (II.xiv, xxxii, xxxiv).

As in Melville's Levantine journal, the barren, stony landscapes of *Clarel* seem both oppressive and hallowed. The Holy Land is consistently imaged as dead, the Judaean wilderness as Hell or Hades, yet between this wasteland and the spirit there is a close connection, clearest in "Of Deserts," which is central to many themes discussed in this book. Melville's subject is the ambiguous power of empty wastes.

> Darwin quotes
> From Shelley, that forever floats
> Over all desert places known,
> Mysterious doubt – an awful one.
> He quotes, adopts it. Is it true?   (II.xi)

In his 1845 *Journal of Researches*, Darwin quotes two and a half lines from Shelley's "Mont Blanc" (75–7), including "The wilderness ... teaches awful doubt," but omitting the rest of the line: "or faith so mild" (Paradis 1981, 97). This bias suits Melville. His "Arabian" pilgrim will have "Small love of deserts, if their power / Make to retreat upon the heart / Their own forsakenness." The desert's value is *not* in the eye of the beholder; it manifests *heaven's* beauty or terror. So Mount Sinai awed the fearful shepherds before Moses. And what landscape could better convey the sense of divine desertion?

Melville is obsessed with the paradoxical holiness of deserts. We call the "caked depopulated hell" of Judah – which rivals Erebus in "horror absolute" and looks like an expression of "settled anger terrible" – the Holy Land. But, he persists,

> *why* does man
> Regard religiously this tract
> Cadaverous and under ban
> Of blastment?   (II.xi; my emphasis)

Biblical history is no answer for Melville; all he can say is that the paradox is ancient, a given of human nature. As Greeks once adored any site scorched by Jove's lightning as "hallowed," so we "adore this ground / Which doom hath smitten. 'Tis a land / Direful yet holy – blest tho' banned": "Exalted in accursed estate," as he puts it later (IV.i). The very contortions that make the land fearful to behold prove supernatural agency and thus evoke a religious response; *any* Divine touch, even an angry one, is better than none. (Geologists also found such lands interesting for the light they shed on "creation.")

Whether or not we find these answers satisfactory, desert landscapes have profound meanings for the characters of *Clarel*. For Nathan, Judaism is "the crag of Sinai," towering "behind man's present lot / Of crumbling faith" (I.xvii). His daughter Ruth is initially made "lorn" by "The waste of Judah" (I.xxvii). The pilgrims to the Jordan (though familiar with the desert writings of Volney, Burckhardt, Chateaubriand, and Lamartine) are shocked by the barrenness of the Dead Sea valley, which is surrounded by "worlds more waste, more bare" (II.xiv). Rolfe observes that nature is "Calvinistic" there, but later asserts that "Man sprang from deserts," and "On deserts he falls back at need" as his "bare abandoned home" (II.xiv, xvi). The prevalent image is extreme bareness: the narrator calls the northern shore of the Dead Sea "null" (II.xxix).

The "holiness" of the land cannot shield it from modern religious scepticism; *et in terra sancta dubitas*. Doubt lives even in Jerusalem, where "All now's revised: / Zion, like Rome, is Niebuhrised" (I.xxxiv). (In the journal of his 1856–57 travels, Melville had "wish[ed] Niebuhr and Strauss," mainstays of the Higher Criticism of the Bible, "to the dogs" for having robbed modern souls of faith [1955, 166–7].) In the Judaean hills, Clarel meets a "Hegelised," "readvised" Jew, "An Apostate" who, having converted to geology, is trying to hammer scientific truth out of the Holy Land (II.xix). In Part Three, "The High Desert" is the setting for a meditation on ancient and modern modes of faith, under "the clear vault of hollow heaven" (III.v). Melville's desert, then, is not a place that necessarily imparts or strengthens faith – may even shake it – but an arena where the great spiritual questions are inevitably raised for serious consideration. It functions like the sea and the whiteness of the whale in *Moby Dick*, whose very blankness leads us to mythmaking.

After finishing his book on the Colorado basin, Major Powell turned to a broader question, both philosophical and practical: what kind of legislation should govern settlement in the West? His *Report on the Lands of the Arid Region of the United States* (1878), "one of the most significant and seminal books ever written about the West," refused to leave the area to fantasy, hope or interest; it tried instead to set out the full geographic truth about the intermountain United States and replace "guesswork with information" (Powell 1962, xxiv; Stegner 1954, viii, 7). Though it lacks the aesthetic dimension of *Exploration of the Colorado*, the *Report* cannot be dismissed as a dry factual document without bearing on the question at hand. It shows Powell's continuing interest in America's arid zone, what Doughty (emerging from Arabia) would call its "vast waterless marches," and his intelligent respect for the verities of that land.

Powell distinguishes the eastern climate ("abundant rainfall for agricultural purposes") from that of the area west of the hundredth meridian, where "agriculture is not successful without irrigation" (Powell 1962, 11), and proceeds to show the consequences of these conditions for settlers. No less than forty percent of the continental United States is arid, he points out, and only a small part of that is irrigable. The greatest portion of this region is "pasturage lands," which "will maintain but a scanty population" on large, widely scattered farms (33). The importance of this report for American history is that it made sensible recommendations for land management based on accurate data. Its importance to the development being traced here is, first, its close attention to a vast tract of mostly empty, barren land, and second, its keen sense of the limits that such a place imposes on human existence. Powell, like most students of desert lands, becomes perforce a minimalist. An illustration of the opening scene of *The Return of the Native* – a broad sweep of sere heath, eventually crossed by a lone human figure – could serve as a frontispiece for Powell's *Report on the Lands of the Arid Region*, making his point about the realities of existence in deserts.

POETS OF WILDNESS

New literary voices in America and England began to pay homage to wild nature. For Walt Whitman, enlarging horizons was an article of faith, and his omnivorous embrace of life included mountains, seas, and stars wherever he went. In *Democratic Vistas* (1871), his prose treatise on America's culture and prospects, Whitman distinguishes between pretty pastoral nature and the outlook that must inform the work of the modern democratic poet: "Nature, true Nature, and the true idea of Nature, long absent, must, above all, become fully restored, and must furnish the pervading atmosphere to poems ... I do not mean the smooth walks, trimm'd hedges, poseys and nightingales of the English poets, but the whole orb, with its geologic history, the kosmos, carrying fire and snow, that rolls through the illimitable areas, light as a feather, though weighing billions of tons" (1968, 252). Liberated writers cannot settle for the tamed landscapes of Cowper and Keats, but will insist on the "whole orb" of the scientists, as Whitman himself did in "Facing West from California's Shores" (1860) and "Passage to India" (1871).

Algernon Charles Swinburne, who admired Whitman's *Leaves of Grass* (1855), included in his own *Songs before Sunrise* (1871) several statements of his own view of nature and a plea "To Walt Whitman in America" to send a song of freedom to the tired Old World. In "Hertha" ("Earth," 1871), the first principle of life ("before God was, I am") tells humanity that she pervades and comprises all, including us (Swinburne 1925, lines 1, 15). Our abject theology does not come from her, "Mother, not maker" (line 66). We must outgrow our present religions; "A creed is a rod" to punish boys, and "the morning of manhood is risen": the "sunrise" of the title (lines 71, 95). Hertha contains all natural phenomena – storm winds, "All shadows and lights / On the world's mountain-ranges / And stream-riven heights" (lines 127–9) – and asks us not to pray "but be" (line 156). God, she says, is finished, replaced by "Man, equal and one with me, man that is made of me, man that is I" (line 200). Many of these views are reiterated in "Hymn of Man" (1871), a Blakean scripture couched in a series of assertions and rhetorical questions to the Ecumenical Council in Rome.

Swinburne gives his philosophy narrative form in "On the Downs" (1871), whose opening scene at "the lip's edge of the down" is not unlike the first chapter of *The Return of the Native*. The speaker remembers looking around at the "faint sea," "dun" sky, and heath dessicated by "dry sea-wind," finding all "stark" and "bare," and searching for "news / Of comfort that all these refuse" (Swinburne 1955, lines 1, 2, 7, 9, 17, 19–20, 23). Now, in his room, he feels as he felt then, but the terrain becomes metaphorical; his mind moving over thought *is* the figure on the downs: "By footless ways and sterile went / My thought unsatisfied" to look with "blank ... eyes" on the "sands of discontent" where "Life hopeless lies" (lines 43–6, 48). Earth seemed, and seems, a captive queen, love and wisdom are dead, and God is absent. Science is never a consideration in Swinburne.

Thus far we have much darker tones than Swinburne usually employs, but then he remembers the "glad mother's song" of nature, "The wise word of the secret earth," which "That day" said, "There is no God, O son, / If thou be none" (lines 92, 97, 107–8, 110). Suddenly (as in T.S. Eliot's *The Waste Land*) "stagnant wells" stir, and an epiphany of "One God," "One forceful nature uncreate," reanimates speaker and scene (lines 112, 126–7). The conviction that "freedom fills time's veins with power, / As, brooding on that sea, / My thought filled me" propels Swinburne to the triumphant conclusion in which "Time's deep dawn rise[s]" (lines 136–8, 156), re-establishing the volume's dominant image. Rejecting the consolations of religion and ignoring the insights of science, Swinburne took nature worship as far as any poet of his century, not in the mountains but on the bare, dry downs, and he was part of Hardy's influential early reading (Rutland 1962, 70). Hardy, however, was drawn to the sere first half of this poem, not to its joyous resolution.

The Scots poet James Thomson generated a darkness deeper than Hardy's in 1874 by using wastelands as bleak as Egdon to symbolize depression. The speaker in "The City of Dreadful Night" (1871), impelled by "cold rage" to deliver "the bitter old and wrinkled truth / Stripped naked of all vesture" that "There is no God," wanders through a city whose king is "Death in Life" and whose queen is "Melencholia [*sic*]" (Thomson 1963, sec. 3, line 25; 14.40; 21.8–10, 42). The setting for this atheist's version of Dante's Hell – "Leave hope behind, all ye who enter here" (sec. 6.21) – is stripped equally naked: "A trackless wilderness," "enormous mountains," "immense wild tracts," "a level upland bleak and bare," "marsh and moorland" surround the city (sec. 1.32–4; 5.2; 21.2, 76). Section four's refrain is, "As I came through the desert." On the River of Suicides, one "Glides drifting down into the desert ocean, / To starve or sink from out the desert world" (sec. 19.13–14). A statue of Melencholia confronts this grim landscape "with a coeval mien" (sec. 21.77).

Thomson blends his feeling that melancholy and nature are "coeval" with his misanthropy. "Wherever men are gathered, all the air / Is charged with human feeling, human thought," "is with our life ... overfraught," he complains, "So that no man there breathes earth's simple breath, / As if alone on mountains or wide seas" (sec. 15.1–2, 7–9). Why not just walk out of the City of No God and climb or sail, then? But no: part of Melencholia's iconography is a "comet hanging o'er the waste dark seas" (sec. 21.36). Similarly, his conviction that "no Fiend ... tortures us; if we must pine, / It is to satiate no Being's gall" (sec. 14.40–2) brings no comfort. Thomson's largest images of Void occur in connection with his denial of God: "How the moon triumphs through the endless nights! / How the stars throb and glitter as they wheel" (sec. 17.1–2). We may "think the heavens respond" to us, but "There is no heart or mind in all their splendour" (sec. 17.7, 20). For Thomson, the salient feature of Great nature is its emptiness. "The empyrean is a void abyss," he asserts flatly; "there is no light beyond the curtain" (sec. 17.28, 21.69). That he could not share the cheerfulness or spirituality of an agnostic such as Tyndall seems more a matter of temperament than of belief.

At the opposite extreme of conviction, Gerard Manley Hopkins's poems on the meaning of the physical world to a devout Christian – which, unpublished at his death, gained recognition only in the twentieth century – show that some of the old deist metaphors and concepts of nature could still be viable for a believer in the 1870s. Several early works in his *Poems* of 1876–89 suggest that Hopkins's intense Catholicism (like Aubrey de Vere's) did not preclude a kind of natural religion. If "the

azurous hung hills *are* his world-wielding shoulder / Majestic" ("Hurrah-
ing in Harvest" [1877] 1970; my emphasis), it does not require Alps or
mountaineering for us to feel God's presence in the high country.

Elsewhere Hopkins's view of nature sounds less traditional. When he
writes, in "The Wreck of the Deutschland" (composed in 1876–78), that
"the infinite air is unkind," he is attributing to material creation what
was once considered a quality of the Deity alone (stanza 13), a leap that
would have been heresy in 1600. The poem seeks meaning in the
deaths of five nuns, shipwrecked in a Channel storm. Hopkins imagines
that the nuns, welcoming their fate as a deliverance in Christ, were "the
keener to come at the comfort for feeling the combating keen" (stanza
25): a Christian counterpart of the belief of some agnostic Alpinists
(such as Tyndall) and desertists (Burton) that there was significance,
perhaps merit, in the hardships of the struggle. Hopkins conceives of
God as the Author of natural phenomena ("master of the tides, / Of the
Yore-flood, of the year's fall") and admires Him in metaphors drawn
from the Great ("Stanching, quenching ocean of a motionable mind; /
Ground of being, and granite of it"), though God is, by definition, "past
all" of these works (stanza 32). It is of course in positing that definition,
in making the theistic assumption, that Hopkins diverges from Hardy.

Coventry Patmore had converted to Catholicism since writing "Sahara"
(see chapter 18), which may explain the change in his use of "desert."
The metaphorical Sahara of 1854 was located in barren passages of
domestic life such as unrequited love or ingratitude. "The Two Deserts"
of 1877–78 (in *The Unknown Eros*) are the macrocosm and the microcosm. Between "these deserts blank of small and great" lies our God-
given "royal-fair estate." The ungrateful-sounding idea that this too
might have its deserts has disappeared. The image is consonant with the
Great Chain of Being as described by eighteenth-century writers; at times
Patmore, like Hopkins, sounds as if he belonged to an earlier stage of English nature writing. Any writer who primarily followed Christian teachings rather than contemporary science *was* apt to sound "eighteenth
century" by this time.

NOVELISTS IN THULE

Victorian novels finally began to treat Great landscape, led by an angry
new voice. In *Erewhon* (1872), Samuel Butler's main purpose is satire –
the book began as "Darwin among the Machines" – but he prefaces the
portrait of Erewhon (i.e., "Nowhere," utopia) with an adventure story

crafted in unusual detail for the genre. The young narrator emigrates to the "Waste Lands" of the Upper Rangitata in New Zealand (where Butler began the book) to become a rancher. Working in the foothills of high mountains whose "utter loneliness" and "vastness" appeal to his imagination, he climbs, Wordsworth-like, through fog until he can look down on a sea of cloud: "I am there now as I write ... Oh, wonderful, wonderful! so lonely and so solemn" (Butler 1961, 20–1). He sets out to explore, following a "terrible" river through a beautiful gorge. There he is happy: the air has "ineffable purity," the "peacefulness" is "delightful and exhilarating," and at night his camp affords "a picture worthy of a Salvator Rosa or a Nicolas Poussin" (28–9). The glaciated mountains look "perfectly worthless" for ranching (31) and his native companion abandons him, yet he climbs to a saddle, from which he sees a deep gorge and a new range beyond.

The narrator crosses the gorge and climbs to another pass, despite the solitude, the "intense silence and gloom" of the "rocky wilderness" (43–4), and a mysterious windborne music. Skirting glaciers, he reaches the pass in fog, but faints when he sees "a circle of gigantic forms, many times higher than myself, upstanding grim and grey through the veil of cloud" (44). These are not cirques or hogbacks but statues, which unnerve the narrator in this "dreadful wilderness" (45), especially when the wind comes up and they begin to produce the Aeolian music he heard. He hastens down to the broad plains below and enters Erewhon. When Butler's satire has run its course, the narrator escapes from the Musical Banks and Colleges of Unreason in a balloon, overflying high mountains and finally dropping into the sea. He expects the worst but is soon picked up, an experience he compares to threading a "sublime and terrible" Alpine gorge and unexpectedly emerging from its dark tunnel to "behold a smiling valley" (223). Thus *Erewhon*'s social ideas are framed by vividly recollected images of mountain travel.

But Thomas Hardy would dominate fictional renderings of the chastened Great in the 1870s. His third novel, *A Pair of Blue Eyes* (1873), includes an episode in which an amateur geologist clings to a steep cliff, facing the earth's history and his own mortality. Combining influences from Darwin, Huxley, Leslie Stephen's "A Bad Five Minutes in the Alps," Arnold's "Dover Beach," and Mantell's *Wonders of Geology*, it shows the extent of Hardy's scientific interests by this time, and the attitudes that they were fostering (Ebbatson, in Hardy 1986, 34, 461–5).

In chapter 21, Elfride Swancourt and Henry Knight walk out on the coastal downs of Cornwall, view the sea from a clifftop, and then confront a higher cliff, "a vast stratification of blackish-gray slate," revealing the "backbone and marrow" of the hill (Hardy 1986, 263). She "cannot bear to look at that cliff. It has a horrid personality, and makes [her] shudder," but they ascend it anyway. At the top, Knight slips a few yards down the slope and cannot get back; trying to aid him, Elfride slips too. They are stayed only by "a bracket of quartz rock," protruding "like a tooth" from "the Cliff without a Name," whose "blackness" gives it "added terror" (265–6). Elfride escapes by standing on Knight's shoulders, but in the process the "igneous protrusion" of quartz is dislodged, and Knight is left hanging by a tuft of grass while she goes for help (267–8). He can only stare at the cliff, whose "grimness" and "desolation" represent "the world in its infancy" and the "inveterate antagonism" of such places to the struggle for life (270–1).

After awhile, Knight, "a fair geologist," realizes that he is looking at the "imbedded fossil" of a trilobite, which has been extinct for millions of years, and that it seems to be regarding him (271). His mind roams back over time to pre-human ages until the trilobite seems comparatively "present and modern"; "there is no place like a cleft landscape for bringing home such imaginings as these" (272). As it begins to rain and the wind rises, nature's "hostility" seems "a cosmic agency, active, lashing, eager for conquest" (273). "Pitiless Nature" has two voices: wind and the ocean, "rubbing its restless flank against the Cliff" (274). Knight is meditating upon Psalm 23 when Elfride returns and saves him with a rope made from her undergarments. Ebbatson argues that in Knight – modelled on Hardy and his friend Horace Moule – we first feel "the ache of modernism," and that the Cliff is an "actant in the story" that overshadows the rest of the action, like Forster's Marabar Caves (in Hardy 1986, 34, 23, 37) – or, it may be added, Hardy's own Egdon Heath.

Hardy's first successful novel, *Far from the Madding Crowd* (1874; serialized by Leslie Stephen in *Cornhill Magazine*), portrays nature as a *force majeure*, source of both good and ill. Chapter 2 places Gabriel Oak in his topographical and cosmic context. Norcombe Hill, "a shape approaching the indestructible," is geologically realized as "a featureless convexity of chalk and soil" that may survive the "great day of confusion" (Hardy 1900, 8). On its summit at night, one feels "the roll of the world eastward" and gets an "impression of riding along": the "epic form" of the "poetry of motion" (9–10). The resulting sense of astronomical expansion can raise "some men" to a "capability for eternity" (10; a phrase omitted from later editions). Oak, "impressed with the speaking loneliness" and beauty of the place, its "complete abstraction" from "the sights and sounds of man," keeps a hut and plays his flute up there (13–14). Thus he can understand nature's messages about the approach of a great storm "in the vast firmamental hollows overhead" that makes "everything human" seem "small and trifling" (291, 294). In Hardy's cosmos, nature links a puny animate creation to the overarching powers.

Hardy admired William Black's popular novel *A Princess of Thule* (1874) enough to take hints from it for *The Return of the Native* (Rutland 1962, 183–5). Black, a Glaswegian, often uses boreal scenery for tonal purposes. His first chapter evokes the somber majesty of Hebridean land- and seascapes as Sheila Mackenzie sails away and her father surveys the "desolate waste of rain-beaten sea." The elements rule; he can see "only wind and water" (Black 1879, 1). As he drives his cart "into the heart of the lonely and desolate land," beyond "the last traces of human occupation," a gloomy late afternoon sky lies "heavily over the dreary wastes of moor and hill. What a wild and dismal country ... not a fence to break the monotony of the long undulations of moorland ... lonely lakes, with not a tree to break the line of their melancholy shores. Everywhere around were the traces of the glacier-drift – great grey boulders of gneiss" amid peat and heather (3). In this bare land the few people stand out starkly and, as in Hardy, are first identified simply as "an old man," "a young girl."

On the isle of Borva, the dark scenery again seems to reflect Mackenzie's sorrow. His isolated stone house is set amidst "dreariness and desolation"; one hears "the breaking of the waves along the hard coast," "rocky and dangerous," where even the music is "sad and sombre" (7–8, 10). Black appears to be using pathetic fallacy to prepare a tragic action, but in fact is manipulating our expectations; his agendum is romance. In chapter 3, "There Was a King in Thule," the imagination of Lavender, a London artist, transforms Mackenzie into the "King of Thule" and Sheila into its Princess. He quickly falls in love both with her and with "this wonder-land" (40). They marry – the first scene is actually the start of their wedding trip and marital troubles – and eventually return there to live, healing the initial wound of separation. It is still a bleak country, of course, but love and imagination transmute or see through its barrenness to wonder, and suffering teaches its value. The novel's real hero is Hebridean nature, its villain, London softness, which almost spoils the romance. Lavender must retire to the solitudes of the Hebrides and realize that they and Sheila are one before he gains his prize.

The Princess of Thule, then, is a homage to the barren Great as well as to Hibernia. Black's Scotland is not Edinburgh and literate country gentlemen, but the primitive wildness of the western isles. He is happiest when entreating visitors and readers to "look at the spacious landscape lying all around" (32): the Atlantic from a cliff at moonrise, the high lonely isle of Mevaig, silent stars, majestic mountains. Beneath this aspect of travelogue, though, is Sheila's yearning towards the sea, towards the Great, frustrated during her time in London. Both she and Cecilia Lorraine are drawn to the amplitude of the Hebrides, "so beautiful and so desolate" (455), which also cures Lavender. Even the house on Borva, with its Cowper-like coziness in winter, has "spacious Tyrolese landscapes" on its wallpaper (37). Black resembles the Hardy of *The Return of the Native* in his penchant for barren vastness and for setting human drama in its geological context, though he was clearly more optimistic, at least in fiction.

An epistolary novel by Winwood Reade the following year warned of the possible social costs (in England) of espousing evolutionary science. *The Outcast* (1875) offers two examples. First, a young man's faith is undermined by Malthus and Darwin. Distraught, he records his opium dreams of space, and composes a dream-vision about a demigod's unfavourable review of the Creator's play "Earth" – shortly before killing himself. Then the narrator, Mordaunt, gives his daughter an account of how her mother came to die young. Mordaunt was a promising young parson when he met her, but during their engagement he read Lyell's *Principles of Geology*, which he found so persuasive that he rejected biblical Christianity and left the Church. With no prospects he could not marry, and his father, a stern pastor himself, turned him away. Mordaunt walked wailing across "moors like a wide black sea," swept by the north wind, under a moon and clouds "pierced by its cold white rays" (Reade 1875, 61). He became a hireling author and married Margaret, but without an adequate income they went from hard times to worse. Shortly after bearing Ellen, she died in a slum.

Thus far *The Outcast* sounds like a warning against the dangers of modern science and free thought, but that is not Reade's drift. Charity by thieves and a bishop sets Mordaunt on his feet again with writing commissions. Sitting on a cliff one night during a sojourn in the country, he envisions the vastness of the universe. Perceiving that humanity is insignificant unless it finds a worthy mission seconding the Creator's work, Mordaunt concludes that we should abandon the hope of personal immortality, battle evil, and "labour for the glory of the planet" and "for posterity" (114). On these foundations he constructs an altruistic religion that does not sound like satire. And in telling the whole story to Ellen, Mordaunt defends scientific doubt, which "dissipates superstition and softens the rancour of religious life ... the history of tolerance is the history of doubt" (116). The Lyellian darkness in the book, then, is actually a tunnel from illusion to enlightenment, fear to hope: "the scales fell from [Mordaunt's] eyes" when he read the *Principles* (48). By the end, uniformitarianism has led him to a higher plane of truth.

Hardy published another land-conscious book in 1876, *The Hand of Ethelberta*. Its chapter titles are settings such as dramatists used to give their scenes, and many of these are topographical: "Sandbourne Moor," "The Shore by Wyndway," "Sandbourne – A Lonely Heath." Chapter 31 ("Knollsea – A Lofty Down – A Ruined Castle") shows Hardy's fondness for natural settings that allow free play to the elements, and whose antiquity dwarfs ours. He describes the landscape minutely as Ethelberta – her name appropriately archaic – rides from the village of Knollsea to an antiquarian society's meeting in the castle. She follows a ridge inland among "prehistoric" barrows, with extensive open country on both sides, "like a map" seen from "the top of a giant's grave." This ridge divides the weather "like a wall": to her right, over the Channel, it is "a fine day," but "dark and cloudy weather" covers the downs, whose "grassed hills rose like knuckles gloved in dark olive." Around these ominously upthrust chthonic fists, the few trees are a "deeper and sadder monochrome," a "zinc sky" meets a "leaden sea" in the distance, "the low wind groaned and whined, and not a bird sang" (Hardy 1927, 273–4).

Ethelberta watches this "battle" of the elements (reading her own problems into it) until the sun prevails. Hardy's interest in atmospheric phenomena was whetted by his early contact with a meteorologist named Martin, who used to observe storms on the actual "Egdon Heath" from one of Hardy's favourite eminences, Rainbarrow (Gittings 1975, 96–7). Arriving at the castle, Ethelberta fends off a suitor, misses Julian, and rides home. The episode resembles the heath-meetings in *The Return of the Native* in that Hardy gives human encounters perspective by setting them within an almost infinitely larger, older, and more powerful context of land, sea, and sky.

The 1870s, then, offer numerous adumbrations of Egdon Heath. Novelists and poets used the barren Great to make statements about the modern spiritual condition, explorers pushed farther into the planet's vast unknown wilds, and many writers took an interest in the earth: what it was in its entirety and how it came to be that way (Whitman's "the whole orb, with its geologic history"), what kind of a home it was, what light it could shed on cosmogony and religion. Great nature interested both the doubtful – Stephen, Tyndall, Arnold, Hardy – and believers such as Hopkins, Patmore, and Ruskin, though the result is a series of monologues rather than a debate. Not everyone was as gloomy as Hardy, but he was correct in saying that "gaunt" and "sombre" locales such as Egdon "appealed to" and were in "harmony with" the sensibilities of his contemporaries.

Epilogue
The Heath Revisited

Seen again after our long excursion, Egdon Heath looks slightly different; a phrase here, an eminence there has acquired new meaning. If we ask why the chapter is written as it is, why the land lies as it does, Hardy's own experiences are one obvious answer. As it took Whistler "all [his] life" to paint "Whistler's Mother," so all of Hardy's went into *The Return of the Native*. The suicide of his friend Horace Moule, who had given him *Essays and Reviews*, Mantell's *Wonders of Geology*, and much more, darkened his outlook on life in 1873, the year that he met Leslie Stephen, a powerful and initially positive influence. Stephen, whose interests spanned literature, theology, philosophy, and mountaineering, gave Hardy access to a broad spectrum of thought and activity: he was an agnostic rationalist (author of *Essays on Freethinking and Plain Speaking*) whose doubts were shared with Hardy, an active Alpinist (the Alps being one destination of Hardy's tourist of the future) who published climbing narratives, and an editor who serialized Hardy's early work in the *Cornhill Magazine*. They parted company over *The Return of the Native*, which Stephen rejected in 1877, but he is nevertheless a part of the book.

Hardy married Emma Gifford in 1874: another ambiguous relationship; by most accounts they were not happy for long. If he indeed "lost all religious faith by thirty-five," that also happened about this time (Rutland 1962, 62). In 1876, when Hardy was writing *The Return of the Native*, his previous novel, *The Hand of Ethelberta*, was coolly received, which discouraged him about the prospects for social reform (Webster 1964, 119). On the other hand, he met William Black, whose novel *A Princess of Thule* he admired, and moved to Sturminster Newton, where he had two good years, despite strained relations with Emma (Millgate 1982, 182–5). Hardy toured Europe in 1876, visiting Scheveningen,

Heidelberg, and Baden: places mentioned in connection with the aesthetics of Egdon Heath.

All this has a certain biographical interest, yet such an approach cannot do justice to the complex historical connections between Egdon Heath and the numerous treatments of Great nature by travellers, poets, and philosophers over the previous two centuries, which formed part of the Victorians' intellectual heritage. Hardy's presentation is saturated with the themes and features we have been tracing. "A Face on which Time makes but Little Impression," Egdon is given the quality of *long endurance* that observers have felt in the Great at least since the voyages of Wood and Marten in the 1670s, being not only unchanged from Roman times, "unmoved, during so many centuries," but "from prehistoric times as unaltered as the stars overhead" (Hardy 1980, 1, 3). Wordsworth in the Alps, Fromentin in the Sahara, Hayes in the Arctic, and Melville in the Galápagos are among those who have been impressed by what Buffon called the 'high antiquity' ("haute ancienneté") of Great nature. And, since the heath's "irregularities" are described as "the very finger-touches of the last geological change" (3), we can add to this list Lyell, Darwin, and other scientists who were demonstrating the earth's great age.

The night sky, the sea, the Alps, and the Arctic ("Thule") all come up in Hardy's first chapter as analogues of Egdon Heath. Such comparisons of one area of the natural Great to other manifestations are the rule and indeed inevitable: as we have seen, the essential coherence or interconnectedness of the various aspects of the Great is attested by a long series of travellers (Thomas Burnet, Windham), aestheticians (Longinus, Addison), and poets (Dante, Albrecht von Haller, Thomson, Arnold).

From the first words of the chapter, Hardy also presents Egdon Heath as a *gloomy* place. He describes it during a November twilight when it is "solemn," makes it a "near relation of night," compares its impressiveness to a prison's and its power to a nightmare's (1–2). In arguing that the attraction of this gloom is peculiarly modern ("Haggard Egdon appealed ... to a more recently learnt emotion"), Hardy might have adduced Ruskin's "mountain gloom," contemporary poets such as Arnold, Thomson, and Mallarmé, and Black's *A Princess of Thule* as support. But in fact the melancholy of the Great – viewed philosophically, as a foil to human transience and weakness – was a tradition that can be traced back through Gothic novelists (Beckford, Radcliffe) to seventeenth- and eighteenth-century poets (Drayton, Young) and travellers: Evelyn in the Alps, Johnson in the Hebrides, Forster in the Antarctic. The parallel between natural barrenness and human unhappiness is at least as old as Eustache Deschamps's "Lay du desert d'Amours" (ca. 1500). Hardy was right, though, to say that "Egdon appealed." The bleakness of these places was not entirely repellent; far from driving observers away, it had fascinated and to some degree attracted them for centuries.

Topographically, Egdon Heath is a "vast tract of unenclosed wild" (1). *Vastness* was a defining trait of Addison's Great, central to the "speculations of eternity and infinitude" that constitute the "pleasure" of this type of imaginative experience. Nearly every traveller to Great landscapes from Conrad Gesner to Tyndall responded reverentially or enthusiastically to their magnitude and the sense of space they convey. The lack of enclosure is what makes a "spacious horizon" an "image of liberty" (Addison, *Spectator* no. 412); desert enthusiasts (Burton, Fromentin) listed *freedom* as part of the appeal, as did writers on the mountains, including Wordsworth, Shelley, and Byron. And Egdon is "wild": "Ishmaelitish" as well as "Titanic." Eighteenth-century European writers had popularized *wildness* as a release from the cultivated or civilized. As Shaftesbury said (and Thacker has reiterated), "The wildness pleases," in and of itself, for reasons we hardly understand.

To say that the heath is "grand" and "majestic" is also to define it as "Great"; most commentators on this aesthetic category have seen *grandeur* or magnificence as essential. That Egdon is "grand in its *simplicity*" (my italics) and "primitive" (2, 3) points to a trait observed less often, but associated with sublimity in the eighteenth century by poets and aestheticians (Mallet, Gerard, Kant). One of the first travellers to note it was Wordsworth, after whom a number of nineteenth-century writers found deserts and seascapes therapeutically simple.

That the heath is "emphatic in its admonitions" is a more esoteric and initially mysterious remark, whose meaning emerges when Hardy explains that the kind of "sublimity" found on Egdon is "chastened" (2). That is, the ecstatic, often deist sublime that Addison and Burke defined has been both "chastised" and "made more chaste" by recent human history, to the point where a gloomy heath or "gaunt waste in Thule" will soon be "all of nature" that will please the more pensive – and eventually everyone. This shift seems to have occurred, or to have begun, during the Romantic period, with Byron and Shelley.

Hardy calls the "subdued" palette and "solemn" mood of Egdon Heath particularly suitable to the "ascetic" temper (2). Asceticism is rarely associated with Great nature before 1878, although it is perhaps implicit in the minimalism of Bashō, Fromentin, and Melville. It does occur later among some mountaineers and desert travellers, a notable instance being Hardy's admirer T.E. Lawrence. The heath's austerity is an aspect of its general gloom, as is its love affair with storms. During one of their trysts, Hardy says, we can see Egdon as "the hitherto unrecognized original" – we might say "archetype" – of "those wild regions of obscurity" that surround us in "midnight dreams of flight and disaster" (2). Few if any travellers saw the Great this way, though the strong reactions of some visitors to vast barrens have an aspect of nightmare: Maundrell in the Holy Land, say, or Hassaurek in the Andes. The usual poetic tropes in this connection were that landscape is a metaphor of some aspect of existence (Browning, Carlyle, Flaubert, Patmore), or a mirror of self (Baudelaire, Swinburne).

Most of Egdon's other traits are better established among Hardy's predecessors. One of the characteristics that make the heath on a calm evening "a place perfectly accordant with man's nature" is its "solitude," its "lonely face" (3). Travellers might feel a kinship with the Great for various reasons – its spirituality and bareness were often adduced – or they might be attracted by its very incomprehensibility, its "otherness," as Gray and Ruskin were. But most testified to a pervasive sense of loneliness and isolation – which might draw or repel them – in desert wastes and on mountains. Writers as diverse as Kinglake in the Mideast, Butler in New Zealand, Irving on the American prairies, Shaw in North Africa, Forbes in the Alps, Hayes in the Arctic, and Black in the Hebrides have identified *solitude* as a salient feature of existence there.

In chapter 2, Hardy adds another detail about the heath that has a familiar ring: the road across it "bisected that dark surface like the parting-line on a head of black hair" (4). The idea that aspects of Great landscape are parts of Earth's body has struck many travellers, sometimes as a revelation, since Maundrell saw the badlands east of Jerusalem as the "bowels" of the earth in 1697. Melville observed of the same area, "You see the anatomy – compares with ordinary regions as skeleton with living and rosy man." The Alps have inspired the most comparisons of this kind. On Mont Blanc, de Saussure seemed to have the "cadavre" of the universe laid out at his feet. Mary Shelley called the Alps the "bones of the world," quoting her mother's Scandinavian letters (she could also have cited her husband); Hugo, Ruskin, and Tyndall use similar images for great mountains. In English poetry, the idea is as old as Donne's "An Anatomy of the World" (1611), where mountains and ocean trenches are the "warts and pock-holes" of the earth's disfigured frame. Hardy is unusual only in specifying the head as the part suggested by a strikingly bare landform.

After this second look at Egdon Heath, it is important to reiterate that I set out to trace, not influences on Hardy, but the development of an aesthetic movement that he was conscious of and participated in, drawing on its themes and images for power beyond his own. Some of the writers discussed here, such as Shelley and William Black, were known and important to Hardy; others were not, though many were being sufficiently read in his time to be considered part of his cultural heritage. It is neither profitable nor necessary to my purposes to ascertain exactly which he had encountered before writing *The Return of the Native*. The issue has been how – on what basis – any western writer could say, in 1878, that "the new Vale of Tempe may be a gaunt waste in Thule." The questions Hardy raises are much wider than whether Black's *Princess of Thule* or his travels suggested a place and a mood to him.

To the extent that chapter 1 of *The Return of the Native* looks backward and says, "Something has happened," Hardy was right. Consider his formulation: "It is a question if the *exclusive* reign of this orthodox beauty [i.e., "Tempe"] is not approaching its last quarter" (my emphasis). The word "exclusive" makes this a conservative statement that must be allowed, the existence of many devotees of "Thule" having been demonstrated. Other than a general loss of joy, Hardy does not explain the dynamics of this paradigm shift in his culture, but we have seen that the roles of religious, aesthetic, and natural philosophy were central. Renaissance thinkers such as Nicholas of Cusa enlarged the conception of the physical universe to a magnitude previously reserved for divinity. This idea begat both deism (wherein the cosmos manifests God) and an "aesthetics of the infinite," of which Addison's Great is a notable instance. From about the same time, scientists studying the heavens (Kepler, Galileo), and later the earth (de Maillet, Buffon, Hutton, Lyell), made a series of discoveries that troubled or complicated faith. Travellers were also important, pressing into unknown areas as they acquired the means, and testing scientific and aesthetic theories, among other interests.

What is least representative about Hardy is his *attitude* towards his perception: the gloom with which he tinges the "aesthetics of Thule." Granted, he had some company – Melville, Arnold, Thomson – but even among poets and novelists his melancholy was extraordinary. His selective use of his favourite sources is telling; we have seen him respond to dark passages in Shelley, Ruskin, Swinburne, and William Black, while ignoring the brighter turns of their images and actions. And it is even harder to find parallels to his mood among scientists and travellers. Lyell and Darwin were not depressed but excited by evolution. High mountains were a source of joy to Tyndall and other Alpinists; Burton and Fromentin found exhilaration in deserts wider and barer than Egdon Heath. Arctic explorers come closest to Hardy's outlook, but not even the polar wastes seemed always or uniformly grim. It comes down to where the emphasis falls in "chastened sublimity"; with Hardy, the adjective dominates. Even in the twentieth century, darkness as deep as his has been rare.

When Hardy tries to extrapolate to the future, he naturally becomes more problematical. After announcing the end of Tempe's "exclusive" hegemony and the rise of Thule, he introduces a complication: "The time seems near, if it has not actually arrived, when the chastened sublimity [of the Great] will be all of nature that is absolutely in keeping with the moods of the more thinking among mankind." To verify this prediction requires that we scrutinize patterns of philosophy, travel, and literary response after 1878, while discriminating between the more and less "thinking" of our subjects. And when Hardy foresees that "ultimately" not only the "more thinking" people but "the commonest tourist" will prefer the Alps and Iceland to the verdant spas of Europe, he is venturing into speculative realms well beyond what he could know, or what we have been able to investigate here.

CHRONOLOGICAL TABLE

A Selection of Dates Mentioned in the Text and Some Others

ca. 388–68 BC	Plato, *Phaedo*
ca. 330–25 BC	Pytheas sails north, reports on "Thule"
ca. 55 BC	Lucretius, *De rerum natura*
3d Century AD?	"Longinus on the Sublime"
ca. 890	Othar rounds North Cape
ca. 1314	Dante, *Purgatorio*
1335	Petrarch climbs Mont Ventoux
ca. 1360	Fazio degli Uberti describes mountain travel
1417	MS of Lucretius, *De rerum natura*, discovered
1432–33	Bertrandon de la Brocquière in Levant
1462	Aeneas Sylvius (Pope Pius II) sojourns on Mount Amiata
ca. 1500	Eustache Deschamps, "Lay du desert d'Amours"
1503	Ludovico de Varthema travels in Arabia
1528	First known tourist in Alps, Aegidius Tschudi
1543	Copernicus, *De revolutionibus orbium caelestium* Conrad Gesner, "The Admiration of Mountains"
1548	Johann Stumpf, *Swiss Chronicle*

1553	First English expedition to seek Northeast Passage
1555	Gesner, *Description of the Riven Mountain*
1572	Tycho Brahe discovers a "new star"
1574	Josias Simler, *Description of Valais*
1576	Frobisher voyages to Greenland and Baffin Bay
1577	Thomas Digges, *Perfit Description of the Celestial Orbes*
1583–85	Giordano Bruno, *La Cena de la Ceneri, De la causa, principio et uno,* and *De l'infinito universo e mondi*
1585–87	Davis voyages to Baffin Island and Greenland
1591	Giordano Bruno, *De immenso et innumerabilibus*
1594–97	Barents voyages to Spitsbergen, winters on Novaya Zemlya
1600	William Gilbert, *De magnete* ..., posits infinite universe
1604	Kepler and others discover a "new star"
1610	Hudson winters, dies in James Bay Galileo, *The Message of the Stars*
1615	Geo. Sandys, *Relation of a Journey* (to Mideast, 1610–11)
1615–16	Baffin, Bylot sail to Hudson Strait and Baffin Bay
1644–46	John Evelyn crosses Alps and Apennines
1646	Henry More, *Democritus Platonissans*
1650	Henry Vaughan, "The World"
ca. 1651–52	Andrew Marvell, "Bill-borow," "Appleton House"
1657	More-Descartes correspondence (1648–49) published in France
1657–60	Pascal, *Pensées*
1667–68	Hooke lectures on geology to Royal Society
1670	(ca.) Thomas Traherne, *Centuries of Meditations*

1671	Frederick Marten, "Voyage into Spitzbergen and Greenland" John Milton, *Paradise Regained* More, *Enchiridium metaphysicum* Thomas Burnet travels in Alps
1674	Boileau translates "Longinus on the Sublime" Milton, *Paradise Lost* (final, 12-book version)
1676	John Wood, "Relation of a Voyage" to find Northeast Passage
1680–81	T. Burnet, *Sacred Theory of the Earth* (in Latin; trans. 1684)
1684–89	Bashō's travels in Japan
1686	Shaftesbury (3d earl) crosses Alps Bernard Fontenelle, *Entretiens* ... (*The Plurality of Worlds*)
1687	G. Burnet, *Letters* (describing Alpine travels 1685–86)
1690	Erasmus Warren, *Geologia* (attacks Burnet)
1691	John Ray, *Wisdom of God Manifested in the Works of Creation*
1692	T. Burnet, *Archeologiae philosophicæ* Ray, *Miscellaneous Discourses ... Changes of the World* Richard Bentley gives Boyle Lectures (published 1693)
1693	John Dennis, *Miscellanies* (includes Alpine travel in 1688) Ray, *Three Physico-Theological Discourses* John Beaumont, *Considerations on* [Burnet's] *Theory*
1694	Royal Society publishes Marten's, Wood's *Accounts* (1671, 1676)
1695	John Woodward, *Natural History of the Earth*
1696	William Whiston, *A New Theory of the Earth*
1699	Joseph Addison crosses the Alps
1700	J.J. Scheuchzer, *Three Alpine Journeys*

1701	Joseph Addison, *Letter from Italy*; letter to Montagu
1702	Archbishop William King, *On the Origin of Evil* (in Latin)
1702–11	Scheuchzer, more *Alpine Journeys*; *Natural History of Switzerland*
1703	Henry Maundrell, *Journey from Aleppo to Jerusalem* (in 1697)
1705	Addison, *Remarks on Several Parts of Italy*
1706	J.H. Hottinger, *Description of Glacial Mountains of Switzerland*
1709	Aaron Hill, *Full and Just Account of the … Ottoman Empire* Shaftesbury, *The Moralists* Thomas Robinson, *Natural History of the Lake District*
1710–12	Pétis de la Croix, *Contes persans*
1712	Addison, *Spectator* nos. 411–21 Leonard Welsted translates Boileau's *Longinus* (1674)
1713	Isaac Newton, 'General Scholium' to the *Principia* Richard Blackmore, *The Creation* William Derham, *Physico-Theology*
1714	George Berkeley, letter to Alexander Pope about Alps Kipseller and Stanyan, *The Pleasures of Switzerland*
1715	J.-P. de Crousaz, *Traité du Beau* Pope, *Temple of Fame*
1715–20	Benoît de Maillet travels in Levant, N. Africa
1717	Berkeley, letter to Arbuthnot about Vesuvius Leibniz-Clarke correspondence (1715–16) published
1722–29	Copies of de Maillet's MS circulate
1726–30	James Thomson, *The Seasons*
1728	Bering sails through Bering Strait to 67° N. latitude
1729	Albrecht von Haller, *Die Alpen*
1730–31	Buffon travels in Alps

1732	Abbé Pluché, *Spectacle de la Nature*
1734	Admiralty offers prize for finding Northwest Passage
1737	"Voyage dans les Montagnes occidentales du Paris de Vaud"
1738	Thomas Shaw, *Travels … to … Barbary and the Levant*
1738–40, 1742–43	De la Verendryes travel to Missouri, Rocky Mountains
1739	Thomas Gray, letters from the Alps
1742 ff.	Edward Young, *Night Thoughts*
1744	Mark Akenside, *Pleasures of the Imagination* Comte de Buffon, *Théorie de la Terre* (*Theory of the Earth*) Joseph Warton, *The Enthusiast* William Windham, *The Glacieres or Ice Alps in Savoy* (in 1741)
1747	John Baillie, "Essay on the Sublime" Thomas Warton, *The Pleasures of Melancholy*
1748	Eliza Haywood, *Life's Progress through the Passions* de Maillet, *Telliamed*
1749	Buffon, *Histoire naturelle* (*Natural History*), vols. 1–3
1751	J.G. Altmann, *Description of the Swiss Ice-Mountains*
1754	Élie Bertrand, *On the Uses of Mountains*
1755	Thomas Amory, *The Life of John Buncle*
1756	J.G. Lehmann, treatise on geological succession
1757	Edmund Burke, … *Enquiry into … the Sublime and the Beautiful* Bartholomew Plaisted, "Journey from Basra to Aleppo" (in 1750) Robert Wood, *The Ruins of Balbec*
1759	Alexander Gerard, *An Essay on Taste*
1760	H.-B. de Saussure visits Chamonix, offers Mont Blanc prize James Macpherson publishes first 'Ossian' poems

1761   J.-J. Rousseau, *La Nouvelle Héloïse*
               Danish (Niebuhr) expedition leaves for Arabia
               (to 1767)

1762   Henry Home, Lord Kames, *Elements of Criticism*
               G.C. Fuchsel argues for geological uniformity

1763   Hugh Blair, *Dissertation on … Ossian*; lectures on
               rhetoric
               Desmarest establishes volcanic origin of Auvergne
               basalt

1767   William Hamilton observes Vesuvius (also 1776–77,
               1791)

1768   Capt. Cook embarks on first voyage (to 1771)
               Pallas begins survey of Russia (to 1774)

1769   Gray's tour of Lake District
               Samuel Hearne's Canadian journeys begin (to 1772)

1770   Deluc brothers climb Le Buet in Alps
               Lyakhov discovers New Siberian Islands
               Baron d'Holbach, *Le Système de la Nature*

1772   Joseph Banks, Solander and von Troil visit Staffa,
               Iceland
               Cook's second (Antarctic) voyage begins (to 1775)
               J.-A. Deluc, *Recherches sur les modifications de l'atmosphère*
               Niebuhr's Arabian travels (1761–67) published in
               German

1773   Banks climbs Mount Snowden
               Cook crosses Antarctic Circle
               Bernardin de St Pierre, *Voyage à l'Île de France*
               Marc-Théodore Bourrit, *Description des glacières de Savoye*

1774   Thomas Pennant, *Tour in Scotland, and … the Hebrides
               1772*
               William Hutchinson, *Excursion to the Lakes*
               Desmarest, essays on basalt and (1775) volcanic epochs

1775   First attempt to ascend Mont Blanc
               Samuel Johnson, *Journey to the Western Islands of
               Scotland*

1776	Cook's third and final voyage begins (to 1779)
	Bourrit, *Description des aspects du Mont Blanc*
	J.-A. Deluc and Dentand, *Voyages dans les Alpes du Faucigny*
1777	Cook, *A Voyage towards the South Pole*
	George Forster, *A Voyage Round the World*
	Goethe climbs Brocken, writes "Harzreise im Winter"
	Joseph Priestley, "On the Sublime"
1778	Buffon, *Époques de la Nature*
	Thomas West, *A Guide to the Lakes* (popular guidebook)
	J.F.W. Charpentier issues first coloured geological map
1779	de Saussure, *Voyages dans les Alpes*, vol. 1
	William Coxe, *Sketches of … Switzerland* (in 1776)
1780	Anna Seward, "Elegy on Capt. Cook"
	Uno von Troil, *Letters on Iceland … in … 1772*
1781	Bourrit, *Description des Alpes Pennines …*
	L. Ramond de Carbonnières, trans. of Coxe (1779), vol. 1
1783	Hugh Blair, *Lectures on Rhetoric and Belles-Lettres*
	George Crabbe, *The Village*
1785	James Boswell, *Journal of a Tour to the Hebrides*
	William Cowper, *The Task*
1786	First ascent of Mont Blanc (Paccard and Balmat)
	de Saussure, *Voyages dans les Alpes*, vol. 2
	Bourrit, *Nouvelle description des glacières de Savoye*
	William Beckford, *Vathek*
1787	de Saussure, *Relation … d'un voyage au sommet du Mont Blanc*
1788	James Hutton, "Theory of the Earth" published in essay form
1789	Ramond de Carbonnières, *Observations sur les Pyrénées*
	Alexander Mackenzie reaches Beaufort Sea (Arctic Ocean)

1790	Wordsworth tours Europe, Alps (also 1791-92)
	Archibald Alison, *Essays on the Nature and Principles of Taste*
	Immanuel Kant, *Critique of Judgement*

1791   Ann Radcliffe, *Romance of the Forest*

1793   Wordsworth, "Descriptive Sketches"
Mackenzie completes overland expedition to Pacific Canada

1794   Radcliffe, *Mysteries of Udolpho*; tours Lake District

1795   Hutton's *Theory of the Earth* (1788) expanded to book
Radcliffe, *A Journey … Tour to the Lakes*

1796   de Saussure, *Voyages dans les Alpes*, vol. 4
Mary Wollstonecraft, *Letters* on Sweden and Norway in 1795

1797   Coleridge, "Kubla Khan," "Ancient Mariner"
J. Michaud, *Voyage littéraire au Mont Blanc*
F. Hornemann travels in Sahara (to 1799)

1799   William Smith begins geological map of England with Bath area
Alexander von Humboldt departs for South America (to 1804)

1801   Ramond de Carbonnières, *Voyage au Mont Perdu*

1802   Coleridge, "Hymn Before Sunrise in the Vale of Chamonix"
John Playfair, *Illustrations of the Huttonian Theory*

1804   Lewis and Clark expedition begins (to 1806)
Sénancour, *Oberman*

1805   Wordsworth completes first version of *The Prelude*

1806   Chateaubriand, "Mont Blanc"; tours Egypt, Holy Land
Desmarest's essay on volcanic epochs (1775) published

1807   Geological Society founded in London

1808   Fraser navigates Fraser River to west coast of Canada
Marie Paradis climbs Mont Blanc (first woman to succeed)

1809   William McClure draws 1st geological maps of eastern
             US

1810   Crabbe, *The Borough*
             Dugald Stewart, "On the Sublime"
             Wordsworth, *Guide through the Lake District*
             Cuvier and Brogniart, *Essai* on mineralogy of Paris basin

1811   First ascent of Jungfrau
             Geological Society begins to publish *Transactions*

1812   Burckhardt reaches Petra
             Lord Byron, *Childe Harold*, cantos 1 and 2

1813   Robert Bakewell, *Introduction to Geology*
             Percy Shelley, *Queen Mab*

1814   Journals of Lewis and Clark published
             Wordsworth, *The Excursion*

1815   William Smith publishes first geological map of England
             Walter Scott, *Lord of the Isles*

1816   Byron and the Shelleys in Alps, May-October
             Byron, *Childe Harold* 3, "Darkness," "Siege of Corinth"
             P. Shelley, "Alastor"
             Frances, Lady Shelley, Alpine diary

1817   Byron, *Manfred*
             P. Shelley, "Mont Blanc"
             Mark Beaufoy, "Narrative ... Summit of Mont Blanc ...
             1787"

1818   Royal Navy sends J. Ross to Melville Bay and Smith
             Sound
             Byron, *Childe Harold* 4
             P. Shelley, "Ozymandias"; visits Vesuvius
             M. Shelley, *Frankenstein*

1819   W. Parry seeks Northwest Passage, winters on Melville
             Island
             J. Franklin leads overland party to Arctic Ocean
             (to 1822)
             Long Expedition to Rocky Mountains (to 1820)
             Capt. G.F. Lyon explores Libyan desert (to 1820)

1820	First sighting of Antarctica Avalanche kills 3 climbers on Mont Blanc W. and Dorothy Wordsworth tour Alps; her *Journal* P. Shelley, *Prometheus Unbound*; "The Sensitive Plant"
1821	Formation of Compagnie des Guides de Chamonix Parry, *Voyage for the Discovery of a North-West Passage*
1822	British expedition across Sahara to Lake Chad
1823	Weddell reaches 74° 15′ S. latitude Humboldt, *Aspects of Nature* (in German) Franklin, *Journey to the Shores of the Polar Sea* (1819–22) E. James, *Account* of Long's Expedition to Rockies (1819)
1824	William Brockedon, *Journals of Excursions in the Alps*
1825	G.P. Scrope, *Considerations on Volcanoes* James Weddell, *Voyage towards the South Pole* Victor Hugo, "Fragment d'un voyage aux Alpes" Alfred Tennyson, "On Sublimity"
1826	Maj. Gordon Laing (first European) reaches Timbuktu M. Shelley, *The Last Man*
1827	Guides discover safer route up Mont Blanc Parry reaches 82° 45′ N. latitude Scrope, *Geology and Extinct Volcanoes of Central France* James Fenimore Cooper, *The Prairie*
1828	Brockedon, *The Passes of the Alps* Lyell and Murchison examine Auvergne region
1830	Charles Lyell, *Principles of Geology*, vol. 1 Tennyson, "Ode to Memory"
1831	James Clark Ross locates North Magnetic Pole Darwin embarks on HMS *Beagle* (to 1836); reads Lyell
1832	*Geographical Journal* (Royal Geographical Society) begins to report on polar voyages Washington Irving's western tour R. Töpffer, *Excursions dans les Alpes*

1833	John Ruskin's first visit to the Alps
	Honoré de Balzac, *Eugénie Grandet*
	Thomas Carlyle, *Sartor Resartus*
1834	A.W. Kinglake travels in Near East (to 1835)
	Ruskin, "Strata of Mont Blanc"
1835	First geological survey of England
	J. Ross, *Second Voyage in Search of a North West Passage* (1829–33)
	Irving, *A Tour on the Prairies*
1836	Ralph Waldo Emerson, *Nature*
	Washington Irving, *Astoria*
	Cooper, *Switzerland*
	Lamartine, *Jocelyn*
1837	Edgar Allen Poe, *Narrative of Arthur Gordon Pym*
	John Lloyd Stephens, *Incidents of Travel in Egypt*, etc.
1838	Lyell, *Elements of Geology*
	Gideon Mantell, *Wonders of Geology*
	Théophile Gautier, "Caravane," "La Tristesse"
1839	E.J. Eyre explores southeast Australian deserts (to 1841)
	James Clark Ross leads expedition to Antarctic (to 1843)
	Darwin, *Journal of Researches* (*Voyage of the Beagle*)
	Hugo, "Les Alpes"
1840	Louis Agassiz, *Études sur les Glaciers*
	Édouard Desors, *Journal d'une course aux glaciers*
1841	Agassiz proves glacial theory in field, climbs Jungfrau
	J.C. Ross sails to 78° 11′ S. in Ross Sea, sights Antarctica
	Hugh Miller, *The Old Red Sandstone*
	Desors, *L'Ascension de la Jungfrau*
	Flaubert, *Les Pyrénées*
1842	Capt. Frémont explores Rocky Mountains (to 1844)
	Nikolai Gogol, *Dead Souls*
	Aubrey De Vere, "The Sea-Cliffs of Kilkee"
1843	James D. Forbes, *Travels through the Alps of Savoy*
	Ruskin, *Modern Painters*, vol. 1
	Hugo, "Pyrénées"

1844	Humboldt, *Cosmos* Kinglake, *Eothen* Wordsworth, letters on future development of Lake District
1845	Franklin expedition to Northwest Passage departs William Bartlett, *Forty Days in the Desert* Eyre, *Journals of Expeditions ... into Central Australia* Eliot Warburton, *The Crescent and the Cross* Robert Browning, "Englishman in Italy"
1846	Ruskin, *Modern Painters*, vol. 2
1847	Cooper, *Crater* J.C. Ross, *Voyage [to the] Antarctic* (1839–43)
1848	Rescue ships sent in search of Franklin expedition Eugène Fromentin first visits Sahara
1849	Bartlett, *Walks about ... Jerusalem* Curzon, *Visits to Monasteries in the Levant* (in 1837) Flaubert, *Tentation de St Antoine* (no. 1); goes to Egypt Herman Melville, *Mardi* Cooper, *The Sea Lions* Francis Parkman, *The Oregon Trail*
1850	Robert M'Clure discovers Northwest Passage Relics of Franklin expedition found near Beechey Island Henry Barth leads British mission to Sahara Melville, *Whitejacket* Tennyson, *In Memoriam* Wordsworth, *The Prelude*
1851	Melville, *Moby Dick*
1852	Matthew Arnold, "Empedocles on Etna," *Switzerland* T. Gautier, "Symphonie en blanc majeur"; crosses Alps Leconte de Lisle, "Midi"
1853	E.K. Kane expedition departs for Arctic (to 1855) Forbes, *Norway and Its Glaciers* (in 1851) Gerrit de Veer, Barents' *Three Voyages* published (Hakluyt Soc.)
1854	England learns of Franklin's death, receives some relics Flaubert's letter on the Bedu

Fromentin, *Un Été dans le Sahara*
Coventry Patmore, *Sahara*

1855   First ascent of Monte Rosa in Alps
Mount Everest established as world's highest
peak
Arnold, "Grand Chartreuse"
Browning, "Grammarian's Funeral," "By the
Fireside"
Burton, *Pilgrimage to Al-Madinah and Meccah* (in 1853)
Leconte de Lisle, "Les Hurleurs," "Les Éléphants"
H. Taine, *Voyage aux Pyrénées*

1856   Flaubert, *Tentation de St Antoine* (no. 2)
Melville, *The Encantadas*; travels in Levant (to 1857)
Ruskin, *Modern Painters*, vols. 3–4
Arthur P. Stanley, *Sinai and Palestine*
Alfred Wills, *Wanderings in the High Alps*

1857   Alpine Club formed
Ch. Baudelaire, *Fleurs du Mal*, trans. *Arthur Gordon Pym*
Miller, *The Testimony of the Rocks* (lectures 1852–55)

1858   Fromentin, *Une Année dans le Sahel*
Ruskin, "Geology of Chamonix"
Leslie Stephen, "The Allalinhorn"

1859   Darwin, *The Origin of Species*
Essays and Reviews
Edward Fitzgerald, *The Rubáiyát of Omar Khayyám*
Alpine Club's *Peaks, Passes and Glaciers*, 1st series
William Thompson, *The Land and the Book*

1860   Isaac Hayes's Arctic expedition (to 1861)
John Tyndall, *The Glaciers of the Alps*
Wills, *The Eagle's Nest*

1861   Baudelaire, *Fleurs du mal* (2d ed.)
"Lyell and Tennyson," *Saturday Review*

1862   Baudelaire, *Mon Coeur Mis à Nu*
Flaubert, *Salammbô*
Peaks, Passes and Glaciers, 2d series
Tyndall, *Mountaineering in 1861*

1863
Alpine Club's *Alpine Journal* begins publication
Italian and Swiss Alpine Clubs formed
Nachtigal reaches Tibesti Mountains in Sahara
Stephane Mallarmé, "L'Azur" (ca.)
Ruskin, "Forms of the Stratified Alps of Savoy"

1864
Browning, "A Death in the Desert," "Prospice"
George Sandie, *Horeb and Jerusalem*
Jules Verne, *Capt. Hatteras*; *Trip to the Center of Earth*

1865
First ascent of Matterhorn (Edward Whymper); 4 of 7 die
Verne, *From the Earth to the Moon*; *Tour of the Moon*

1866
Thomas Hardy, "In Vision I Roamed"
Mallarmé's letter on the "deux néants"
Christina Rossetti, "The Prince's Progress"

1867
John Wesley Powell's first expedition to Rocky Mts
Arnold, "Dover Beach"
Hardy, "Neutral Tones"
Friedrich Hassaurek, *Four Years among the Ecuadorians*
A.W. Moore, *The Alps in 1864*

1868
Powell, John Muir climbing in West, Moore in Caucasus
Ernst Haeckel, *Natural Creation* (in German)

1869
German Arctic expedition reaches 77° N. (to 1870)
Austrian and German Alpine Clubs formed
Opening of Suez Canal brings many visitors to Egypt
Nachtigal travels in Sahara (to 1874)
Fromentin, *Voyage en Égypte*
Science journal *Nature* begins publication with Huxley, Goethe
T. Gautier, *Les Vacances de lundi*

1870
Doane-Washburn expedition to Yellowstone
A.G. Girdlestone, *The High Alps without Guides*

1871
E.M. Palmer, *The Desert of the Exodus*
Stephen, *Playground of Europe*
A.C. Swinburne, "Hertha," "Hymn of Man," "On the Downs"
Tyndall, *Hours of Exercise in the Alps*

Walt Whitman, *Democratic Vistas*
Whymper, *Scrambles among the Alps*

1872   Austrian Arctic expedition (to 1874)
Samuel Butler, *Erewhon*
Hayes, *The Land of Desolation*
Joaquin Miller, *Songs of the Sierras*

1873   Hardy, *A Pair of Blue Eyes*; meets Stephen
French expedition to Timbuktu (wiped out in 1874)

1874   Club Alpin Français formed
Nares Antarctic expedition
William Black, *A Princess of Thule*
Flaubert, *Tentation de St Antoine* (final version)
Hardy, *Far from the Madding Crowd*
James Thomson, *City of Dreadful Night*

1875   Nares, Markham explore Arctic Ocean (to 1876)
Powell, *Exploration of the Colorado River* (in 1869)
Ruskin, *Deucalion* (glaciology lectures, 1874–)
begins pub.
Winwood Reade, *The Outcast*

1876   Charles Doughty's travels in Arabia begin (to 1878)
Hardy, *Hand of Ethelberta*; meets William Black
Melville, *Clarel*

1878   Swedish expedition traverses Northeast Passage
(to 1879)
Powell, *Report on Lands of the Arid Region of the US*
Gerard Manley Hopkins, "Wreck of the Deutschland"
Hardy, *The Return of the Native*

Lexicon

A DICTIONARY AND GRAMMAR
OF RESPONSES TO THE GREAT

What kinds of interest did early travellers, philosophers, and poets take in the Great? What motivated them to seek it, and what reactions did they feel in its presence? While the main text of this book takes a discursive approach to the testing of Hardy's thesis about a modern aesthetic of nature, treating authors and genres within national and chronological parameters, a more formal analysis here may help to elucidate some features of the material. This "Lexicon" sorts through the heterogeneous mass of data on the appeal and qualities, conceived or perceived, of the Great and barren in nature that had accumulated by the late nineteenth century, trying to identify recurrent patterns of preconception and response.

Of course there were many differences between individuals' reactions, nor were the five spatial areas (mountains, deserts, skies, seas, poles) at all equal or constant in their appeal. Although every entry in this lexicon was important to some observer at some time, the following discussions do not imply that any writer experienced all of these responses for each area or for all areas, but rather delineate a spectrum along which commentators ranged themselves. Pooling data in this way brings out some large tendencies that do not emerge in studies of individuals, works, or even periods.

Each entry has two paragraphs. The first (the "dictionary") begins by giving in parentheses the number of primary works from the bibliography in which the response or quality occurred before 1878. The term is then defined and its meanings illustrated with the aid of the writers themselves. Chronological development is also indicated. If an idea or type of appeal was operative for only a few travellers in a certain period, or for one or two areas and not others – i.e., was not general – those limitations are stated. In the second paragraph, the "grammar," the entry's connections with other ideas are briefly indicated. The most idiosyncratic responses (those appearing in fewer than four works) have been omitted; for the record, they are ASCETICISM, ECSTASY, FAME, INDIFFERENCE OF NATURE, MORALITY, NOBILITY, and USEFULNESS.

The trees being fairly numerous here, it may be helpful to point out the major sections of the forest. Most responses fall into one of ten clusters. That is, at a certain level of generalization, ignoring fine distinctions, the seventy-odd discriminations that are required to describe individuals' reactions resolve themselves into one-seventh as many broad classes. Of these, by far the largest is the *Spiritual Group*, comprising several of the most frequent responses – Awe, Natural Theology, Sublimity – as well as subtypes like Holiness of Mountains and God in Desert. A *Minimal Group*, linked by a willingness or desire to settle for less, is surprisingly large: Bareness, Barrenness, Emptiness, Silence, Solitude, and Void. The *Spacious Group* has fewer members – Infinity and Vastness, chiefly – but they are some of the most frequently mentioned. A *Temporal Group*, including Antiquity, Elements, and Eternity, is also important. These appear to be the central categories.

The *Adventure Group* (Awareness, Challenge, Enjoyment, Self-Knowledge) has fewer adherents than one might expect. A *Science Group* is obvious: Astronomy, Geology, Knowledge; so is a *Metaphorical Group*, including Earth's Body, Land/Self, Mirror, Whiteness, and Wintriness. There is both a *Pleasure Group* – Beauty, Calm, Usefulness – and a larger *Dark Group*, consisting of qualities (Chaos, Gloom, Indifference of Nature) and responses (Fear, Incomprehension, Pain for Gain) not ordinarily sought or found attractive in western culture. (The Oxymoron response in a sense mediates between these two groups.) There remains a *General Group*, where the writers themselves are so vague about their motives that one must resort to such terms as Fascination, Lure of Desert, or Mystique to describe them.

ADVENTURE (4): Few travellers (none before the Victorian era) admit that simple love of "daring enterprise," "unexpected incident" or "hazardous activity" (*OED*) drew them to the Great, though that love is sometimes inferred. Claire Engel argues that adventure is the leading motive of every mountaineer, but also mentions other motives, and doubts that any two Alpinists climb for the same reason. Tyndall is one of the few early climbers who can confidently be described as driven (partly) by love of adventure; in desert travel, Burton was certainly an adventurer. But the response is more typical of novelists (e.g. Jules Verne) and later explorers such as Shackleton and Hillary.

ADVENTURE is part of a group of interests that collectively motivate a fair number of travellers, however. The most important of these are love of LIBERTY and a willingness to feel FEAR. Less often mentioned are heightened AWARE-NESS, the CHALLENGE of hardship, and a sense of ENJOYMENT or SELF-KNOWLEDGE.

ANTIQUITY (25): Some travellers and writers (mostly on science) were impressed by an aura of great antiquity approaching permanency in manifestations of the Great. Capt. Wood observed in 1676 that the snow on the mountains of Novaya Zemlya "hath lain there ever since the Creation," and most later visitors to polar wastes make similar remarks. Travellers to the desert frequently noted its ancient appearance. Antiquity is one of the themes of Buffon, who refers to the "haute an-cienneté" of nature, of Melville in the Galápagos and the Middle East, and of Hardy on "antique," "venerable" Egdon Heath. Darwin wrote feelingly on this theme, which burgeoned in the 1850s with the growth of interest in geology.

ANTIQUITY, part of the *Temporal Group*, has close ties to PRESERVATION and primordial ELEMENTS. It can be regarded as a cautious, secular approach to the idea of ETERNITY.

ASTRONOMY (12): The development of astronomical science from the early sev-enteenth century and the interest taken in it by the intellectual community at large played an important role in forming the aesthetics of the Great. Vaughan's poem "The World" (1650) and Fontenelle's *Entretiens sur la pluralité des mondes* show how excited (and terrified) amateurs were by the sense of vast space inher-ent in the new science. Addison's *Spectator* no. 420 (1712) identifies astronomi-cal speculation as one of the "pleasures of the imagination" and shows its aesthetic connection with the Great. It is rarely mentioned by travellers, except those who wintered in the Arctic, and the occasional scientist such as Tyndall.

ASTRONOMY, a member of the *Science Group*, is linked to the concepts it pro-motes – ETERNITY, VASTNESS, INFINITY – and to the emotion it often inspires, SUBLIMITY. INFINITY and ETERNITY, originally attributes of the Deity, came to be applied to the material universe through astronomical discoveries.

AWARENESS (6): A few sources say or imply that in the presence of the Great they are more fully aware of themselves and their surroundings, that they live more intensely. Whymper lists this feeling as a benefit of mountaineering; Fro-mentin seems to imply it. The idea has eighteenth-century roots in Thomson's "Winter," where cold days "refine the spirits" and make the brain "swifter." Kant associated sublimity (i.e., the experience of the Great) with a "momentary check to the vital forces" followed by their strong return, which suggests increased awareness.

AWARENESS belongs to the *Adventure Group*. It tends to occur in company with CHALLENGE, SELF-KNOWLEDGE (one of the objects of AWARENESS), and, less often, FEAR.

AWE (61): One of the most widespread early responses to the Great was the quasi-religious sense of wonder, reverence, and fear known as AWE. It occurs – often in the form "awful" = "awing" – widely: in seventeenth-century travellers (Dennis) and philosophers (Fontenelle); in Georgian poets such as Thomson, Young, and Gray; in Capt. Cook; in Romantic and Victorian traveller-poets (Wordsworth, Shelley, Tennyson, Arnold); in novelists and mountaineers. By the nineteenth century, sensitive men like Bartlett and Palmer felt awe in the desert. Powell in the Grand Canyon, Eyre before the cliffs of the Australian Bight, re-acted with fearful admiration. AWE was most frequently mentioned in the sup-posedly sceptical 1860s and 1870s.

AWE, a neighbour of NATURAL THEOLOGY and SUBLIMITY in the *Spiritual Group*, is often produced by ASTRONOMY and GEOLOGY. It usually accompanies a sense of VASTNESS or GRANDEUR.

BARENESS (45): A considerable number of early travellers and poets considered nakedness or starkness a striking feature of mountains and deserts. This quality became more popular with time, at least through the 1850s, yet it is impossible to assign a single value to it. Christian hermits were drawn to the desert by a sym-pathy with its austerity, and this was sometimes an attraction with secular travel-lers; Fromentin says of the Sahara's bareness, "c'est précisément cette nudité qui m'encourage." Mountain bareness, on the other hand, celebrated in Bashō's haiku, elicited a mixed reaction from Thomas Burnet in the seventeenth cen-tury, and negative ones from Shaw and Johnson in the eighteenth. Yet in the next century the painterly eye of Ruskin could see any "bare ground" as the landscapist's nude. Overall the only tenable generalization is that writers on the subject were fascinated by this multivalent quality.

BARENESS is part of the *Minimal Group*, itself quite ambiguous. It has the gen-erally positive connotations of SIMPLICITY, SELF-KNOWLEDGE and sometimes LIBERTY, but can shade to the darker qualities of BARRENNESS, EMPTINESS and VOID if too much is taken away. There are as well links to the neutral response called ELEMENTS, when the landscape seems primordial.

BARRENNESS (82): Early travellers termed mountains, deserts, and the Arctic "barren," "desolate," or "waste" even more often than they called them "bare."

Usages date from the 1590s. Barrenness is ambiguous. Dr Johnson was "repelled" by the "wide extent of hopeless sterility" in the Scottish Highlands, but large-scale barrenness tended to prey on the imagination; travellers often felt that there was a virtue in the waste. The desolation of the Galápagos caused a movement of human sympathy in Melville, and near Jerusalem he wondered if "the desolation of the land" was "the result of the fatal embrace of the Deity": a frequent note in the Bible lands. George Sandie noted that wandering in the Sinai Peninsula strengthened the Hebrews and made them mindful of God. This purifying quality appealed to poets. Shelley says that a religious sect fled from the Roman army to mountains whose "desolate recesses possessed peculiar attractions" for them. Barrenness is a theme in Byron's *Manfred,* Poe's *Arthur Gordon Pym,* in Verne, and in Hardy, among others.

Part of the *Minimal Group,* BARRENNESS is associated with BARENESS, EMPTINESS, and SIMPLICITY. It has a scientific side, linking it to GEOLOGY and ELEMENTS, and a symbolic one, where it dovetails with METAPHORS and WINTRINESS. For some it discloses physical or spiritual REALITY.

BEAUTY (58): BEAUTY, which Addison *distinguishes* from the Great and Burke from sublimity, is nevertheless mentioned by numerous writers and travellers in connection with the Great. Traherne contrasted the "great and beautiful" world made by God with that made by men. BEAUTY (rarely defined in the field) is some grace that pleases the eye of the beholder, usually in deserts or on mountains, although Forster noted icebergs of a "beautiful sapphirine or ... berylline blue" in the Antarctic Ocean. Hayes and Kane concede beauty to the Arctic at times. Mountains impressed observers with their beauties as early as Gray's Alpine letters (1739); Shaw called the desert "beautiful" in 1738. From the 1820s on, as the distinction between the Great and the beautiful lost strength, examples are numerous, especially from the Alpine Club's climbers in the 1860s.

BEAUTY may arise from pleasing sense data or qualities (PURITY, RICHNESS), or from what is seen as a superhuman order (COSMOS, NATURAL THEOLOGY). With FEAR or revulsion as a foil, it forms part of OXYMORON.

CALM (14): Some itinerant writers have attested to a sense of peace and serenity in the presence of the Great. This note, audible in Rousseau, is often sounded by the English Romantics. Poe, Ruskin, and Tyndall also associate peace with mountains, but of early desert travellers only Fromentin claims to have found tranquillity there. From the 1790s, "oblivion," "relief," seclusion, and retirement from the world are sometimes mentioned as motives or effects of travel to the Great.

CALM is linked with SILENCE and SOLITUDE (less often with VOID) as desirable states. It can either cause, or result from, EMPTINESS. CALM is often sought as a response to feelings of MISANTHROPY or WEARINESS of the world.

CHALLENGE (4): Not until the 1850s did any travellers seek the Great *because* it was exacting and demanding. Burton exulted in the harshness of the Arabian desert, Tyndall in the challenges of the Alps. The explorer and historian Clements Markham implies that this has been a motive of polar voyagers. Browning's "Prospice" welcomes "the Arch Fear in a visible form" as the traditional heroic quest.

CHALLENGE, part of the *Adventure Group*, has links to AWARENESS and SELF-KNOWLEDGE. FEAR seems an integral part of the psychology, and a certain degree of asceticism (in Burton, masochism) is implicit.

CHAOS (7): A few travellers found Great landscapes chaotic. Thomas Burnet described the Alps as "indigested heaps," shapeless, disordered, and confused, and Gray called the mountains of the Lake District a "turbulent Chaos." Kane saw the Arctic as "a world unfinished by the hand of its Creator." Verne applies the term to Iceland in *Voyage au centre du monde*.

CHAOS, a member of the *Dark Group*, is closely tied to the desolate aspect of BARRENNESS. It tends to come up in connection with GEOLOGY, and to produce FEAR.

COSMOS (10): A feeling of inclusion within a larger order, of sympathetic identification with a whole (as in Freud's "oceanic feeling"), was part of the experience of the Great for a few theorists and mountain-climbers. Before Humboldt popularized the term (applying it to the entire natural universe), de Saussure pronounced Mont Blanc "la clef d'un grand système"; from its summit a whole range's structure could be grasped. Wordsworth went beyond this limited scientific reference in identifying the source of mountains' power over us as a feeling of "intense unity," an idea that recurs in Browning. Both the scientific and the mystical senses appear in Tyndall.

COSMOS is related to several terms in the *Spiritual Group*, especially NATURAL THEOLOGY and SPIRITUALITY, and is usually accompanied by a sense of BEAUTY. It is the opposite of CHAOS.

DESERTNESS (5): DESERTNESS, an oppressive, almost obsessive sense of the desert as a threat to or reflection of human existence, appears among a scattering of nineteenth-century writers. Critics have often noted it in the work of Flaubert and Melville. Swinburne's "On the Downs," with its real and metaphorical "sands of discontent," also exhibits DESERTNESS.

DESERTNESS affiliates with both the *Minimal Group* (BARE, BARREN) and the *Metaphorical Group* (MIRROR, LAND/MIND), which it links to the *Dark Group* (GLOOM, WEARINESS).

DULLNESS (13): A few travellers to (mainly) polar and desertic landscapes in the 1770s and from the 1820s on describe them as dreary, tedious, uninteresting, or monotonous. This attitude, however, is not necessarily inconsistent with interest or respect (e.g. Cooper's *The Prairie*).

DULLNESS is the blandest member of the *Dark Group*; it has few associations with any other qualities.

EARTH'S BODY (15): The idea that mountains and deserts are the body, organs, or skeleton of the earth underlies Donne's idea that "the world's whole frame" became disjointed at the Fall. Thomas Burnet, impressed by the Alps, drew topographical diagrams of "Nature undrest" and wished for "natural maps" of "the Skeleton of the Earth." Maundrell called the wilderness of Judaea the "bowels" of the earth. High up on Mont Blanc, de Saussure seemed to see the "cadavre" of the world at his feet. The image also occurs in a few nineteenth-century writers.

EARTH'S BODY, a member of the *Metaphorical Group*, has links with terms in other groups: GEOLOGY, BARENESS, GRANDEUR, VASTNESS, and (when the observer is a Deist) SPIRITUALITY.

ELEMENTS (16): An interest in the Great as constituting the most basic elements, the primordial building blocks, of the earth appears in early writers such as Thomas Burnet, who argued that mountains are remnants of the prelapsarian world. The scientific version appears in de Saussure, who saw in the high Alps "les premiers et les plus solides ossements de ce Globe, qui ont mérité le nom de *primitives*," interesting because so near to the origin of things, and in Goethe's "Essay on Granite." This feeling for primeval landforms also shows up in Arnold's "Switzerland," Melville's *Encantadas*, and in Hardy.

ELEMENTS has close ties with other members of the *Temporal Group* and with several ideas in the *Minimal Group*, as well as with GEOLOGY.

EMPTINESS (16): The vacancy or EMPTINESS of Great nature receives less attention before than after Hardy, but elicits more comment from the 1840s on, especially from desert travellers (Bartlett, Melville, Flaubert, Fromentin). The theme begins in seventeenth-century scientific and religious responses to the vast empty reaches of the universe (Fontenelle, Pascal), but Romantic and Victorian poets and nineteenth-century European novelists were also interested in earthly and metaphorical vacancies. In Gogol's *Dead Souls*, the "flat emptiness" of the steppe mirrors Chichikov's "empty" stare.

EMPTINESS, the terrestrial version of cosmic VOID, has obvious affinities with other terms in the *Minimal Group*. For some it is metaphorical, a (usually disturbing) MIRROR of mind and spirit; for others it engenders a sense of CALM.

ENJOYMENT (24): A fair number of travellers, philosophers, and poets (mostly after 1830) found contact with the Great "enjoyable," "joyful," "exciting," or "exhilarating." Gesner's "admiration of mountains" sometimes took the form of simple happiness. Gray found the mountains of Scotland "most pleasing." Fromentin and Burton enjoyed the desert's extreme bareness, Hayes was charmed by the Arctic summer, and many tourists and climbers exulted in the Alps.

ENJOYMENT is frequently accompanied by other emotions of the *Adventure Group*, such as sensations of HEALTH and increased AWARENESS, less often by a sense of SELF-KNOWLEDGE.

ETERNITY (46): Intimations of eternity form part of the original definition of the Great and occur fairly often among early travellers and skywatchers. Vaughan saw "Eternity" in a dream vision of the nocturnal heavens (1650). Addison parallels Great horizons and eternity as pleasures of the imagination. "Eternity" became almost a stock response to Arctic wastes and high mountains, "eternal snows" being a cliché from Pope to at least Byron and Shelley. Sea and sky (but rarely desert) also engendered such feelings; Carlyle's Teufelsdroeckh has a sensation of eternity at Nordkapp. Scientists (Buffon, de Saussure, Goethe, Darwin) also sensed the Great as eternal.

ETERNITY is the extrapolation of the *Temporal Group*, being the infinite projection of ANTIQUITY and the temporal counterpart of INFINITY. It tends to come up in connection with ASTRONOMY, and to produce feelings of INCOMPREHENSION. Because ETERNITY is one of the traditional attributes of God, it occurs in conjunction with NATURAL RELIGION.

FASCINATION (9): This unsatisfactory term refers to a broadly positive preoccupation with the Great among some writers. Engel cites fascination with the Alps as one of the themes of Ramond de Carbonnières's books. When Hayes had to turn back from the Arctic Ocean, he said that he did so reluctantly, because of the region's "fascination." Tyndall and Whymper use the word to describe their reaction to certain Alpine scenes. In Poe's *Arthur Gordon Pym*, Verne's novels, and Powell's writings on the arid lands, something like FASCINATION must be posited in order to explain a persistence in uncomfortable or dangerous activities.

FASCINATION seems to have no grammar; it is a vague, general response that the traveller does not trouble to analyse, but that probably comprises several other more precise reactions.

FEAR (42): Burke made fear a prominent part of "the sublime" in his influential essay, and (despite the objections of some aestheticians) a good number of early travellers found the Great fearful, terrible, or dangerous. Well before Burke, this was a common reaction to mountains (Donne, Marvell, Evelyn, Gilbert Burnet), and there is a steady trickle of examples from the 1790s on. Tennyson used a sentence of Burke's – "The sublime always dwells on great objects and terrible" – as the epigraph to "On Sublimity," while Ruskin defined "mountain gloom" as "the terror of God's wrath." Deserts and polar wastes also inspired fear, though less often. Explorers and scientists at the level of Cook and Lyell found the Great fearful.

Besides its historical connection with SUBLIMITY, FEAR touches the *Adventure Group*, often accompanying CHALLENGE and AWARENESS. It is also a close neighbour of GLOOM. Paired with BEAUTY, FEAR becomes half of OXYMORON.

GEOLOGY (46): The rise of empirical studies of the earth roughly paralleled the formation of Great aesthetics, and dozens of writers associated these interests, especially after Lyell began publishing *Principles of Geology* in 1830. Fontenelle discusses marine fossils found on inland mountains, a phenomenon observed by Leonardo. Both de Saussure and Ruskin studied the Alps' geology, a topic broached by Thomas Burnet, and most of the Alpine Club's members were geological *amateurs*. Hugh Miller lectured and wrote on "Christian geology," the effort to harmonize the two fields. Tennyson devoted several stanzas of *In Memoriam* to the issues raised by evolutionary geology, and Whitman distinguished the pastoral nature of English poets from "the true idea of Nature," comprehending "the whole orb, with its geologic history."

GEOLOGY has many connections: with the general quest for KNOWLEDGE, with several members of the *Temporal Group*, and with BARE and BARREN in the *Minimal Group*. For the pious it leads to SPIRITUALITY and NATURAL RELIGION, and for the metaphorical to the idea of EARTH'S BODY.

GLOOM (50): The tendency to find Great landscapes gloomy or melancholy was common among writers after 1820. Not just a response to Ruskin's "mountain gloom," it began centuries earlier and embraced deserts and polar wastes as well. Most references come from poetry and fiction, which may have had a role in shaping travellers' responses, as did some theologians' dislike of mountains. Drayton's *Poly-Olbion* (1622) depicts "grim Hills" in "sterne" country, a scenario and mood later exploited by Gothic novelists (Beckford, Radcliffe). The French tradition runs from Deschamps' "Lay du desert d'Amours" (ca. 1500) to the bleakness of Théophile Gautier, Leconte de Lisle, and Balzac's *Eugénie Grandet*, whose provincial houses inspire a melancholy like that of barren lands. Arnold ("Switzerland"), Melville (*Clarel*), Butler (*Erewhon*), and Black (*A Princess of Thule*) use a grim version of the Great, too. Travellers provided ample support: Forster found the Antarctic "dismal," Fraser thought British Columbia's Coast Range "gloomy," Bartlett encountered "melancholy" in the Sinai Peninsula, and so on.

GLOOM overlaps with moods such as WEARINESS and MISANTHROPY (less often with FEAR) in the *Dark Group*. It is frequently a concomitant of the metaphors DESERTNESS and WINTRINESS.

GLORY (14): A broad, vaguely religious term used by a few travellers, mostly with reference to mountains, GLORY gained prominence in Ruskin's *Modern Painters*, where "mountain glory" connotes aesthetic beauty and a cathedral-like function. It occurs earlier in Gray's letters, when he has a view of the Lake District's mountains "all in their glory." Powell says that part of the Grand Canyon "opens ... to a region of glory," evidently referring to the light: the root religious meaning, as in a halo. When Whymper calls the Weisshorn "glorious" he may mean a different kind of splendour, and when he quotes "a crowded hour of glorious life," or lists glory among the values of mountaineering, we seem to be closer to heroic endeavour.

GLORY, then, has a SPIRITUAL side, and may be a form of BEAUTY. A sense of spaciousness (VASTNESS or GRANDEUR) is implicit in most uses.

GOD IN DESERT (8): That God is present in the desertic parts of creation is asserted by a few travellers and writers before 1878. The biblical tradition is developed in Milton's *Paradise Regained* as Satan tempts Christ in the wilderness. Thomson's "Hymn to the Seasons" gives the classic statement: "God is ever present, ever felt, / In the void waste as in the city full." Melville's *Clarel* maintains that the waste is God-touched, "exalted in accursed estate." Burton notes that pious Muslims say, in the desert "there is nothing but He."

GOD IN DESERT belongs to the *Spiritual Group*; like HOLINESS OF MOUNTAINS, it is a special case of NATURAL THEOLOGY.

GRANDEUR (97): One of the defining characteristics of the Great, grandeur, majesty, or magnificence was the most frequent response to it before Hardy; in fact, aesthetic philosophers who developed Addison's ideas (Gerard, Kames) preferred the term "grand" to "great." Poets helped establish it: Young's *Night Thoughts* finds the "gloomy grandeur" of the night sky well suited to prepare the soul for God, and Akenside's *Pleasures of the Imagination* defines the Great as "vast majestic pomp" that the mind leaps to embrace. Scott said that the "savage grandeur" of Scotland's wild landscapes "wakes / An awful thrill." Explorers responded similarly. In *The Journals of Lewis and Clark*, the mouth of the Columbia River is a scene of "grandeur," a word Eyre applies to the cliffs of south Australia. Curzon felt "something grand" in the Egyptian desert, Hassaurek a "grave majesty" in the Andes. Climbers often found "grandeur" in the Alps. The term (or its counterpart) also appears in many European writers: von Haller, Rousseau, Sénancour, Hugo, and Flaubert.

GRANDEUR has numerous relations in the *Spacious* and *Spiritual Groups*. Often inspired by a sense of VASTNESS, INFINITY, or ETERNITY, it may give rise to feelings of AWE and INSIGNIFICANCE, or to a sensation of LIBERTY. In the eighteenth century, SUBLIMITY was virtually a synonym of GRANDEUR.

HEALTH (8): A few climbers have claimed that mountaineering promotes mental and physical health. One reason for Gesner's "admiration of mountains" is the "exercise" they provide (including spiritual refreshment). Tyndall is the great Victorian advocate of this idea; mountains, he says, "improve us totally ... we return ... wiser as well as stronger." Whymper also felt that mountaineering brought him strength. Some travellers have spoken similarly of the salubrity of desert air.

HEALTH belongs to the *Adventure Group* of relatively uncomplicated, positive responses. It is only marginally aesthetic, but does understand BEAUTY in metaphysical as well as physical ways.

HOLINESS OF MOUNTAINS (26): The ancient and widespread idea that mountains are sacred places – found among Greeks, Africans, and Asians, and in Dante's Mt Purgatory, "which sets us free from evil as we climb" – occurs in a good many writers from the 1770s on. Goethe's "Harzreise im Winter" culminates in the discovery of an altar and a mysterious deity on the summit of the Brocken, Byron says in *Childe Harold* that the Persians were right to make their mountains altars, and Browning sent a Renaissance funeral procession towards an Italian summit. Irving reported that American Plains Indians place their Supreme Being and happy hunting grounds "at the crest of the world." Mountains' holiness is often asserted by Ruskin.

HOLINESS OF MOUNTAINS, part of the *Spiritual Group*, is (like GOD IN DESERT) a subset of NATURAL THEOLOGY. Closely associated with AWE and SUBLIMITY, it is often accompanied by a sense of VASTNESS or ETERNITY.

INCOMPREHENSION (4): A few writers stress the strangeness or incomprehensibility of Great phenomena. Gray found the Alps as "strange" as his idea of Greenland. Kant built this quality into his definition of the sublime, which refers to what is "beyond all comprehension"; Ruskin argued likewise that infinity (a standard component of the Great or sublime) is incomprehensible.

INCOMPREHENSION arises from qualities that exceed the observer's "normal" sense of space and time: ETERNITY, INFINITY (sometimes VAST), and VOID. Feelings of INCOMPREHENSION commonly occur in ASTRONOMY.

INFINITY (33): Even before Addison compared the impact of Great landscape on the imagination to that of infinity on the mind, travellers were making the connection; Thomas Burnet's description of the Alps may be the source of *Spectator* no. 412. The heavens were the venue of choice for this quality. Thomson's *Seasons* helped popularize the idea of the "infinite Extent" of space, containing "infinite worlds," and Kant made infinity a defining characteristic of natural sublimity, which by his time had subsumed the Great. Many nineteenth-century poets spoke of an infinite sky: Shelley in "Mont Blanc," Tennyson in "Ode to Memory," and Baudelaire often. In Thomson's "City of Dreadful Night," the sphinx has a "cold majestic face / Whose vision seemed of infinite void space." The infinity of the Great is also asserted by Sénancour, Darwin, and the Alpine Club's climber-writers.

INFINITY is often paired with ETERNITY – both attributes of divinity and of the Great – and therefore connected with NATURAL THEOLOGY, but it belongs to the *Space Group*, with VASTNESS and INSIGNIFICANCE. Depending on the writer, it may arouse feelings of GRANDEUR, or of VOID.

INSIGNIFICANCE (29): A feeling of being rendered insignificant by the scale of the Great was a fairly common reaction of early writers. It is at least as old as Vaughan's "The World" (1650), in which the miserable pettiness of earth is "hurled" along in Time's "vast shadow," beneath Eternity's "great Ring" of light. In the nineteenth century, Joaquin Miller found an ocean beach a good place to meditate, a place "Where man must own his littleness": the feeling that can be inferred from many of Turner's seascapes. Powell felt that the Grand Canyon's walls "shrink the river into insignificance," let alone man. J.S. Mill noted that we are awed by "the greater natural phenomena" – storm, mountains, desert, ocean, solar system – which dwarf humanity.

INSIGNIFICANCE is a response to the mind-stretching concepts (INFINITY, ETERNITY, VOID), spaces, and time-spans of ASTRONOMY and GEOLOGY, and to some manifestations of the natural Great. It may be accompanied by a spiritual response such as AWE.

KNOWLEDGE (12): A desire to learn something previously unknown brought some pioneer travellers to the Great, especially after 1860. De Saussure and Tyndall were serious scientists who carried out research during their climbs; Engel believes that the quest for knowledge has been a general motive with Alpinists. Powell's run of the Colorado was a scientific expedition. Palmer and other "sacred geographers" sought knowledge about the "Scriptural topography" of the Mideast. Most early polar explorers enlarged geographical knowledge, though this seldom seems their principal motive. Jules Verne's fictional travellers are usually seeking scientific knowledge.

KNOWLEDGE relates to all members of the *Science Group*. Its historical dimension leads inquirers to ANTIQUITY and ELEMENTS. For the pious, KNOWLEDGE is a stepping stone to NATURAL THEOLOGY; others simply hope that they are coming nearer to REALITY.

LAND/SELF (18): The idea of a relation between land and mind (or body) is much older than Kant's argument that sublimity is in the mind, or Ruskin's "pathetic fallacy." The eighteenth-century feeling for nature as the force uniting inner and outer realities led poets in this direction; in *Night Thoughts*, Young states that the "naked waste" of the world is "a true map of man." But the idea's popularity dates from the 1830s. Emerson's *Nature* develops the notion of a "radical correspondence between visible things and human thoughts." Versions of this "correspondence" appear in most of Melville's works and in Flaubert's *Salammbô*, Mallarmé's "L'Azur," and Fromentin's *Un Été dans le Sahara*.

Part of the *Metaphorical Group*, LAND/SELF is often difficult to distinguish from MIRROR. It is one type of METAPHYSICS, and is sometimes accompanied by a conviction of SELF-KNOWLEDGE.

LIBERTY (18): The association of freedom with the Great dates from Addison's assertion that "a spacious Horison is an Image of Liberty." In *Tatler* no. 161, Thomson's "Liberty," and Wordsworth's "Descriptive Sketches," the Alps (for Johnson, mountains generally) are the home of the goddess Liberty. The connection is made regularly from the Romantics on. Shelley set his epic of liberation, *Prometheus Unbound*, in the mountains of the Caucasus. Both he and Hopkins refer to "wilderness" as "free." The nineteenth century discovered the desert's liberty mainly through the Bedu or the Australian aborigines, though in the Sahara, Fromentin found just what Addison had predicted: "cet énorme horizon libre de toutes parts." For Byron's Corsair, it is the sea that is "boundless" and "free."

Addison's theory relates LIBERTY to the *Spacious Group*, but most of its associates are in the *Minimal Group*, where entities or restrictions are taken away: BARENESS, EMPTINESS, SIMPLICITY, SOLITUDE. A sense of SELF-KNOWLEDGE is sometimes reported.

LURE OF THE DESERT (10): Only a few writers before Hardy (most of them post-1850) were attracted to the desert. This must have been the case, however, with early Christian hermits such as St Anthony, who kept moving deeper into the Egyptian desert as visitors disturbed him. Shaftesbury provided a defence of deserts (1709) – "hideous as they appear, they want not their peculiar beauties. The wildness pleases" – and Addison placed their power above mere beauty. Some of the "deserts" that lure poets like Byron and Arnold are just "deserted places" (the old sense), but Burton's paean to "the glorious desert," where nature returns to us and "man meets man," concerns the real thing, as does Melville's attribution of beauty and spirituality to the Judaean waste in *Clarel.* Fromentin provides the period's best example of a traveller lured by the desert.

LURE OF THE DESERT is a vague term covering several different types of appeal: sometimes BEAUTY or SUBLIMITY, sometimes SPIRITUALITY. In Byron and others it is related to MISANTHROPY. At times the lure is a kind of self-testing.

METAPHORS (33): A substantial number of travellers and poets treat the Great metaphorically. Deschamps's "Lay du desert d'Amours" is a late mediaeval allegory playing on the idea of the "garden of love." For Donne and others in the seventeenth century mountains were ugly signs of Original Sin and the Fall, but in the eighteenth, Addison, von Haller, and Rousseau used them to symbolize *desiderata.* Most examples postdate 1810. In Carlyle's translation of Goethe's *Wilhelm Meister's Apprenticeship,* "all was desolate" in "the waste of [Wilhelm's] imagination" when Mignon died, and his *Sartor Resartus* uses mountains and deserts allegorically. Byron's *Childe Harold, Manfred,* and letters often make deserts and the Alps metaphors of life and moral qualities. Théophile Gautier's "La Caravane" depicts "La caravane humaine au Sahara du monde," by then a common image. Gogol's *Dead Souls,* Flaubert's *Salammbô,* Thomson's "City of Dreadful Night," and Fitzgerald's *Rubáiyát of Omar Khayyám* provide other instances of metaphorical deserts.

METAPHORS is the centre of the *Metaphorical Group.* It can be distinguished from the simpler MIRRORS, the more self-referential LAND/SELF, and the more abstract METAPHYSICS. The qualities most frequently allegorized are BARENESS, BARRENNESS, and VOID.

METAPHYSICS (6): A few early travellers tried to read Great landscapes metaphysically, a tendency with roots in the Bible and in Conrad Gesner's feeling that mountains constitute another world, one in which the spirit is lifted to God. Such readings increased in the nineteenth century. The metaphysical strain in Romantic poetry includes passages on the Great in Wordsworth, Coleridge, and

Shelley. Hayes found the long night of the Arctic winter more than the sum of its physical discomforts and terrors; he took solitary walks through its silent desolation, noting how "The mind ... wanders into space." By the 1860s, English climbers tended to wax metaphysical in the higher Alps.

With several near relations in both the *Spiritual Group* (GOD IN DESERT) and the *Metaphorical Group* (LAND/SELF), METAPHYSICS may be said to bridge the two.

MINIMALISM (4): In the West, MINIMALISM is usually viewed as a movement in twentieth-century art, but a tendency to seek out bare essences and enjoy less appears earlier in some travel-writers. The seventeenth-century Japanese poet Bashō, minimal both in his haiku form and his subject matter – hard travel to desolate places – searched for the essential, eternal truths in scenes of barren nature. Fromentin is the best example of an early desert minimalist; what he loved in the Sahara is stated in terms of lack: "le ciel sans nuages, au-dessus du désert sans ombre." Minimalism can also be felt in Melville's *Encantadas,* especially in the account of the hermit Oberlus's existence.

MINIMALISM is the central term of the *Minimalist Group.* Searches for ELEMENTS, or for SELF-KNOWLEDGE, are often minimal in style. It is also associated with WINTRINESS.

MIRROR (6): A few writers treated manifestations of the Great as mirrors of some kind. In *Centuries of Meditations,* Traherne contemplates the night sky and observes, "The world is a mirror of infinite beauty." Baudelaire specifies just one quality that oceans will reflect; a *free* man will love the sea, for "La mer est ton miroir." In Flaubert's *Salammbô,* deserts mirror the characters' barrenness. Swinburne's "On the Downs" is more complex: the narrative of a figure walking the downs reflects the narrator's mind moving over thoughts.

MIRROR, part of the *Metaphorical Group,* is closely akin to LAND/SELF (although here self need not be the image). There is usually a sense of gaining SELF-KNOWLEDGE or of discovering another REALITY.

MISANTHROPY (22): An antipathy to human civilization, or to too much of it, sometimes sent travellers to the wilderness. This impulse can be seen in the early Christian desert hermits, in Bashō, and in Georgian primitivists such as Joseph Warton, but did not become popular in Europe until the nineteenth century. Wordsworth could feel the "secret Power" in an Alpine canton because "no trace of man the spot profanes." Byron's Childe Harold fled from crowded Lac Léman into the Alps; Poe's Julius Rodman, finding no peace among men, "fled to the desert as to a friend." Stephen praised the Alps as a "safe asylum" from "our fellow-creatures," who "come about us like bees." Burton's *Pilgrimage* to Mecca, Arnold's "Empedocles on Etna," and Thomson's "City of Dreadful Night" provide other examples.

Part of the *Dark Group*, MISANTHROPY arises from feelings of GLOOM and WEARINESS of the world; it seeks more CALM, LIBERTY, SOLITUDE, and PURITY. The more extreme cases move towards VOID.

MUSIC (4): Few writers before 1878 make the connection between Great phenomena and music that has since been established. Gesner praised the silent mountainous solitudes because there you can hear "orbium harmonium": the music of the spheres. Baudelaire asserts that "La musique donne l'idée de l'espace." Butler uses music effectively in *Erewhon*; the gigantic statues in the mountain pass are Aeolian (wind-blown) pipes, emitting a mysterious natural music among cloudy peaks and glaciers.

MUSIC's syntax is sparse. It usually involves some kind of MYSTIQUE, and there is an historical connection with ASTRONOMY.

MUTABILITY (5): In 1709 Shaftesbury noted that mountains teach us the "incessant changes" and "fleeting forms" of the earth's surface, but this note of mutability is heard more often in the nineteenth century, with its geological consciousness of change. For Humboldt and Darwin, South American earthquakes showed the instability of the earth's crust; for Forbes, Alpine glaciers were the teacher. As Tennyson's *In Memoriam* put it, "O earth, what changes hast thou seen!"

MUTABILITY's grammar varies with the writer and period. For Shaftesbury, it was affiliated with the *Spiritual Group*. In the nineteenth century it becomes part of the *Science Group*, cousin to GEOLOGY.

MYSTIQUE (13): Beginning with the Romantics, some travellers and poets stress the mysterious or magical aspects of the Great. Wordsworth's "Descriptive Sketches" are heavy with an Alpine mystique compounded of holiness, transcendental experience, and silence. Shelley represents the Assassins' mountain refuge as a wilderness "hallowed ... to a deep and solemn mystery." Tyndall was not the only member of the Alpine Club fascinated by the "mystic pinnacle" of the Matterhorn. Darwin found a "mysterious grandeur" in Tierra del Fuego's mountains. Kane viewed the Arctic as a "desolate, mysterious" land, while Hayes called northern Greenland a "land of enchantment." He longed to reach the "mystic sea" around the pole.

MYSTIQUE is a *General* affiliate of some responses in the *Spiritual Group*; it may arise from a sense of approaching INFINITY or ETERNITY. Often it combines feelings of UNCANNINESS and INCOMPREHENSION, sometimes with a metaphysical dimension.

NATURAL THEOLOGY (37): A frequent response to the Great in the eighteenth and nineteenth centuries was natural theology, in which the Creator is inferred from the creation. *Natura codex est Dei*, as St Bernard said; the world "discovers the being of God unto you," wrote Traherne. Addison thought that we delight in the Great because it raises the mind to the Creator. Subsequent examples are numerous and broadly based, ranging from Wollstonecraft through Arctic explorers to Ruskin. Sometimes the connection is implicit (St-Pierre speaks of nature's "divins ouvrages"), sometimes explicit, as when Buffon calls nature "le trône extérieur de la magnificence Divine." Natural theology permeates Thomson's *Seasons*, Young's *Night Thoughts*, Hugh Miller's books, and Cooper's *Crater.*

   NATURAL THEOLOGY, the broad phenomenon of which GOD IN DESERT and HOLINESS OF MOUNTAINS are parts, has numerous relatives, mostly in the *Spiritual Group*. Often it arises from intimations of divine attributes – ETERNITY, INFINITY, POWER – or approaches to them (VAST). In some cases there is a vague sense of GRANDEUR and of one's own INSIGNIFICANCE.

OXYMORON (24): The Great can elicit quite different, even contradictory, responses in the same observer at the same time: usually BEAUTY/TERROR. Psychologically, this is an approach / avoidance conflict arising from emotional overload and aesthetic confusion; stylistically, it is OXYMORON. Dennis's "delightful Horrour, terrible Joy" while crossing the Alps in 1688 begins the English tradition. Addison's reaction was similar, and a French or Swiss traveller ascribed "horribles beautés" to the Alps in 1737. Instances occurred almost regularly among poets, explorers, and adventurers after Burke's seminal essay (1757) made FEAR an important part of the sublime. Cook resorted to OXYMORON in the Antarctic, von Troil in Iceland. Boswell called a night storm at sea "grandly horrible," and Crabbe exclaimed of a similar scene, "gloom in glory drest!" Byron found in the Alps "All that expands the spirit, yet appalls." Hayes saw that Arctic icebergs had both "terrible aspects" and "wondrous beauties."

   Typically, OXYMORON combines BEAUTY and FEAR into the mood called AWE, later part of the sublime. Usually springing from contact with natural GRANDEUR or VASTNESS, it links the *Spiritual, Dark*, and *Spacious Groups*.

PAIN FOR GAIN (5): Only a few travellers, mostly in the 1850s and 1860s, valued their hardships as a reward. Fromentin insisted that he must share "la lenteur et la fatigue extrême" of a Sahara journey or lose something. Burton, anxious to test his "powers of endurance" on the desert, welcomed hardship. Browning's

St John, enduring his "Death in the Desert," reflects, "When pain ends, gain ends too." This is mostly a desert phenomenon, although one may infer it in some polar explorers, and Engel lists asceticism or masochism among the motives of Alpinists. Von Haller says that the rigours of Alpine life purify the morals and increase the happiness of the peasantry.

PAIN FOR GAIN, a form of asceticism in which pain is deemed beneficial or essential, belongs to the *Dark Group*. It often seeks out BARRENNESS, and a mood of CHALLENGE is common.

POWER (27): The strength or power of the Great, which would seem as inherent to its definition as VASTNESS or GRANDEUR, is mentioned only about a third as often. While some early theorists (Locke, Gerard, Kant) discuss power, most citations come from nineteenth-century poets, scientists, or explorers. Byron speaks of "the power and the Glory" of the Alps, and Shelley's Mont Blanc is above all the home of "Power." Browning, Swinburne, and Joaquin Miller provide other poetic examples. "Power" also occurs in writings on science (Lyell), aesthetics (Ruskin), Alpine climbing (Will, Whymper), and polar exploration (the Rosses). Hayes found the Tyndall Glacier "evidence of the greatness and the power of the Almighty hand."

POWER is akin to several members of the *Spiritual Group* – AWE, INFINITY, NATURAL THEOLOGY – but responses to it vary. For some it engenders feelings of FEAR or INSIGNIFICANCE; for others, POWER is an aspect of GRANDEUR, another enigmatic quality.

PRESERVATION (6): A scattering of early sources remarked on the preservative qualities of Great landscapes, usually in connection with ice, snow and cold. Capt. Wood's account of permafrost (1676) worked into Pope's description of the "Temple of Fame" (1711), while Victorian climbers such as Forbes and Wills noted that Alpine glaciers preserved everything from straw to corpses. Shaw reported (1738) that the dry air of the desert also protected bodies against decay, and Darwin observes how geological exposures preserve the past.

PRESERVATION, a member of the *Temporal Group*, tends to come up in connection with GEOLOGY or WINTRINESS.

PROFUNDITY (7): Beginning in the 1790s, a small number of travellers to Great landscapes (mostly the Alps) discovered therein a deeply moving seriousness, which they sometimes projected onto the landscape as its wisdom. This is seen in both climbers (de Saussure, Wills, Tyndall) and tourists (Wordsworth, Hugo). Fromentin reacts thus to the Sahara, "dont la première influence est de rendre sérieux."

PROFUNDITY has affiliations with NATURAL THEOLOGY in the *Spiritual Group*, with INFINITY in the *Space Group*, and with ETERNITY in the *Temporal Group*. It often accompanies ELEMENTS, and sometimes produces feelings of INSIGNIFI-CANCE.

PURITY (37): One of the most widely distributed reactions to the Great has been that it is extraordinarily pure, clean, clear, or rarefied. Such remarks appear in the mid-seventeenth century (with harbingers in Plato's *Phaedo* and Dante's Mt Purgatory), and are made regularly from the late eighteenth century on about all areas of the Great, usually with reference to air, water, ice or snow. Vaughan's poem "The World" envisions eternity as "a great Ring of pure and endless light" in the night sky. Capt. Marten's account of the clear water and pure air of Spitsbergen (1671) was broadened to the Arctic by nineteenth-century explorers such as Parry. Von Haller, de Saussure, Wordsworth, Coleridge, Sénancour, Forbes, and others depicted the Alps as a realm of natural and social purity, a view later extended to other mountains. Plaisted found the air of the Syrian desert "always pure and serene" in the 1750s; a century later, Fromentin celebrated the Saharan sky, "d'un bleu de cobalt pur."

PURITY tends to occur in connection with BARENESS in the *Minimal Group* or with HOLINESS OF MOUNTAINS in the *Spiritual Group*. It is part of the LURE OF THE DESERT, and, if perceived as "inhuman," can contribute to feelings of IN-SIGNIFICANCE.

REALITY (4): A few travellers understood the Great as a higher, sterner, or different reality: a truth not hidden by appearances. This is a theme of de Saussure's *Voyages*, from his interest in granitic mountains as near the origin of things and his feeling that the high Alps are "un autre monde" (a point foreshadowed in Gesner) to his revelation of the truth about the range's structure atop Mont Blanc. Burton and Fromentin represent the desert as bringing out truths elsewhere concealed.

REALITY may arise in connection with GEOLOGY or general KNOWLEDGE in the *Science Group*, or as part of SELF-KNOWLEDGE, wherein it acts as a MIRROR. When the reality perceived partakes of ETERNITY, the observer may feel his or her INSIGNIFICANCE.

RICHNESS (8): A few visitors found Great landscapes (mostly in the north) rich and precious, actually or visually. In the 1670s Capts. Wood and Marten mention black marble and the appearance or colours of silver, sapphire and emerald on Arctic islands, which may have suggested to Pope the precious stones of his "Temple of Fame." Later both Kane and Hayes perceived icebergs as "gemwork." Powell noted many occurrences of real jasper and marble in the Grand Canyon.

RICHNESS belongs to the *Pleasure Group*, next to BEAUTY. It has a more distant connection with the *Spiritual Group*, by way of Moses' vision of heaven's jeweled pavement (Ex 24).

SELF-KNOWLEDGE (5): A few nineteenth-century writers found that contact with or meditation on the Great gave them a keener sense of their own identity as individuals or as human beings. Usages shade from the aggressive self-reliance of Burton ("in the Desert man meets man") to the philosophical humanism of Shelley's "Queen Mab" and Swinburne's "Hymn of Man."

Burton's kind of SELF-KNOWLEDGE is affiliated with the *Adventure Group*, but for most it is an aspect of KNOWLEDGE in general. In all cases the Great is a MIRROR and confers greater LIBERTY of thought, resulting in a new AWARENESS of REALITY.

SILENCE (36): Quiet became one of the Great's most popular attributes in the nineteenth century; after 1786, when de Saussure hailed the "majestic silence" of the Alps, it is welcomed regularly. Romantic poets made celebration of Alpine stillness one of their themes, and mountaineers concurred. As the pressures of population intensified in Europe, travellers commented more frequently, more favourably, and more widely on silence, especially in the desert (Curzon, Stephens, Fromentin, etc.); Darwin reports that the "stillness" of the Patagonian plain gave him a "strong sense of pleasure." Shelley and Hardy emphasize the silence of space, Parry and Kane that of the Arctic. Silence also figures prominently in the verse of de Lisle and Baudelaire.

SILENCE is related to other themes of sensory deprivation and absence (EMPTINESS, SOLITUDE, VOID) in the *Minimal Group*. It is frequently associated with CALM as pleasures of the Great. On a vast or cosmic scale it may cause feelings of INSIGNIFICANCE.

SIMPLICITY (15): The appeal of Great simplicity is acknowledged more often in literature and aesthetic philosophy than in accounts of travel, though there are notable exceptions (Fromentin, Irving, Kane). In the 1750s, Gerard made simplicity part of his definition of sublimity (a point accepted by Kant), but it was such 'Romantic' texts as Radcliffe's *Journey* to the English Lakes, Sénancour's *Oberman*, Shelley's "Alastor," and Wordsworth's *Prelude* that gave currency to the idea that a "naked and severe simplicity" (Shelley) was an essential part of the Great. Egdon Heath is "grand in its simplicity."

SIMPLICITY belongs to the *Minimal Group*, where its nearest relatives are BARENESS and SOLITUDE. It often arises from ELEMENTS and produces a mood of CALM.

SOLITUDE (57): A strong sense of loneliness and isolation during contact with the Great was noted in the seventeenth and eighteenth centuries by Bashō, by Thomson and Shaw, by Rousseau, and by Kant. In the nineteenth century, as time spent alone became rarer in Europe, its significance increased, and depictions of solitude burgeoned (a development parallel to that of SILENCE, though solitude is mentioned more often). Its value varies. In Sénancour, Byron's *Childe Harold* and "Manfred," and Baudelaire, the protagonist is isolated and unhappy, though we can infer that society was problematical and that solitude is the best condition for him. In Wordsworth and in Browning's "Englishman in Italy," solitude is part of the appeal of the mountains; in Shelley's "Alastor," part of the hero's nobility. Victorian climbers such as Tyndall and Stephen rejoiced in the loneliness of the Alps. But few desert travellers besides Fromentin affirmed its solitude, and most explorers of the Arctic found its loneliness oppressive.

SOLITUDE is a member of the *Minimal Group*, closely allied to BARENESS and SILENCE. It is highly variable: it may arise from a desire for LIBERTY and produce feelings of SELF-KNOWLEDGE or CALM, or stem from MISANTHROPY, and adopt a mood of GLOOM.

SPIRITUALITY (67): Few perceptions of the Great have been as enduring or as widespread as that which finds it spiritual, inspiring piety or reverence in the beholder. A broad range of the planet's aboriginal peoples treated mountains as holy places, a response corroborated by Gesner in the sixteenth century and Evelyn in the seventeenth. The eighteenth century provided further examples of the spiritual Great (gradually extended to include the heavens, the polar oceans, and the desert), but the most frequent attestations come from the supposedly sceptical nineteenth century. These range from literary devices such as Flaubert's and Melville's desert settings for spiritual tests or Arnold's yearnings towards the Alps, through Emerson's assertion that the stars inspire reverence, to the discoveries of serious climbers or explorers (Burton, Hayes, Tyndall) that the Great was a spiritual realm. Scientists were not immune to these feelings; de Saussure said that the 'soul ascends' and the 'spirit grows' on a clear night at the Col du Géant.

SPIRITUALITY, the centre of the largest group of responses to the Great, including AWE and SUBLIMITY, has links with qualities in other groups as well: chiefly ETERNITY and INFINITY.

SUBLIMITY (86): Since Burke's sublime succeeded Addison's Great, poets, travellers, and theorists naturally saw sublimity in Great landscapes more often than they did almost any other quality. Early users were mindful of the word's Latin root, *sublimis*, 'lifted up,' and while later uses are more general, a sense of exaltation and spiritual expansion remained. Burke's *Enquiry* and Kant's *Analytic* were the highlights of eighteenth-century discussions, but the word's general currency dates from the 1790s, when Wordsworth, Radcliffe, and Wollstonecraft applied it to mountains. Byron said that the Alps enthroned "Eternity in icy halls / Of cold sublimity" ("All which expands the spirit, yet appalls"). The word was used and discussed throughout the nineteenth century in aesthetics, explorers' narratives, desert travel, mountaineering, poetry, novels, and science.

SUBLIMITY, the leading member of the *Spiritual Group*, is an associate of AWE. It often comes up in connection with ASTRONOMY, ETERNITY, INFINITY, and VASTNESS. As Byron's quotation suggests, it involves an OXYMORON, more than does GRANDEUR, which has many of the same values and connections.

TIME (5): For a few writers, contact with the Great was a kind of time travel. De Saussure said that Alpine rocks showed the primitive foundations of the earth, and Darwin was whirled far back in time by various South American formations. The temporal implications of Great landscapes also intrigued some imaginative writers, notably Swinburne and Jules Verne.

TIME is related to the other members of its group: ANTIQUITY, ELEMENTS, ETERNITY, and PRESERVATION. It tends to come up in discussions of ASTRONOMY and GEOLOGY.

UNCANNINESS (28): Some eighteenth- and nineteenth-century writers found that the Great transcended ordinary experience in weird, deceptive, or unique ways. This theme begins as early as de Veer's account of Arctic islands (1596), develops in the eighteenth century with Shaw's narrative of desert travel and the poems of Thomson, and becomes regular from the 1770s, when de Saussure described the Alps as "un monde nouveau": a view endorsed by Hugo and several Alpinists. Von Troil likewise found Iceland "a new world," and Arctic explorers emphasized the optical illusions that made it seem "dream-like and supernatural" (Kane). Powell noted similar phenomena in the "strange, weird" Grand Canyon. Creative writers such as Cooper and Verne were glad to dwell on this aspect of the Great.

UNCANNINESS has an obscure syntax. It can be as general as FASCINATION, or as spiritual as METAPHYSICS. Its dark side can produce FEAR or INCOMPREHENSION.

VASTNESS (83): The immensity of Great nature has always been one of its most striking features; only GRANDEUR and SUBLIMITY are mentioned more often. Citations begin in the 1640s with Evelyn and appear sporadically until about 1800, when they become regular and more frequent. Though some debated whether mere vastness should be considered sublime, observers in the field continued to marvel at the size of Great natural phenomena. Nineteenth-century poets (Byron, Shelley) and Alpinists (Tyndall, Whymper) were as struck by the scale of the Alps as Thomas Burnet had been in the seventeenth; a parallel statement could be made of the line of Arctic navigators from Wood and Marten to Hayes and Kane. The vastness of deserts and prairies impressed visitors as disparate as Plaisted and Flaubert. Fontenelle evokes the "grand espace vide" of the universe, the largest physical phenomenon we know, and had many followers, including Addison. In the nineteenth century, poets such as Byron, Baudelaire, and Hardy took a darker view of the vast empty reaches of space, which seemed devoid of God and meaning.

VASTNESS belongs in the *Space Group*, as viceroy to INFINITY. It may give a sense of LIBERTY, call forth spiritual responses (SUBLIMITY), or engender feelings of INSIGNIFICANCE. Often it comes up in connection with ETERNITY or GRANDEUR. At first associated with ASTRONOMY, it later arises from GEOLOGY.

VOID (17): The nullity or void of nature was a theme of nineteenth-century writers such as Sénancour, Gogol, Poe, de Lisle, Baudelaire, Melville, and Mallarmé (as Robert Adams showed in *Nil*). It was discussed by earlier writers and travellers as well, not always with fear or despair. Thomson's "Autumn" sought knowledge of the "Void immense" of space, which it affirmed as part of God's Creation; Wordsworth's "voids" are wild sections of the Alps and great deserts. As late as the 1850s Fromentin embraced "le rien, le vide" of the Sahara, but most literary discussions of void from Byron's "Darkness" to Thomson's "City of Dreadful Night" find the idea of nothingness terrifying.

VOID is central to the *Minimal Group*, where its closest kin are BARENESS, EMPTINESS, and SILENCE. It most often comes up in connection with ASTRONOMY.

WEARINESS (4): A few nineteenth-century sources use the Great as a way of escaping from lives of which they are weary, as Menelik I did in the Ethiopian legend about Kilimanjaro. Arnold's Empedocles on Mt Etna and Flaubert's St Anthony in the desert have both withdrawn from societies that distract them from the essential concerns of the mind and spirit. The only traveller who presents himself thus is Burton, who treats the desert as a relief from European civilization.

WEARINESS is part of the *Dark Group*, with GLOOM and MISANTHROPY. It seeks SOLITUDE and SILENCE. Its metaphorical cousin is DESERTNESS.

WHITENESS (21): The colour most often associated with the Great is not sea-blue or space-black but white. This began with the poets: Bashō in the blizzards of Japan, Pope in an imagined Arctic. Later, polar voyagers such as Forster, Parry, and Hayes dwelt on the dominant whiteness of those environments. Poe's *Arthur Gordon Pym* uses white as a symbol of the inscrutability of the universe, a device developed by Melville, especially in "The Whiteness of the Whale" chapter in *Moby Dick*. Nineteenth-century poets such as Arnold, Théophile Gautier, Baudelaire, Hardy, and Swinburne repeatedly used the white or dun of snow, sand, or bare earth to stand for the opacity of nature to human inquiry.

WHITENESS, a member of the *Metaphorical Group*, has strong links to minimal qualities (BARENESS, EMPTINESS). Its connotations range from INCOMPRE-HENSION to PURITY.

WILDNESS (36): Shaftesbury announced in *The Moralists* (1709) that "The wildness [of deserts] pleases," and Thomson wrote about "fractured mountains wild" and the Arctic's "wild stupendous scene" in "Winter." 'Great' and 'wild' were often coupled thereafter. Sometimes, as in Shaftesbury, or Thoreau's "In wildness is the preservation of the world," 'wild' simply means natural as opposed to artificial, but as explorers reached less accessible areas and applied it to the fringes of Creation, 'wild' came to connote 'savage' and 'stern.' The Alps were central to this development, from Gray's letters through Rousseau to Victorian mountaineers, but the wildness of Arctic and Antarctic islands (von Troil, Cook), the Canadian north (Franklin), the American prairies (Parkman), and other areas was also noted. In early nineteenth-century uses 'wild' may be coupled with 'romantic,' but by the 1870s Whymper, Black, and Hardy were using 'wild' for harsh, unfriendly landscapes that seemed outside Divine benevolence.

WILDNESS has such diverse affiliates – e.g. CHAOS and MISANTHROPY in the *Dark Group*, and LIBERTY (itself quite ambiguous) – that it must be placed in the *General Group*.

WINTRINESS (12): A few sources (beginning with Bashō) dwell on the wintriness or sereness of some Great landscapes. Early on, in Pope and Thomson, the main interest is scenic (although in the preface to "Winter" the "world of letters" is termed "wintry"). Most later uses are more ominous. Alpine tourists and high-latitude voyagers were taken aback by winter's dominance there; Forster noted that the country around Cape Horn "looked wild and horrid in its wintery [*sic*] dress" even at midsummer. Nineteenth-century writers employed late fall or winter as a symbol of inner sterility (Sénancour, Verlaine) more often than they were exhilarated by it (Emerson, *Nature*), especially after scientists suggested that the world might end in ice after the sun expired. Hardy associates Egdon Heath (and 'Thule') with the spiritual wintriness of modern humanity.

WINTRINESS, a member of the *Metaphorical Group*, also has kin in the *Minimal Group*, including BARENESS. It can evoke feelings of CHALLENGE or PURITY, or, more darkly, of GLOOM and MASOCHISM.

Works Cited

Abrams, M.H. [1953] 1958. *The Mirror and the Lamp.* Oxford Univ. Press. Reprint. New York: Norton.

– 1971. *Natural Supernaturalism.* New York: Norton.

Account of Several Late Voyages and Discoveries to the South and North. [1694] 1711. London: Royal Society. Reprint. New York: Da Capo, 1969.

Adams, Brooks. 1981. "Turner: the Chastened Sublime." *Art in America* 69, no. 5 (May): 114–22.

Adams, Richard P. 1954. "Emerson and the Organic Metaphor." *Publications of the Modern Language Association of America* (*PMLA*) 69:117–30. In *Interpretations of American Literature*, ed. Charles Feidelson, Jr, and Paul Brodtkorb, Jr, 137–52. New York: Oxford Univ. Press, 1959.

Adams, Robert Martin. 1966. *Nil. Episodes in the Literary Conquest of Void during the Nineteenth Century.* London: Oxford Univ. Press.

Addison, Joseph. 1893. *The Works of Joseph Addison.* 5 vols. London: Bell, Bohn's Library.

– 1965. *The Spectator.* Ed. Donald F. Bond. 5 vols. Oxford: Clarendon Press.

Akenside, Mark. [1744] 1857. *The Poetical Works of Mark Akenside.* Ed. Rev. George Gilfillan. Edinburgh: James Nichol.

Albritton, Claude C., Jr. [1980] 1986. *The Abyss of Time. Changing Conceptions of the Earth's Antiquity after the Sixteenth Century.* San Francisco: Freeman, Cooper. Reprint. Los Angeles: Jeremy P. Tarcher.

Alison, Archibald. [1790] 1971. *Essays on the Nature and Principles of Taste.* In *Criticism and Aesthetics 1660–1800*, ed. Oliver F. Sigworth. San Francisco: Rinehart.

Allott, Kenneth, and Miriam Allott, eds. See Arnold, Matthew. 1979.

Amory, Thomas. [1755] 1904. *The Life and Opinions of John Buncle, Esq.* Intro. Ernest Baker. London: Routledge.

Armstrong, Neil. 1969. [First moon-walk.] *Time* (25 July): 12.

Arnold, Matthew. [1965] 1979. *The Poems of Matthew Arnold.* Ed. Kenneth Allott (1st ed.), Miriam Allott (2d ed.). London: Longman.

Ashmun, Margaret. 1931. *The Singing Swan.* New Haven: Yale Univ. Press.

Atkinson, Geoffrey. 1960. *Le Sentiment de la nature et le retour à la vie simple (1690–1740).* Paris: Minard.

Aubin, Robert A. 1934. "Grottoes, Geology and the Gothic Revival." *Studies in Philology* 31:408–16.

Augustine. *The Confessions.* [1961] 1964. Trans. R.S. Pine-Coffin. Harmondsworth: Penguin.

Bailey, Sir Edward. 1962. *Charles Lyell.* London: Nelson.

Baillie, John. [1747] 1953. "An Essay on the Sublime." Ed. Samuel H. Monk. Augustan Reprint Ser. no. 43. Berkeley and Los Angeles: Univ. of California Press.

Balzac, Honoré de. [1833] 1972. *Eugénie Grandet.* Paris: Librairie Générale Française, Le Livre de Poche.

– 1985. "A Passion in the Desert." Trans. Ellen Marriage. In *Story,* ed. Boyd Litzinger and Joyce Carol Oates. Lexington, MA: Heath.

Bartlett, Phyllis. 1955. "Hardy's Shelley." *Keats-Shelley Journal* 4:15–29.

Bartlett, William. [1845] N.d. *Forty Days in the Desert on the Track of the Israelites.* 4th ed. London: A. Hall.

Bashō, Matsuo. 1966. *The Narrow Road to the Deep North and Other Travel Sketches.* Trans. with an intro. by Nobuyuki Yuasa. Harmondsworth: Penguin.

Baudelaire, Charles. 1975. *Oeuvres Complètes.* Ed. Claude Pichois. Paris: Gallimard.

Beach, Joseph Warren. [1936] 1956. *The Concept of Nature in Nineteenth-Century English Poetry.* New York: Macmillan. Reprint. New York: Pageant.

Beaufoy, Mark. 1817. "Narrative of a Journey ... to the Summit of Mt-Blanc ... 1787." *Annals of Philosophy* 9 (February): 97–103.

Beckford, Willam. [1786] 1930. *Vathek.* London: Dent, Dutton.

Beechey, Capt. F.W. 1831. *Narrative of a Voyage to the Pacific and Beering's Strait ... 1825–28.* 2 vols. London: Colburn and Bentley.

Bergin, Thomas G. 1970. *Petrarch.* New York: Twayne.

Berkeley, George. 1848. *The Works of George Berkeley.* 2 vols. London: Tegg.

Bernardin de St Pierre. [1773] 1983. *Voyage à l'Île de France.* Paris: La Découverte/Maspero.

Berton, Pierre. [1988] 1989. *The Arctic Grail.* Toronto: McClelland and Stewart. Reprint. Markham, Ontario: Penguin.

Bertrandon de la Brocquière. 1848. *The Travels of Bertrandon de la Brocquière.* In *Early Travels in Palestine,* ed. Thomas Wright. London: Bohn.

Bietenholz, Peter G. 1963. *Desert and Bedouin in the European Mind.* Khartoum: Univ. Press.

Bishop, Morris. 1963. *Petrarch and His World*. Bloomington: Indiana Univ. Press.

Black, William. [1874] 1879. *A Princess of Thule*. London: Macmillan.

Blackmore, Richard. [1712]. N.d. *Creation. A Philosophical Poem*. In *Blackmore's Works*. London: Cooke.

Blair, Hugh. [1783] 1824. *An Abridgment of Lectures on Rhetoric [and Belles Lettres]*. London: Brattleborough, Holbrook and Fessenden.

Bonney, T.G. 1895. *Charles Lyell and Modern Geology*. London: Cassell.

Boswell, James. [1785] 1970. *The Journal of a Tour to the Hebrides, with Samuel Johnson, LL.D.* 3d ed., 1786. Ed. R.W. Chapman. London: Oxford Univ. Press [1924].

Boulton, James T., ed. See Burke, Edmund. [1759] 1987.

Brockedon, William. [1824] 1833. *Journals of Excursions in the Alps*. New ed. London: Duncan.

Brontë, Charlotte. [1847] N.d. *Jane Eyre*. New York: Random House.

Brown, Hamish M. [1978] 1980. *Hamish's Mountain Walk*. London: Granada.

Browning, Robert. 1970. *Browning. Poetical Works 1833–1864*. Ed. Ian Jack. London: Oxford Univ. Press.

Buffon, George-Louis Leclerc, Comte de. [1744] 1854. "Histoire et théorie de la terre." In vol. 1 of *Oeuvres complètes de Buffon*. 10 vols. Paris: Dufour, Mulat and Boulanger.

– [1778] 1854. "Des Époques de la nature." In vol. 3 of *Oeuvres complètes de Buffon*. 10 vols. Paris: Dufour, Mulat and Boulanger.

Burckhardt, John Lewis. 1822. *Travels in Syria and the Holy Land*. London: Murray.

– [1822] 1978. *Travels in Nubia*. London: Murray. Reprint. New York: AMS.

– [1829] 1968. *Travels in Arabia*. London: Colburn. Reprint. N.p.: F. Cass.

Burd, Van Akin. 1981. "Ruskin's Testament of His Boyhood Faith: Sermons on the Pentateuch." In *New Approaches to Ruskin. Thirteen Essays*, ed. Robert Hewison. London: Routledge and Kegan Paul.

Burke, Edmund. [1759] 1987. *A Philosophical Enquiry into the Origin of Our Ideas of the Sublime and the Beautiful*. [1757] 2d ed. Ed. James T. Boulton. Oxford: Blackwell.

Burnet, Gilbert. 1687. *Some Letters, Containing An Account of … Switzerland, Italy, Some Parts of Germany, &c. In the Years 1685 and 1686*. 3d ed. Rotterdam.

Burnet, Thomas. [1684] 1965. *The Sacred Theory of the Earth*. Intro. Basil Willey. London: Centaur.

Burton, Richard F. [1855] 1964. *Personal Narrative of a Pilgrimage to Al-Madinah & Meccah*. Ed. Isabel Burton. London: Tylston & Edwards. 1893. Reprint. 2 vols. New York: Dover.

Butler, Samuel. [1872] 1961. *Erewhon*. New York: New American Library, Signet Classics.

Byron, George Gordon, Lord. [1821] 1968. *Lord Byron's "Cain."* Ed. Truman G. Steffan. Austin: Univ. of Texas Press.

– 1976. *Byron's Letters and Journals.* Ed. Leslie A. Marchand. 11 vols. Vol. 5. Cambridge: Harvard Univ. Press, Belknap Press.

– 1980. *Lord Byron. The Complete Poetical Works.* Ed. Jerome J. McGann. 7 vols. Vol. 2. Oxford: Clarendon Press.

– 1981. *Lord Byron. The Complete Poetical Works.* Ed. Jerome J. McGann. 7 vols. Vol. 3. Oxford: Clarendon Press.

– 1986. *Lord Byron. The Complete Poetical Works.* Ed. Jerome J. McGann. 7 vols. Vol. 4. Oxford: Clarendon Press.

Cameron, Ian. 1974. *Antarctica: The Last Continent.* Boston: Little, Brown.

Carlyle, Thomas. [1833–34] 1987. *Sartor Resartus.* Ed. Kerry McSweeney and Peter Sabor. New York: Oxford Univ. Press.

– [1923] 1970. *Letters of Thomas Carlyle to J.S. Mill, John Sterling and Robert Browning.* Ed. Alexander Carlyle. Reprint. New York: Haskell.

Carozzi, Albert V., ed. and trans. See de Maillet, Benoit. [1748]

Carré, Jean-Marie. [1932] 1956. *Voyageurs et écrivains français en Égypte.* 2 vols. 2d ed. Cairo: Imprimerie de l'Institut Français d'Archéologie.

Carritt, E.F. 1925. "The Sources and Effects in English of Kant's Philosophy of Beauty." *Monist* 35:315–28.

Carruthers, Douglas, ed. 1929. *The Desert Route to India.* London: Hakluyt Society.

Carter, Paul. 1987. *The Road to Botany Bay.* London and Boston: Faber and Faber.

Cate, George A., ed. 1982. *The Correspondence of Thomas Carlyle and John Ruskin.* Stanford: Stanford Univ. Press.

Chadwick, Douglas H. 1979. "Our Wildest Wilderness." *National Geographic* 156, no. 6 (December): 740–69.

– 1981. "Nahanni: Canada's Wilderness Park." *National Geographic* 160, no. 3 (September): 396–420.

Chase, Richard, ed. 1950. Herman Melville. "The Encantadas." [1856] In *Selected Tales and Poems by Herman Melville.* New York: Holt, Rinehart and Winston.

Chateaubriand, F.A.R. de. [1806] 1948. "Voyage au Mont-Blanc." In *Chateaubriand. Oeuvres Choisies*, ed. Charles Florisoone. 10th ed. Paris: A. Hatier.

– 1948. *Chateaubriand. Oeuvres Choisies.* Ed. Charles Florisoone. 10th ed. Paris: A. Hatier.

– [1811] 1877. *Itinéraire de Paris à Jerusalem.* Nouvelle Edition. Paris: Garnier.

Clark, Harry H. 1959, 1960. "Fenimore Cooper and Science." *Transactions of the Wisconsin Academy of Science, Arts and Letters* 48:179–204; 49:249–82.

Clough, Wilson O. 1964. *The Necessary Earth.* Austin: Univ. of Texas Press.

Coleridge, Samuel T. 1895. *The Letters of Samuel Taylor Coleridge*. Ed. E.H. Coleridge. 2 vols. London: Heinemann.

– [1817] 1907. *Biographia Literaria*. Ed. J. Shaucross. 2 vols. Oxford: Clarendon Press.

– 1912. *The Poems of Samuel Taylor Coleridge*. Ed. E.H. Coleridge. London: Oxford Univ. Press.

Collier, Katherine B. [1934] 1968. *Cosmogonies of Our Fathers*. Reprint. New York: Octagon.

Cook, Capt. James. 1777. *A Voyage towards the South Pole*. 2 vols. London: W. Strahan and T. Cadell.

– 1961. *The Journals of Captain James Cook*. 4 vols. Vol. 2. *The Voyage of the "Resolution" and "Adventure," 1772–1775*. Cambridge: Cambridge Univ. Press/Hakluyt Society.

Cooper, James Fenimore. [1827] 1985. *The Prairie*. Ed. James P. Elliott. Albany: State Univ. of New York Press.

– [1836] 1980. *Gleanings in Europe. Switzerland*. Ed. Robert E. Spiller and James F. Beard. Albany: State Univ. of New York Press.

– [1847] 1962. *Crater: or, Vulcan's Peak*. Ed. Thomas Philbrick. Cambridge: Harvard Univ. Press.

– 1849. *The Sea Lions; or, The Lost Sealers*. 2 vols. New York: Stringer and Townsend.

Cornford, Stephen, ed. See Young, Edward. [1742–46] 1989.

Cowper, William. [1785] 1934. *The Task*. In *The Poetical Works of William Cowper*. 4th ed. Ed. H.S. Milford. London: Oxford Univ. Press.

Cowper, William. 1995. *The Poems of William Cowper*. 3 vols. Vol. 3, *1785–1800*. Ed. John D. Baird and Charles Ryskamp. Oxford: Clarendon Press.

Coxe, William. 1779. See Ramond de Carbonnières, Louis. 1781–82.

Crabbe, George. 1988. *The Village* [1783]; *The Borough* [1810]. In *George Crabbe. The Complete Poetical Works*. Ed. Norma Dalrymple-Champneys and Arthur Pollard. 3 vols. Oxford: Clarendon.

Curley, Thomas M. 1976. *Samuel Johnson and the Age of Travel*. Athens: Univ. of Georgia Press.

Curzon [Zouche], Robert. [1849] 1955. *Visits to Monasteries in the Levant*. London: Barker.

Cust, Lionel, intro. John Ruskin. *Modern Painters*. New York and London: Dent, Dutton, n.d.

Dante Alighieri. 1954. *Purgatory*. In *The Divine Comedy*. Trans. H.R. Huse. New York: Holt, Rinehart & Winston.

Darrah, William C. 1951. *Powell of the Colorado*. Princeton: Princeton Univ. Press.

Darwin, Charles. [1839] 1972. *The Voyage of the Beagle. (Journal of Researches into the Geology and Natural History of the Various Countries Visited by HMS Beagle.)* Intro. Walter Sullivan. New York: Bantam.

– [1859] 1962. *The Origin of Species.* New York: Collier.

Davidson, Edward H. "The Tale as Allegory." In *Interpretations of American Literature,* ed. Charles Feidelson, Jr, and Paul Brodtkorb, Jr. New York: Oxford Univ. Press, 1959.

Dean, Dennis. 1981. "'Through Science to Despair': Geology and the Victorians." In *Victorian Science and Victorian Values: Literary Perspectives,* ed. James Paradis and Thomas Postlewait. *Annals of the New York Academy of Science* 360 (20 April): 111–36.

De Beer, Gavin. 1930. *Early Travellers in the Alps.* London: Sidgwick and Jackson.

Debenham, Frank. 1959. *Antarctica: The Story of a Continent.* London: Herbert Jenkins.

De Bruyn, Frans. 1996. *The Literary Genres of Edmund Burke.* Oxford: Clarendon Press.

de Crousaz, Jean-Pierre. 1715. *Traité du beau.* [Paris?] Fayard.

Deluc, Jean-André. 1772. *Recherches sur les modifications de l'atmosphère.*

de Maillet, Benoît. [1748] 1968. *Telliamed.* Trans. and ed. Albert V. Carozzi. Chicago: Univ. of Illinois Press.

Dennis, John. [1693] 1943. "Letter describing his crossing the Alps." In *The Critical Works of John Dennis,* ed. Edward N. Hooker. 2 vols. Vol. 2. Baltimore: Johns Hopkins Univ. Press.

de Saussure, Horace Bénédict. 1779. *Voyages dans les Alpes.* Vol. 1. Neuchatel: Fauche-Borel, 1803.

– 1786. *Voyages dans les Alpes.* Vol. 2. Neuchatel: Fauche-Borel, 1804.

– 1796. *Voyages dans les Alpes.* Vols. 3 and 4. Neuchatel: Fauche-Borel.

Deschamps, Eustache. 1880. "Lay du desert d'Amours." In *Oeuvres complètes de Eustache Deschamps.* 11 vols. Vol. 2. *Lais,* no. 2 (CCCV). Paris: Didot.

Desors, Édouard. 1840. *Journal d'une course aux glaciers du Mont-Rose et du Mont Cervin.* Geneva.

– 1841. *L'Ascension de la Jungfrau.* Geneva.

de Veer, Gerrit. [1853] 1876. "The True and Perfect Description of Three Voyages." In Gerrit de Veer. *The Three Voyages of William Barents to the Arctic Regions (1594–96).* 2d ed. London: Hakluyt.

De Vere, Aubrey. [1842] 1875. "The Sea-Cliffs of Kilkee." In *A Song of Faith.* Reissued in *Sonnets by Aubrey De Vere.* London.

Dickens, Charles. [1860] 1953. *Great Expectations.* London: Oxford University Press.

Donne, John. [1611] 1978. "An Anatomy of the World: The First Anniversary." In *John Donne. The Epithalamions, Anniversaries and Epicedes*, ed. W. Milgate. Oxford: Clarendon Press.

Drachman, Julian M. 1930. *Studies in the Literature of Natural Science*. New York: Macmillan.

Drayton, Michael. [1622] 1889. *Poly-Olbion*. 3 vols. [Manchester:] Spenser Society.

Dryden, John. [1667] 1966. "Dedication" to *The Indian Emperor*. In *The Works of John Dryden*. 20 vols. Vol. 9. Ed. John Loftis and Vinton A. Dearing. Berkeley and Los Angeles: Univ. of California Press.

Dutton, Geoff. 1967. *The Hero as Murderer. The Life of Edward John Eyre*. Sydney: Collins.

Eagleton, Terry. 1990. *The Ideology of the Aesthetic*. Oxford: Blackwell.

Ebbatson, Roger, ed. See Hardy, Thomas. [1873] 1986.

Eliade, Mircea. [1957] 1959. *The Sacred and the Profane. The Nature of Religion*. Trans. Willard R. Trask. New York: Harcourt, Brace.

Elioseff, Lee Andrew. 1963. *The Cultural Milieu of Addison's Literary Criticism*. Austin: Univ. of Texas Press.

Emerson, Ralph Waldo. 1886. *The Poems of Ralph Waldo Emerson*. London: Scott.

– 1912. *The Journals of Ralph Waldo Emerson*. Ed. Edward W. Emerson and Waldo E. Forbes. 10 vols. Vol. 8. Boston and New York: Houghton Mifflin.

– 1957. *Selections from Ralph Waldo Emerson*. Ed. Stephen E. Whicher. Boston: Houghton Mifflin.

Engel, Claire-Éliane. 1930a. *Byron et Shelley en Suisse et en Savoie*. Chambéry: Dardel.

– 1930b. *La Littérature alpestre en France et en Angleterre aux XVIIIe et XIXe siècles*. Chambéry: Dardel.

– [1950] 1971. *Mountaineering in the Alps. An Historical Survey*. Rev. ed. Foreword John Hunt. London: Allen & Unwin.

Essays and Reviews. See Goodwin, C.W.

Evelyn, John. 1889. *Diary and Correspondence of John Evelyn*. Ed. William Bray. 4 vols. Vol. 1. London: Bell.

Eyre, Edward John. [1845] 1964. *Journals of Expeditions of Discovery into Central Australia ... in the Years 1840–1*. 2 vols. London: Boone. Reprint. Australiana Facsimile Eds. no. 7. Adelaide.

Feidelson, Charles, Jr. [1953] 1959. *Symbolism and American Literature*. Chicago: Univ. of Chicago Press.

Feidelson, Charles, Jr, and Paul Brodtkorb, Jr, eds. 1959. *Interpretations of American Literature*. New York: Oxford Univ. Press.

Fitzgerald, Edward, trans. [1859, 1879] 1934. "The Rubáiyát of Omar Khayyám." In *Victorian and Later English Poets*, ed. James Stephens, Edwin L. Beck, and Royall H. Snow. New York: American Book Company.

Fitzgerald, Margaret M. 1947. *First Follow Nature. Primitivism in English Poetry 1725–1750*. New York: King's Crown.

Flaubert, Gustave. [1849–56] 1908. *La Première "Tentation de Saint Antoine."* Ed. Louis Bertrand. Paris: Charpentier.

– [1862] 1953. *Salammbô*. Ed. Édouard Maynial. Paris: Garnier.

– [1874] 1936. *La Tentation de Saint Antoine*. Ed. Édouard Maynial. Paris: Garnier Frères.

– [1886] 1910. "Pyrénées." In *Par les champs et par les grèves* (1841). Paris: Conard.

– 1927. *Correspondance. Oeuvres complètes de Gustave Flaubert.* 9 vols. Vol. 4. Paris: Conard.

Fontenelle, Bernard le Bovier de. [1686] 1955. *Entretiens sur la pluralité des mondes*. Ed. Robert Shackleton. Oxford: Clarendon.

Forbes, James D. [1843] 1845. *Travels through the Alps of Savoy*. 2d ed., rev. Edinburgh: Black.

– 1853. *Norway and Its Glaciers Visited in 1851*. Edinburgh: Black.

Forster, George. 1777. *A Voyage Round the World*. 2 vols. London: B. White.

Franklin, John. [1823] 1969. *Narrative of a Journey to the Shores of the Polar Sea … 1819–22.* Reprint. New York: Greenwood.

Fraser, Simon. 1960. *The Letters and Journals of Simon Fraser, 1806–1808*. Ed. W. Kaye Lamb. Toronto: Macmillan.

Frasso, Giuseppe. 1974. *Travels with Francesco Petrarca*. Padua: Antenore.

Freshfield, Douglas W. 1920. *The Life of Horace Bénédict de Saussure*. London: Arnold.

Fromentin, Eugène. [1857?] 1938. *Un Été dans le Sahara*. Paris: Conard.

– [1858] 1909. *Une Année dans le Sahel*. 12th ed. Paris: Plon-Nourrit.

– [1881] 1935. *Voyage en Égypte*. Paris: Editions Montaigne.

Froude, James A. 1847. "The Lieutenant's Daughter." In James A. Froude. *Shadows of the Clouds*. London: Oliver.

Gadsby, John. [1860–61] 1867. *My Wanderings. Being Travels in the East*. 2 vols. London: A. Gadsby.

Gautier, Théophile. [1869] 1881. *Vacances de lundi. Tableaux de montagnes*. Paris: G. Charpentier.

– 1932. *Poésies complètes de Théophile Gautier*. 3 vols. Paris: Firmin-Didot.

Geikie, Archibald. 1897. *The Founders of Geology*. London: Macmillan.

Gerard, Alexander. [1759] 1764. *An Essay on Taste*. 2d ed. Edinburgh: A. Millar, A. Kincaid, and J. Bell.

Gesner, Conrad. [1543, 1555] 1937. *On the Admiration of Mountains ... Zurich ... 1543. A Description of the Riven Mountain, commonly called Mt. Pilatus ... Zurich ... 1555*. Trans. H.B.D. Soule. San Francisco: Grabhorn.

Gilfillan, George. 1857. "Memoir and Critical Dissertation." In *The Poetical Works of Mark Akenside*. Edinburgh: James Nichol.

Gillispie, Charles C. [1951] 1959. *Genesis and Geology*. Cambridge: Harvard Univ. Press. Reprint. New York: Harper.

Girdlestone, Arthur G. 1870. *The High Alps without Guides*. London.

Gittings, Robert. 1975. *Young Thomas Hardy*. Harmondsworth: Penguin.

Glacken, Clarence J. 1967. *Traces on the Rhodian Shore*. Berkeley: Univ. of California Press.

Goethe, Johann Wolfgang von. [1777] 1957. "Harzreise im Winter." In *Poems of Goethe*, trans. Edwin H. Zeydel. *Studies in the Germanic Languages and Literatures*, no. 20. Chapel Hill: Univ. of North Carolina Press.

– 1897. "Nature." In *Library of the World's Best Literature*, ed. Charles D. Warner. Trans. Bailey Saunders. 30 vols. Vol. 11. New York: Peale.

– 1958. "Essay on Granite." Trans. Norbert Guterman. In *The Permanent Goethe*, ed. Thomas Mann. New York: Dial.

Gogol, Nikolai. [1842] 1961. *Dead Souls*. Trans. Andrew R. MacAndrew. New York: New American Library, Signet Classics.

Goldberg, M.A. 1959. "Moral and Myth in Mrs Shelley's *Frankenstein*." *Keats-Shelley Journal* 8:27–38.

Goodwin, C.W. [1859] 1860. "The Mosaic Cosmogony." In *Essays and Reviews*. London: Parker.

Gracyk, Theodore A. 1986. "Kant's Shifting Debt to British Aesthetics." *British Journal of Aesthetics* 26, no. 3 (Summer): 204–17.

Gray, Thomas. 1935. *The Correspondence of Thomas Gray*. Eds. Paget Toynbee and Leonard Whibley. 3 vols. Oxford: Clarendon.

– 1966. *The Complete Poems of Thomas Gray*. Ed. Herbert W. Starr and J.R. Hendrickson. Oxford: Clarendon.

Grean, Stanley, intro. See Shaftesbury, earl of. [1709] 1964.

Greene, Mott T. 1982. *Geology in the Nineteenth Century*. Ithaca: Cornell Univ. Press.

Grenberg, Bruce. 1989. *Some Other World to Find*. Urbana: Univ. of Illinois Press.

Griffin, Andrew. 1979. "Fire and Ice in *Frankenstein*." In *The Endurance of Frankenstein*, ed. George Levine and U.C. Knoepflmacher. Berkeley and Los Angeles: Univ. of California Press.

"Grotte de Balme, La." 1827. Geneva.

Grube, G.M.A., trans. See Plato. 1981.

Haeckel, Ernst H. 1903. *The History of Creation, or the Development of the Earth and Its Inhabitants by the Action of Natural Causes. An Exposition of the Doctrine of Evolution.* Trans. E. Ray Lankester. 2 vols. 4th ed. New York: Appleton.

Hansen, Thorkild. [1962] 1964. *Arabia Felix: The Danish Expedition of 1761–1767.* Trans. James and Kathleen McFarlane. London: Collins.

Hardy, Thomas. [1873] 1986. *A Pair of Blue Eyes.* Ed. Roger Ebbatson. London: Penguin.

– [1874] 1900. *Far From the Madding Crowd.* Wessex Ed. New York: Harper.

– [1876] 1927. *The Hand of Ethelberta.* London: Macmillan.

– [1878] 1980. *The Return of the Native.* London: Zodiac.

– 1982. *The Complete Poetical Works of Thomas Hardy.* Ed. Samuel Hynes. 5 vols. Vol. 1. Oxford: Clarendon.

Hassaurek, Friedrich. [1867] 1967. *Four Years among the Ecuadorians.* Ed. C. Harvey Gardiner. Carbondale: Southern Illinois Univ. Press.

Hayes, I[saac] I. 1867. *The Open Polar Sea. A Narrative of a Voyage of Discovery towards the North Pole.* New ed. London: Sampson Low and Marston.

Haywood, Eliza. [1748] 1974. *Life's Progress through the Passions.* Reprint. New York: Garland.

Hearne, Samuel. [1795] 1958. *A Journey from Prince of Wales's Fort in Hudson's Bay to the Northern Ocean, 1769–72.* Ed. Richard Glover. Toronto: Macmillan.

Heath-Stubbs, John F.A. 1950. *The Darkling Plain: A Study of the Later Fortunes of Romanticism.* London: Eyre & Spottiswoode.

Henkin, Leo J. [1940] 1963. *Darwinism in the English Novel 1860–1910.* New York: Russell.

Hewison, Robert, ed. 1981. *New Approaches to Ruskin. Thirteen Essays.* London: Routledge & Kegan Paul.

Hill, Aaron. 1709. *A Full and Just Account of the Present State of the Ottoman Empire.* London: the author. Microfilm.

Hill, Robert W., Jr, ed. See Tennyson, Alfred. 1971.

Hipple, Walter J., Jr. 1957. *The Beautiful, the Sublime, and the Picturesque in Eighteenth-Century British Aesthetic Theory.* Carbondale: Southern Illinois Univ. Press.

Hogarth, David G. [1904] 1966. *The Penetration of Arabia.* Khayat's Oriental Reprint, no. 22. Beirut: Khayat.

Holbach, Baron d'. [1770] 1970. *Système de la nature; or, Laws of the Moral and Physical World.* Trans. H.D. Robinson. New York: Ben Franklin.

Hooke, Robert. [1705] 1969. *The Posthumous Works of Robert Hooke.* London: Richard Waller. Reprint. New York: Johnson.

Hopkins, Gerard M. 1970. *The Poems of Gerard Manley Hopkins.* 4th ed. Ed. W.H. Gardner and N.H. Mackenzie. London: Oxford Univ. Press.

Horsford, Howard C., ed. See Melville, Herman. 1955.

Hugo, Victor. [1825, 1839, 1843] 1910. *Oeuvres complètes de Victor Hugo. Voyages II: France et Belgique, Alpes et Pyrénées, Voyages et Excursions.* Paris: L'Imprimerie Nationale.

Humboldt, Alexander von. 1849a. *Cosmos: A Sketch of a Physical Description of the Universe.* Trans. E.C. Otté. London: Bohn.

– 1849b. *Aspects of Nature, in Different Lands and Different Climates, with Scientific Elucidations.* Trans. Mrs Sabine. 2 vols. London: Longman, Brown, Green.

– (and Aimé Bonpland). 1852. *Personal Narrative of Travels to the Equinoctial Regions of America during the Years 1799–1804.* Trans. Thomasina Ross. 3 vols. London: Routledge.

Hussey, Christopher. 1927. *The Picturesque.* London: Putnam.

Hutchinson, William. 1774. *An Excursion to the Lakes, in Westmoreland and Cumberland.* London: Wilkie. Microprint.

Huth, Hans. 1957. *Nature and the American.* Berkeley and Los Angeles: Univ. of California Press.

Huxley, T.H. [1869] 1870. "Nature: Aphorisms by Goethe." *Nature, A Weekly Illustrated Journal of Science,* no. 1 (4 November): 9–11. London: Macmillan.

Hyde, Walter W. 1915. "The Ancient Appreciation of Mountain Scenery." *Classical Journal* 11, no. 2 (November): 70–84.

Irving, Washington. [1835] 1967. *A Tour on the Prairies.* (Rev. ed. 1865.) Preface James P. Wood. New York: Pantheon.

– [1836] 1961. *Astoria.* Intro. William H. Goetzmann. 2 vols. Philadelphia: Lippincott.

– [1836] 1964. *Astoria or Anecdotes of an Enterprise beyond the Rocky Mountains.* Rev. ed. 1860–61. Ed. Edgeley W. Todd. Norman: Univ. of Oklahoma Press.

– 1986. *Journals and Notebooks.* Ed. Sue Fields. Vol. 5 of *The Complete Works of Washington Irving,* ed. Richard D. Rust. 30 vols. Boston: Twayne.

Iseman, Peter A. 1978. "The Arabian Ethos." *Harper's* 256, no. 1533 (February): 37–56.

James, Edwin. 1822–23. *Account of an Expedition from Pittsburgh to the Rocky Mountains.* 2 vols. Philadelphia: Carey and Lea.

Johnson, Samuel. [1775] 1970. *A Journey to the Western Islands of Scotland.* Facsimile, ed. R.W. Chapman [1924]. London: Oxford Univ. Press.

Johnson, S.F. [1958] 1959. "Hardy and Burke's 'Sublime.' " *English Institute Essays 1958.* In *Style in Prose Fiction,* ed. Harold C. Martin. New York: Columbia Univ. Press.

Jones, A.G.E. 1982. *Antarctica Observed.* Whitby: Caedmon of Whitby.

Journal of a Voyage of Discovery to the Arctic Regions. By an Officer of the "Alexander" [Alexander Fisher]. [1821] 1964. London: Phillips. Reprint. Seattle: Shorey.

Joyce, James. [1916] 1976. *A Portrait of the Artist as a Young Man.* Harmondsworth: Penguin.

Kallich, Martin. 1948. "The Meaning of Archibald Alison's *Essays on Taste.*" *Philological Quarterly* 27:314–24.

Kames, Henry Home, Lord. [1762] 1824. *Elements of Criticism.* London: G. Cowie.

Kane, Elisha K. [1856] 1971. *Arctic Explorations in 1853, 1854, 1855.* Reprint. 2 vols. New York: Arno Press.

Kant, Immanuel. [1790] 1952. *The Critique of Judgement.* Trans. James C. Meredith. Oxford: Clarendon.

Keats, John. 1935. *Complete Poems and Selected Letters.* Ed. Clarence D. Thorpe. New York: Odyssey.

Kendall, Henry. [1861] 1966. "The Fate of the Explorers." In *The Poetical Works of Henry Kendall,* ed. T.T. Reed. Adelaide: Libraries Board of South Australia.

Kinglake, Alexander W. [1844] 1961. *Eothen.* London: Dent.

Koyré, Alexandre. [1957] 1994. *From the Closed World to the Infinite Universe.* Reprint. Baltimore: Johns Hopkins Univ. Press, Softshell Books.

Lamartine, A.M.L. de. [1836] 1960. *Jocelyn.* Paris: Garnier.

Langbaum, Robert. [1959] 1970. "The New Nature Poetry." *The American Scholar* 28, no. 3 (Summer): 323–40. Reprint. In Robert Langbaum. *The Modern Spirit.* New York: Oxford Univ. Press.

Langford, Nathaniel P. [1905] 1972. *The Discovery of Yellowstone Park.* Lincoln: Univ. of Nebraska Press.

Leconte de Lisle, C.M.R. [1927] 1974. *Poésies complètes.* Ed. Maurice de Becque. Paris. Reprint. 2 vols. Geneva: Slatkin.

Levin, Harry. 1958. *The Power of Blackness. Hawthorne, Poe, Melville.* New York: Vintage.

Levine, George. 1988. *Darwin and the Novelists.* Cambridge, Mass., and London: Harvard Univ. Press.

Lewes, George H. [1855] 1965. *The Life of Goethe.* Reprint. New York: Ungar.

Lewis, C.S. [1936] 1958. *The Allegory of Love.* Reprint. New York: Oxford Univ. Press.

Lewis, Meriwether, and William Clark. 1814. *The Journals of ... Lewis and Clark.* Ed. Nicholas Biddle and Paul Allen. 2 vols. Philadelphia. Reprint. *The Lewis and Clark Expedition.* Intro. Archibald Hanna. 3 vols. Philadelphia: Lippincott, 1961. Facsimile. *The Expedition of Lewis and Clark.* Ann Arbor, MI: Univ. Microfilms, 1966.

– 1904. *Original Journals of the Lewis and Clark Expedition.* Ed. Reuben G. Thwaites. 8 vols. (1904–05). New York: Dodd, Mead.

– 1953. *The Journals of Lewis and Clark.* Ed. Bernard DeVoto. Boston: Houghton Mifflin.

– 1986. *The Journals of the Lewis and Clark Expedition.* Ed. Gary E. Moulton. 7 vols. (1986–91). Lincoln: Univ. of Nebraska Press.

Littlejohn, David. 1965. *Dr Johnson: His Life in Letters*. Englewood Cliffs, NJ: Prentice-Hall.

Litzinger, Boyd, and Joyce Carol Oates, eds. 1985. *Story*. Lexington, MA: Heath.

Lokke, Kari Elise. 1982. "The Role of Sublimity in the Development of Modern Aesthetics." *Journal of Aesthetics and Art Criticism* 40, no. 4 (Summer): 421–9.

'Longinus.' 1965 [3d century AD?]. *On Sublimity*. Trans. and ed. D.A. Russell. Oxford: Clarendon.

Loomis, Chauncey C. 1977. "The Arctic Sublime." In *Nature and the Victorian Imagination*, ed. U.C. Knoepflmacher and G.B. Tennyson. Berkeley and Los Angeles: Univ. of California Press.

Lopez, Barry. 1986. *Arctic Dreams*. New York: Scribner's.

Lovejoy, Arthur O. [1936] 1960. *The Great Chain of Being*. Cambridge: Harvard Univ. Press. Reprint. New York: Harper.

Lowes, John L. [1927] 1959. *The Road to Xanadu*. Houghton-Mifflin. Reprint. New York: Vintage.

Lyell, Charles. 1838. *Elements of Geology*. London: Murray.

– [1863] 1873. *The Geological Evidences of the Antiquity of Man*. 4th ed. London: Murray.

Lyell, Katherine M., ed. 1881. *Life, Letters and Journals of Sir Charles Lyell*. 2 vols. London: Murray.

"Lyell and Tennyson." 1861. *The Saturday Review* 11 (22 June): 631–2.

Lyotard, Jean-F. [1991] 1994. *Lessons on the Analytic of the Sublime*. Trans. Elizabeth Rottenberg. Stanford: Stanford Univ. Press.

Mackenzie, Alexander. [1801] 1911. *Voyages from Montreal through the Continent of North America to the Frozen and Pacific Oceans in 1789 and 1793*. Reprint. 2 vols. Toronto: Courier.

Macpherson, James. [1760] 1970. *Fragments of Ancient Poetry, Collected in the Highlands of Scotland*. 2d ed. Reprint. Edinburgh: Thin.

Mallarmé, Stephane. 1945. *Oeuvres complètes*. Paris: Gallimard.

Mallet, David. 1759. *The Works of David Mallet, Esq*. 3 vols. London: A. Millar and P. Vaillant.

Mantell, Gideon A. 1838. *The Wonders of Geology*. 2 vols. London: Relfe and Fletcher, Cornhill.

Manwaring, Elizabeth W. [1925] 1965. *Italian Landscape in Eighteenth-Century England*. Reprint. London: Cass.

Markham, Clements. 1921. *The Lands of Silence*. Cambridge: Cambridge Univ. Press.

Marten, Frederick. 1671. *Voyage into Spitzbergen and Greenland*. See *Account* [1694] 1711.

Marvell, Andrew. 1979. Michael Craze. *The Life and Lyrics of Andrew Marvell.* London: Macmillan.

Matthews, G.M. 1957. "A Volcano's Voice in Shelley." *English Literary History* 24 (September): 191–228.

Maundrell, Henry. [1703] 1963. *A Journey from Aleppo to Jerusalem in 1697.* Ed. David Howell. Khayat's Oriental Reprints, no. 3. Beirut: Khayat.

Maynard, Temple. 1979. "The Landscape of the *Arabian Nights* and the *Persian Tales.*" *Transactions of the Samuel Johnson Society of the Northwest for 1978.* Ed. Camille la Bossière. Victoria, BC: Queen's Printer for the Johnson Society.

Melville, Herman. [1849] *Mardi and a Voyage Thither.* 2 vols. London: Chapman and Dodd, n.d.

– [1850] [1892?]. *Whitejacket: The World in a Man-of-War.* Boston: L.C. Page, n.d.

– [1851] 1991. *Moby Dick.* Intro. Larzer Ziff. New York: Knopf.

– [1856] 1950. "The Encantadas, or Enchanted Isles." In *Selected Tales and Poems by Herman Melville.* Ed. Richard Chase. New York: Holt, Rinehart and Winston.

– [1876] 1963. *Clarel.* In *The Works of Herman Melville.* Standard Ed. [1924] 16 vols. Vols. 14 and 15. Reprint. New York: Russell & Russell.

– 1955. *Journal of a Visit to Europe and the Holy Land* [1856–57]. Ed. Howard C. Horsford. Princeton: Princeton Univ. Press.

Meryon, Charles. [1846] *Travels of Lady Hester Stanhope.* 3 vols. London: H. Colburn, n.d.

Miall, David S. 1980. "Kant's *Critique of Judgement:* A Biased Aesthetics." *British Journal of Aesthetics* 20 (Spring): 135–45.

Michelet, Jules. [1868] 1930. "La Montagne." In *La Nature. Oeuvres de Jules Michelet.* 6 vols. Vol. 6. Paris: Larousse.

Mill, John Stuart. [1873] 1874. *Three Essays on Religion.* 3d ed. New York: Holt. Reprint. New York: Greenwood, 1969.

– [1924] 1944. *The Autobiography of John Stuart Mill.* Ed. John J. Cross. New York: Columbia Univ. Press.

Miller, Hugh. [1841] 1857. *The Old Red Sandstone.* 7th ed. Edinburgh: T. Constable.

– [1857] 1876. *The Testimony of the Rocks.* London: William P. Nimmo.

Miller, Joaquin. [1871] 1872. *Songs of the Sierras.* Boston: Roberts.

Millgate, Michael. 1982. *Thomas Hardy. A Biography.* New York: Random House.

Milton, John. 1953. *Paradise Lost* [1674]; *Paradise Regained* [1671]. In *The Poems of John Milton,* ed. James H. Hanford. 2d ed. New York: Ronald.

Miyoshi, Masao. 1969. *The Divided Self. A Perspective on the Literature of the Victorians.* New York: New York Univ. Press.

Monk, Samuel H. [1935] 1960. *The Sublime.* Modern Language Association. Reprint. Ann Arbor: Univ. of Michigan.

Monk, Samuel H., ed. 1953. See Baillie, John. [1747] 1953.

Moore, A.W. [1867] 1939. *The Alps in 1864. A Private Journal.* Privately printed, 1902. 2 vols. Oxford: Blackwell.

Moore, Cecil A. [1917] 1953. "The Return to Nature in English Poetry of the Eighteenth Century." *Studies in Philology* 14:243–91. In his *Backgrounds of English Literature 1700–1760.* Minneapolis: Univ. of Minnesota Press.

Mornet, Daniel. 1907. *Le Sentiment de la nature en France de J.-J. Rousseau à Bernardin de Saint-Pierre.* Paris: Hachette.

Nansen, Fridtjof. 1911. *In Northern Mists.* Trans. Arthur G. Chater. 2 vols. London: Heinemann.

Nash, Roderick. [1967] 1982. *Wilderness and the American Mind.* 3d ed. New Haven: Yale Univ. Press.

Nicolson, Marjorie H. [1959] 1963. *Mountain Gloom and Mountain Glory. The Development of the Aesthetics of the Infinite.* Ithaca: Cornell Univ. Press. Reprint. New York: Norton.

Norton, Charles E., ed. 1883. *The Correspondence of Thomas Carlyle and Ralph Waldo Emerson.* 2 vols. Boston: Osgood.

Noyes, Russell, ed. 1956. *English Romantic Poetry and Prose.* New York: Oxford.

Ogden, H.V.S. 1947. "Thomas Burnet's *Telluris Theoria Sacra* and Mountain Scenery." *English Literary History* 14:139–50.

Ogden, H.V.S., and Margaret S. Ogden. 1955. *English Taste in Landscape in the Seventeenth Century.* Ann Arbor: Univ. of Michigan Press.

Oppé, A.P. 1954. *Alexander and John Robert Cozens.* Cambridge: Harvard Univ. Press.

Palgrave, Francis T. 1897. *Landscape in Poetry from Homer to Tennyson.* London: Macmillan.

Palmer, Edward H. 1871. *The Desert of the Exodus: Journeys on Foot in the Wilderness of the Forty Years' Wandering.* 2 vols. Cambridge.

Paradis, James. 1981. "Darwin and Landscape." In *Victorian Science and Victorian Values: Literary Perspectives,* eds. James Paradis and Thomas Postlewait. *Annals of the New York Academy of Science* 360 (20 April): 85–110.

Parke, John. 1959. "Seven Moby-Dicks." In *Interpretations of American Literature,* eds. Charles Feidelson, Jr, and Paul Brodtkorb, Jr. New York: Oxford Univ. Press.

Parkman, Francis. [1849] 1991. *The Oregon Trail.* Ed. William R. Taylor. New York: Library of America.

– 1947. *The Journals of Francis Parkman.* Ed. Mason Wade. 2 vols. New York: Harper.

Parry, William E. [1821] 1968. *Journal of a Voyage for the Discovery of a North-West Passage ... 1819-20.* London: Murray. Reprint. New York: Greenwood.

– [1824] 1969. *Journal of a Second Voyage for the Discovery of a North-West Passage ... 1821–23.* London: Murray. Reprint. New York: Greenwood.

– 1889. *Journal of the Third Voyage for the Discovery of a North-West Passage.* London: Cassell.

Pascal, Blaise. [1670] 1976. *Pensées.* Intro. Dominique Descotes. [Paris:] Garnier-Flammarion.

Patmore, Coventry. [1854] 1892. *The Angel in the House.* London: Bell.

– [1877–78] 1897. *The Unknown Eros.* 4th ed. London: Bell.

Paulson, Ronald. 1996. *The Beautiful, Novel, and Strange. Aesthetics and Heterodoxy.* Baltimore and London: Johns Hopkins Univ. Press.

Peaks, Passes, and Glaciers; being excursions by members of the Alpine Club. 1862. 2d series. Ed. Edward S. Kennedy. 2 vols. London: Longman, Green, Longman, and Roberts.

Piccolomini, Aeneas Sylvius [Pius II]. [1959] 1962. *Memoirs of a Renaissance Pope ... An Abridgment.* Trans. Florence A. Gragg. Ed. Leona C. Gabel. Reprint. New York: Capricorn.

Pine-Coffin, R.S., trans. 1961. Augustine. *Confessions.* Harmondsworth: Penguin.

Piper, Herbert W. 1962. *The Active Universe.* London: Athlone.

Plaisted, Bartholomew. [1757] 1929. "Narrative of a Journey from Basra to Aleppo in 1750." In Douglas Carruthers, ed. *The Desert Route to India.* London: Hakluyt Society, 1929.

Plato. 1981. *Phaedo.* In *Five Dialogues.* Trans. G.M.A. Grube. Indianapolis: Hackett.

Pluché, Abbé Noel A. [1732–33] 1749–54. *Le Spectacle de la nature.* 8 vols. Paris: Estienne.

Pococke, Richard. 1743–45. *A Description of the East, and Some Other Countries.* 2 vols. London: Knapton.

Poe, Edgar Allan. [1837] 1975. *The Narrative of Arthur Gordon Pym of Nantucket.* Ed. Harold Beaver. Harmondsworth: Penguin.

– [1838] 1857. Review of J.L. Stephens, *Incidents of Travel in Egypt, Arabia Petraea and the Holy Land.* In *The Works of the Late Edgar Allan Poe.* Vol. 4. New York: Redfield.

– [1840] 1902. "The Journal of Julius Rodman." *Burton's Gentlemen's Magazine.* In *The Complete Works of Edgar Allan Poe,* ed. James A. Harrison. New York: Crowell.

– 1857. *The Works of the Late Edgar Allan Poe.* 4 vols. Vol. 2. New York: Redfield.

Pope, Alexander. [1963] 1968. *The Poems of Alexander Pope.* Ed. John Butt. Reprinted with corrections. London: Methuen.

Pourtales, Count de. 1968. *On the Western Tour with Washington Irving. The Journal and Letters of the Count de Pourtales.* Ed. George F. Spaulding. Trans. Seymour Feiler. Norman: Univ. of Oklahoma Press.

Powell, J[ohn] W. 1875. *Report of J.W. Powell. Exploration of the Colorado River of the West and Its Tributaries ... 1869 ... 1872.* Washington: Government Printing Office.

– [1878] 1962. *Report on the Lands of the Arid Region of the United States.* Ed. Wallace Stegner. Cambridge: Harvard Univ. Press, Belknap Press.

Priestley, Joseph. [1777] 1971. "A Course of Lectures on Oratory and Criticism." In Sigworth, Oliver, ed. 1971.

Ra'ad, Basem. 1991. "Melville's Art: Overtures from the Journal of 1856–57." In *Savage Eye: Melville and the Visual Arts.* Ed. Christopher Sten. Kent, Ohio: Kent State Univ. Press.

Radcliffe, Ann. [1791] 1904. *The Romance of the Forest.* Reprint. London: Routledge.

– [1794] 1963. *The Mysteries of Udolpho.* Ed. and abridged Andrew Wright. New York: Holt, Rinehart and Winston.

– 1795. *A Journey Made in the Summer of 1794, through Holland ... to which are added observations during a tour to the Lakes.* London: Robinson.

Ramond de Carbonnières, Louis F.-E. 1781–82. *Lettres sur l'État politique, civil et naturel de la Suisse.* 2 vols. Trans. with commentary of William Coxe. *Sketches of the Natural, Civil and Political State of Switzerland.* London, 1779.

Ray, John. [1691] 1735. *The Wisdom of God Manifested in the Works of Creation.* 10th ed. London: Royal Society.

Read, H.H. [1949] 1963. *Geology: An Introduction to Earth-History.* Rev. ed. London: Oxford Univ. Press.

Reade, Winwood. [1875] *The Outcast.* London: Watts, n.d.

Reusch, Richard R. [1928] 1965. "The Menelik Legend." *Tanganyika Times* (10 February). Reprint. *Tanganyika Notes and Records,* no. 64 (March).

– 1954. *History of East Africa.* Stuttgart: Evang. Missionsverlag.

Robertson, David. 1977. "Mid-Victorians among the Alps." In *Nature and the Victorian Imagination,* ed. U.C. Knoepflmacher and G.B. Tennyson. Berkeley and Los Angeles: Univ. of California Press.

Ross, Ian. 1965. "A Bluestocking over the Border: Mrs Elizabeth Montagu's Aesthetic Adventures in Scotland, 1766." *Huntington Library Quarterly* 28, no. 3 (May): 213–33.

Ross, James C. [1847] 1969. *A Voyage of Discovery and Research in the Southern and Antarctic Regions in the Years 1839–43.* 2 vols. Reprint. New York: Kelley.

Ross, John. [1835] 1969. *Narrative of a Second Voyage in Search of a North West Passage ... [1829–33] and the Discovery of the Northern Magnetic Pole.* Reprint. New York: Greenwood.

Rossetti, Christina. [1866] 1979. "The Prince's Progress." In *The Complete Poems of Christina Rossetti* (Variorum ed.), ed. R.W. Crump. Vol. 1. Baton Rouge: Louisiana State Univ. Press.

Rousseau, Jean-Jacques. [1761] 1960. *Julie; ou La Nouvelle Héloïse. Lettres de deux amants habitants d'une petite ville au pied des Alpes.* Paris: Garnier Frères.

Ruskin, John. 1903. *The Works of John Ruskin.* Ed. E.T. Cook and Alexander Wedderburn. 39 vols. Vols. 3 and 4. London: Allen.

– 1904. *The Works of John Ruskin.* Ed. E.T. Cook and Alexander Wedderburn. Vol. 6. London: Allen.

– 1906. *The Works of John Ruskin.* Ed. E.T. Cook and Alexander Wedderburn. Vol. 26. London: Allen.

Russell, D.A., ed. See Longinus. 1965.

Rutherford, Andrew. 1961. *Byron. A Critical Study.* Stanford: Stanford Univ. Press.

Rutland, William R. [1938] 1962. *Thomas Hardy: A Study of His Writings and Their Background.* Oxford: Blackwell. Reprint. New York: Russell.

Said, Edward W. 1978. *Orientalism.* New York: Random House.

Saint-Pierre, Jacques H.B. [1789] 1804. *Études de la Nature.* Rev. ed. Paris: Crapelot.

Sambrook, James, intro. 1981. *James Thomson. The Seasons.* Oxford: Clarendon.

Sandie, George. 1864. *Horeb and Jerusalem.* Edinburgh.

Sandys, George. [1615] 1621. *A Relation of a Journey Begun An. Dom: 1610.* 2d ed. London: Barrett.

Savage, Richard. [1729] 1962. *The Wanderer.* In *The Poetical Works of Richard Savage,* ed. Clarence Tracy. Cambridge: Cambridge Univ. Press.

Schaller, George B. 1993. "In a High and Sacred Realm: Tibet's Remote Chang Tang." *National Geographic* 184, no. 2 (August): 62–87.

Schama, Simon. 1995. *Landscape and Memory.* New York: Knopf.

Scott, Walter. 1904. *Scott. Poetical Works.* Ed. J. Logic Robertson. London: Oxford Univ. Press.

Scudder, Harold H. 1947. "Cooper's *The Crater.*" *American Literature* 19:109–26.

Sénancour, Étienne Pivert de. [1804] 1984. *Oberman.* Paris. Reprint. N.p.: Livre de Poche.

Shaftesbury, Anthony Ashley Cooper, 3d Earl of. [1709] 1964. *The Moralists.* Ed. John M. Robertson. 2 vols. Intro. Stanley Green. Indianapolis: Bobbs, Merrill, Library of Liberal Arts.

Shaw, Thomas. [1738] 1972. *Travels, or Observations Relating to Several Parts of Barbary and the Levant.* Oxford. Reprint. Farnborough: Gregg.

Shelley, Frances [Winckley], Lady. [1816] 1912. *The Diary of Frances Lady Shelley 1787–1817.* Ed. Richard Edgcumbe. London: Murray.

Shelley, Mary W. [1818] 1980. *Frankenstein; or the Modern Prometheus.* 3d ed. 1831. Ed. M.K. Joseph. Oxford: Oxford Univ. Press.

– 1826. *The Last Man.* 3 vols. London: Colburn.

Shelley, Percy B. 1921. *The Complete Poetical Works of Percy Bysshe Shelley.* Ed. Thomas Hutchinson. London: Oxford Univ. Press.

– 1954. *Shelley's Prose.* Ed. David L. Clark. Albuquerque: Univ. of New Mexico Press.

– 1964. *The Letters of Percy Bysshe Shelley.* 2 vols. Vol. 1. *Shelley in England.* Ed. Frederick L. Jones. Oxford: Clarendon.

– 1965. *The Complete Works of Percy Bysshe Shelley.* Ed. Roger Ingpen and Walter E. Peck. 10 vols. Vol. 2. New York: Gordian.

– 1989. *The Poems of Shelley.* 2 vols. Ed. Geoffrey Matthews and Kelvin Everest. Vol. 1. London: Longman.

Shepard, Paul. 1967. *Man in the Landscape. A Historic View of the Esthetics of Nature.* New York: Knopf.

Sherburn, George, ed. 1956. *The Correspondence of Alexander Pope.* 5 vols. Oxford: Clarendon.

Short, R.W. 1959. "Melville as Symbolist." In *Interpretations of American Literature,* ed. Charles Feidelson, Jr, and Paul Brodtkorb, Jr. New York: Oxford Univ. Press.

Siegrist, Christoph. 1967. *Albrecht von Haller.* Stuttgart: Metzlersche.

Sigworth, Oliver, ed. 1971. *Criticism and Aesthetics 1660–1800.* San Francisco: Rinehart.

Sloan, Kim. 1986. *Alexander and John Robert Cozens. The Poetry of Landscape.* New Haven and London: Yale Univ. Press.

Smith, Bernard. 1960. *European Vision and the South Pacific, 1768–1850.* Oxford: Clarendon.

Smith, Henry N. 1950. *Virgin Land: The American West as Symbol and Myth.* New York: Random House.

Smythe, F.S. 1940. *Edward Whymper.* London: Hodder and Stoughton.

Stafford, Barbara M. 1976. "Rude Sublime: The Taste for Nature's Colossi during the Late Eighteenth and Early Nineteenth Centuries." *Gazette des Beaux Arts,* ser. 6, 87 (April): 113–26.

Stanhope, Lady Hester. See Meryon, Dr Charles. 1846.

Stanley, Arthur P. [1856] 1863. *Sinai and Palestine.* London: Murray. New ed. New York: Widdleton.

Steegmuller, Francis, trans. and ed. 1972. *Flaubert in Egypt ... from Gustave Flaubert's Travel Notes.* Chicago: Academy Chicago.

Stegner, Wallace. 1954. *Beyond the Hundredth Meridian. John Wesley Powell and the Second Opening of the West.* Boston: Houghton Mifflin.

Stephen, Leslie. [1871] 1874. *The Playground of Europe.* A New Edition. London: Longmans, Green.

Stephens, John L. [1837] 1991. *Incidents of Travel in Egypt, Arabia Petraea, and the Holy Land.* Ed. Victor W. von Hagen. Norman: Univ. of Oklahoma Press, 1970. Reprint. San Francisco: Chronicle Books.

Stevenson, Lionel. 1932. *Darwin among the Poets.* Chicago: Chicago Univ. Press.

Stewart, Dugald. [1810] 1818. *Philosophical Essays*. 3d ed. Edinburgh: Constable.

Swinburne, Algernon C. [1871] 1925. *The Complete Works of Algernon Charles Swinburne*. Bonchurch ed. Ed. Edmund Gosse and Thomas J. Wise. 20 vols. Vol. 2. London: Heinemann.

– 1955. *A Swinburne Anthology*. Ed. Kenelm Foss. London: Richards.

Taine, Hippolyte A. 1855. *Voyage aux Pyrénées*. Paris.

Tennyson, Alfred. 1971. *Tennyson's Poetry*. Ed. Robert W. Hill, Jr. New York: Norton.

– 1987. *The Poems of Tennyson*. 2d ed. Ed. Christopher Ricks. 3 vols. London: Longman.

Tennyson, Hallam. 1897. *Alfred, Lord Tennyson. A Memoir By His Son*. 2 vols. London: Macmillan.

Thacker, Christopher. 1983. *The Wildness Pleases. The Origins of Romanticism*. London: Croon Helm.

Thomson, James. [1726–46] 1981. *The Seasons*. Ed. James Sambrook. Oxford: Clarendon.

– [1736] 1908. "Liberty." In *James Thomson. Poetical Works*. Ed. J. Logic Robertson. (Reprint, 1971.) London: Oxford Univ. Press.

Thomson, James. (1834–82) [1874] 1963. *Poems and Some Letters of James Thomson*. Ed. Anne Ridler. London: Centaur.

Thomson, William. [1859] 1880. *The Land and the Book*. N.p.

Thorpe, Clarence D. 1935a. "Two Augustans Cross the Alps: Dennis and Addison on Mountain Scenery." *Studies in Philology* 32:463–82.

Thorpe, Clarence D., ed. 1935b. *John Keats. Complete Poems and Selected Letters*. New York: Odyssey.

Tillotson, Geoffrey, ed. 1954. *The Twickenham Edition of the Works of Alexander Pope*. 2d ed. Vol. 2. London: Methuen.

Traherne, Thomas. 1908. *Centuries of Meditations*. Ed. Bertram Dobell. London: The editor.

Tuveson, Ernest L. 1951. "Space, Deity, and the 'Natural Sublime.'" *Modern Language Quarterly* 12:20–38.

– 1960. *The Imagination as a Means of Grace. Locke and the Aesthetics of Romanticism*. Berkeley and Los Angeles: Univ. of California Press.

Tyndall, John. [1860] 1906. *The Glaciers of the Alps*. New York: Dutton; London: Dent, Everyman.

– [1862] 1906. *Mountaineering in 1861*. New York: Dutton; London: Dent, Everyman.

– [1871] 1899. *Hours of Exercise in the Alps*. 4th ed. London: Longman.

Ueda, Makoto. 1970. *Matsuo Bashō*. New York: Twayne.

Unrau, John. 1981. "Ruskin, the Workman and the Savageness of Gothic." In *New Approaches to Ruskin. Thirteen Essays*, ed. Robert Hewison. London: Routledge & Kegan Paul.

Unwin, Timothy. 1979. "Flaubert's First *Tentation de Saint Antoine.*" *Essays in French Literature* 16 (November): 17–42.

Uren, Malcolm, and Robert Stephens. [1941] 1945. *Waterless Horizons.* 4th ed. Melbourne: Robertson and Mullens.

Vaughan, Henry. [1650] 1963. *Poetry and Selected Prose.* Ed. L.C. Martin. London: Oxford Univ. Press.

Verendrye, Pierre G., Sieur de la, and Chevalier de la Verendrye. 1925. *The Verendrye Overland Quest to the Pacific. Oregon Historical Society Quarterly* 26, no. 2 (June).

Verne, Jules. [1864] 1911a. *A Trip to the Center of the Earth* and *Adventures of Captain Hatteras.* In *The Works of Jules Verne*, ed. Charles F. Horne. 15 vols. Vols. 2 and 3. New York: Parke.

– [1865] 1911b. *A Trip from the Earth to the Moon* and *A Tour of the Moon.* In *The Works of Jules Verne*, ed. Charles F. Horne. 15 vols. Vol. 3. New York: Parke.

Villarejo, Oscar M., intro. and afterword. 1965. In Johan G.C. Petersen. *Dr Kane's Voyage to the Polar Lands.* Philadelphia: Univ. of Pennsylvania Press.

von Haller, Albrecht. [1729] 1965. *Die Alpen.* Stuttgart: Reclam.

von Troil, Uno. 1780. *Letters on Iceland ... Made, during a Voyage Undertaken in the Year 1772 by Joseph Banks.* Dublin.

"Voyage dans les Montagnes occidentales du Paris de Vaud." 1737. In *Journal helvétique.*

Warburton, Eliot. [1845]. *The Crescent and the Cross.* 2 vols. London: Colburn. 2 vols. in 1. London: Maclaren, n.d.

Warton, Joseph. [1744] 1973. *The Enthusiast.* In *Late Augustan Poetry*, ed. Patricia M. Spacks. Englewood Cliffs, NJ: Prentice-Hall.

Warton, Thomas, Jr. [1747] 1973. *The Pleasures of Melancholy.* In *Late Augustan Poetry*, ed. Patricia M. Spacks. Englewood Cliffs, NJ: Prentice-Hall.

Webster, Harvey C. [1947] 1964. *On a Darkling Plain. The Art and Thought of Thomas Hardy.* Chicago: Univ. of Chicago Press. Reprint. London: Cass.

Weddell, James. 1825. *A Voyage towards the South Pole, Performed in the Years 1822–24.* London: Longman, Hurst, Rees, etc.

Whitman, Walt. [1871] 1968. *Democratic Vistas.* In *Complete Works of Walt Whitman.* Deathbed Ed. 2 vols. Vol. 2. Intro. Malcolm Cowley. New York: Funk and Wagnalls.

Whymper, Edward. [1871] 1981. *Scrambles amongst the Alps.* Reprint. Berkeley: Ten Speed Press.

Willey, Basil. [1934] 1955. *The Seventeenth-Century Background.* Reprint. New York: Doubleday Anchor.

– [1940] 1962. *The Eighteenth-Century Background.* Reprint. Harmondsworth: Penguin Peregrine.

– [1949] 1964. *Nineteenth-Century Studies.* Chatto and Windus. Reprint. Harmondsworth: Penguin.

Wills, Alfred. [1856] 1858. *Wanderings among the High Alps.* 2d ed., rev. London: Bentley.

Wilson, Leonard G. 1972. *Charles Lyell. The Years to 1841: The Revolution in Geology.* New Haven: Yale Univ. Press.

Windham, William. [1743] 1744. *A Letter from an English Gentleman ... giving an Account of ... the Glacieres ... in Savoy, written in 1741. Translated from the French.* [London.]

Wollstonecraft, Mary. [1796] 1976. *Letters Written during a Short Residence in Sweden, Norway, and Denmark.* Ed. Carol Poston. Lincoln: Univ. of Nebraska Press.

Wood, Captain John. 1676. *A Relation of a Voyage for the Discovery of a Passage by the North-East, to Japan and China.* See *Account* [1694] 1711.

Wood, Robert. 1757. *The Ruins of Baalbec, otherwise Heliopolis in Coelesyria.* London.

Woodrow, Alain. 1979. "Alone in the Sahara." *Le Monde.* Reprint. *Manchester Guardian Weekly* (7 January).

Wordsworth, Dorothy. [1820] 1941. *Journals of Dorothy Wordsworth.* Ed. Ernest de Selincourt. 2 vols. London: Macmillan.

Wordsworth, William. [1805, 1850] 1971. *The Prelude. A Parallel Text.* Ed. J.C. Maxwell. London: Penguin.

– [1810] 1974. *A Guide through the District of the Lakes in the North of England.* 5th ed. Kendal: Hudson and Nicholson. In *The Prose Works of William Wordsworth,* ed. W.J.B. Owen and Jane W. Smyser. 3 vols. Vol. 2. Oxford: Clarendon.

– [1844] 1896. "Kendal and Windermere Railway." Two letters to the *Morning Post.* In *Prose Works of William Wordsworth,* ed. William Knight. 2 vols. Vol. 2. London: Macmillan.

– [1904] 1936. *The Poetical Works of Wordsworth.* Ed. Thomas Hutchinson. Oxford Standard Authors Edition. New ed., rev. Ernest de Selincourt. London: Oxford Univ. Press.

Wright, Thomas, ed. 1848. *Early Travels in Palestine.* London: Bohn.

Young, Edward. [1742–46] 1989. *Night Thoughts.* Ed. Stephen Cornford. Cambridge: Cambridge Univ. Press.

Yuasa, Nobuyuki, trans. and intro. See Bashō. 1966.

Zeydel, Edwin H., trans. See Goethe [1777] 1957.

Index